THE BYZANTINE EMPIRE 1025–1204

THE BYZANTINE EMPIRE
1025–1204

A political history

Michael Angold

LONGMAN
London and New York

LONGMAN GROUP LIMITED
Longman House, Burnt Mill, Harlow
Essex CM20 2JE, England
Associated companies throughout the world

*Published in the United States of America
by Longman Inc., New York*

© Michael Angold 1984

First published 1984

BRITISH LIBRARY CATALOGUING IN PUBLICATION DATA
Angold, Michael
　The Byzantine empire 1025–1204.
　1. Byzantine Empire – History – 527–1081
　2. Byzantine Empire – History –　1081–1453.
　I. Title.
　949.5′03　　DF601
　ISBN 0−582−49060−X
　ISBN 0−582−49061−8

LIBRARY OF CONGRESS CATALOGING IN PUBLICATION DATA
Angold, Michael.
　The Byzantine Empire 1025–1204

　Bibliography: p.
　Includes index.
　1. Byzantine Empire – History – 1025–1081.
2. Byzantine Empire – History – Comneni Dynasty, 1081–1185.
I. Title.
DF596.A54　　1984　　949.5′03　　84–4407
ISBN 0–582–49060–X
ISBN 0–582–49061–8 (Pbk)

Printed in Singapore by
Selector Printing Co (Pte) Ltd

CONTENTS

LIST OF MAPS

PREFACE

This is a political history, but not one that aims only at providing a straightforward account of the main events and personalities. The object has been to set the political history of the Byzantine Empire in the eleventh and twelfth centuries in its social, economic, and intellectual context. It concentrates on those who exercised power and influence, both individually and collectively, and it tries to chart those changing forces and assumptions that helped to determine the possibilities of action. It sets out to explore Professor Paul Lemerle's dictum: 'To represent Byzantium as unchanging over eleven centuries would be to fall into the trap, which it has itself laid'. Never perhaps did Byzantium's external situation and internal structure change so quickly as over the eleventh and twelfth centuries. The fascination of the period lies in the way the Byzantines strove to adapt to new circumstances. It was a heroic effort, but one that failed.

Another of the traps which Byzantium has laid for the unwary comes in the shape of that splendid succession of histories which cover our period. It is all too easy to neglect the rich variety of other sources and to fall back on the narratives provided by Michael Psellos, Anna Comnena, and Nicetas Choniates, to mention only the best-known historians of the period. To guard against this danger, I have not treated their histories as mere repositories of facts, but have sought out their opinions, their prejudices, and their discussions of the issues of the day, in the hope that these will illuminate the political process at Byzantium. I have accordingly, if paradoxically, advanced historians to the front of the political stage. There seems to be nothing wrong in this, for they were often considerable political figures in their own right. I have tried to test their prejudices and questionable judgements against a whole range of other sources – legal, literary, ecclesiastical, documentary. I hope that this has made it possible to strike a reasonable balance between the different kinds of source material.

This book has very largely been written out of the primary sources, though I have obviously gained much from the secondary material. I have tried to indicate my debts by citing by name in the text those scholars whose work I have found particularly useful. There is, however, one name that I was not able to work in – that of Paul Gautier. I was extremely sorry to learn that he had died in July 1983. I never met him, nor ever corresponded with him, but like all Byzantinists working on the eleventh and twelfth centuries I was greatly in his debt. His scrupulous editions of such a variety of new sources opened up a body of material, which is almost justification in itself for taking a fresh look at the history of the Byzantine Empire during those centuries.

I should like to thank Paul and Ruth Magdalino of St Andrews University for going through a draft of this book, which I sent them early in 1983. They saved me from a number of mistakes and gave me the encouragement needed to press on to a conclusion. I should also like to thank my wife for her forbearance, as papers, books, and typewriters came cascading down the stairs from my attic study.

I have dedicated this book to my mother as a small token of love and affection.

MICHAEL ANGOLD
Edinburgh
February 1984

A NOTE ON THE TRANSLITERATION OF GREEK

I have tried, where I have thought appropriate, to follow the traditional transliteration of proper names, but I have preferred a direct transliteration from the Greek for names that are not in common English usage – for example Eustathios instead of Eustathius or even Eustace, which seems a shade bizarre. In place names I have, where possible, transliterated the Greek letter χ by kh rather than the more usual ch, because the latter represents such a confusing range of sounds.

Chapter 1

BASIL II AND HIS LEGACY

The shadow of Basil II hangs over the eleventh century. In the evenings men recounted his achievements and wise sayings. He came to symbolize the imperial grandeur which was slipping away. His rule seemed to have consummated a period of Byzantine history. He attained most of the political objectives for which Byzantine emperors had been striving since the middle of the ninth century. His Empire may not have rivalled that of Justinian in size, but its frontiers ran once more along the Danube and the Euphrates, and the Russian lands were at long last drawn firmly within the Byzantine sphere of influence. On the graph of Byzantine political history his reign marks one of the peaks.

The pattern of Byzantine history is one of peaks and troughs; of triumph, swift decline, and dogged recovery. This sequence was rooted in Byzantium's very being with its combination of enduring strengths and extreme vulnerability. The key is the city of Constantinople. As the seat of imperial government and through its sheer wealth and weight of numbers it provided the Empire with an impressive concentration of material resources. As the setting for the imperial office and the patriarchal church, it contributed spiritual and ideological strengths. But it was difficult to control, if clear direction from the emperor was lacking. This might happen when the succession was in doubt or the emperor at cross-purposes with the church. Constantinople also placed an immense burden upon the provinces, which was the cause of resentment. For any of these reasons the apparently solid facade of imperial power might suddenly crack open. The greatest dangers came when a period of internal division and unrest coincided with difficulties abroad, for Constantinople was not only a seat of empire, it was also the crossroads and the point of balance of the medieval world. This offered its emperors great opportunities, but also presented them with considerable dangers, depending upon the nature and aims of the peoples and powers that came within its orbit. Most Byzantine emperors possessed the experience and resources to meet any external challenge, but they became extremely vulnerable, if they allowed foreign powers to be drawn into the internal politics of the Empire.

Basil II seemed to have inherited from his predecessors, the soldier emperors, Nicephorus Phokas (963–69) and John Tzimiskes (969–76), a ring of secure frontiers. They conquered Bulgaria and restored the frontier to the Danube, which was protected by a series of great fortresses and a special fleet. In the east they pushed the frontiers of the Empire beyond the Euphrates and into northern Syria, where in 969 the city of Antioch was conquered. To the south Nicephorus Phokas's conquest first of Crete (961) and then of Cyprus (965) more or less sealed off the Aegean from enemy attack.

There remained the danger from the north. The Russians had threatened Constantinople from across the Black Sea on a number of occasions since their first appearance beneath the walls of the city in 860. Efforts to convert them to christianity had met with no great success. It was left to Basil II to find a solution, which ironically he improvised out of sheer desperation. In 987 the two greatest families of Anatolia, the Phokas and the Skleros, united in rebellion against him. They had at their back the bulk of the imperial armies of the East. Basil II needed troops and was willing to give almost anything for them. He turned to the Russians of Kiev who had provided the Empire with mercenaries in the past. Their Prince Vladimir offered a corps of 6,000 Varangians. He was also willing to be baptized, but the price demanded was unprecedented, nothing less than the hand of the emperor's sister, Anna. This marriage gave the Russian prince immense prestige, for his bride was not merely a Byzantine princess, but one born to a reigning emperor, a Porphyrogenite princess, the ultimate status symbol of the time. It has only to be remembered that the great German Emperor Otto I (961–73) was fobbed off with a princess, who was not even of imperial stock, for his son Otto II.

The arrival of the Russian troops gave new heart to the imperial forces. The rebels were defeated on 13 April 989 near Abydos at the mouth of the Hellespont. For the time being the power of the Anatolian families was crushed. These families had been a problem for the imperial government from the turn of the ninth century. Their power was solidly based in the Anatolian provinces. They were lords of broad estates and owners of vast flocks; they controlled the local military organization. The success of the Byzantine campaigns against the Arabs from the middle of the ninth century was largely their work and they benefited in the form of booty and new lands. Both Nicephorus Phokas and John Tzimiskes came from this background.

Normally, a grudging alliance existed between these families and the central government. This turned into something more concrete, when in 963 the Emperor Romanos II died, leaving two young sons, the future Basil II and Constantine VIII, to succeed him. The commander-in-chief Nicephorus Phokas seized power and was crowned emperor, but on the understanding that the rights of the imperial princes would be respected. This arrangement was continued after Phokas's assassination in 969, when he was succeeded by his nephew John Tzimiskes. For the Anatolian families it was a most satisfactory state of affairs. Lip service continued to be paid to the rights of the legitimate dynasty, the house of Macedon, while real power rested in the hands of one of their number. This constitutional compromise could not outlast the death of John Tzimiskes in 976 and the accession to power of Basil II, who was now of age. The Anatolian families tried to recover their position under the leadership of Bardas Skleros, the brother-in-law of Tzimiskes, but his rebellion was put down in 979 thanks to the intervention on the emperor's side of the ruler of Georgia. This did not break the power of the magnates. As we have seen, they challenged Basil II once again, but with Russian help were completely defeated in 989. The emperor now had no rivals within the Empire; his position was unassailable.

Tradition records that the defeated leader of the Anatolian armies, Bardas Skleros, was led before his conqueror, who enquired of him how he should in future rule. Back came the rather surprising advice: 'Destroy the highest commands. Do not allow the common soldiers to prosper; rather exhaust them with unjust exactions, so that they remain occupied at home. Don't introduce women into the imperial palace. Don't be approachable. Few should know of the plans you are brewing.'[1] Whether this piece of advice was ever given or was just *ben trovato,* Basil II's rule became increasingly harsh and arbitrary. He set out to curb the power of the great families by attacking its foundations: their control over peasants and their property. Existing legislation designed to protect peasant property had remained very largely a dead-letter. In 996 Basil II revived and extended it. He underlined his seriousness of purpose by including the cautionary tale of one Philokales. This man had succeeded in buying up all the property in his native village. In the process he must have offended against the existing legislation. The matter came to the emperor's notice. 'Passing through the village, my majesty considered the matter on the request of the villagers. We had his luxurious villa levelled to the ground and returned his property to the peasants, leaving him with what he had to begin with and reducing him to the level of the peasants.'[2]

Peasant property now received effective protection from the attentions of the magnates. Whether, apart from one or two spectacular examples, much peasant property was recovered from the magnates is another matter, but it was a threat hanging over them and would have made them reluctant to challenge the emperor, even when he proceeded to yet another measure directed against them. In the past the arrears owed by a tax district were shared out among the peasants. Now Basil II forced the magnates to pay the arrears owed by the peasantry. Taxation was the chief burden upon the peasantry and the passage of teams of tax-collectors was feared and resented. Heavy taxation was one of the major causes forcing peasants either to abandon their holdings or to sell up. It was therefore indirectly responsible for peasant property passing into the hands of the magnates. It was in the interests of the state to have a prosperous and contented peasantry, for their well-being, in the words of an imperial novel, 'has many and necessary advantages: the payment of taxes and the performance of military service, which things will always be wanting, as long as the general population abandons its holdings'.[3]

The condition of the peasantry was to be improved by shifting the arrears of taxation on to the shoulders of the 'powerful'. In this way, much of their surplus wealth would be soaked up by the state. They would have less money for the purchase of peasant property. The defence of the peasantry was not merely an exercise of imperial philanthropy. It went to the heart of the question of imperial authority. In the past, buying up of peasant property had very often meant that the peasantry were reduced to dependent status; they virtually became serfs bound to great estates. Real power at the local level was passing more and more into the hands of the magnates. They dominated local military organization: the provincial armies, known as themes, were almost turning into private armies. It was a trend which for much of the tenth century the imperial government was willing to overlook, but it almost cost Basil II his throne. The rebellions at the beginning of his reign showed all too clearly that the loyalty of these armies was to the magnates of Anatolia and not to the emperor.

Basil II's solution was to generalize commutation of military service in the armies of the themes for a money payment and to rely for his military power on a standing army, the flower of which was his Varangian Guard. It was this army that enabled him to defeat the Bulgarians who had recovered their independence, while he was embroiled with the Anatolian magnates. It took nearly twenty years of campaigning to grind down Bulgarian resistance and to reincorporate the Bulgarian lands in the Empire. When in 1016 booty gained in the Bulgarian wars was shared out, the Varangians received as much as the rest of the army put together: a good reflection of their importance in Basil II's armies. They provided him with the military backing that would make his ideal of autocracy a reality.

Something of its spirit exudes from the frontpiece of the Psalter he commissioned to celebrate his final victory over the Bulgarians in 1018. He stands with the conquered Bulgarians cowering at his feet. In his right hand he holds a spear; in his left a sword. At his side are medallions of warrior saints. Around his head hover the archangels Michael and Gabriel, the one touching his spear in blessing and the other his crown, while from above Christ lowers the imperial circlet. Nothing could more clearly express the concept of military might sanctioned by divine power. It was the consummation of an extreme version of Byzantine autocracy.

It found its expression on the battlefield, whereas it was more usual for Byzantine autocracy to find its clearest expression in the ceremonial of the court. Basil II had no time for ceremonial. He was more interested in action. There was a drive and sense of purpose behind his rule, which bordered on the fanatical and accorded ill with the more cautious and diffident, if obstinate, approach favoured by most of his predecessors. He ruled through fear and was not receptive to the advice of others. He was the complete autocrat. As the historian Michael Psellos was to put it: 'He alone decided policy, he alone supervised strategy. He conducted his administration not according to the written laws, but according to the unwritten dictates of his intuition.'[4]

Such a ruler was hard to follow. He had created a style of government, which he alone could manage. It is not in the least surprising that his immediate successors did not measure up to his example. He made their task still more difficult by failing to make adequate provision for his succession. For a very great ruler it was a fearful omission, which it is now impossible to explain. Basil II never married. This can be explained by a conversion to an ascetic way of life early in his reign, as he sought to master both himself and his opponents. His successor was to be his elderly brother Constantine (1025–28), a brave man, whose talents had been sapped by years of indolence, but he only left daughters to succeed him. For the last twenty years of Basil II's reign it must have been clear that the succession would eventually go with the hand of the eldest, Zoe. Yet Basil took no real steps to find her a husband, and by the end of his reign she was probably past child-bearing age. Only when her father, Constantine VIII, was on his death-bed was she hastily married off to Romanos Argyros (1028–34), who then succeeded to the throne. There were to be no children of the marriage.

Thereafter the throne went with Zoe. The constitutional arrangement with Zoe in her dotage resembled that existing with Basil II during his minority, only power now rested not with the magnates of Anatolia, but the great families of Constantinople. Romanos Argyros, her first husband, was the scion of an old aristocratic house. Her next husband, Michael IV the Paphlagonian (1034–41) was the brother of the chief minister John the Orphanotrophos, who was able to induce Zoe to adopt a nephew of his, also called Michael, as her son. He reigned for scarcely six months. Zoe's last husband, Constantine Monomachos (1042–55) was another aristocrat. He outlived her. On his death Theodora, Zoe's younger sister, who never married, reigned briefly. She was the last of the imperial house of Macedon and the succession would remain in doubt until the end of the century, when Alexius I Comnenus (1081–1118) succeeded in establishing the dynastic rights of his family.

Basil II must take much of the blame for the problems of succession that bedevilled Byzantine politics for most of the eleventh century. But, even if he had taken all necessary precautions to protect the succession, there would still have been great difficulties, for the very nature of his rule stored up trouble for the future. He continued even more brutally the imperialist policies of the soldier emperors, Nicephorus Phokas and

John Tzimiskes. These had already strained the resources of the Empire. Nicephorus Phokas was obliged to issue debased gold coins. Basil II tried to minimize these strains by straitjacketing the economy and society. They were to be organized to support the war effort, which meant rigid imperial control. Basil sought to halt changes which he considered weakened the basis of imperial authority, rather than to follow the usual Byzantine practice of bowing to change. As we have seen, he hoped to rebuild a free peasant society with a simple, rather primitive, economy, because this was thought to provide strong foundations for imperial government. In doing so he was going counter to the forces of change, which had been building up for at least a century.

In the early middle ages the Byzantine economy was relatively primitive. It was essentially agrarian. With the exception of Constantinople, Thessalonica, and one or two other places, there was no city life. The great cities of late antiquity had either been swept aside by the invasions of the seventh century or had been reduced to fortresses. The theme, rather than the city, became the focus of local government. It rested on a society of peasant communities. The peasantry supplied the bulk of the troops for the theme armies and paid the bulk of the taxation, which was siphoned off to Constantinople only to be redistributed in the form of wages and other government expenditure. The money economy was thus largely a matter of recycling. Money was used mainly for the payment of taxes and salaries. It cemented a system of government, rather than having any clear economic purpose. Market forces had little impact. There was relatively little trade; the peasantry were more or less self-sufficient. Anything they needed might be obtained at the local fair, where they would take their surplus produce, sell some of it, to obtain money for the payment of taxes, and barter the rest. While gold coins, the staple of state finance, continued to be issued in the early middle ages, there was a distinct falling away in the issues of bronze and copper coinage, which were needed for local and petty transactions. What surplus there may have been was mostly spent in Constantinople, where the supply of petty currency did not dry up. Foreign trade and the manufacture of luxury articles, such as silks, were concentrated in the capital, which on a reduced scale preserved the metropolitan character it possessed in late antiquity.

Constantinople's economic pre-eminence was just a facet of a system of imperial government. Both were predicated upon the continued existence of a primitive economic system, but change was being induced by the growing demands of the imperial administration. When in the middle of the eighth century new taxes were imposed to help pay for the restoration of the Aqueduct of Valens at Constantinople, it was observed that the peasantry had to put more of their produce on the market in order to pay these new impositions. By the middle of the ninth century large issues of bronze coinage were being made to meet and fuel an upsurge in local exchanges. Already at the end of the previous century there is clear evidence for the success of local fairs. At the same time, the appearance of families, whose local power was based on the military organization of the themes, meant that more disposable wealth was retained in the provinces, thus quickening local markets. The fortresses began to acquire some of the marks of a town.

The balance between the market and the state as the determinant of economic activity was shifting imperceptibly towards the former. As this happened, so the provincial towns grew more important. While the greatest of the provincial magnates lived out on their estates in the country, lesser families, whose fortunes were connected with service in the themes and the provincial administration, came to congregate in the towns, thus enhancing their position. The towns became the motors of more marked social differentiation, expressed most clearly in the way that the more powerful or successful families invested in peasant property and began to build up retinues and clientele. It was this which alerted Byzantine emperors of the early tenth century to the changes which were taking place in the structure of the economy and society. As we have seen, their reaction took the form of agrarian legislation designed to protect peasant property. It was hoped in this way to halt changes, which were considered detrimental to the exercise of imperial authority. In practice, it was applied patchily. It would seem that many of the emperors of the tenth century saw it as a screen which would allow them to come to terms with changes in the economy and society, while enabling them to retain much of their authority. Basil II may have been tempted by such an arrangement at the beginning of his reign, but the lesson he learnt from the revolts of the Anatolian armies was that he must suppress all internal opposition and deprive it of its sources of strength. The revival of the agrarian legislation offered the best hope of this.

Basil II was activated by a desire to restore and assert imperial authority to the full. He would not have had much interest in the underlying economic structure of his Empire. There is some evidence that there were civil servants with a reasonably sophisticated understanding of the workings of the economy. They are not likely to have had much influence upon the emperor's policies, which were conceived in terms of the exercise of power, even if presented as acts of philanthropy. The deflationary effects of his agrarian policies were unlooked for, but welcome. It was a way of slowing down the pace of economic and social change.

By the time of his death Basil II had been able to accumulate a massive treasure of 200,000 talents of gold, excluding precious stones and other valuables. This was the largest treasure of any Byzantine emperor since Anastasius back in the early sixth century, when the Empire still included the rich provinces of Syria and Egypt. It is difficult to give an idea of how vast this treasure was. At today's value (450 dollars per ounce) it would be worth 1,440 million dollars, even today quite a respectable sum for an undeveloped country to have put away in gold reserves. This treasure was amassed despite the long and costly wars against the Bulgarians. Apart from windfalls such as the tsar's treasure captured at Ohrid, these wars cannot have yielded much in the way of booty given the primitive level of the Bulgarian economy. There was almost no money in circulation. As part of his peace settlement, Basil II agreed that in Bulgaria taxes should continue to be collected in kind, not in money.

The size of Basil II's treasure is testimony to the harsh character of his fiscal policies and to the success of his measure extending responsibility for the payment of tax arrears to the magnates. It must have meant that a significant proportion of gold currency was withdrawn from circulation. Given that there were few, if any, credit facilities, this would have had a deflationary effect. The consequences can be judged from the fact that at the end of his reign Basil II left two years' taxes uncollected out of pity for the poor. Any beneficial results were immediately cancelled by his brother Constantine VIII's decision to exact the uncollected taxes. Five years' taxes were got in within the space of three years. This measure hit both the poor and the well-to-do and was the cause of hardship and discontent throughout society. There was a rebellion in protest centred on mainland Greece. In Anatolia the condition of the peasantry deteriorated. They showed little resilience in the face of a series of natural disasters and abandoned their holdings. The magnates were expected to shoulder the mounting tax arrears.

It was left to Romanos Argyros, Constantine VIII's son-in-law and successor, to deal with the consequences of these harsh fiscal policies. In the face of the bitterness which they produced, he could hardly continue with them. He met the criticism of the magnates by repealing Basil II's measure which burdened them with the payment of the tax arrears of the peasantry. He treated the starving Anatolian peasants with great humanity, giving them sums of money so that they would return to their native villages. The intention was to restore stability to a peasant society, which harsh taxation threatened to undermine. Basil II's policy of tight fiscal control was abandoned. Any relaxation was likely to benefit the economy, but, unless carefully managed, it could easily get out of control. The first casualty was likely to be government finance. If no effort was made to cut expenditure to meet a fall in revenues, there would be budgetary difficulties. Romanos Argyros remained unaware of the dangers. He not only lavished great sums of money on the church of the Peribleptos, which he was building in Constantinople, as his memorial; worse, he continued Basil II's aggressive foreign policy.

Romanos seems to have been even more ambitious than Basil II. He contemplated the conquest of Syria and Egypt. In 1030 he led an expedition into Syria against Aleppo. He suffered a humiliating reverse, which did much to confirm the view abroad that the strength of the Empire was on the wane. It was then followed in 1033 by an attack on

Egypt. This maritime venture was another failure. The casualties were heavy. 6,000 Byzantine troops are said to have perished. The conquest of Edessa beyond the Euphrates in 1032 was small consolation for these disasters. It was the work of George Maniakes, who continued the brutally heroic spirit of Basil II. He was then sent to Sicily, the conquest of which Basil II had been contemplating at the very end of his reign. Maniakes appeared to be on the point of wresting the island from its African emirs, when he was recalled in 1040 and the initiative was lost. These ambitious undertakings had cost a great deal. Nothing had been gained except Edessa and that was expensive to defend.

The increasingly difficult financial position of the Byzantine government is apparent from a measure taken by Michael the Paphlagonian (1034–41). Despite the pledge given by Basil II, he converted the taxes paid by the Bulgarians in kind into money payments. This sparked off a rebellion in 1040, which spread all over the Bulgarian lands and even affected northern Greece. A scion of the old ruling house of Bulgaria escaped to join the rebels. That the movement did not lead to the restoration of Bulgarian independence was due to the energy and purpose of the Byzantine emperor. He was ill, suffering from epilepsy, and had not long to live, but he left the capital and set up his headquarters at Thessalonica. The Bulgarians attacked the Byzantine camp. Their indiscipline and open order made them an easy target for the imperial troops. The rebellion was crushed. It was nevertheless proof that the Bulgarians remained disaffected, awaiting an opportunity to regain their independence.

An earlier event should have brought home to the Byzantines the difficulties they were likely to face in the Balkans. In 1027 the Petcheneks who had been loyal allies of the Empire for nearly a century crossed the Danube and attacked the Balkans. This invasion was repulsed without much difficulty, but it was a pointer to the future. If the Bulgarians had had their nuisance value and had occasionally been a real threat to the Empire, they had also acted as a buffer which protected Byzantium from the turmoil existing on the Black Sea steppes. The beginnings of the Turkish raids along the eastern frontier in the 1040s would teach a similar lesson about Armenia. While Basil II was reigning, conditions on the steppes seemed set fair. The Petcheneks were the dominant power and respected their treaties with Byzantium. The distant movements of the Seljuq Turks, who were beginning to threaten eastern Iran, hardly registered. There seemed no good reason to abandon the policy of annexing the Armenian principalities, which had been going on in a piecemeal fashion since the early tenth century. Basil speeded it up. By a mixture of force and diplomacy he was able to persuade the Armenian rulers to agree to the reversion of their principalities to the Byzantine Empire after their deaths. It seemed the most effective way of safeguarding Byzantine interests in an area of great strategic importance. Buffer states had become a thing of the past.

Time would show the dangers which Basil II's expansionism held for the Empire.

The annexation of Bulgaria and Armenia provided Basil II's successors with other problems. It meant that substantial minorities distinguished by race, church, and language were introduced into an Empire which had not only been fairly homogeneous but had also displayed a marked capacity for assimilating foreigners. By the early eleventh century the Slavs, who two centuries earlier had formed a very substantial proportion of the population of the Peloponnese, had been absorbed except for two tribes confined to the fastnesses of the Taygetos mountains. Armenians flocked to take service at Constantinople and in the Byzantine armies; they too became good Byzantines, whose Armenian origins were only betrayed by their surnames. But from the time of Basil II's conquests the Byzantines found it more and more difficult to assimilate foreigners. One of its great strengths was starting to wane.

Is there a connection between the two phenomena? Perhaps there is. Basil II is usually congratulated on the far-sightedness of his treatment of the Armenians and the Bulgarians, once peace had been made. As we have seen, the Bulgarians continued to pay their taxes in kind, which was a sensible measure in view of the primitive state of the Bulgarian economy. It was also an earnest that Basil II was not interested in altering the basic conditions prevailing in Bulgaria. This is even clearer in his treatment of the Bulgarian church. It was to retain its old privileges and organization. The Bulgarian identity was closely bound up with its church, with the use of Old Church Slavonic as its liturgical language. It would seem that Basil II saw no reason to assimilate the Bulgarians.

At least, the Bulgarian church was not heretical, even if there were many heretics in Bulgaria. The Armenian church, on the other hand, was in Byzantine eyes heretical. It followed the Monophysite persuasion, refusing to accept the creed of Chalcedon. The Armenians were still more of a problem because they had taken advantage of the Byzantine conquests along the Euphrates to spread southwards into Cilicia and northern Syria. Armenians, who in the past sought their fortunes in Byzantine service, usually found themselves cast adrift from their church and were thus more willing to accept orthodoxy. In the new conquests the Armenian settlers remained in contact with their homeland. By the end of the tenth century the Armenian church was beginning to establish bishoprics for the Armenian colonists. The result was that the majority of them remained true to their own church. It might have been possible to avoid any serious religious conflict in the new conquests, because the bulk of the native population were Syrians, who were also Monophysites. Basil made the mistake of favouring both the Armenian and the Syrian churches, which aroused orthodox suspicions. He also settled Armenian princes and their retainers in

Cappadocia, where they soon clashed with the native Byzantine inhabitants. Religion was the principal cause.

Basil II was interested in effective government. He understood the nature of the price which had to be paid for the annexation of Bulgaria, Armenia, and the lands along the Euphrates: that the customs and religion of the native peoples must be respected. Perhaps he was less conscious of how radically he was altering the character of the Empire. It looked set to become multi-racial, multi-lingual, and multi-confessional. This was not easy for the Byzantine élite to accept. However varied its ethnic origins, it preserved the old Greek contempt for the barbarian, though now investing it with a religious as well as a cultural complexion. At the same time areas vital for the defence of the Empire along the Danube and the Euphrates were inhabited by people not fully reconciled to rule from Constantinople. They became the object of suspicion on the part of the Byzantine government, which in due course would take the form of persecution.

Both internally and externally Basil II bequeathed his successors a poisoned legacy. They were left with a series of extremely hard choices, but it is most unlikely that they realized how hard these choices were. They continued an expensive policy of military aggression, partly because the state was on a military footing, partly as a matter of prestige, largely because they could not think in other terms. Faced with the mounting resentment at the fiscal policies followed by Basil II they had to make concessions, which only produced budgetary difficulties. It was becoming increasingly clear that the attempt to continue Basil II's foreign policy while abandoning his fiscal policy was condemned to failure. It was time to work out new lines of policy, both at home and abroad. In the usual manner of Byzantine reforms the existing machinery of government would be overhauled, in order to make these new policies work. This was going to be the task of Constantine IX Monomachos (1042–55), Zoe's last husband, and the clever young men that he assembled about him.

NOTES

1.   Michael Psellus (transl. by E R A Sewter), p. 43
2.   Zepos, *Jus*, I, p. 265
3.   *Ibid.*, p. 209
4.   Michael Psellus (transl. by E R A Sewter), pp. 43–4

Chapter 2

BYZANTIUM'S PLACE IN THE WORLD, 1025–1071

In the tenth century external conditions favoured Byzantine expansion. Neighbouring powers were all experiencing a greater or lesser degree of political fragmentation. A series of events in the 1040s signalled that these favourable conditions were coming to an end. Byzantium's hold on its northern, eastern, and western frontiers was challenged by new and formidable enemies. In southern Italy the Normans, brigands that they were, began to establish themselves as an independent power. Beyond the Danube, as we have seen, the Petcheneks ceased to play their traditional role as the linchpin of Byzantine diplomacy, while along the eastern frontier pressure began to build up as more and more Turkish tribesmen pushed westwards. Byzantium would need to reorientate itself, if it was to come to terms with this new set of circumstances.

THE RUSSIAN ATTACK OF 1043

The Byzantines should have been alerted to the changes which were taking place beyond their frontiers by the Russian attack on ple in 1043. This was reminiscent of those Russian expeditions against Byzantium of the early tenth century, before the Byzantines had fully worked out a strategy for dealing with the dangers which threatened from the north. Since then they had made it their business to monitor conditions to the north of the Black Sea. They knew that the Russian steppe supported a way of life very different from that of the forest zone to the north. The steppes were given over to herding and a nomadic way of life; the forests to hunters and gatherers. They were also well aware that the Slavs of the forest zone were ruled by Scandinavian traders and marauders, known as the Ros, or more conveniently as Russians, who controlled the river routes leading from the Baltic to the Black Sea and the Caspian.

An alliance with the Petcheneks gave the Byzantines some protection against these Scandinavians. The Petcheneks controlled the lower reaches of the Don and the Dnepr, which the Russians had to navigate if they were to reach the Black Sea. But increasingly it became clear that both the Byzantines and the Russians had much more to gain from trade than from war. A series of commercial treaties were concluded. They gave the Russians a special trading quarter, just across the Golden Horn from Constantinople. There were special payments to Russian merchants bringing goods with them from their homeland. Russian wax was in particular demand at Constantinople to provide candles for its countless churches. These ties were consolidated by Vladimir's conversion to christianity in 989. The success of the Byzantine strategy is apparent. There had been no direct Russian attack on Constantinople since 944 and the last serious conflict with the Russians was in 971, when they were completely defeated by the Byzantines near the mouth of the Danube. The Russian attack on Constantinople in 1043 signalled that Byzantium's northern strategy was beginning to break down.

The exact reasons for the Russian expedition remain mysterious. There is no conclusive evidence to support the two most popular explanations: that it was either an attempt by the Russians to assert complete independence of Byzantium or in response to an appeal for aid from the Byzantine general, George Maniakes, who was preparing a rebellion against the reigning emperor, Constantine IX Monomachos. The first is rather more plausible than the second. One consideration, in particular, more or less rules out the second explanation: Maniakes would not have been in a position to appeal for help until the autumn of 1042, while Russian preparations had started well before this. Troops were recruited from as far afield as Scandinavia. Yaroslav the Wise, the prince of Kiev, put his son Vladimir, the ruler of Novgorod, in command of the expedition. It was not a success. The Russian fleet was worsted in the narrow waters of the Bosporus by the Byzantines, who made effective use of Greek fire. Those Russian troops that got ashore were easily rounded up and many of them were blinded. Another Russian force, which attempted to breach the Danube frontier, was defeated.

Relations between the two powers were soon patched up. In 1046 a marriage was arranged between Maria, daughter of the Emperor Constantine Monomachos, and Vselevod, the younger son of Yaroslav the Wise. The Byzantines agreed to pay compensation for damage done during the period of hostilities to the Russian monastery on Mount Athos and for injuries to Russians resident in the Byzantine Empire. This willingness to pay reparations combined with the reticence of Byzantine accounts of the affair suggests that the Byzantines were not entirely without blame. How exactly it is now impossible to say. It is clear that the rapid development of Kievan Russia under Yaroslav the Wise (1036–54) must have imposed severe strains on Byzantium's relations with the Russian ruler. It lost its barbarian quality and quickly acquired the trappings of an independent Christian polity. Much that Yaroslav did was in pure imitation of Byzantium. He had a Golden Gate built at Kiev and a new church of St Sophia constructed. The growing confidence of the Russians is reflected in the *Sermon on Law and Grace* of the future metropolitan of Russia, Hilarion. In it he acknowledges that the gift of christianity came from Byzantium, but stresses the independence of the ruler of Kiev. This was only too apparent, when in 1051 Yaroslav appointed Hilarion metropolitan of Russia, the first native-born Russian to hold this post, which in the past had always been held by a Greek appointed from Constantinople. Yaroslav died in 1054, dividing his territories among his sons, and the church in Russia returned once again under the direct control of the patriarchate of Constantinople. The appointment of Hilarion as metropolitan of Russia has therefore normally been regarded as something of an aberration, of little significance for the general course of Byzantine relations with Russia. But it sheds some light back on the mood in which Yaroslav undertook the 1043 expedition against Constantinople. He had no time for any Byzantine claims to tutelage, and his great victory at Kiev in 1036 over the Petcheneks meant that he enjoyed a freedom of action unknown to his immediate predecessors.

After Yaroslav's death there is very little information about Byzantine–Russian relations. This is no accident. It reflects the growing distance between the two powers. The various Russian princes looked westwards rather than to Byzantium for their political and matrimonial alliances. The supply of Russian mercenaries to the Byzantine armies began to fall off. This may be part of the explanation why fewer Byzantine gold coins appear to have been in circulation in the Russian lands. It may also be that trade between Russia and Byzantium was now better balanced. There was always at Byzantium a strong demand for the products of the Russian forests, but it was only once Russia was thoroughly christianized that there would be an equivalent demand for the wares and services offered by the Byzantines.

THE PETCHENEKS

Constantine Monomachos had reason to congratulate himself on how well he had dealt with the Russians. His forces had gained a notable victory and the ties between the Byzantine emperor and the ruling family of Kiev appeared to have been re-established. This success for Byzantine arms and diplomacy may have convinced the emperor that he had the situation to the north of the Danube well under control. In the past, the Byzantines used the Petcheneks to police the steppes in their interests; they could be used to threaten not only the Russians, but also the

Bulgarians and the Hungarians. The conquest of Bulgaria and the conversion of the Russians to christianity had lessened their importance in Byzantine eyes. When their position on the steppes began to be challenged by another Turkic people, the Oguz Turks, the Byzantines were not over-concerned. They may even have welcomed the way that pressure from the Oguz was undermining the political stability of the Petcheneks. The inactivity of their leader, Tyrakh, in the face of this threat weakened his ascendancy. He found himself challenged by a minor chieftain, Kegen, who had won a number of victories against the Oguz. In the confrontation that followed the old chieftain was able to reassert his power, and Kegen was forced to flee with his followers, reckoned to be 20,000 all told, to the safety of the Byzantine territories across the Danube. This occurred in either 1045 or 1046. Constantine Monomachos decided to accept a *fait accompli.* Kegen was brought to Constantinople, where he was baptized and given the rank of patrician. He was granted three fortresses along the Danube and his followers were given lands in the vicinity. A monk was sent to preach to them and many were baptized in the waters of the Danube. Once settled Kegen's tribesmen carried out a series of raids against the other Petchenek tribes. Tyrakh protested that these contravened the pacts existing between his people and the Byzantine Empire.

Constantine Monomachos continued to back Kegen. He put the Danube fortresses in order and sent a squadron of the fleet to patrol the Danube. These precautions failed in the face of the harsh winter of 1046–47. The Danube froze over and the Petcheneks rode across the ice to invade Byzantine territory. As so often happened to nomads in the Balkans, the Petcheneks were attacked by disease and became easy prey for the Byzantine forces. Kegen was all for massacring his former compatriots, but the Byzantine government viewed them as potential colonists for the still comparatively empty Balkans. They were settled between Sofia and Nish, astride the main route across the Balkans. Tyrakh and other Petchenek chieftains were taken to Constantinople, baptized, and given high-ranking positions.

Almost at once Constantine Monomachos was faced with an attack on the eastern frontier by the Seljuq sultan. The Petcheneks were excellent mounted archers and were thought capable of matching the Seljuqs who employed similar tactics. A force of 15,000 was raised from the newly settled Petcheneks and in 1048 they were despatched eastwards under their own chiefs. Uncertain about their reception by the people of the eastern provinces of the Empire and uneasy about the foe that awaited them, they mutinied and made their way back across the Bosporus to their families. This act of disobedience soon turned into a full-scale rebellion. The Petcheneks abandoned the hilly wooded country which they had been given to settle. They could never have been very happy in such alien surroundings. Making their way over the Balkan mountains they finally established themselves in a region known as the Hundred Mountains, just inland from the Black Sea coast. It lay very close to the centres of early Bulgarian settlement. Preslav, the old Bulgarian capital, became a Petchenek stronghold. It was all uncomfortably reminiscent of the establishment of the Bulgarians in the Balkans at the end of the seventh century.

Constantine Monomachos was aware of the dangers. At first, he relied on Kegen to deal with the Petcheneks. While on a visit to the emperor, Kegen was the victim of an attempted assassination. This left him and his people suspicious of the emperor's intentions and they hurried back to join up with the main body of Petcheneks. The Byzantine army sent against them failed to dislodge them. This encouraged the Petcheneks in the following summer to cross the Balkan mountains and attack Thrace. They were checked before Adrianople in June 1050 and the Byzantines concentrated on keeping them at bay behind the Balkan mountains. In 1052 the Byzantine forces were once again ready to attack the Petcheneks in their strongholds. They penetrated to Preslav, but were not able to drive the Petcheneks out. As they retreated, the Byzantine forces were completely defeated. It was now clear that the Byzantines were not going to solve the Petchenek problem by military means. There was a wave of popular indignation at the way Byzantine youth was being so needlessly sacrificed in the wars against the Petcheneks. Constantine Monomachos gave in to this pressure and in 1053 a thirty years' truce was arranged with the Petcheneks. The Byzantines had to accept Petchenek settlement south of the Danube as a *fait accompli*. It meant that the Petcheneks were able to keep their chiefs and their tribal structure. They remained a permanent threat to direct Byzantine control of the old Bulgarian lands. Constantine Monomachos hoped to establish them in the Balkans as military colonists; they succeeded in settling on their own terms, as an independent people.

The existence of a truce with the Petcheneks did not prevent the Emperor Isaac Comnenus (1057–59) from launching a campaign against them in the summer of 1059. It had some temporary success. During the reign of his successor Constantine X Doukas (1059–67) the terms of the truce seem to have been respected. All the time, the Petcheneks' old enemy, the Oguz Turks, were encroaching on the Danube frontier, which they finally breached in 1065. They ravaged the whole of the Balkans as far south as Thessalonica. Constantine Doukas's inactivity in the face of this new enemy outraged public opinion. He was criticized for his parsimonious treatment of the army, which meant that there were no effective forces to put into the field against the Oguz. To still criticism he undertook a token expedition against these Turks. He is said to have taken only 150 men with him. This excited the people of Constantinople to unkind comparisons with the army which Dionysius was said to have led against India. The emperor had almost certainly received word that the Oguz were in a bad way. They were being decimated by plague and desired only to extricate themselves from the Balkans. As they retreated they were harassed by Bulgarians and Petcheneks. Constantine Doukas was able to claim a share in this triumph. Soon afterwards some of the Oguz asked to be allowed to settle on Byzantine territory. Constantine agreed and gave them public lands in Macedonia, where they were to protect Byzantine interests.

Byzantine influence in the northern and central Balkans was now very largely exercised through a series of local communities, enjoying a greater or a lesser degree of autonomy from the central government. This was not how Basil II had intended his Balkan territories to be organized. He hoped to establish a regular provincial administration based on themes, which would cover the whole of the Balkans. There was even very briefly in the 1030s a theme of Serbia, but it could not be maintained in the face of Serbian hostility. The Bulgarian uprising of 1040–41 revealed how weakly based Byzantine provincial administration was in other parts of the Balkans. The pacification of the Bulgarians was left to Constantine Monomachos. The Petcheneks must have seemed to him one solution. They had policed the steppes for Byzantium; they could now keep the recalcitrant natives of the Balkans in order. The experiment soon got out of control. The Petcheneks proved to be an uncertain quantity, much more interested in preserving their independence and way of life, than acting as imperial agents and mercenaries. When they finally established themselves in north-eastern Bulgaria, their presence stimulated the local populations of Latin speakers along the Danube to seek greater autonomy from the imperial government. The net result was that Byzantine control in the northern and central Balkans was largely indirect. It was not what Constantine Monomachos had envisaged, but neither was it a complete disaster for the Byzantine Empire. Byzantine garrisons still held some of the key points, notably Sofia and Sirmium. To all intents and purposes a broad frontier region had been created to the south of the Danube, which provided some degree of protection for the rich provinces to the south of the Balkan mountains.

THE SELJUQS

The problems posed by the defence of Byzantium's eastern frontier turned out to be very similar to those along the Danube, but they were complicated by the Armenian question, to which there was no exact parallel in the West. It had been opened up once again by the death in 1040 of John-Smbat III, the ruler of the Armenian kingdom of Ani. He died without issue, but as long ago as 1022 he had designated the

Byzantine emperor as his heir. Byzantine claims to the kingdom did not go uncontested. Gagik, a nephew of the dead ruler, was put on the throne of Ani. He capitulated before a show of force; his abdication sweetened by the promise of estates in Cappadocia, where he retired with many leading Armenian families in 1045. Exactly twenty years later the Byzantines also annexed the Armenian principality of Kars. This was not mindless aggression. Pressure from the Turks on the Armenian lands was building up. In 1053 Kars had been sacked by the Turks and the Armenians were happy to seek Byzantine protection. On the Byzantine side it was a way of ensuring that the strongpoints that dominated the invasion routes from Iran to Anatolia were in Byzantine hands. At first, this strategy seemed to pay off. If in 1048 the Armenian trading centre of Artze was sacked by the Turks, in September of that year the Byzantine forces under the command of Kekavmenos Katakalon were able to force the Seljuq sultan to evacuate Armenia. His attack on Mantzikert, which controlled one of the main invasion routes to the north of Lake Van, was decisively beaten off. Two years later the Seljuq sultan made another thrust into Armenia and again failed to achieve anything. At this stage the Byzantines were more than holding their own. In 1055 the two sides came to terms. The Seljuq Sultan Tugrul Beg had just conquered Baghdad and the Caliphate now came under his protection. The Byzantines recognized his claims by arranging that in future the name of the Seljuq sultan should be commemorated in the Friday prayers at the mosque in Constantinople. The Byzantines abandoned their alliance with the Fatimids of Egypt. The Byzantines imagined that they could look forward to a new era of stability in their dealings with the Muslim world, now that a strong power controlled the lands of the Caliphate.

Any such hopes were to be disappointed. This was not entirely a matter of bad faith on the part of the Seljuq sultan. He needed some measure of ascendancy in the Armenian uplands, not because he had any grand design for the invasion of Byzantine Anatolia, but because he needed to protect the western flank of his dominions. It was his policy to shunt large numbers of Turkish tribesmen in this direction, in order to protect his Iranian territories from their depredations. They pressed westwards into Armenia. In 1058 their warbands gained their first major success when they managed to penetrate the Byzantine defences and sack the city of Melitene. The next year they managed to get as far as Sebastea and sacked it too. It looked as though the sultan might be losing control over these warbands. Their exploits threatened to involve him in war with the Byzantines, who might be expected to renew their old alliance with his bitter enemies, the Fatimids of Egypt. To restore his ascendancy over the Turkish warbands, the sultan needed a measure of authority in the Armenian lands. In 1064 as an earnest of his intentions he captured Ani, the old capital of the Armenian kingdom.

From a Byzantine angle what needs to be explained is this: why did the

Byzantine defences which had coped so well with the Turkish attacks suddenly break down in 1058–59? Superficially, it was just a matter of temporary weakness. The eastern defences had been depleted of troops in 1057, when Isaac Comnenus drew off many of the Anatolian units to help him in his successful bid for the throne of Constantinople. It soon became apparent that it went deeper than this. The whole Byzantine defensive strategy was suspect because it was too static. It depended on a few key positions being held in strength by professional troops. The Turkish warbands soon learnt to make use of their superior mobility: they were able to skirt round these obstacles and attack more vulnerable targets further inland.

The sack of Melitene in 1058 must have alerted the Byzantine government to the shortcomings of their strategy, but its options were limited by the policy of financial retrenchment followed under Constantine X Doukas (1059–67). It was, in any case, far from certain that another strategy would have worked any better. The strategy adopted was not without its merits and resembled that followed in the Balkans. It aimed at the creation of a broad frontier zone covering the Armenian uplands and the Euphrates lands, where Byzantine control would rest on a few key positions. If this strategy was to work, the loyalty of the local people was essential. They were mostly Armenians and Syrians, whose first allegiance was to their churches. These were of the Monophysite persuasion and therefore, in Byzantine eyes, heretical. In a polity where church and society were indistinguishable, this naturally produced grave suspicions about the loyalty of the Armenians and Syrians. One response of the Byzantines to the Turkish invasions was to try and secure their loyalty. This they tried to do by ending the schism separating the churches. The Armenians and Syrians were suspicious of the Byzantine intentions and refused to cooperate. Under the Patriarch Constantine Leichoudes (1059–64) Byzantine patience gave out and persecution began in an attempt to force the Armenian and Syrian churches into communion with Constantinople. This only reinforced the resentment of the Syrians and Armenians. In the face of such disaffection the Byzantine hold on the borderlands became increasingly precarious. In 1067 the Turks were able to penetrate further westwards then ever before and sacked the great city of Cappadocian Caesarea. The nomads took particular delight in plundering the cathedral of St Basil. This disaster stemmed from the failure of the Byzantine garrison at Melitene to oppose the Turks as they crossed the Euphrates. The Byzantine government could not have anticipated such a total failure of morale.

It was alarming how easily the Turks were able to penetrate the border defences and ravage the lands of Byzantine Anatolia. For nearly two centuries this region had suffered only minor incursions. The defensive system built up to resist the Arab invasions was allowed to run down. The Turks found that once across the Euphrates they had little to fear from the Byzantines. It was no wonder, then, that when Constantine Doukas died in 1067 there was a clamour for a military man to run the Empire. The choice was in the hands of his Empress Eudocia Makrembolitissa, whom he had left to govern the Empire on behalf of their young sons. She soon gave in to the agitation to associate in the imperial office a man capable of restoring the Empire's military fortunes. Her choice fell on Romanos Diogenes, who had enjoyed a reasonably distinguished military career in the Balkans. He came from an Anatolian family, which had done well under Basil II. He was crowned emperor on 1 January 1068 and immediately set about reversing the policies and strategy followed by his predecessor. Romanos realized that the existing Byzantine forces would never be able to recover the initiative against the Turks. They consisted mainly of small numbers of foreign mercenaries, who might be able to conduct a defensive war, but were in no position to take the offensive. Romanos needed other sources of troops. He hoped to find these by the simple expedient of restoring the armies of the themes. These had been allowed to run down since the reign of Basil II and had become more or less moribund in the previous twenty odd years. Romanos mustered what was left of the armies of the themes in the summer of 1068. It was a depressing sight; the levies were poorly armed and ill-disciplined. They did not look a particularly promising foundation for the re-establishment of the eastern frontiers of the Empire.

Romanos seemed undismayed. His campaign of 1068 was directed towards clearing the Turkish marauders out of central Anatolia. He then moved on to secure the frontiers around the fortress city of Antioch. This he achieved by a thrust against Aleppo. The Turks simply took advantage of this preoccupation with the Syrian frontier to invade Asia Minor once again, reaching as far west as the fortress of Amorion. The emperor was beginning to learn how slippery an enemy the Turks were. It was difficult to devise any satisfactory tactics to counter their exceptional mobility. The cumbersome army, which Romanos had got together, hardly seemed to be the answer. In 1069 he made his base at Cappadocian Caesarea, from which he could survey most of the invasion routes into Anatolia. He achieved some small successes and felt that he had secured his primary objective, which was to clear central Anatolia of the Turkish warbands. There can be little doubt that Romanos, like other Byzantine emperors before him, was mainly interested in the security of Byzantine Asia Minor. This was the area where his family had its estates, as did the aristocratic families on whose support he relied. It was equally clear that unless the border regions were properly secured Byzantine provinces of Anatolia would once again have to face centuries of raiding, and in such conditions it was far from certain that the great families would be able to keep their estates together. There were therefore sound reasons underlying the strategy which Romanos now adopted. His plan was to recover possession of

Khliat, the key to the main invasion routes through Armenia, which passed to the north of Lake Van. Romanos's circle of advisers argued that if Khliat and the surrounding fortresses, including Mantzikert, could be recovered and garrisoned in force, then the Turkish invasions would be blocked at source.

The strategy was sound, but not the logistics. It proved impossible to move a large and encumbered army from the Euphrates to the region of Lake Van. It is very difficult country and food was hard to come by. It was decided that the army must be divided. One section was then defeated by the Turks; the other under the command of the emperor never reached Khliat. The best the emperor could do was to extricate his troops from the Armenian foothills and lead them back to the comparative safety of Sebastea. The Turks had in the meantime cut through to Ikonion, which they sacked. An attempt to cut them off as they returned through Cilicia failed.

The next year Romanos did not take the field, but left the defence of Asia Minor to Manuel Comnenus, a nephew of the late Emperor Isaac Comnenus. He tried to intercept the Turks near Sebastea, but was defeated and captured. Worse was to follow: another Turkish warband broke through and reached the great pilgrim city of Chonai in western Asia Minor. They ransacked the church of St Michael the Archangel, one of the most venerable places of worship in the Empire. Nowhere in Asia Minor now seemed safe from the Turks. The emperor gathered a force, but because of uncertainty about the fate of Manuel Comnenus and the whereabouts of the enemy he disbanded it almost immediately. His aggressive strategy on which so much hope had been placed was in tatters. Asia Minor seemed to be even more open to Turkish raids than had been the case when a passive, defensive approach had been the order of the day.

MANTZIKERT 1071

So meagre had been the success enjoyed by Romanos that, when Manuel Comnenus reappeared with a Turkish chieftain, his erstwhile captor, in tow, it was greeted as a minor triumph. The chieftain was fêted and given the high rank of *proedros*. This was to be an insidious precedent. It pointed forward to the day when the only means the Byzantines had of counteracting the Turkish threat was by attracting Turkish chieftains into imperial service. For Romanos it was a way of distracting attention from his lack of success against the Turks and hiding how weak his position at Constantinople was becoming. He had been brought to the throne to deal with the Turkish invasions. His promises of a military solution had been shown to be hollow. Opposition to him, centring on the Caesar John Doukas, the late emperor's brother, was gathering strength. If Romanos was to hold on to power he needed a resounding success.

So, in the summer of 1071 he gathered his forces, by now better trained, for what was to be the decisive campaign. He returned to the strategy which had failed so abysmally in 1069: to secure control over the Lake Van fortresses. This time he was not going to approach the region from the direction of Melitene on the Euphrates, but from Theodosioupolis, the modern Erzerum. This route was rather shorter and offered better supplies for a large army. The size of Romanos's army is difficult to estimate. The only figures given are ludicrously large. All that can be said is that it was a considerable force, perhaps as many as 40,000 soldiers. The bulk was made up of native troops, but there were also foreign contingents: Petcheneks, Oguz, Normans, and Armenians. Most of these were sent with the *Magistros* Joseph Tarchaneiotes to besiege the fortress of Khliat. Romanos commanded the main body of the army, which included some Oguz and a strong detachment of Armenian infantry. He laid siege to Mantzikert, which had recently been captured by the Seljuq Sultan Alp Arslan.

The fortress fell to the Byzantine emperor with surprising ease; and a Byzantine garrison was installed. The main body of the army encamped on the plain outside. It was only at this point that foragers brought news of the approach of a substantial Turkish army. Romanos immediately sent word to Joseph Tarchaneiotes instructing him to join forces with the emperor. There was no reply, because Tarchaneiotes and his troops were already in headlong flight towards the safety of Melitene. They had learnt that they were facing the full might of Seljuq power and that the sultan himself was in command. The emperor was left to face the sultan alone. The sultan offered a peace treaty, which the emperor turned down. He felt that the sultan was probably playing for time, waiting for reinforcements. He decided that he had more to gain from immediate action. The longer he delayed the greater the danger that his Oguz troops might desert to the Seljuqs; they were of the same Turkish stock. Battle was joined on 26 August 1071. The Byzantines moved forward cautiously, keeping their ranks. They seemed to be having the better of the fight. As evening drew on, the emperor judged it prudent to disengage and seek the safety of his camp. He did not wish to spend a night out in the open, where his troops would be at the mercy of the Turkish archers.

From the moment that the retreat was sounded things began to go disastrously wrong for the Byzantines. Retreat is a difficult manoeuvre at the best of times and Romanos's men were far from being veterans. As they retreated they had to endure the Turkish arrows and there was nothing they could do to counter the Turks. The uncertainty in the Byzantine ranks was only increased by rumours that the emperor had been defeated. There is the strongest suspicion that these rumours and the panic which ensued were deliberately fostered by Andronicus Doukas, the eldest son of the Caesar John Doukas. He had been taken on the campaign as a virtual hostage and had been put in command of the rearguard, where in normal circumstances he could do least harm. Once the retreat had started and the Turks began their usual encircling tactics, command of the rearguard assumed the greatest importance. As long as it remained intact, the main body of the army had some protection from the Turks. If it broke, then the army would almost certainly break up and find itself at the mercy of the Turks. There were good reasons why Andronicus Doukas should have wanted the defeat of Romanos. If the emperor emerged from this campaign with credit, then there was every chance that the Doukas family would lose its position at Constantinople. The sons of Constantine X Doukas would be ousted from the line of succession in favour of the sons borne by Eudocia Makrembolitissa to Romanos.

The defeat at Mantzikert was not solely a matter of treachery. It was also a failure of military discipline and skills. There are signs of faulty intelligence: the appearance of the sultan and his army took the Byzantine emperor by surprise. There was a lack of coordination among the different army commanders. Finally, the army did not have the discipline nor the experience to execute the relatively complicated manœuvre of retreat to camp. Byzantine commanders had been used to working with small bodies of troops. The skills of command needed for deploying large bodies of troops had grown rusty. It was only because of these military deficiencies that Andronicus Doukas's treachery could have the devastating effect that it had.

The Byzantine army does not appear to have suffered very heavy casualties at Mantzikert. The army commanders were able to escape with the bulk of their troops. The full brunt of the Turkish onslaught fell upon the *corps d'élite* around the emperor. When he saw what was going wrong, he tried to save the day by turning and making a stand. It was in vain. He was captured and led before the sultan who treated him with great generosity. The two rulers spent eight days together. A peace treaty was drawn up. The Byzantines lost little or no territory, except for the vital fortresses to the north of Lake Van. It confirmed Seljuq ascendancy in the Armenian lands. It is not likely that Alp Arslan wished for more than this. His great rival was not the Byzantine emperor, but the Fatimid caliph of Egypt; and his ambitions lay in that direction.

The defeat at Mantzikert has always been taken as one of the turning points of Byzantine history. Its repercussions were certainly far more serious than they should have been. At the most, it should have meant that the Armenian uplands and the Euphrates lands passed out of the Byzantine sphere of influence; with frontiers following much the same lines along the Taurus mountains, as they had before the Byzantine advance in the tenth century. Byzantine Anatolia would have become a

23

marcher land once again, open to foreign invasion, but these lands had been successfully held against the Arabs. There was nothing in the defeat of Mantzikert, which pointed to the unbelievably swift conquest of Anatolia by the Turks, which followed. It is not, therefore, by itself a satisfactory explanation of the fall of Asia Minor. It is altogether more complicated than that. Perhaps the best way of putting it is this: by their victory at Mantzikert the Turks were given the opportunity of exploiting the political weaknesses of the Byzantine Empire.

The nature and the causes of these weaknesses have already been briefly touched upon and they will be considered in more detail below. For the moment it is enough to say that Byzantium, like so many other imperial powers, was always at its most vulnerable when a period of conquest and expansion was coming to an end. It took time to realize that the aggressive foreign policy inherited from Basil II had little to recommend it. The cost of maintaining the Empire on a permanent war footing was becoming exorbitant and the gains were negligible. The deficiencies of Byzantine foreign policies were starkly revealed by a series of events in the early 1040s. There were serious revolts in the Byzantine territories in southern Italy and the Balkans. A punitive expedition sent against the Serbs was a complete fiasco. The Byzantine hold in these areas was nothing like so secure as the Byzantine government had imagined. Then, the Russian attack in 1043 brought home the dangers of neglecting old alliances. The emperor called upon to refashion Byzantine foreign policy in the light of these events was Constantine IX Monomachos (1042–55). At first sight, he and his advisers adopted sound and sensible solutions to the problems facing the Empire. They wanted to create buffer zones in southern Italy, along the Danube, and beyond the Euphrates. In these regions, they were willing to tolerate a reasonable level of local independence, but intended to hold on to the main fortresses and towns, which would be garrisoned with professional troops. They hoped to protect these buffer zones by cultivating friendly relations with neighbouring powers. Embassies were exchanged with the German Emperor Henry III; an alliance was forged with the papacy; the Serbian ruler accepted a Byzantine court title; a crown was sent to the ruler of Hungary; an imperial bride to the son of the prince of Kiev; feelers were put out for an alliance with the Seljuqs, while at the same time efforts were made to keep the friendly relations with the Fatimids of Egypt in being. At the very end of his reign Constantine Monomachos authorized the despatch of 400,000 *artabae* of corn to Egypt to help relieve the terrible famine there.

What went wrong? For on the face of it, at least, it all looked eminently sensible. The fashioning of any new line of policy is easier done on paper than in practice. The problems are immense. The state has to be reorganized to meet a new set of objectives. In the process established interests see their position being threatened. In the present case, it was the army which suffered. Recourse to diplomacy rather than force as a way of regulating relations with the outside world did away with the necessity of maintaining very large numbers of troops under arms. We shall see how Constantine Monomachos disbanded the army of Iberia. He also dismissed units of the army based on Adrianople. This was much resented; and the disaffected troops fomented the rebellion of Leo Tornikios in 1047. This in turn helped to create the conditions which made possible the successful Petchenek uprising.

The settlement of the Petcheneks was mismanaged. The Byzantines had long adopted the expedient of establishing foreign military colonies in order to protect their interests in the Balkans. John Tzimiskes (969–76) established heretical Paulicians from Asia Minor at Philippopolis to protect Thrace from the Bulgarians. Hungarians were settled in the middle reaches of the Vardar valley to survey the approach routes to Thessalonica. The Petcheneks were to be used in a very similar manner. They were settled along a section of the military road across the Balkans to the north of Sofia. This would both drive a wedge between different groups of Bulgarians and ensure control of one of the vital arteries of the Balkans. What the government of Constantine Monomachos did not take into account was that the lands they gave the Petcheneks were quite unsuited to their traditional way of life. In addition, it was dealing with vast numbers of people, far in excess of other military colonies established in the Balkans. The failure to deal with the Petcheneks by force discredited the policies embraced by Constantine Monomachos and his advisers.

As a result, there was not that consistency in the execution of a new line of policy which was essential, if it was to succeed in the face of numerous obstacles. Isaac Comnenus (1057–59) tried to reverse the approaches adopted by Monomachos, but he did not stay in power long enough to elaborate his own line of foreign policy. Constantine Doukas (1059–67) returned to the Monomachos line, but failures in Asia Minor, where many of the great families had their landed base, discredited his defensive strategy; and, as we have seen, Romanos Diogenes came to power on a wave of popular indignation. If a defensive strategy had not worked all that well, the aggressive strategy adopted with such energy and singlemindedness by Romanos Diogenes was a total failure. This was apparent before the defeat of Mantzikert. Romanos's search and destroy tactics had little success against a guerrilla enemy, such as the Turks. They found it all too easy to evade the clutches of the cumbersome armies the emperor led across Anatolia. For the future the most insidious lesson seems to have been that the Petchenek episode was not quite the disaster it had seemed. The settlement of a Turkic people retaining their tribal organization was seen to be compatible with the maintenance of some semblance of imperial control of the regions where they were established. This was a precedent that might be applied to the Turkish tribesmen in Anatolia.

Byzantium tried to extricate itself from the legacy of Basil II's foreign policy by substituting flexible frontiers for fixed ones, but by the 1070s found itself with no clear frontiers. It was more than ever a matter of trying to find ways of controlling a recalcitrant native population and of creating a *modus vivendi* with foreign settlers. It became for a time almost impossible to separate the strands of domestic and foreign policy. Byzantium would have to operate with a system of frontiers which had become permeable. Nowhere would this be clearer than in its relations with the West, but until the late eleventh century the West hardly impinged directly upon Byzantium, except for a single incident, the schism of 1054. Even in this case, both sides hurriedly tried to forget what had happened.

BYZANTIUM AND THE WEST

Byzantium and the West touched in southern Italy, where the Byzantines retained a foothold. Their presence there at first sight seems to be a historical accident, all that remained from the reconquests of Justinian. It seemed to have little relevance to an empire based on Constantinople. Yet the Byzantines showed extraordinary skill and tenacity in holding on to their territories in southern Italy. It might be argued that they had some strategic value as a cover for Byzantine interests in the Adriatic region, but it was much more a matter of prestige. In the face of the papacy and the western Empire a presence in southern Italy was an earnest of Byzantium's claims to a universal empire. This was the cause of plenty of bickering with both the papacy and the western Empire. On a number of occasions western emperors had laid claim to the Byzantine territories, but from the late tenth century Byzantine relations with both the papacy and the western Empire had been surprisingly good. If the German emperors still tried on occasion to assert their suzerainty over the Lombard duchies of Capua, Salerno, and Benevento, which lay on the frontiers of Byzantine rule, they respected Byzantine territory. While, strictly speaking, a state of schism existed between the Roman and Byzantine churches from the pontificate of Sergius IV (1009–12), this was only discovered long after the event. At the time, nobody seemed to care.

The relative indifference of the papacy and the western Empire to the Byzantine presence in southern Italy gave the Byzantines the best opportunity they would have to recover Sicily from the Arabs. By 1040 the reconquest of Sicily seemed to be within the grasp of the Byzantine commander, George Maniakes, but he was dismissed from his post and the initiative lost. Thereafter events moved too quickly for the Byzantines, and they found it increasingly difficult to keep control of their Italian territories. The recall of Maniakes was the signal for a revolt by the armies of the themes of southern Italy. Norman freebooters who had been terrorizing the Lombard duchies for nearly twenty years invaded the Byzantine territories and defeated the Byzantine governor. This was the opportunity that Argyros had been waiting for. Despite his Greek name he was the head of the leading Latin family of Bari, the chief city of Byzantine Italy. His father had earlier rebelled against the Byzantines and had been forced to seek refuge at the German court. Argyros seized control of Bari in the wake of the Byzantine defeat by the Normans. He soon came to an understanding with the Norman chiefs and in February 1042 he was jointly elected 'Prince and Duke of Italy' by the Normans and the militia of Bari. The Byzantine government reacted with energy and decisiveness. Maniakes was reinstated as governor and commander-in-chief of Byzantine Italy. Argyros was won over to the Byzantine side by the promise of the rank of patrician and drove the Normans out of Bari, while Maniakes crushed any further local resistance. Byzantine control reasserted, Maniakes almost immediately began to plan rebellion. He was convinced that he had nothing to lose because he had powerful enemies at court. In the early spring of 1043 he crossed from southern Italy to Albania, taking with him most of the available forces. Argyros remained aloof, thus further commending himself to the Emperor Constantine Monomachos. In 1045 the emperor called him to Constantinople where he became one of his most trusted supporters.

By prompt action the Byzantine government had averted the loss of its territories in Italy, but in retrospect the events of 1040–43 were ominous. They brought into the open the weaknesses of Byzantine rule. These sprang from a combination of a growing awareness of local interests and the presence of the Normans on the northern frontiers of the Byzantine lands. The comparatively rapid economic and commercial development of southern Italy from the turn of the tenth century meant that there was more at stake. By the middle of the eleventh century southern Italy was enjoying a level of prosperity, not seen since the fall of the Roman Empire and probably long before that. Byzantine Italy became one of the main centres for the production of raw silk in the Mediterranean. In the early middle ages such towns as there were depended upon agriculture and functioned as centres of defence. Now they were orientated towards production and trade and had developed a strong artisan class. The towns were gaining in bargaining power with the Byzantine authorities. The town of Troia, for instance, was exempted from the payment of commercial dues in its local theme by the Byzantine governor. The grant of such a privilege presupposes that the town must have had some organization of its own. Real power was passing into the hands of an urban patricate.

Local interests were further complicated by confessional and ethnic differences. The population of southern Italy was very mixed. The Greek element had been much strengthened since the turn of the ninth century by the transfer of populations from the eastern and Balkan provinces of the Empire. The founding of many Byzantine monasteries, which had then become the centres of rural life, also went to strengthen the Greek element. In general terms the further east and south that you went, the larger the number of Greek speakers and followers of the orthodox rite, difficult as it now is to disentangle the pattern of ecclesiastical geography. Orthodox and catholic bishoprics existed cheek by jowl, though no city had both an orthodox and a catholic bishop. A further complication lay in the way that some Greek churches followed the Latin rite and Latin churches the Greek. During the iconoclast controversy of the eighth century jurisdiction over the church in southern Italy and Sicily had been unilaterally transferred by the Byzantine Emperor Leo III from Rome to Constantinople and had remained a bone of contention ever since. In 1024 the Byzantine church hoped to persuade the papacy to recognize this transfer of ecclesiastical jurisdiction, but had failed. It remained a sore point. There was always potential in southern Italy for division, but effective Byzantine rule from the mid-tenth century had concealed the fact.

The Normans were the power most likely to benefit from these divisions. The Byzantine Emperor Constantine Monomachos was fully conscious of the threat from these soldiers of fortune. In 1051 he raised Argyros to the rank of *magistros* and appointed him duke of Italy, with the widest possible powers, in the hope that he would be able to impose some solution on southern Italy. The Normans had support in Bari and Argyros hoped that he would be able to attract the Normans into Byzantine service. Suddenly the possibility of a different approach opened up. The people of the Lombard duchies rose up against the hated Normans. Argyros put himself at their head and allied with Pope Leo IX against the Normans. The enemy proved too formidable. Argyros was defeated in the spring of 1053 and in the summer of that year the pope was captured by the Normans at Civitate. The Byzantines failed in their attempt to drive the Normans out of their bases in southern Italy, but these defeats hardly pointed to the fall of Byzantine Italy to the Normans. Other factors came into play.

The patriarch of Constantinople, Michael Keroularios (1043–58), had been following events in southern Italy with a jaundiced eye. Argyros he regarded as his mortal enemy. During his stay at the Byzantine court from 1045 to 1051 he had been the patron of the Latin churches in Constantinople. He had taken part in debates with the patriarch over the differences of rite separating the Orthodox and Latin churches and the patriarch regarded his views as heretical. He was suspicious of the influence which Argyros and his supporters at Constantinople appeared to wield with the emperor. His appointment as viceroy of Byzantine Italy in 1051 concentrated the patriarch's attention on the problems of the church in those lands. He would have been disturbed to discover that the senior bishop of southern Italy, John of Trani, was also a Latin. It was also becoming clear to him that Latins used unleavened bread or 'azymes', while the Byzantines used leavened bread. The patriarch found the Latin custom uncomfortably reminiscent of Jewish practice, and at the end of 1052 he closed down the Latin churches in Constantinople. At the same time, Leo, archbishop of Ohrid, despatched a letter to John of Trani indicating in no uncertain terms what Byzantine practice was in the matter and condemning the use of 'azymes'. John of Trani passed the document on to the papacy, where it was assumed that the letter was inspired by the patriarch. It remains a plausible assumption.

The patriarch's actions over the 'azymes' were to produce a wave of indignation at Rome. Pope Leo IX suspended the negotiations with the patriarch over the question of regularizing the relations between their churches, and in January 1054 commissioned papal legates to investigate the patriarch's conduct. Keroularios was simply mystified. This was partly because he regarded it as a domestic matter and partly out of sheer ignorance of the Roman church. He cast round for an explanation of the papacy's apparently inexplicable behaviour and his suspicions came to rest on his old enemy Argyros. He accused him of tampering with his correspondence with the papacy in a deliberate effort to undermine good relations between the patriarch and the pope. There is no doubting the strength of the patriarch's conviction that Argyros was to blame for the whole affair. It is now impossible to establish the truth of the accusation, but prompting Keroularios's actions was a firm belief that the 'azymes' controversy was being used by his political opponents to attack him personally. He was afraid that they would be quite willing to sacrifice the well-being of the Orthodox church to gain their political ends.

His suspicions even reached as far as the Emperor Constantine Monomachos, whose welcome for the papal legates led by Cardinal Humbert of Silva Candida was rather too cordial. The direction of imperial favour was all too evident, when on 24 June 1054 Constantine ordered a pamphlet directed against Roman teachings to be burnt. The emperor realized how delicate the situation was in Italy. The Normans were triumphant and Pope Leo IX had recently died on 15 April, a prisoner of the Normans. He wished to preserve the alliance with the papacy and this meant making concessions. He urged that communion between the two churches should be restored and that differences should be tolerated. Keroularios decided that this might produce a situation where the church of Constantinople accepted communion with a pope whose views were heretical. He turned down any compromise as unthinkable: 'If the head of a fish is rotten, how can the rest be healthy' was his final opinion.

The patriarch's obduracy vexed both the emperor and the papal legates. The impasse was breached in the most dramatic fashion on 16 July 1054 when the papal legates entered the cathedral of St Sophia and laid upon the altar a bull anathematizing the patriarch and all who supported him. Once again, it is impossible to say what induced the legates to take this precipitate action, which was out of keeping with anything which had gone before. Strictly speaking, their actions had no validity. With the death of the pope their commissions had lapsed. The news must have reached Constantinople by the end of May at the very latest, given the relative ease of communication between southern Italy and the Byzantine capital. It is something of a mystery why the papal legates remained so long at Constantinople. It can only have been at the prompting of the emperor; they enjoyed his favour and they may well have believed that their action against the patriarch enjoyed his tacit support.

The patriarch retrieved the bull and had it translated into Greek. Its purport was deliberately altered in translation, so that it became a charge not just against the patriarch, but the whole Byzantine church. The legates had already left Constantinople with the emperor's blessing, bearing with them gifts for St Peter. Keroularios protested and demanded that they be brought back to the capital, so that their conduct could be investigated. The emperor did his best to protect them by insisting that he should be present at any meeting between the patriarch and the legates. The patriarch would not countenance this. He fomented a riot and the emperor was forced to climb down. Constantine despatched a delegation to the patriarch, which included his enemy, Michael Psellos. It delivered an imperial letter authorizing the patriarch to punish those responsible for the incident. The blame was placed on the supporters of Argyros, whose son and son-in-law, both resident in Constantinople, were imprisoned. Two Latin interpreters were beaten and tonsured and handed over to Keroularios. The contents of the bull were anathematized, as were those responsible. The legates were finally allowed to depart for Rome. It was a triumph for the patriarch, a setback for the emperor, whose Italian policy was now in ruins, and a humiliation for the papal legates and the Roman church.

The events of 1054 are often singled out as of pivotal importance in the history of the middle ages. In retrospect, they probably were, even if contemporaries, both Latin and Byzantine, seem to have done their best to forget about them. They were embarrassing and confusing; and it would take a little while for their meaning to emerge. It was even then difficult to decide exactly what had happened. The motives on both sides appear petty and personal, hardly inspired by great issues of principle. Only slowly were the principles involved perceived. It was part of a process of rediscovery. For nearly two centuries the two churches had only had occasional contact. The events of 1054 revealed that neither church matched up to the image the other required of it. For the reformers around Pope Leo IX, men convinced of the primacy of the see of St Peter, the recalcitrancy of the Byzantine patriarch was literally anathema. For their part the Byzantines began to discover what papal primacy meant to these reformers. It seems that it was only during the exchanges which occurred in 1054 that the Byzantines learnt of the existence of the Donation of Constantine and the doctrine of papal primacy based upon it. This was deeply disturbing to the Byzantines. They willingly accepted that the pope enjoyed a primacy of honour among the five patriarchs of the church universal. They could not, however, countenance the idea that the unity of the church depended upon submission to the papacy. This would have undermined the authority of the general council of the church, which was in Byzantine eyes the one true guarantor of the unity of the Christian church. In the aftermath of the schism of 1054 Byzantine theologians slowly became convinced that the two churches were separated not so much by questions of doctrine or liturgical practice, more by papal claims to primacy of jurisdiction over the whole Christian church.

Over many centuries the relations of the two churches had been characterized by countervailing currents of interest and indifference, of attraction and repulsion. There had been schisms before 1054 and they had been patched up, because the sentiment of a common brotherhood in Christ proved to be stronger than any points of doctrine or practice which separated them. Such sentiments were not destroyed by the schism of 1054, but they were weakened. As a result, the crusades which grew, in part, out of a desire on both sides to renew, in a positive way, a unity of faith were undermined from the beginning by a lack of trust engendered by the events of 1054.

This was for the future. In the short term, the main effect of the schism of 1054 was to hasten a political realignment in Italy. After some hesitations the papacy sought an alliance with the Normans. This was sealed at the council of Melfi in 1059. Pope Nicholas II invested the Norman leader, Robert Guiscard, with Apulia and Sicily, since they formed, in theory, part of the patrimony of St Peter, and he also bestowed upon him a papal banner. Overnight, the Normans were transformed from brigands into agents of St Peter. They acquired instant respectability. As the chronicler Amatus of Monte Cassino observed, 'Duke Robert repented of his past sins and guarded against present and future sins and thus he began to love the priests.'[1] It is difficult to overestimate the importance of the support of the monastery of Monte Cassino, because of the moral influence it possessed. It was the abbot of Monte Cassino, Desiderius, who was chiefly responsible for the *rapprochement* of the Normans and the papacy. The change in Norman fortunes which followed the Investiture of Melfi was staggering. The Normans had been in southern Italy for almost exactly forty years, but they still held no more than a few strongholds, of which Melfi was one of the most important. They had not fully succeeded in breaking out to the south into Byzantine territories. Then, in 1060 Robert Guiscard was able to secure the towns of Reggio on the toe of Italy and Brindisi and Taranto on the heel. Byzantine Italy was now caught in the Norman net.

It would only be a matter of time before other towns were reduced one by one. The dangers were apparent to Gisulf II, the Lombard duke of Salerno, who saw his own position threatened should the Byzantines be driven out of Italy. In 1062 he arrived in Constantinople disguised as a pilgrim on his way to Jerusalem. He sought an alliance with the Emperor Constantine Doukas against the Normans. There was little response from the Byzantine government. It was economizing and the southern Italian territories were left to survive as best they could. As long as Bari, the chief Byzantine stronghold, held out, there was every chance that the situation might be restored at a more favourable opportunity. The city was put under siege by the Normans in 1068. It would fall in 1071. The Emperor Romanos Diogenes was preoccupied by the eastern frontier and could only despatch a small naval squadron, which accomplished nothing. Otherwise, the best he could do was to keep on good terms with the abbot of Monte Cassino and give him some help with the rebuilding of the abbey church. He was looking ahead to the time when the Normans would be forced to come to terms with the Byzantine government. Then the offices of the abbot might prove to be very useful. There was nothing for the present but to accept what had happened. The loss of southern Italy could hardly be construed as the loss of a region vital to the safety of the Empire.

This defeatism was realistic, but it stands in contrast to the energetic measures taken by the Byzantine government in 1042 after Bari had fallen; in contrast, even, to the perceptive, if unsuccessful, attempt to drive the Normans out of southern Italy between 1051 and 1054. This was the crucial failure. It was not simply due to that peculiar combination of qualities displayed by the Normans, for it was only afterwards that their drive, military flair, and lack of scruples became decisive. Even then, the path to conquest was eased by papal backing. The root causes of Byzantine failure are to be explained differently. At the local level, the mechanisms of Byzantine rule had been allowed to run down, as power passed into the hands of leading urban families. Their interests were not identical with those of the Empire as a whole. The circulation of the *tari* in southern Italy rather than the official Byzantine coinage suggests that the region was developing economic interests which separated it from the rest of the Empire. These might well be better nurtured by a local power rather than by the imperial authorities. This was recognized by Constantine Monomachos, when in 1051 he appointed Argyros viceroy of Byzantine Italy. Monomachos's attempt to work through local interests failed on this occasion because it aroused the opposition of the patriarch, who suspected that the interests of his church were being sacrificed for short-term political gains. The patriarch was able to paralyse imperial policy. Until his deposition in 1058 he was to remain the most powerful figure at Constantinople, almost always at loggerheads with successive emperors. Once again, Constantine Monomachos sought to fashion policies which took account of the conditions existing along the frontiers of the Empire. In retrospect, they look very perceptive, but, as with so much else he attempted, they failed. They failed not because they were without merit, but because they offended powerful interests within the Byzantine polity.

NOTE

1.   Amato di Montecassino, *Storia dei Normanni,* edited by V de Bartholmaeis (*Fonti per la storia d'Italia,* 76) (Rome, 1935), p. 194

Chapter 3

BYZANTIUM 1041–1071: THE SEARCH FOR A NEW POLITICAL ORDER

The early 1040s marked a turning point in Byzantine history. It was then that attempts were made to fashion new policies, both at home and abroad, more in tune with the needs of the time. The events of the brief reign of Michael V (1041–42) form a watershed. He succeeded to the throne on the death of his uncle Michael the Paphlagonian (1034–41). The Empress Zoe had previously been induced to adopt him as her son, in order to give him the necessary legitimacy. This was the work of another uncle, John the Orphanotrophos, who was the architect of his family's fortunes. He controlled the machinery of government. He was a eunuch, who had risen to power in the first place as a loyal and able servant of Basil II. He managed to preserve the essentials of his master's policies. Like him, he was suspicious of the great aristocratic families, who had regained much of their power and prominence under Romanos Argyros (1028–34). He had numbers of them exiled, including the future Emperor Constantine Monomachos and the future Patriarch Michael Keroularios. There seemed to be no reason why the Paphlagonians should not succeed the house of Macedon as the ruling dynasty of Byzantium and continue, if in modified form, the traditions and policies of Basil II. Michael the Paphlagonian was a much respected ruler and John the Orphanotrophos a minister of consummate ability.

That this did not happen was outwardly the fault of Michael V. He resented the ascendancy of his uncle, John the Orphanotrophos, in much the same way that Basil II chafed under the tutelage of his uncle, Basil the Chamberlain. His solution was the same. He drove John the Orphanotrophos into exile. He then turned on other members of his family. Later generations were amazed at the way he thus deprived himself of the natural support of his family. Like Basil II he wanted 'to make his realm "subject" to himself'.[1] He did not wish to share his authority. It was therefore inevitable that he would proceed against the Empress Zoe. He also moved against the Patriarch Alexius of Stoudios, accusing him of plotting his overthrow. Zoe was hustled off into a nunnery, but Alexius escaped his clutches. The emperor had tried to win over the people of Constantinople, but he had miscalculated their mood. News that their beloved empress had been sent into exile produced a spontaneous uprising by the people of the capital. In the confined spaces around the palace the imperial guards found it impossible to resist the fury of the mob. Michael V was frightened that the palace defences would not hold and lost his nerve; he fled from the palace by boat, hoping to find some safer place, but was caught by the mob and blinded. By that time supporters of Zoe's sister Theodora had taken charge of the uprising.

The historian Michael Psellos was an eyewitness of the whole affair. He would have been in his early twenties at the time and had just entered imperial service. He found it difficult to explain the overthrow of Michael V except in terms of the rage of the people at the way Zoe had been treated by an upstart. One can now see that Michael V was particularly vulnerable to attack from this quarter. He had ridded himself of his natural supporters. He turned instead to the people of Constantinople, for 'he would then have the support of the people, who were many, rather than of the nobility, who were few',[2] to use Michael Psellos's words. His appeal was dictated by his background. His father was a caulker and made a fortune out of his activities. He was very much a representative of the new wealth at Constantinople. It was here that Michael V looked for support, but the people rejected him with their terrible cry, 'Dig up the Bones of the Caulker'. His background ironically told against him.

The people of Constantinople were once again a political force to be reckoned with and were to remain so down to the end of the eleventh century, when Alexius I Comnenus managed to curb their power. It is impossible to detect any organization behind the uprising which overthrew Michael V. It was a spontaneous outburst of popular indignation. Even women took part, much to Michael Psellos's amazement. It was something quite unheard of. It, was only later that the various popular associations from guilds to confraternities came into political prominence. Such was their influence that a shrewd contemporary observer would advise his sons to have spies posted in the guilds of Constantinople. Emperors openly courted their support, for the apparent lesson of Michael V's fate was that the people of Constantinople had to be carefully managed. They were to be mollified by the grant of court titles and other imperial favours. In the process the guilds and other associations found their prestige much enhanced. Emperors would explain their policies and justify themselves to their people before assemblies composed of guildsmen. The overthrow of Michael V taught that it was dangerous to offend the susceptibilities of the people of Constantinople or to attack their darlings, such as the Empress Zoe, 'Our Mother', as they used to call her.

There was every expectation that Zoe would return from the nunnery where she had been incarcerated to take up the reins of government, but this did not please the supporters of her sister Theodora, who had secured control of the palace. It was finally agreed that the sisters should reign jointly. This arrangement did not last very long. The two sisters tended 'to confuse the trifles of the women's quarters with pressing matters of state'.[3] The business of government required an emperor. Zoe cast around for yet another husband to take on this responsibility. Her choice finally fell on Constantine Monomachos, who had been prominent at the court of the Emperor Romanos III Argyros (1028–34), but was exiled under Michael IV. He came from a Constantinopolitan family of note, closely related to the Argyros and Skleros families. His aristocratic connections made him suspect in the eyes of the Paphlagonians.

Constantine Monomachos was an exceedingly attractive ruler, but his intimates found him indolent and irresponsible. Michael Psellos, for a time one of his closest confidants, was convinced that for him 'the exercise of power meant rest from his labours, fulfilment of desire, relaxation from strife. He had entered the harbour of the palace, so to speak, to enjoy the advantages of a calm retreat and to avoid the duties of helmsman in the future.'[4] A poem of another contemporary, Christopher of Mitylene, addressed to the emperor, catches the indulgent mood of his court.

> 'Who needs pearls with a skin as fair as yours
> What price gold with hair as blond as yours
> Precious stones are just a bore
> With riches such as yours
> A plague on the base world
> Now that you have a realm such as yours.'[5]

After his death he was almost universally blamed for the disasters which overtook the Byzantine Empire. He was taken to task for his frivolity, his ludicrous generosity, his lack of attention to the details of government, his needless waste of the Empire's resources, his running down of the frontier defences of the Empire, for tolerating backstairs intrigue, for allowing his womenfolk to control the workings of government. In the words of the highly reliable twelfth-century chronicler Zonaras, 'that man will be judged responsible by the impartially minded for the subjection of the eastern parts of the Empire to the barbarian spear'.[6]

Constantine Monomachos was the obvious scapegoat for the loss of Anatolia to the Turks. His very amiability told against him. He was not taken seriously by those close to him and later historians pounced on their critical judgements of this emperor, as they tried to make sense of the disasters that overtook the Empire in the second half of the eleventh century. To those of his contemporaries further removed from the intimacies of the palace he seemed a more impressive figure. The historian Michael Attaleiates, who only held minor office in his reign, took pains to stress the seriousness of purpose that lay behind the reforms he initiated and the efforts he made at the end of his reign to restore the finances of the Empire. Even his detractors had to allow that he faced the crises of his reign with admirably cool displays of courage.

The first came in 1043. It was as serious a challenge as any faced by previous emperors. George Maniakes's rebellion coincided with Russian preparations for an attack on Constantinople. The possibility of collusion has already been raised, but there is no clear proof of any communication between the rebel and the Russian prince. In any case, both acted independently. George Maniakes crossed the straits of Otranto and advanced down the Via Egnatia towards Thessalonica, where the imperial army barred his way. Maniakes's initial charge carried all before it, but in mysterious circumstances he fell from his horse mortally wounded and the imperial forces won the day. Whether Maniakes's death was the result of treachery or just an accident of war, the outcome was the same: the Empire lost its best general and the emperor came to regard other commanders with the deepest suspicion. The death of Maniakes made no difference to the plans of the Russians. As we know, they were completely defeated before Constantinople. Monomachos increased his prestige still further by suppressing a rebellion on the island of Cyprus in the same year. His position seemed unassailable.

The next challenge to his rule came in the autumn of 1047 from a relative of his, Leo Tornikios. It seems to have started as a family quarrel. There was dislike on both sides, which was fanned by the emperor's sister, who encouraged Tornikios's ambitions. The emperor relieved him of the governorship of Iberia and forced him to become a monk. Tornikios's stand against the emperor, for whatever reasons, caught the attention of those opposed to the emperor's policies. The chief centre of disaffection was Adrianople, the main military base of Thrace. The cause of dissension was the settlement of the Petcheneks in the central Balkans some months previously. This had produced deep resentment among the western armies, when they found that they were being pensioned off. Their leaders got in touch with Leo Tornikios and persuaded him to head a rebellion. He was then spirited out of Constantinople to Adrianople and proclaimed emperor. He led the western armies on Constantinople. Monomachos had almost no regular soldiers with which to defend his capital. He armed the people; he opened up the gaols and got together a scratch force out of the prisoners. They were sent out against the rebels and were completely defeated. The city lay open to Tornikios but he failed to press home his attack, perhaps because he expected the city to be betrayed from within. That this did not happen was largely the result of the coolness that the emperor at all times displayed. He was conspicuous on the walls of the city. He gave no sign that his nerve would fail him. This encouraged his supporters and the defence held. News soon came that the eastern armies were coming to the emperor's rescue and the rebel retreated to his base at Adrianople. He tried once more to march on Constantinople, but this was an utter fiasco. His army just melted away. He was captured and blinded. There were to be no more rebellions for the rest of his reign. Well might a contemporary counsel his sons against taking part in a rebellion: 'the Emperor resident in Constantinople always wins'.[7] That certainly seemed to be true in Monomachos's reign. The greatest advantage enjoyed by the emperor over any rival was possession of Constantinople. As long as he could count on the support of the people of Constantinople, then his position was more or less secure. The loyalty of Constantinople was at a premium and had to be paid for. More than ever, imperial government had to be seen to foster Constantinopolitan interests.

The needs of the provinces were neglected. Did the two major rebellions against Constantine Monomachos simply reflect provincial dissatisfaction with rule from Constantinople? The usual answer is that they should be seen as the product of the growing rivalry between the military establishment centred in the provinces and a civilian-dominated government in Constantinople. Constantine Monomachos was the scion of a Constantinopolitan family and has therefore been regarded as the epitome of this civilian government, while Maniakes and Tornikios are held to be representatives of a military aristocracy. This is an over-simplification. Maniakes was something of an outsider. He did not come from any ancient lineage, but had risen to the forefront of Byzantine life as a result of his military abilities. His rebellion was prompted first and foremost by the hostility of his neighbour in Anatolia, Romanos Skleros, who came from one of the greatest and most renowned of the old military families. But Skleros had strong connections with the court at Constantinople and with Constantine Monomachos. Much the same is true of Leo Tornikios. By this time, there was already coalescing a network of noble families with a claim to political power. Most of these families had their roots and estates in the provinces, but increasingly they gravitated to Constantinople, which was the centre of the political stage. They were families, which in some cases could trace their origins back to the mid-ninth century; families which had borne the brunt of Basil II's animosity. After his death they had been able to recover their influence. They assured their positions in Constantinople by marrying into the patrician families of the capital, old wealth buttressed by position at court and in the administration.

Constantine Monomachos's accession represented the reassertion of the power of these families. With the triumph of the opposition to Basil II, politics threatened to revolve around the competition of a handful of families, which provided the natural leaders of Byzantine society. They had great estates and were immensely rich; they possessed powerful households and had built up a network of clients. This in itself gave them a large measure of political influence, but it had to be safeguarded by some say in government, by position at court, and a degree of control over the military organization. To ensure this they needed the support of a series of groups, both in the provinces and in the capital. In the provinces they tended to work through the army, which was divided into the eastern and western armies. The latter seemed the more powerful political force, because its base at Adrianople was within easy striking distance of Constantinople. Rarely, if ever, was there any cooperation between the two armies. One of the strengths of the central government was that it was possible to play them off against one another. The most powerful force in Constantinople should have been the bureaucracy, but it was split into a number of cliques, which might try to dominate the workings of government on their own account, but rarely succeeded for long. As we have seen, the guilds and confraternities of the capital were becoming more important. In the background was the patriarch, who might on occasion intervene decisively. Normally speaking, the emperor was able to hold the balance between these competing groups, none more adroitly than Constantine Monomachos. He could do so, because he had the support of the people of Constantinople, even if he had to purchase it by opening up the senate to a wide range of Constantinopolitan society. He sought to strengthen his position still further by a series of reforms. They were intended to provide a sound foundation for an effective civilian government, which did not have to rely on the sanction of military power.

These reforms were carried out between 1043 and 1047. There were two major components. The first was the creation of a new ministry under the *epi ton kriseon*. The second was a reorganization of higher education. This was the classic pattern of Byzantine administrative reorganization. There was no question of a thoroughgoing overhaul of the system. No departments of state would be wound up; they would just be allowed to atrophy. Instead, new ministries would be created in order to meet new pressures and new areas of governmental business, which existing departments could not cope with. It was part of that long Byzantine tradition of 'economy', of adapting to new circumstances as they arose. But a willingness to adapt was not to compromise the Byzantine ideal of good government, with its twin aims of providing charity and justice. Theoretically, the emperor was the guarantor of the quality of government, but, practically, this was seen to depend upon the system of education; whence the need for educational reforms, such as those carried out by the Caesar Bardas in the mid-ninth century and by the Emperor Constantine VII Porphyrogenitus a century later.

The creation of the new ministry under the *epi ton kriseon* was designed to coordinate provincial administration. Since the death of Basil II there had been a whole series of provincial rebellions, few of them very serious, but they pointed to shortcomings in the administration of the provinces. These were seen to be connected with the piecemeal changes which had been effected over the past fifty odd years. These had meant that more and more of the business of provincial government had passed into the hands of the judge of a theme, who was originally subordinate to the military governor. In the past, one of the characteristic features of Byzantine provincial government was the way the military governor of a theme combined both military and civil powers. Now, in practice, his authority was limited to military matters, while the judge controlled the administration and was an altogether more influential figure, but their respective competences were not clearly delineated, which must have been the cause of some confusion at the local level. From the point of view of the central government the main problem was that there was no ministry to which the judge was specifically responsible. The creation of the new ministry, therefore, met a series of administrative needs. It allowed the central government a greater degree of supervision over provincial administration and made possible the coordination of the judge's activities. At the same time, it was a recognition of the independence he enjoyed in his theme. He was no longer to be considered subordinate to the military governor.

The creation of this ministry meant that the military side of provincial government was now only of secondary importance beside the civilian administration. This measure was therefore yet another step in the piecemeal dismantling of the military organization of the theme armies. Most of these armies had long been on a peacetime footing: that is to say, apart from certain professional regiments or *tagmata* recruited from the themes, which are found serving abroad, no use was made of the theme armies, which effectively existed on paper only; their soldiers commuting the military service they owed. The border themes were another matter. Their armies continued to exist and formed a valuable home guard. At some point in his reign Constantine Monomachos took steps which led to the disbanding of the army of the border theme of Iberia. It was a measure which caught the imagination of contemporaries, who blamed it for the collapse of the defences of the region before the Turks. Contemporaries only mention this one measure, but a later historian, who is usually well informed, suggests that the emperor proceeded to a general demobilization of the armies of the border themes. It was felt at the time that the treatment meted out to the borderers was perhaps the chief cause of the failure of the Byzantine Empire to hold its frontiers.

On the face of it, Constantine Monomachos's measure was sound and logical. There were professional troops stationed in the border regions under their own commanders. The existence of theme armies meant a duplication of military organization and was an unnecessary expense. Disbanding the army of Iberia was a measure which saved the imperial government significant sums of money. It was, in any case, prompted by the very poor performance this army put up against the Turks in the campaigns of 1048/49. Its commander was captured by the Turks and did not meet the professional standards of the other Byzantine commanders, notably Kekavmenos Katakalon. This seemed to confirm the argument that not only were the border theme armies an unnecessary expense; they were also ineffective. The creation of the new ministry under the *epi ton kriseon* must therefore be seen as part of a series of measures to restructure provincial administration and local military organization. They were the culmination of long-term changes, which produced the demobilization of the armies of the themes and confirmed that effective authority in the themes was wielded by a civil governor, the judge. They represented a clear shift within the Byzantine system of government to the civil authorities and promised tighter control over the provinces from the capital.

Constantine Monomachos and his advisers identified two areas of government where reorganization was needed: provincial government, including local military arrangements, and legal education. As we have seen, this was a usual choice for reforming emperors, but it was usually complemented by legislation. Constantine Monomachos, in contrast, issued almost no legislation. This does not mean that he saw reform of the government in strictly administrative terms. Like all emperors before him, his concept of government remained a legal one; that is to say, the laws were the foundation of government. If it was not functioning effectively, this was to be ascribed to the failure of the law, but Constantine Monomachos did not see legislation as the answer. As far as he was concerned, the laws the Byzantines had at their disposal were quite excellent. What was wrong was the system of legal education. Its neglect since the middle of the tenth century had meant that the laws were neither easily nor clearly understood. The teaching of law was in the hands of the guild of notaries. To judge by its description in the Book of the Prefect, it was at a fairly rudimentary level. Its main aim was to turn out notaries with the practical skills that their calling required. An important part of their final exam was to give proof that they could draft basic legal documents. Whether judges, barristers, and assessors received any specific legal education is not clear. The presumption is that they learnt on the job.

A legal compilation, known as the *Peira,* gives a vivid glimpse of the state of Byzantine jurisprudence and legal practice around the time of the accession of Constantine IX Monomachos. It was put together soon after 1040 by a judge of the Hippodrome, the central law court of the capital. The intention was to provide a practical manual, which would guide the judges, assessors, and clerks of the court in matters of legal procedure. It consisted of the judgements and opinions given by various judges of the court. The emphasis is not on the details of the cases tried, but on the framing of legal decisions and the basis on which they were made. It is the only surviving Byzantine legal collection which allows us an insight into the practice of Byzantine law. In terms of jurisprudence it left much to be desired in the sense that it was far removed from the norms of Justinianic law. In theory, the Byzantines looked back to

Justinian's codification of the laws as the foundation of their legal system. Reform-minded emperors would attempt to put theory into practice. A concerted effort in this direction was made at the end of the ninth century. Its chief monument was the law code known as the Basilics, which was designed to meet a pressing need: the lack of any officially approved Greek version of the *Codex Justinianus.* This deficiency was made good by the Basilics.

The judgements preserved in the *Peira* make constant reference to the Basilics, but this does not mean that they were arrived at on the basis of a strict interpretation of its norms. They were used to justify decisions often reached on purely pragmatic grounds. The great legal historian Zachariae von Lingenthal condemned the judgements of the *Peira* as 'completely arbitrary and without any reference to the laws'. 'Total casuistry' is how a modern writer describes them.[8] He insists that rhetoric provided the principle and methods underlying Byzantine justice, just as with so much else in Byzantine public life. Judgements did not depend upon the application of clear legal principles, but upon the weight and plausibility of arguments. The numerous lawbooks which circulated in the Byzantine Empire served only as a quarry from which arguments could be garnered. Specious grounds were easily found for circumventing or disregarding inconvenient articles of law. It was very much a matter of arguing with the law, rather than applying its norms. The law of the *Peira* comes closest to that vulgar Roman Law, which circulated from the fifth century in the lands of the western Roman Empire. In both cases use was made of codifications of the law, but in the absence of any coherent system of legal interpretation judgements were inconsistent and justice arbitrary. Local custom and practices were allowed to seep in.

It is quite possible that the justice meted out at the court of the Hippodrome before Constantine Monomachos's accession met the needs of the time. There seems to have been no widespread demand for legal reforms, but it would have appeared differently to a reforming emperor, confronted with the problems of provincial government. Now that it revolved around the judge, rather than the military governor of a theme, the administration of justice became the key concern. Yet it must have been clear that there was a shortage of adequately trained men to serve as thematic judges. For example, Michael Psellos was appointed judge of a theme, soon after he had left school in the mid-1030s. His knowledge of the law seems to have been no more than what he had managed to pick up from one of his schoolfellows. Such inadequacy underlined the need for the creation of a ministry to supervise the activities of the thematic judges. As we have seen, the office of the *epi ton kriseon* made good this deficiency. It produced a greater degree of central control over the provincial administration, but it would also have highlighted the need for much greater uniformity in the enforcement of the laws.

These practical requirements – the need for better-trained judges and for a clearer and more consistent application of the laws – might have been enough in themselves to suggest the need for a reorganization of legal education, but the form this took depended upon another consideration, which was more ideological. Reform had to be justified in terms of *Renovatio* – the return to the ideal of the Christian Roman Empire of Constantine and Justinian. *Renovatio* was largely a matter of propaganda and Byzantine history is punctuated with a series of these propaganda campaigns. The ideal proclaimed varied from time to time, but it helped to shape the measures of reform. Under Constantine Monomachos the Roman element in *Renovatio* was especially marked. It was evident in the interest in Roman law, but it manifested itself in other ways as well. Attention was paid to the position of the senate, people, and army within the constitution. There was renewed interest in Roman history. An epitome was made of Dio Cassius's *Roman History.* Michael Psellos began his world history not with the creation of the world, which was a usual starting point, but with the foundation of Rome. For the first time since the sixth century there was serious study of Latin at Constantinople, for legal purposes. *Renovatio* was conceived in terms of a return to Roman law as the foundation for Byzantine justice. Such a perspective could only have intensified dissatisfaction with the shortcomings of the system of justice exemplified in the *Peira.*

The root cause was the state of legal education. Constantine Monomachos compared it to 'a rudderless ship abandoned in the midst of the sea of life, either to founder or to be swept away'.[9] To remedy this deficiency he proceeded to found a law school. He attached it to his foundation of St George of the Mangana, which he hoped would be the monument of his rule, while the law school would make possible his ideal of good government. The man chosen to head the school was John Xiphilinos, a boyhood friend of Michael Psellos. He had already built up a reputation as a legal expert while serving in the court of the Hippodrome. He was given the title of *nomophylax.* The school was officially opened in April 1047 at the same time that the monastery church of St George of the Mangana was inaugurated, but it had been conceived some time before this. A certain amount of preliminary organization was involved. Books had to be assembled, for instance, for the library which was attached to the school. The main duty of the *nomophylax* was to instruct students in law. In return he received a salary and subsistence from the emperor. He was expected to teach free of charge, but could accept additional fees from scions of noble houses. His competence also included supervision of the training and examination of notaries and barristers. It was hoped that in this way 'the laws would be protected against those who did not hesitate to use blatant sophistry to pervert the course of justice'.[10]

For a number of reasons this measure was the cause of much dissatisfaction. Students of rhetoric felt that the creation of a school of law under imperial patronage was likely to diminish their chances of preferment in the imperial administration. The emperor gave in to this pressure and appointed Michael Psellos to the new post of consul of the philosophers. His duties paralleled those of the *nomophylax*. He taught rhetoric and philosophy under imperial patronage and exercised general supervision over the various private schools operating in the capital. He might be described very roughly as a Byzantine minister of education.

More serious opposition to the creation of the law school came from a different quarter. It was led by a former judge of the Hippodrome and was directed against John Xiphilinos personally. Michael Psellos came out in defence of his friend. He suspected that there were more powerful figures behind the attack, but he has not left any clear pointers that might enable us to identify them. The case made against Xiphilinos concerned his teaching of law. In his opponents' eyes it was far too academic. It centred on the Basilics and consisted of a systematic exploration of the law it contained. He would explain a text and then seek to prove that his intepretation conformed with the ancient texts underlying the Basilics. This was then completed by an exercise known as a *thematismos,* in which a hypothetical case was used to show how the particular ruling considered might have worked in practice. This method approximated to that used in the law school of Beirut in Justinian's time. Constantine Monomachos made it plain that his foundation was intended to make good the lack of such a law school. Its merit had lain in the way it ensured some degree of uniformity both in legal education and in the interpretation of the law. This was what Constantine Monomachos expected of his law school and John Xiphilinos's teaching enshrined in his commentary on the Basilics went some way to meet his hopes. The aim was to bring order to the legal system. This was to be achieved by a consistent interpretation of the law of the Basilics. John Xiphilinos was not interested in the current legal problems and must have been quite out of sympathy with the kind of legal procedures he had known while serving in the court of the Hippodrome. It is easy to see that his lack of interest in practical legal problems would have infuriated the day-to-day practitioners of the law, the guild of notaries especially. They were unhappy at the way they had been deprived of control over legal education and were justifiably alarmed at the highly academic training that future notaries were receiving.

The attack against John Xiphilinos failed. He was confirmed in his office by the emperor, but the bitterness of his opponents had been unsettling. Around 1050 Xiphilinos decided to abandon a career in public service for a monastic vocation on Mount Olympus. The office of *nomophylax* continued to exist, but his duties became administrative. The teaching of law reverted to the guild of notaries. The exact fate of the law school is unknown. It is not likely to have survived Xiphilinos's departure. Its creation may have succeeded in tipping the balance within government towards those trained in the law, because young men continued to seek legal training in increasing numbers. It offered the best opportunity of entry into the civil service. It is only a guess that, had the law school survived, the quality of government and the effectiveness of imperial control would have been improved. Its failure was mainly symbolic. It showed that Constantine Monomachos's plans for the reorganization of the Empire were running into difficulties, as were those most closely associated with these plans.

These men formed a clique around Constantine Leichoudes, who was Constantine Monomachos's chief minister at the beginning of his reign. They included Michael Psellos, John Xiphilinos, and their teacher John Mavropous, who were bound by the closest ties of friendship. John Mavropous held no official position at the imperial court, but he acted as the emperor's spokesman. It fell to him to present and justify the programme of reform and he may well have been the moving spirit behind it. The new men prided themselves on their intellectual abilities rather than on their family connections. Michael Psellos puts it thus: 'It pleased this emperor not to advance office holders and judges according to birth nor to fill the senate and various magistracies only from the first families, but also from other sections of society ... for he believed it absurd that it should be an essential law and an unchangeable rule to allow entry into the senate on grounds of family alone; or that access to the palace should be the preserve only of those revered for their lineage, even if their mental faculties were marred and they could do little more than breathe; not able to belch forth anything except for their family's great name.'[11] This passage raises many problems, not least that elsewhere Michael Psellos repudiates the meritocratic notions that he espouses here. He draws a veil over his own humble but respectable guild background and would claim after the antiquarian fashion of the day that his father's family could claim descent from consuls and patricians. He would also criticize Constantine Monomachos for the way he opened up the senate to people from all walks of life. These inconsistencies can possibly be explained by changing circumstances. Psellos insisted that the supreme human virtue, which he possessed in abundance, was the ability to adapt to shifts in fortune.

More difficult to explain, at first sight, is the apparently meritocratic basis on which Constantine Monomachos allowed entry into the senate and administration. It hardly squares with the view already expressed that his accession marked the return to favour of the old families, who had opposed Basil II. This inconsistency is not likely to have disturbed Constantine Monomachos. He needed the support both of the old families and of the people of Constantinople. He also required new men to help him carry through his administrative reforms. These reforms could hardly have been construed as a threat to the position of these old families, but, the meritocratic notions espoused by Psellos and his friends would have been irritating and would have aroused suspicions at court about their intentions

Constantine Monomachos took care to remain on good terms with the most powerful families. The Skleroi are an example. Their influence at court continued after the death in 1044 of Maria Skleraina, the emperor's official mistress. At the end of the reign her brother, Romanos Skleros, was the duke of Antioch. Michael Psellos, for his part, was soon taking pains to cultivate his acquaintance. 'My lord, ancient and modern' is how he addressed him. After the death of Constantine Monomachos in 1055, when the position of the family was less secure, Michael Psellos was able to repay members of the family for past favours by intervening on their behalf. Michael Psellos must have been disabused of any meritocratic notions he may have entertained by his experience of Byzantine political life. A successful administrative career depended upon imperial favour, which was capricious, and meant that survival at court demanded great skills. It required the cultivation of contacts at all levels of government and the goodwill of the grandees of the imperial court, men such as Romanos Skleros or the Caesar John Doukas, both of whom were at one time or another patrons of Michael Psellos. Without such support a clique of civil servants soon became isolated. This must have become apparent to Michael Psellos, once the reforms with which he and his group were identified began to run into difficulties. One by one they were forced out of office. In 1048 John Mavropous accepted much against his will the bishopric of Euchaita in deepest Anatolia. He treated his appointment as a form of exile, as it indeed was. He was being made a scapegoat for the way the settlement of the Petcheneks had backfired. He had been one of the keenest advocates of the project. Soon afterwards, as we have seen, John Xiphilinos decided to become a monk in the face of sustained criticism of his conduct of the office of *nomophylax*. Michael Psellos had bound himself by oath to follow suit, but avoided doing so for as long as he could. His position at court became increasingly precarious. At some point, his mentor Constantine Leichoudes was dismissed from his post as chief minister and replaced by a eunuch. Psellos found himself relieved of certain responsibilities he had previously been entrusted with in the field of foreign affairs. Still he clung on.

The fall from favour of Michael Psellos and his friends was an admission by the Emperor Constantine Monomachos that his attempt to restructure the imperial government had failed. It had been predicated upon a period of lasting peace and prosperity. Any such hopes were dashed by the Petchenek wars. They were very costly and left the Empire's finances in a precarious condition. Some two years before his death in 1055 the Emperor Constantine Monomachos embarked on a policy of financial retrenchment. The accounts of tax-collectors were examined and heavy fines were imposed on those who had failed to render their due. Payments made by the imperial treasury to churches and monasteries were carefully checked. Those found enjoying imperial gifts illegally were deprived of them. There was clearly a thoroughgoing inquest into the financial side of government. The new chief minister, the eunuch John, was a financial expert. A pattern was now set. The main aim of government was to curb expenditure, rather than to meet any other challenges.

Even with the advantage of hindsight Constantine Monomachos's foreign and domestic policies appear eminently sane. They seemed to provide the Empire with the best hope of escaping from the options imposed by the legacy of Basil II. In retrospect, their failure can almost be said to have sealed the Empire's fate, because thereafter for some fifty years there seems to have been almost no direction to imperial policy, beyond reacting to events. Constantine Monomachos's reign seems to mark that point when the Byzantine Empire lost control of its destiny. Why then did his reforms fail? Contemporaries singled out the ludicrous extravagance of the early part of his reign. Since this involved the permanent alienation of imperial revenues in the shape of tax exemptions and the creation of perpetual pensions to monasteries, it is not an explanation which should be dismissed lightly, nor should the cost of the Petchenek wars. It was also that the reforms were not allowed to work. They aroused opposition both from the officers of the western armies and within the judiciary and legal profession. It is natural to suspect that this was a matter of self-interest and nothing more, but from a different direction there came a clear challenge to imperial authority.

By the end of his reign Constantine Monomachos was at loggerheads with the Patriarch Michael Keroularios. The immediate cause was the schism of 1054. Until this episode there is nothing to suggest that there was any hostility between the emperor and the patriarch, though there was some friction between the patriarch and members of the imperial entourage. We have already seen that Argyros, one of the emperor's trusted men, was the bitter personal enemy of Keroularios, while the patriarch's relations with Michael Psellos had been deteriorating for some time. Nor could those economy measures directed against the church have been to the patriarch's liking. With these considerations in mind it is easy to understand the suspicions created in the patriarch's mind by the emperor's overtures to the papacy. They seem to have been confirmed by some of the sentiments expressed to the emperor by the pope: 'Mother Rome has properly decorated your forehead with the diadem of earthly authority.'[12] The papal assumption that in return the Byzantine emperor was obliged to recover the rights of St Peter must have seemed to the patriarch like a direct challenge to his authority. The exact nature of papal claims was to become still clearer, when a copy of the Donation of Constantine came into the patriarch's hands. We have seen that the Byzantines had previously been unaware of its existence. It was against this background that Michael Keroularios set about redefining patriarchal authority. He understood that the papacy had a claim to all imperial privileges, the coronation excepted. He therefore started to effect the red buskins of an emperor: not in itself perhaps very important, but a symbol of his claim to parity with the papacy and even a kind of equality with the emperor. The latter had a duty to govern, while the patriarch, as spiritual head, had the responsibility of moral supervision. 'Not even emperors', he would proclaim, 'were exempt from a patriarch's duty to rebuke and reprove.'[13] To carry out such a responsibility he could call on the people, as he did in July 1054, to force the emperor to end his support for the papal legates. This reliance on the people of Constantinople left him open to the charge formulated by Michael Psellos: 'and you, being a democrat, disapprove of the monarchy'.[14] If nothing else, it was a recognition of the power wielded by the patriarch over the people of the capital.

After his victory over Constantine Monomachos in 1054 Michael Keroularios was the most powerful figure in Constantinople. At this point Michael Psellos wisely discovered that he had a monastic vocation and retired to a monastery on Mount Olympus. He was thus able to avoid entanglement in the intrigues which followed Constantine Monomachos's death in 1055. His successor was the ageing Empress Theodora, who had outlived her sister Zoe, but she could only be a very temporary solution to the problem of the succession. She duly died in August 1056. Who would reign now that the last of the Macedonian line was dead? In the absence of any obvious candidate Theodora's chief minister, Leo Paraspondylos, raised to the imperial dignity an ageing nonentity, Michael Stratiotikos. He belonged to a distinguished civil service family, the Bringas, which gave him a respectability that his abilities could not command. The clique in power still further ensured their position by forcing him to swear that he would do nothing contrary to their wishes and advice. The only direct opposition came from a cousin of the late Emperor Constantine Monomachos. He was backed by a strong force of family retainers, but he failed to win the support of the patriarch which was vital and his coup fizzled out.

Michael Keroularios was on bad terms with the Empress Theodora. He objected to the way the Empire was being ruled by a woman. He was equally opposed to the regime of Michael Stratiotikos and fostered popular discontent against it. There was also opposition to the regime from the aristocracy who worked through the army chiefs. They claimed that they had not been consulted in the choice of the new emperor, whereas constitutionally an emperor should be elected by the senate, people, and army. A deputation of the chiefs of the eastern armies, headed by Isaac Comnenus and Kekavmenos Katakalon, came up to Constantinople, seeking imperial favour. They were sent away unsatisfied. The emperor did not even make the usual donatives to the troops. The army commanders decided to try once again, but this time they approached Leo Paraspondylos, the power behind the throne. Once again they met with a point-blank refusal to entertain their requests. They went away to the church of St Sophia where they exchanged solemn oaths that if their demands were not met they would rebel. Since the army commanders chose to seal their pact in the patriarchal church, it is to be assumed that Michael Keroularios knew what was afoot and gave their action his tacit approval.

Isaac Comnenus was chosen to head the conspiracy. He and the other leaders went back to their country estates to bide their time. The preparations for the revolt nearly came to grief because of the actions of the military governor of Cappadocia. He was a Bryennios from Adrianople in Thrace. He was therefore an outsider, but it was felt that he should be brought into the conspiracy because he held such a key position. He moved too precipitately. He tried to win over his troops to the conspirators by the payment of a higher donative. This was opposed by one of his subordinates; and an independent commander, who was encamped near by with his troops, arrested and blinded Bryennios and sent him back to Constantinople. The heads of the great families of the neighbouring Anatolic theme were party to the conspiracy and were frightened that Bryennios would implicate them. They included Romanos Skleros, Michael Bourtzes, the sons of Basil Argyros, and the future Emperor Nicephorus Botaneiates. It reads like a list of the old aristocracy. They hurried to Kastamon in Paphlagonia where Isaac Comnenus had his residence. They forced him much against his will, as he would later claim, to raise the standard of revolt and on 8 June 1057 they proceeded to have him proclaimed emperor. Kekavmenos Katakalon at first tried to back out, but once he saw that the rebellion had sufficient support, he joined it with troops he had collected around his home town of Koloneia in north-eastern Anatolia.

This rebellion was not a general rising of the army in the eastern provinces against the central government. Many units stationed in Asia Minor remained loyal to the emperor in Constantinople. Their commanders, in the few cases where their names are known, appear to come from undistinguished families, whereas the leaders of the rebellion, with the single exception of Kekavmenos Katakalon, were drawn from old families prominent in the affairs of the Empire since the reign of Basil II at the latest. They were accustomed not just to enjoying great influence locally, but to playing a dominant role at court as well. The rebellion was forced on them because the ruling clique led by Leo Paraspondylos had deprived them of the position at court which they had enjoyed under Constantine Monomachos. Leo Paraspondylos began his career as a servant of the Emperor Michael IV (1034–41) and his policy towards the old families repeats that favoured by his master. But they were now well entrenched in the capital and the leaders of the rebellion could count on support from within Constantinople. The brothers Constantine and John Doukas were sympathetic to their cause. They did not take part in the rebellion, but they had formed part of the original deputation of generals to Michael VI. Constantine Doukas was married to a niece of the patriarch, who, as we have already seen, was favourably disposed towards the rebels.

The rebel army advanced towards the capital. Towards the end of August 1057 it came face to face with the imperial army near Nicomedia. There was a bitterly contested battle with heavy casualties on both sides. The rebels carried the day. There was little they could do thereafter, but wait on events in Constantinople. Opponents of Michael VI within the capital gathered in the church of St Sophia. The patriarch made a pretence of opposing their occupation of the patriarchal church, but before long he had been persuaded to put himself at their head. He was in control of events. He had Isaac Comnenus acclaimed emperor. He sent a delegation to Michael VI demanding that he abdicate. He even handed out positions in government. The emperor appeared to have no room for manœuvre. Leo Paraspondylos was discredited and disappears into the background. The emperor turned more and more to Michael Psellos for advice. His solution was to reach an accommodation with the rebels before the patriarch managed to. A deputation composed of Psellos, his old mentor Constantine Leichoudes, and the leader of the senate was accordingly despatched to Isaac Comnenus's camp. They offered him the rank of Caesar and recognition as the heir apparent to the throne. Comnenus turned this offer down. They next offered him the imperial title on condition that Michael VI remained titular emperor. Comnenus was tempted but Kekavmenos Katakalon forced him to refuse this offer as well. He may well have been informed that Michael VI was on the point of abdicating. The emperor was an old man and he had no desire to be the cause of further bloodshed. He asked the prelates sent to him by the patriarch, 'And what will the patriarch provide me with instead of the imperial office?' Back came the reply, 'the heavenly kingdom'.[15] That was sufficient. He gave up the palace and the imperial title and became a monk. The patriarch could now offer Isaac Comnenus Constantinople.

On 1 September 1057 Michael Keroularios crowned Isaac Comnenus emperor. Michael Psellos expresses the slightly puzzling opinion that it was this act of coronation which legalized Isaac's position as emperor. Strictly speaking, the coronation was not supposed to be an institutive ceremony. The acclamation was the essential act in the making of an emperor. In practice, usurpers were in a slightly difficult position, because in their case acclamation was also an act of rebellion. In the previous century John Tzimiskes, who had overthrown the Emperor Nicephorus Phokas, was not just crowned emperor after his coup; he was also anointed. This was held to have washed away the stain of usurpation. Keroularios felt that Isaac Comnenus owed the throne to him. He was alleged to have later threatened the emperor with the following words: 'I raised you up ... and I can break you.'[16] The patriarch may even have believed that through the act of coronation he was conferring upon the emperor his God-given authority, for Michael

Psellos would go out of his way to emphasize to him that the imperial crown 'comes not from men nor through men, but perfectly naturally from on high'.[17] The elevated conception which Keroularios had of the nature of patriarchal authority is graphically displayed in the iconography of a cross that belonged to him. There are three panels. The first shows the Emperor Constantine bowing his head in reverence before the icons of St Peter and St Paul held up before him by Pope Sylvester; signifying the supremacy of spiritual authority over secular power and incidentally proof of how well the patriarch had absorbed the lessons of the Donation of Constantine. In the second panel we see the Archangel Michael, the patriarch's patron saint, rescuing his church at Chonai from the floodwaters; symbolizing the patriarch's triumph over the flood of heresy. The final panel depicts the Archangel Michael appearing before Joshua at Jericho and demanding his obeisance. It can be no mere coincidence that the day on which Michael Keroularios crowned Isaac Comnenus was none other than the feast of the death of Joshua. This panel must therefore proclaim not just Isaac's debt to the patriarch, but also his subordination.[18]

At first, Isaac went out of his way to honour and conciliate the patriarch. He gave the patriarch the right to appoint the two key officers of the patriarchal administration, the *oikonomos* and the *skevophylax,* appointments which had previously been within the emperor's gift. He also raised the patriarch's nephews to high positions of state. But, at the same time, he made Michael Psellos his chief minister. This choice had much to recommend it. Psellos had been away from the centre of government since the end of Monomachos's reign and was not tainted, like so many other bureaucrats, by the measures taken by Michael VI against the generals. Rather was he on good terms with one of the leaders of the rebellion, Romanos Skleros. Isaac Comnenus, too, had reason to appreciate Psellos. He admired the way he had conducted negotiations on behalf of Michael VI. His apparent loyalty to the reigning emperor was commendable, but still more commendable was his known dislike of the patriarch. Psellos insisted, in a letter to the patriarch, that they were complete opposites: 'I love, you hate; I conciliate, you bring hatred; I propitiate, you disdain; I praise, you denigrate.'[19] By choosing Psellos as his chief minister Isaac hoped to find a balance against Keroularios, to whom he owed the throne. He was the spokesman of those who thought that the patriarch was exceeding the powers allotted to him. Psellos's dislike and distrust of the patriarch pointed to a breach between emperor and patriarch, but contemporaries are very coy about revealing the exact issue which brought this about. Reading between the lines it is most likely to have been Isaac Comnenus's revival of Nicephorus Phokas's anti-monastic legislation. The patriarch was a great patron of monks and a devotee of mysticism. He would have construed the emperor's action as an infringement of his authority. The emperor, for his part, could not tolerate the patriarch's obstructionism, because it might jeopardize his whole programme of reform.

Isaac acted swiftly. On 8 November 1058 the patriarch was hustled out of Constantinople on a trumped-up charge and Michael Psellos was put in charge of the prosecution. He first tried to get the patriarch to abdicate voluntarily, because he knew that a public trial would be an opportunity for his supporters to mobilize public opinion on his behalf. Keroularios refused to abdicate. The government began to get jittery and it was arranged that the patriarchal synod should meet to hear charges against Keroularios, not in Constantinople, as might have been expected, but in an obscure town in Thrace, far from the publicity of the capital. The speech which Michael Psellos composed for the prosecution in the case against the patriarch still survives, but it was never delivered, because the patriarch died before the trial could begin.

Far from being overjoyed Isaac Comnenus was downcast by the news of the patriarch's death. There was a danger that dead he might be more powerful than he had been alive. He was close to becoming a martyr. His death was soon surrounded by miraculous occurrences. A few days before he died he visited the shrine of St Euthymios at Madyta and spent the night there. The saint appeared to him in a dream and foretold his death. When he was being buried it was observed that his hands seemed to be making the sign of the cross. This was taken as proof of his sanctity. Isaac did what he could to mollify public opinion in the capital. He allowed the patriarch to be buried in his monastery of St Michael in Constantinople. The patriarch's closest relatives who had also been exiled were reinstated at court and in the emperor's favour. But his true intentions were revealed by his appointment of Constantine Leichoudes, Psellos's friend and patron, as patriarch in succession to Keroularios. He hoped that a political appointment of this sort would allow him a greater measure of control over the church. It did not work. His hold on power became weaker. Keroularios's supporters remained unappeased, while the emperor found himself increasingly isolated once his grand schemes for the regeneration of the Empire began to run into difficulties.

The main plank of Isaac's programme was the restoration of the military might of the Empire. He had a *stele* set up showing himself with a naked sword in his hand. The same design appears on his coinage. As he was soon to discover, such an undertaking was only possible if the finances of the Empire were completely overhauled. Retrenchment became the order of the day. Arrears of taxation were got in; pensions paid to court dignitaries were cut back; grants of property made from the imperial demesne were rescinded. Isaac was determined to build up the imperial demesne. Before becoming patriarch Constantine Leichoudes was obliged to give up the imperial foundation of St George Mangana, over which he enjoyed rights of administration. Isaac saw himself in the tradition of those soldier emperors of the tenth century, who had secured the Empire's greatness. We have seen how he tried to revive the anti-monastic legislation of Nicephorus Phokas, by which the monasteries were deprived of their excess property.

In principle, Michael Psellos was sympathetic to these reforms. He may well have had overall charge of their implementation. He claimed that they were admirable in themselves. All that was wrong was that the emperor tried to push them through too quickly and consequently alienated all sections of opinion, from the church to the army. Office-holders of all kinds suffered from the economies. Their salaries and pensions were cut back and opportunities for the exercise of patronage began to dry up. The army did not benefit from a military emperor on the throne. Isaac did his best to disassociate himself from the other leaders of the rebellion. Kekavmenos Katakalon was sent back to his estates in Anatolia in disgrace. He was suspected of plotting against the emperor and was forced to become a monk. Romanos Skleros also seems to have been in bad odour at court at this time. Isaac distanced himself from the heads of the great families of the Empire. At the same time, he did little to promote his own family's interests. His brother John was left very much in the background. He found himself more or less isolated, once his chief minister, Michael Psellos, started working against him.

His overthrow in the autumn of 1059 is therefore not as surprising as it first appears. He returned to his capital in September 1059 from a not unsuccessful campaign against the Petcheneks, which should have confirmed his hold on the reins of power. Michael Psellos, a keen observer of royalty, noted that he was becoming more aloof, paid less attention to the details of government, and devoted most of his time to hunting. He suddenly fell ill. Making full play with his medical knowledge Michael Psellos persuaded him that he was seriously ill and should retire to a monastery. Isaac's brother John Comnenus refused to press his claim to the throne. He must have realized that outside his immediate family he could expect very little support. In his place, Michael Psellos persuaded Isaac to nominate Constantine Doukas as his successor. This was a logical choice. He was the natural nominee of those loyal to the memory of the Patriarch Michael Keroularios, whose niece he had married. He had been a potential candidate for the throne back in 1057, but had bowed to Isaac Comnenus's superior military backing.

Michael Psellos modestly begins by disclaiming any decisive role in the transfer of the imperial dignity from Isaac Comnenus to Constantine Doukas: 'If the latter was assisted in any way by myself, it is surely not for me to say so.'[20] But he is soon at pains to assure his audience that his intervention was indeed conclusive. The bitter remark of Isaac's empress would seem to bear this out: 'Pray Heaven we benefit from your advice as much as you hope, philosopher! But what a fine way to show your gratitude – planning to convert your emperor to the life of a monk!'[21] Despite her pleas, the emperor accepted Psellos's advice.

Why should Psellos have exercised this ascendancy over the emperor? Part of the answer is that Psellos presented him with a version of imperial absolutism, which caught his imagination: he would be the complete autocrat with a philosopher as his guide. Psellos compared him to Caesar and Augustus: 'He combines the purple robe of office with the cloak of a philosopher and endeavours to introduce philosophy into the imperial palace, just as formerly Caesar and Augustus had, as counsellors and advisers, Arrian and Rusticus respectively. They appointed them governors of nations and ruled their subjects according to the laws of political philosophy.'[22] This style of government left Isaac not merely isolated but also dependent upon his philosopher, Psellos, who would betray him.

Not surprisingly, Psellos is not very forthcoming about his reasons for abandoning his emperor. Again it is necessary to read between the lines. The emperor's illness was a threat to Psellos's position. His identification with the prosecution against the Patriarch Michael Keroularios must have made for unpopularity, which his advocacy of the emperor's reform programme can only have increased. His survival depended upon having the emperor's fullest backing. He remembered all too vividly how the Emperor Constantine Monomachos's last illness had deprived him of the political protection he needed. He did not wish to see history repeating itself. Bringing Constantine Doukas to power seemed to offer him a way out. The new emperor would be beholden to him and likely to keep him at court. There would be less danger of having to retreat to a monastery once again. His experience of the monastic life had not appealed to him. A change of emperors would also allow a change of policies: something that Psellos would have welcomed, now that he was beginning to doubt the efficacy of Isaac Comnenus's reform programme.

To an extent Michael Psellos had miscalculated. He was not for a time welcome at court. His part in the downfall of Michael Keroularios could not be overlooked. He found it prudent to retreat to the monastery of Narses, which had the twofold advantage of being situated in the capital and under Psellos's patronage. He was able to rehabilitate himself by delivering an encomium of his old enemy. He became tutor to the imperial children and recovered charge of the institutions of higher education, but he was never again to be the political force he had been under Isaac Comnenus. He attached himself to the new emperor's brother, the Caesar John Doukas, and acted as one of his political advisers.

Constantine Doukas shared the responsibilities of government with his brother, the Caesar John. He had learnt from his predecessor's downfall that it was essential to associate the imperial family in power. He also realized how important the goodwill of the great families of the Empire was and set about securing it. The Comneni, for instance, enjoyed his favour and protection. His government was deliberately to be one of reconciliation. In a speech he made to the assembled guilds of the capital shortly after becoming emperor, Constantine Doukas emphasized that truth and justice, not the sword, would be the keynote of his reign. He restored to their honours those deprived of them by Isaac Comnenus. He also made a number of new promotions both of people from the guilds and from the senate. It was a return to the policies pursued by Constantine Monomachos at the beginning of his reign. They flew in the face of the financial facts, but his was in many ways a successful reign. There was little opposition to his rule. He governed very much with Constantinopolitan interests in mind. The mild criticism there was of his rule centred on his neglect of the army and his lack of concern for the provinces. He imposed tax surcharges on the provinces, which were the cause of a rebellion in Thessaly. This was easily mopped up. The emperor was accused of parsimony. Economies had to be made and the army suffered. It was run down still further, leaving the defences of the eastern frontier particularly vulnerable. The loss to the Turks in 1064 of Ani, one of the keys to the defence of Armenia, was attributed at the time to the way the garrison had been cut down as a result of economies.

The success of the Turks went to feed a mood of public disquiet, that had been heightened by a series of earthquakes and confirmed by the famous appearance of Halley's comet in May 1066, which spread gloom and despondency. The emperor who was nearing his sixtieth birthday fell ill, but the succession seemed secure enough. His brother, the Caesar John, was quite capable of safeguarding the family interest, while his eldest son, Michael, was in his mid-teens, old enough to succeed to the throne, but when his father died in May 1067, he was passed over. He was not considered capable of taking up the burdens of imperial office. In the words of a contemporary, he was 'affable and pliable; he was considered old among the young'.[23] There was no disguising that he was an incompetent weakling. Constantine Doukas therefore vested his empress by the terms of his will with imperial authority. She was to wield it on behalf of her sons, but she was forced to take an oath before the patriarch that she would not remarry, would not put the interests of her own family first, and would rely for counsel on the Caesar John Doukas.

This attempt to protect the Doukas interest was not a success. The empress persuaded the Patriarch John Xiphilinos to release her from her oath, perhaps by holding out to him the prospect that his cousin would be her choice as husband and emperor. As we know, she instead married the general, Romanos Diogenes. She was under considerable pressure to abandon the policies followed by Constantine Doukas. Her marriage to Romanos Diogenes was a sign that more warlike policies would be pursued. This is not likely to have been the whole story. Eudocia Makrembolitissa was agreed to be a shrewd, capable woman: 'an exceedingly clever woman' in Michael Psellos's opinion. A scene from his *Chronographia* suggests that she aimed at holding on to the substance of power. The empress and Michael Psellos were praying together in the same church. Psellos claimed that he was so moved by her evident piety that he started to pray fervently that she would enjoy power as long as she lived. His prayer was so fervent that it carried to the empress. She turned to him and insisted that this was the last thing she wanted. This has all the marks of a ploy by Michael Psellos to sound out the empress's intentions. Her denial has the ring of a guilty conscience. Psellos insists that she expected to be able to control her new husband and to retain the reins of power. The failure of Constantine Doukas's policies was every day becoming clearer and Eudocia needed to distance herself from them. In these circumstances, her choice of Romanos Diogenes would seem to have been a shrewd move.

It did not quite work out as she had planned. Biology was against her. She bore her new husband two sons in quick succession and was forced more and more into the background. Romanos Diogenes was soon well in control of the government. The Doukas family and their adherents found themselves out of favour. The Caesar John retreated into semi-exile on his country estates, while Michael Psellos was hauled off as a virtual hostage to accompany the emperor on campaign. The defeat of Mantzikert was heaven-sent as far as the Doukas family and their supporters were concerned.

We have seen how the search for a new political order consistently failed over the period from 1042 to 1071. Why should this have been? Constantine Monomachos's reforms may seem to have been sensibly designed, but underlying them were ideas which would have made these measures less palatable. There was a strongly antiquarian flavour to them, in which one detects the hand of Michael Psellos and his cronies. The aim was to realize an abstract notion of imperial authority, which made the emperor little more than a figurehead. Psellos had a very elevated view of the imperial office and a very low opinion of emperors. Opponents not unnaturally suspected that his grand words only disguised an attempt by yet another civil service clique to secure ascendancy over the emperor and the apparatus of government; whence the surprisingly hostile reception accorded to apparently innocuous measures.

Constantine Monomachos was aware of the need for careful political management. This normally took the form of securing the support of influential sections of society through the grant of honours, pensions, and privileges. They were doled out almost indiscriminately to the great families and to monasteries. The church of St Sophia received special funds from Constantine Monomachos so that mass could be celebrated daily. It had previously been usual only to celebrate mass on Saturdays and Sundays and on the great feast days. All these concessions required a vast outlay of public revenues. The result was a financial crisis that, ironically, more or less ruled out reform.

Savings could most easily be made by cutting back on the army, which had hardly distinguished itself under Constantine Monomachos. Isaac Comnenus came to power pledged to restore the military might of the Empire. He could only find the necessary funds for this by dismantling the system of political management that had grown up under Constantine Monomachos. He soon found himself quite isolated. His worst mistake was to challenge the patriarch.

Under the Patriarch Michael Keroularios (1043–58) the church became a real political force and the patriarch dominated the political scene from 1054 until his death in 1058 and some might say even afterwards. The strange thing is that the early part of his patriarchate gave no indication of this. He remained in the background and at critical moments, such as Leo Tornikios's rebellion in 1047, loyally supported Constantine Monomachos. He came from much the same aristocratic background as the emperor and his appointment to the patriarchal throne has a political complexion to it. He was, however, a devout man, a patron of monks and an adept and promoter of the new mysticism associated with the teaching of St Symeon the 'New Theologian'. He must have absorbed from this source a certain distrust of imperial authority and a strong belief in his moral responsibilities as the upholder of orthodoxy. This seems only to have been strengthened by his belated discovery of papal ideology. The events leading to the schism of 1054 must have confirmed his suspicions of imperial intentions and made him more aware than ever of the need to defend the church against imperial encroachments. In trials of strength between emperors and patriarchs it was usually the latter who came off worse. Keroularios was more formidable an opponent because of the way he could count on the support of the people of Constantinople. Why they should have backed him remains slightly mysterious. It was not as though the emperors of the time neglected the people of their capital. Leaving aside considerations of the esteem in which they held him, it is not impossible that the secret of the patriarch's ascendancy within the capital was that he had grasped an essential point: the power wielded by the guilds and confraternities of the capital.

Michael Keroularios's posthumous victory over Isaac Comnenus put an end to the more strident claims for imperial authority. Michael Psellos would not again proclaim with Homer and Aristotle before him, 'Let there be one lord and one emperor' or entreat 'the most holy emperor to gird his sword on his thigh, and in his comeliness and beauty to extinguish this sulphurous and sterile conflagration',[24] by which he meant the patriarch's opposition to the emperor. Imperial authority would for the time being be presented in a more muted fashion. Constantine X Doukas made mild play with justice and truth as the guide to his rule, but these were slogans with little substance behind them. Only in one particular did his reign seem to mark a new departure. The emphasis of imperial propaganda shifted from the ideal of the imperial office to the dynastic ideal. His glorious ancestry, descending, it was claimed, from the great Doukas generals of the turn of the ninth century, was much embroidered. His marriage first into the Dalassenos family and then into the Makrembolites was also cause of pride, and incidentally recognition of the political importance of the aristocratic network. If nothing else, it was acceptance of the reality of political power and pointed the way to the future.

NOTES

1. Michael Psellos (transl. by E R A Sewter), p. 131
2. *Ibid.*
3. *Ibid.*, p. 157
4. *Ibid.*, p. 179
5. E Kurtz (ed.), *Die Gedichte des Christophoros Mitylenaios* (Leipzig, 1903), no.54
6. John Zonaras, *Epitomae Historiarum Libri XIII–XVIII,* III (Bonn, 1897), p. 647
7. Kekavmenos, *Strategikon* (ed. Wassilievsky–Jernstedt), p. 74; (ed. Litavrin), p. 268
8. D Simon, *Rechtsfindung am byzantinischen Reichsgericht* (Frankfurt, 1973), p. 17
9. Zepos, *Jus,* I, p. 620
10. *Ibid.,* p. 625
11. Sathas, IV, pp. 430–1
12. Migne, PL, 143, c. 178
13. A Michel, *Humbert und Kerullarios,* II (Paderborn, 1930), p. 242
14. Sathas, V, p. 512
15. John Skylitzes, *Synopsis Historiarum* (ed. I Thurn) (Berlin/New York, 1973), p. 499
16. *Ioannes Skylitzes Continuatus* (ed. E T Tsolakes) (Thessalonica, 1968), pp. 104–5
17. Sathas, V, p. 512
18. R J H Jenkins, 'A Cross of the Patriarch Michael Cerularius', *Dumbarton Oaks Papers,* 21 (1967), pp. 233–40
19. Sathas, V, p. 512
20. Michael Psellos (transl. by E R A Sewter), p. 330
21. *Ibid.,* p. 325
22. Sathas, V, p. 509
23. Michael Attaleiates, *Historia* (Bonn, 1853), p. 180
24. Sathas, V, p. 511

Chapter 4

ECONOMY AND SOCIETY IN ELEVENTH-CENTURY BYZANTIUM

At first sight the failures of the Byzantine Empire in the half-century following Basil II's death were political in origin. There was a lack of purpose at the centre of government and a willingness to bow to circumstance. Imperial authority was in danger of being compromised, as government came to be more and more an exercise, not of power, but in holding the balance between different interests and families. The price was the alienation of the rights and revenues of the state, so that a say in government came to be looked upon as a right or a prize to be exploited. The uncertainties that surrounded the succession must have contributed to this state of affairs, but they are hardly an explanation in themselves. A glance back at earlier Byzantine history reveals that the succession was often in doubt without this producing a prolonged crisis of the sort met in the eleventh century.

Many of the difficulties facing the Byzantine government in the eleventh century were financial in origin. It found it impossible to balance its books, whence the periodic attempts at retrenchment; whence, too, the need felt by different emperors to cut back on spending on the army and navy; whence, finally, the debasement of the gold coinage, which was a feature of the mid-eleventh century.

Modern historians have viewed this debasement of the gold coinage as perhaps the clearest indicator of the long-term decline of Byzantium. It may not at first have been apparent where the debasement of the gold coinage was leading, but today it looks very much like the first step down the slippery slope of permanent economic decline. It was a sign that the Byzantine government was finding it increasingly difficult to finance an international currency and that its economic ascendancy was coming to an end. The debasement of the Byzantine gold coinage can be traced back to the reign of Constantine Monomachos (1042–55). At the beginning of his reign the fineness of the gold coinage still stood at a notional twenty-four carats. In practice, it was likely to be a little less, since not even Byzantine moneyers could eliminate all impurities. Over the course of his reign the fineness was reduced to eighteen carats of gold. This debasement was carried out with extreme care. No less than five types of gold *nomismata* were issued and two types of *tetartera*, a coin of the same fineness, but weighing less. Each type represented a different fineness, so that it was possible to distinguish the stages of the debasement. There does not seem that there was any intention of passing off these debased coins as of full value and therefore misleading the public. Constantine's immediate successors kept their coins at the same finenesses. It was only under Romanos Diogenes that there was further debasement. After the battle of Mantzikert there was chaos and the fineness of the gold coinage plummeted. By the reign of Nicephorus Botaneiates (1078–81) it was down to eight carats of gold and the silver and copper currencies had suffered equally. The debasement from the time of Romanos Diogenes was a matter of necessity, but that effected under Constantine Monomachos is more difficult to explain.

It is often said that this was the first serious debasement of the Byzantine gold coinage since Constantine the Great had set the standard in the early fourth century. The maintenance of the gold coinage at a notional twenty-four carats of gold was a watchword of Byzantine tradition; a matter of prestige as much as anything else. If Byzantine emperors sometimes tampered with the currency, striking lightweight issues, they almost never resorted to debasement. The great exception was Nicephorus Phokas (963–69), who at a time of great financial difficulty struck a new coin, known as the *tetarteron*, with a fineness of only twenty-two carats of gold. According to his critics he hoped to collect taxes in full-value coins and pay out government pensions and salaries in the new debased coins and thus make a considerable profit. It was an expedient which caused understandable resentment and contributed to his unpopularity in Constantinople and his eventual overthrow. His successor John Tzimiskes (969–76) did not continue the practice. It had been an object lesson in the perils of debasement. Short-term financial gains hardly compensated for the odium they generated. With this example before him Constantine Monomachos is unlikely to have embarked on a much more serious debasement of the coinage than that carried out by Nicephorus Phokas, unless there was pressing need. There is, however, something quite surprising. This debasement appears to have occasioned no protest among Constantine Monomachos's subjects. While we know about Nicephorus Phokas's debasement from the chroniclers of the time, it is only the work of modern numismatists that has revealed Monomachos's debasement. This is all the more surprising because he came in for harsh and often unfair criticism from his contemporaries and near contemporaries. There are therefore two questions: why did he resort to debasement and why did this apparently not produce open criticism? The first is rather easier to answer than the second.

Financial embarrassment is the most obvious explanation for debasement in a medieval context and is the most likely cause of

Constantine Monomachos's debasement. Constantine and Zoe were ludicrously extravagant in their private lives and pursuits. They were overgenerous in their grant of offices and dignities. These had to be paid for in the hard cash of the pensions and salaries that went with them. Inflation of honours and debasement of the coinage went together. On top of this, there were rebellions to face and wars to be fought. The long struggle with the Petchenegs would have strained the Empire's finances. Revenues would have been falling if only because of Romanos Argyros's repeal of the *allelengyon,* that measure instituted by Basil II, whereby landowners undertook to pay arrears of taxation incurred by the peasantry. Its reimposition would have gone some way to meet the financial difficulties confronting Constantine Monomachos, but it would have earned him the hatred of the ruling class. Given his still uncertain position, this was not a real option. Other emperors faced with similar difficulties merely added a surcharge to the basic land tax, thus shifting the burden very largely on to the shoulders of the peasantry. But there were clearly problems just getting in the basic land tax. From the reign of Romanos Argyros it had been necessary to resort to tax farmers to collect back taxes. Between the late 1020s and 1040 there were a series of rebellions caused by resentment at heavy taxation. When Constantine X Doukas sought to impose a surcharge on the basic land tax in the 1060s it produced a rebellion in Thessaly. Debasement really was the least painful solution.

But why was there no outcry of the sort provoked by Nicephorus Phokas's rather milder debasement? The most likely answer is that those that counted did not suffer as a result. Office-holders saw themselves threatened by Nicephorus Phokas's measure because it meant a real reduction in salaries and pensions, but under Constantine Monomachos debasement was compensated by an inflation of honours, which offered the possibility of readier access to higher dignities and a correspondingly higher pension. Promotion was a way of allaying discontent. If used subtly it could strengthen support for the government, but there were dangers: after Constantine Monomachos's death it was resentment at the way promotion was blocked by the new government which led to Isaac Comnenus's rebellion.

Under Nicephorus Phokas office-holders were still a fairly small, tightly knit group, conscious of their place in society and likely to react strongly against any threat to their position. By the reign of Constantine Monomachos it was a broader, less well defined group. Court dignities were widely distributed among the guildsmen and businessmen of Constantinople. They were probably more interested in the status their dignities brought rather than the value of the pensions. They were prospering, and the increased amount of money in circulation as a result of debasement may have seemed to quicken trade and to have been to their advantage.

Such reasoning is in line with a fashionable desire to see more sophisticated considerations underlying Monomachos's debasement. The argument goes as follows: supplies of precious metals in the middle ages were inelastic. The existing coinage in circulation was quite insufficient to meet any rapid increase in the number of exchanges. Credit still had only a small role to play. Debasement was therefore the only practical means of increasing the amount of currency in circulation. It goes without saying that this line of argument is rooted in modern economic theory. Could Byzantine bureaucrats have thought in such terms? It is most unlikely to have been the case at the time of the debasement, since civil service wisdom stressed the advantages of maintaining the value of the coinage. The debasement itself gave rise to a debate in court circles over the management of the currency. It may even have produced a deeper understanding of the laws of economics, to judge by the historian Michael Attaleiates's penetrating account of the relationship between the price of grain and the level of other prices and wages. This tends to point to the conclusion that debasement produced consequences for good and for ill that were not anticipated at the time when the decision to debase was taken and only became clear with the passage of time. If debasement did turn out to be a way of relieving an inelastic money supply, this can only have been an unlooked-for bonus.

The argument is anyway dangerously circular: there was not enough money in circulation, therefore it was necessary to debase; the need to debase proves that there was not enough money in circulation. How can we be sure that there was not a sufficient money supply? Again the argument advanced to support such a contention is a dangerous one: since the money supply was inelastic, it could not meet the demands placed on it by economic growth, whence the need to debase; since there was debasement, this must have meant that there was economic growth. Therefore the money supply was insufficient, or there would have been no need for debasement. These arguments are backed up by impressive-looking equations, which only show that debasement can be a solution to some of the problems created by rapid economic growth, but they are hardly proof that Byzantium experienced any such thing in the eleventh century. The condition of the Byzantine economy in the eleventh century has to be approached not from the direction of modern economic theory, but through the few pieces of solid evidence that we possess.

The first is that the money supply was not quite so inelastic as assumed. Precious metals shifted from western Europe, to Byzantium, to Islam in response to the prevailing gold–silver ratios, but these movements are difficult to pin down. It was also possible to withdraw precious metals from circulation by the simple process of hoarding. This is what Basil II did on a grand scale by building up his vast treasure. His successors squandered it. It had all been disgorged by the time Constantine Monomachos came to the throne. It seems to have been a time of dehoarding. Michael IV made the archbishop of Thessalonica give up his treasure amounting to 3,300 lb of gold and distribute it to his clergy and to the poor of his diocese. At his death in February 1043 the Patriarch Alexius Stoudites had 2,500 lb of gold stored in his monastery, which was seized by the Emperor. Opinion in court circles at this time was opposed to the hoarding of wealth. Christopher of Mitylene was contemptuous of a *nouveau riche,* who had no idea what to do with his money except bury it:

'Having gazed on money, much as a polecat does on fat
You accumulate gold just to bury it in a vat
What good does it do you under the ground
When that is where you are bound?'[1]

Just as the unlooked-for consequence of building up treasure was to damp down economic activity, so its disgorging was to quicken it. The conditions for a growth in local trade already existed, especially around Constantinople. The shores of the sea of Marmora were cluttered with small ports, which prospered from provisioning the capital. Petty tradesmen – greengrocers, bakers, gardeners – and small merchants engaged in coastal traffic were beginning to do well. The career of Michael V's father provides evidence that there were fortunes to be made out of shipbuilding around Constantinople in the early eleventh century. His trade was that of caulker. His skills came into demand just at this time because of changes in shipbuilding techniques. The traditional method had been the expensive and time-consuming shell construction. In the course of the early middle ages this slowly gave way to the cheaper frame construction, but the Byzantine shipwrights did not clad the frame with overlapping planks clinkerwise, they preferred to build in carvel fashion with the planks set flush. If the vessel was to remain watertight, caulking with pitch was essential. This method of construction only seems to have been perfected around the turn of the tenth century. It produced a cheap serviceable boat, ideal for coastal trade and fits nicely into the upsurge of local trade in the early eleventh century.

Archaeology suggests that this was not just limited to Constantinople and its surrounding region, but also occurred in the Greek provinces, where a sustained growth in urban life seems to have occurred in the eleventh century. The evidence is clearest from Athens and Corinth. These had been more or less abandoned in the course of the early middle ages. Some sort of Byzantine presence may have been maintained in their citadels, but their *agorai* were left deserted. In the eleventh century they began to be built over. The building was not impressive. There was no clear plan to it, just a maze of rather mean houses. Workshops and living quarters were jumbled together. There were no *piazze* in the Italian style. Quarters centred on churches and monasteries. They were almost always small, as at Athens with its numerous medieval churches,

most of them dating to the eleventh and twelfth centuries: in themselves
testimony to the growth of the city at that time. Other Greek cities which
are known to have prospered at this time were Thebes and Sparta (or
Lakedaimon, as it was known to the Byzantines) even though their sites
have not been thoroughly explored by archaeologists.

How is one to account for the apparent prosperity of the cities of
Greece in the eleventh century? Their wealth was largely agricultural in
origin. By the eleventh century most of the land surrounding Thebes
seems to have passed into the hands of rich families from Thebes itself
and from other neighbouring towns, such as Athens and Chalkis or
Eurippos, the main place in Euboea. The same people also showed
interest in buying up mills in the neighbourhood of Thebes. There
seems, at least in Greece, to have been considerable investment by
landowners in agriculture. Kekavmenos, who approved of very little,
approved of investments designed to improve estates. His own were
centred on Larissa, the capital of Thessaly. These landowners almost
invariably had their residence in a town or city and the wealth of their
estates flowed into the towns and cities to be consumed. Their presence
and spending power attracted local manufactures. Corinth and Thebes
were both centres of cloth and silk manufacture, and Corinth was also a
centre of glassmaking. Athens developed purple-fishing and soap-
making, both activities geared to the cloth and silk trades. The silk
industry in Corinth and Thebes was, at this time, very largely in the
hands of Jews, who sought refuge in the Byzantine Empire from
persecution in Fatimid Egypt and brought their skills in silk
manufacture and perhaps, glassmaking, too, with them. They found in
the Greek cities conditions which allowed them, if not to prosper, at
least to ply their trades and skills. It would have been more or less
impossible for them to settle in Constantinople with its guild regulations
and restrictions. There was nothing of this sort in the Greek cities.

Neither Jews nor manufactures are much in evidence in the cities of
Asia Minor. Of the cities which have been thoroughly excavated Sardis
shows considerable building activity from the end of the tenth century,
both in the citadel and in the plain below. Ephesus, on the other hand,
does not display the same signs of rebuilding, almost certainly because
this came earlier in the ninth century. Generally speaking, Anatolia
seems to have been a land of wide open spaces with a few prosperous
market towns, such as Ikonion, which was a centre for trade in livestock,
or Euchaita in the Pontus region, to which John Mavropous was sent as
bishop in 1048. He arrived in the depths of winter and was intimidated
by the bleakness of the surrounding countryside. It took on a different
aspect in spring. It produced wheat on a big scale. The city itself seems to
have been populous and possessed impressive buildings in addition to
the cathedral. It was a great centre of pilgrimage, containing the chief
shrine of St Theodore the Recruit, one of the most popular of
Byzantium's military saints. Connected with this was an annual fair,

which brought in people and livestock from the surrounding countryside.

The wealth of Anatolia was agricultural. In the middle of the eleventh century there were still good opportunities for investment in land, as the experience of Eustathios Boilas suggests. He came from a Cappadocian family and achieved some modest success in public life, attaining the middling rank of *protospatharios*. At some point, he was forced to leave his native land and settle in the border region around Edessa. He is rather coy about giving reasons for this, but it is to be assumed that he was in disgrace. He found the land so wild that not even intrepid Armenians would settle it. Slowly, he brought it back into cultivation. He built mills and irrigation channels; he planted vineyards, meadows, and gardens. He constructed a country-house and built an adjoining church. He also acquired a number of villages in the area. By the time he drew up his will in 1059 he was a man of some substance, with an impressive range of property and ready money at his disposal.

Against this has to be set the inventory drawn up in 1073 of part of some imperial estates situated near the mouth of the river Maiander in the western coastlands of Asia Minor. It reveals years of neglect and lack of investment. Farm buildings were in a state of disrepair. Arable land had been inundated by the river and had been allowed to turn into marshland. The peasants settled on the villages belonging to the estate do not seem to have been especially prosperous and were burdened with heavy taxation. This may well have been a failure of the administration of the imperial demesne, and should not be taken as solid evidence of economic decline.

The hard evidence, such as it is, about the state of the Byzantine economy in the eleventh century turns out to be contradictory. It suggests that the Byzantine Empire was not getting significantly poorer. The reverse, in fact: in most areas agriculture was prospering, because landowners were willing to invest in their estates; local trade largely in agricultural products was thriving and supported a network of ports and market towns. But outside a handful of Greek towns, where some manufacturing capacity was developing, there was no transformation of the economy. It remained what it had always been: agricultural, localized, with such manufactures as there were heavily concentrated in Constantinople. This hardly suggests that the upsurge in economic activity was so intense that debasement was a necessary means of easing the inelasticity of the money supply. In any case, if this had been so, the government would have stood to gain on a grand scale, since it took a tax of 10 per cent on every commercial transaction. This would hardly square with the evidence there is for its financial difficulties.

What was the nature of these financial difficulties? We have already seen that there were problems getting in basic taxation. The imperial administration resorted to tax farmers to collect the arrears and then under Constantine X Doukas the ordinary revenue. This suggests that all was not well with the fiscal administration. Though only properly appreciated by an income tax inspector, the Byzantine fiscal system had been one of the glories of Byzantium and one of the foundations of its enduring strength. By the eleventh century it was becoming less effective, largely because of long-term changes in the organization of Byzantine society.

Like so much else in Byzantine government, the fiscal system rested on the village community of peasant proprietors. Over more than a century peasant property had come under pressure from landowners. Landowners bought into the village community and sometimes bought it up. In some regions this would have meant exappropriation as the land was turned into ranches or large farms run by slave or hired labour. In the majority of cases, though, the peasant would almost certainly have stayed on his holding, but would have been responsible for his rent and taxation to a lord rather than to the state and its agents. The peasant community continued to exist. It remained a very largely self-regulating body, responsible for most of its own affairs. The village court continued to function, the village elders sitting in judgement on petty crime and peasant squabbles. The real difference was that the village was represented before the state by a lord or patron. This was often, perhaps usually, to the advantage of the peasants. There are plenty of examples of villages submitting voluntarily to a lord. We have some in the letters of Michael Psellos. The inhabitants of the village of Atzikome approached him, desiring that he become their patron. In return they agreed to furnish him with agricultural services. Before long Psellos was intervening with a local judge on their behalf.

No one should underestimate how difficult it was to squeeze taxes out of the peasantry, but once a village acquired a patron and a lord it became still harder. A man, such as Michael Psellos, would have known all the loopholes in the system, all the weak points and where, how, and when pressure should be applied. There was another reason why the yield of the basic land tax was likely to fall. The Byzantine tax system was regressive, that is to say, the richer you were the less proportionately you paid in taxes. A village which had passed under the control of a lord, even if the same peasants continued to farm their old holdings, would pay less tax than one where the peasants continued to pay their taxes directly to the state.

The agrarian legislation of the tenth century was brought in to protect the interest of the state in peasant property against the encroachments of the 'powerful', as they were called: the direct control exercised by the state over the peasant and his property was considered to be one of the Empire's basic strengths. Even after Basil II's death the Byzantine judiciary made some effort to enforce this legislation, but it was a losing battle. It is conceivable that judges could maintain a detached attitude to the problem, but not those responsible for carrying out their decisions, for they were almost invariably landowners themselves. In any case, the agrarian legislation was very often not in the peasant's best interests, in the sense that a lord might offer better protection than the state. Under Basil II the state became increasingly predatory. It aimed at a more direct exploitation of public lands. This was put in the hands of a new ministry under the presidency of the *epi ton oikeiakon*. In the past, when deserted lands came into the hands of the state, it was usual to sell them off relatively cheaply. A quick sale, it was reckoned, was the most effective way of bringing them back into production. The sooner this happened the better, as far as raising taxes was concerned. Under the new regime the state exploited such lands by settling peasants on them on its own account. There is even an instance of the *epi ton oikeiakon* buying up land for the purpose. The peasants settled on these public lands were known as *demosiarioi* or state *paroikoi*. They were of exactly the same semi-servile status as the peasants settled on the estates of the 'powerful'. The advantage to the state was that they not only paid the basic tax, but also a rent at the relatively high rate of 1 *nomisma* per 10 *modioi* – the rough equivalent of a tithe. They also owed labour services.

The legal position of the dependent peasantry increasingly became a matter for debate among the Byzantine judiciary. It was an important problem now that such a large proportion of the Byzantine peasantry was made up of *paroikoi*. A ruling on the subject has been preserved in the *Peira,* that legal collection put together in the early 1040s. It gave *paroikoi* security of tenure after thirty years' occupation of a holding, but in return they owed their lord rent and services. There was an assumption, which did not always hold good, that dependent status would be passed on to their children. It is difficult to judge whether reduction to semi-servile status automatically produced a deterioration in the economic position of the Byzantine peasantry. The condition of the *paroikoi* on the imperial estates of Alopekai near the mouth of the river Maiander was in 1073 less favourable than that of *paroikoi* in the twelfth century. There was some resistance to the encroachments of landowners and the state, not so much from peasants as from the inhabitants of *kastra* or fortresses: small country towns, with markets which were locally important. With their easy access to markets and the opportunities of local trade they were perhaps those with most to lose by reduction to dependent status.

The agrarian legislation of the tenth century was consciously designed to combat a danger that the imperial government recognized in the growth of a dependent peasantry: its loss of control over rural society. The administration of the Byzantine Empire was built on the village community. Its effectiveness would automatically be impaired, should it be denied direct access to the village. This would happen with the growing domination of peasant society by lords and patrons. The policy of direct exploitation of public lands associated with the creation of the office of the *epi ton oikeiakon* was a reaction against this danger, but it did not prevent the grant of exemptions from taxation and the creation of immunities on an increasingly large scale. Total immunities from the payment of taxation and the interference of the imperial administration are only attested for a few highly favoured monasteries, such as Constantine Monomachos's foundation of Nea Moni on the island of Chios, or for members of the imperial family, such as Andronicus Doukas, the son of the Caesar John. They were created out of the imperial demesne or the pious foundations attached to it, not out of public lands – that was for the future.

In many ways rural society in eleventh-century Byzantium was coming to resemble that of the later Roman Empire with great landowners exercising rights of patronage and enjoying exemptions from taxation. In the later Roman Empire the imperial government did not exercise any very close control over the countryside. It had little need to, because it worked through the cities. The dangers that this held in store became apparent with the swift decline of city life from the early seventh century. The administrative system was undermined. Out of the chaos that ensued there emerged the theme system, which rested on the village community and a few garrison towns. Power resided with the army of the theme under its *strategos* or military commander. As we have seen, conditions changed decisively from the turn of the tenth century. The theme armies became more or less redundant; the *strategos* lost much of his authority to the civil governor, and the towns grew in importance. If the late Roman pattern is anything to go by, the towns should now have become the key to local government, but almost nothing was done to evolve new patterns of provincial administration, based upon the town. Instead, the towns were allowed to develop their own informal organization around their *archontes*. These came for the most part from landowning families, who increasingly preferred to live in the towns rather than out on their estates. They often held positions in local government and might provide the bishop with some of his officials. Some members of these families might well go to Constantinople to further their own careers and to protect family and local interests at the imperial court. The emergence of a group of landowners associated with each town meant that local interests could be fostered and local people were less likely to be overawed by the might of the local governor, who was, in any case, outside the provincial capitals a remote figure.

Each town had its own cults, such as that of St Nikon at Lakedaimon. He was a holy man, who had wandered far from his native Cappadocia, with the monotonous cry of 'Repent, Repent' always on his lips. He stumbled into Lakedaimon at the end of the tenth century, to find the place suffering from plague. Begged by the people to deliver them, he decided that the Jews settled there were to blame and drove them out of the town. The plague went too. In gratitude they helped him to build a church. He chose a site on the edge of the ancient *agora*. The *archontes* who used the place as a polo ground let him have the site and two of their number donated an antique column apiece. The townspeople down to the very poorest provided food and drink for the workforce that assembled, while the *archontes* found the wages of the masons. The building of St Nikon's church was very much a communal effort. His reputation was confirmed by miracles both before and after his death. There is no firm evidence, however, that his cult gave rise to a confraternity of the sort attested in Thebes. It was founded in 1048 and devoted to an image of the Mother of God kept in a local nunnery. Each month the brotherhood went in procession to the nunnery and took the image to a place of honour which had been prepared for it by one of the number, perhaps in his own home or in another church. The purpose of this association seems to have been purely religious, but with its prayers, processions, and burial services it gave comfort and solidarity. It was around such associations that much of urban life revolved.

The sense of community existing in these provincial towns is caught in the word *synkastritai* that might be applied to their inhabitants. *Kastron* was the usual word for a provincial city, although its literal translation is fortress: the rough meaning of *synkastritai* therefore being fellow-citizens. It was used by Kekavmenos of the citizens of Larissa in Thessaly, who rose in rebellion against Constantine X Doukas. At its centre was Nikoulitzas Delphinas, one of Kekavmenos's relatives. He belonged to the archontic ascendancy of Larissa. He discovered that other local leaders were organizing a rebellion in protest against a tax surcharge imposed by the government. Nikoulitzas, perhaps to cover himself, tried to warn the emperor, but was sent away. He returned to his native town, where, apparently against his will, he was placed at the head of the rebellion. The rebels moved against Servia, a fortress commanding the main route northwards out of Thessaly. Nikoulitzas felt that he was now in a strong enough position to negotiate. The emperor promised to remit the taxes and gave Nikoulitzas a guarantee of personal safety. The rebellion came to an end; the emperor disregarded his promise to Nikoulitzas and had him imprisoned in far-off Amaseia.

The most instructive part of this episode is the willingness of the citizens of Larissa to engage in communal action to protect local interests. Pressure for rebellion did not come from above, but from within the community. Nikoulitzas was forced to head the rebellion simply because he came from the most influential local family. The growth of towns gave a much sharper focus to local interests. At some point in the eleventh century these came to be seen as of greater moment than respect for imperial authority. One of the first steps in this direction was the appearance in one or two towns of a 'dynast', as he was called. He was the lord or patron of a town. His position was quite unofficial. He was able to impose his authority over the town because he could protect its interests. In some cases, it might just be a matter of military strength, but we have the example of one, Noah, who around the middle of the eleventh century became the 'dynast' of the Thessalian port of Demetrias. It was his business acumen which recommended him to the citizens of the place. The existence of these petty local rulers was testimony to the way towns were slipping away from the direct control of the central government. By the reign of Michael VII Doukas (1071–78) the imperial government was being forced to recognize their authority. It granted out lordship over *kastra*, which might be either fortresses or towns. Too late it was realized that this often meant the permanent alienation of imperial authority, and legislation was introduced to the effect that such grants were for a single life only and could not be inherited.

Worst of all, the emperors of the eleventh century were losing their ascendancy over their capital of Constantinople. We have seen how in the eleventh century the people of Constantinople became an important factor in Byzantine politics. They took part in the overthrow of Michael V in 1042. They intervened decisively on the patriarch's side in 1054; they had a role to play in the events which led up to Isaac Comnenus's accession in 1057 and they would have again in those which brought Nicephorus Botaneiates to power in 1078. The overthrow of the Emperor Michael V was a spontaneous outburst of popular fury at the treatment of the Empress Zoe, one of the darlings of the people. Constantinople was always liable to explode. For a medieval city it was densely populated with great extremes of wealth and poverty. There was a proletariat, only too happy to exploit any opportunities for plunder, violence, and excitement. Christopher of Mitylene vividly describes how easy it was for a church festival to get out of hand and turn into a violent riot. This was a perennial feature of Constantinopolitan life. The anarchic urges of the mob might explode harmlessly or they might be channelled against the government, as happened in the early sixth century with the circus factions.

There were still circus factions in eleventh-century Constantinople and the chariot races in the Hippodrome still excited the enthusiasm of the people of Constantinople, rich and poor alike, but the circus factions had long lost any political role. Their function was, apart from putting on races, purely honorific. The Hippodrome was the scene of much imperial ceremonial with the circus factions acting as a chorus. It created that illusion of popular involvement in imperial government that did much to reconcile the people to autocracy. Its impact is hard to gauge, but it probably contributed to the relatively peaceful condition of the capital for most of the tenth and early eleventh centuries.

A more concrete contribution was made to this state of affairs by the guild organization, which was perfected in the early tenth century. It was then that the Emperor Leo the Wise codified the guild statutes in a piece of legislation known as the Book of the Prefect. It certainly did not cover all guilds, the less prestigious trades, such as cobblers, blacksmiths, ropemakers (the list could be extended almost endlessly), were not included. The Book of the Prefect was more concerned with what we would call professions rather than trades. Much space was devoted to the workings of the notaries, the bankers and money-changers, the silversmiths and the silk merchants. They represented the professional backbone of the city, the sort of people vital to keep the city functioning smoothly. The guilds were private, self-regulating bodies, with their own officers, ultimately responsible to the prefect of the city. It was a system that worked very well, in a number of different ways. It ensured that the capital was supplied with basic foodstuffs; that legal business and commercial transactions could be carried out reasonably efficiently. The aim was stability, to be achieved by way of price controls, fixed profit margins, and limitations on competition. These were not to be enforced by the government, which would have been almost impossible, but by the trades and professions themselves, organized into private associations. These in return enjoyed monopoly rights. There were of course weaknesses. It was difficult for such a system to respond rapidly to change; it was indeed designed to hobble it. The limited extent of economic activity is betrayed by a single detail from the Book of the Prefect. The total number of notaries allowed to operate in the city was fixed at a mere twenty-four. This was regarded very seriously: any prefect of the city attempting to increase this number was to be stripped of his office and dignity. When one thinks of the hundreds of notaries who operated in the Italian cities in the twelfth and thirteenth centuries, it is immediately apparent how this lack of notaries must have restricted business in Constantinople.

The Book of the Prefect was drawn up at the beginning of the tenth century, when the Byzantine economy was still fairly rudimentary. Growing demand put some strain on the guild system. The silk guilds could not meet the demand for Byzantine silks. They had to tolerate competition from workshops, particularly at the cheap end of the market, which escaped their regulation. Generally, it was the unregulated trades which did best out of the growth of local exchanges from the beginning of the eleventh century. A legal ruling included in the *Peira* draws a clear distinction between professional guilds, composed of those such as silk merchants, 'not working with their hands', and the associations of tradespeople, such as smiths and cobblers, who did. It was a matter of some importance in the early eleventh century, reflecting a division between professional groups, almost invariably included in the Book of the Prefect, and trades associations which were normally absent. The latter were the ones who had gained most from the upsurge of local trade, and there is plenty of evidence that the educated élite of Constantinople found this disturbing. The feeling was that they did not know their station in life and were aspiring to positions that belonged to their betters. They wanted to go into the church. 'Gatekeepers, vineyard workers, cattle merchants, greengrocers, bakers, blacksmiths, gardeners, cobblers, peddlars', so Christopher of Mitylene[2] assures us in horrified tones, all wanted to become priests, but they were so ignorant, scarcely literate, that they could not conduct church services properly and kept introducing into the solemnities of the liturgy words used in their own trades. The same sort of people aspired to be court dignitaries. Michael Psellos records with scorn how Constantine Monomachos conferred honours indiscriminately on those 'who had no right to them, especially the vulgar sort'. 'The doors of the senate were thrown open to the rascally vagabonds of the market.'[3] The sort of man he had in mind was very much Michael V's father, the 'Caulker'. His wealth brought him high position, but he just looked ridiculous. Everything about him was out of place. 'It was as if a pygmy wanted to play Hercules and was trying to make himself look like a demi-god.'[4] That was Psellos's supercilious opinion.

Psellos came from a guild background. A chance remark he dropped suggests that his family were silversmiths and so belonged to that professional élite among the gilds. His strictures were not directed against members of the 'professional' guilds, but against *nouveaux riches,* the people of the market as he called them. There was an element of snobbery, but there was also distress at the way traditional order was being undermined by the indiscriminate grant of honours. He accuses Constantine Monomachos of reducing the *cursus honorum* to confusion with excessive promotions and honours doled out to the undeserving tradesmen. The system of honours was getting out of hand. It was not so much that new individual titles were being created, but new orders of titles and ranks, which might be granted out in their hundreds. *Proedros* and *nobellisimos* had been high-ranking titles, now you find above them *protoproedros* and *protonobellisimos*. It was literally an inflation of honours. By the reign of Nicephorus Botaneiates (1078–81), according to one contemporary, the number of court dignitaries had reached tens of thousands. The pensions that they were entitled to draw would bankrupt the state, thus reinforcing the view that there was a direct connection between inflation of honours and debasement of the coinage.

The inflation of honours also debased the currency of political ascendancy, to judge by Psellos's charge against Constantine X Doukas: that he swept away the traditional distinction between ordinary citizen and senator. 'Henceforward no discrimination was made between worker and senator and they were all merged into one body' is how he puts it.[5] Psellos was almost certainly being sarcastic: honours had been distributed so widely and so indiscriminately that it was difficult to tell the difference between citizens and senators, but there was some truth in his hyperbole. You find guild officers who also held positions in the imperial administration. Businessmen claiming senatorial privileges, such as testifying in the privacy of their own homes; tradesmen able to purchase honours for their children. It is this blurring of clear social distinctions that Psellos is criticizing.

The result was in a purely Byzantine sense an extension of the franchise; a much wider circle was brought into Byzantine political life. The guilds came to play a political role. This was officially recognized by Constantine Doukas when he made his address on taking up the imperial dignity not just to the senate as he might have done in the past, but to the assembled guilds. Politicized in this way the guilds ceased to contribute to the stability and docility of the capital as they had done in the past. The craft guilds did not have that tradition of deference to imperial authority associated with the professions. They also brought their rivalries. Constantine X Doukas made a lavish grant of honours at the beginning of his reign to the people of the market. This was followed two years later by a plot against the emperor headed by two bankers, no doubt incensed by the favours showered upon the craftsmen.

Why should Constantine Monomachos and Constantine Doukas have gone out of their way to grant honours to the people of the market? It can only have been that they needed their support. They had turned themselves into the representatives of the people of Constantinople. The ill-fated Michael V had calculated that he could found his authority on the people rather than on the élite of office-holders. Constantine Monomachos and Constantine Doukas may have made a rather similar calculation: that control of the capital depended upon the support of the people of the market, who represented the new wealth of Constantinople. Wealth did not by itself bring status. This was conferred by position in the imperial administration or at court or by entry into the patriarchal administration. The emperors surrendered to this demand for status at a time when their hold on authority was weak. Promotions and the doling out of honours were at their most lavish at the beginning of an emperor's reign. The consequences were a dilution of imperial authority, a lack of effective control over the capital.

Both Michael Attaleiates and Michael Psellos have left clues that help solve the puzzle presented by Byzantine economy and society in the eleventh century. They approach the problem from different directions. They complement one another very well, Attaleiates providing the economic dimension and Psellos the social and political side. Attaleiates has left us an account of how the Byzantine government made an attempt during the reign of Michael VII Doukas (1071–78) to recover some direct control over the economy. This was to be done by regulating the corn trade of Thrace through the creation of a state monopoly. The results were disastrous. Imperial officials intervened to fix the price of corn, which immediately disappeared from the market. The shortage of corn had a critical effect on the price of other commodities and on wages. It was proof that the state could not intervene in the economy without upsetting the workings of the market. The economy had become too complicated. The Byzantine government evolved to meet the needs of a society which combined a relatively primitive rural economy with a capital which monopolized virtually all urban functions. It was very successful at imposing a large measure of central control.

It was done through self-regulating institutions: the village in the provinces and the guild in the capital. The long-term changes in the economy began to undermine the workings of these institutions in the course of the eleventh century. They continued to exist, but they no longer sustained an effective system of government. They became vehicles of private and sectional interest rather than remaining amenable to imperial control. Basil II had tried to keep change in check, but his successors had neither his will nor his assured position. They preferred to condone the changes which had occurred by the granting of honours and imperial rights. They gave recognition to new power and new wealth.

It was this that Michael Psellos saw and deplored, even though he was a major beneficiary of the new order of things. In his opinion 'two things in particular contribute to the hegemony of the Byzantines, our system of honours and our wealth'.[6] The two things went together. The breakdown of the honours system meant a depletion in the Empire's wealth. This is easy to see, because of the pensions that went with a title. It also meant a loss of control over patronage, which was one of the cements of Byzantine society. Honours were granted in perpetuity to monasteries and to foreign potentates, such as Robert Guiscard, and probably to members of the great families of the Empire. This seems to be a reasonable inference from a passage of Michael Attaleiates, where he mentions that Constantine Doukas restored the private honours, which had been taken away by Isaac Comnenus. The use of the word 'private' brings home how the honours system was being infiltrated by private interests. So, an influential minister, such as Michael Psellos, had in his gift a number of court titles and the pensions which went with them and could distribute them as he saw fit, even as a way of making up the dowry of his adopted daughter.

There was no clear shape to Byzantine society, now that social distinctions were becoming blurred. There were many opportunities for advancement; there were more for graft and intrigue. All this is reflected in the *Book of Advice* that Kekavmenos compiled out of his own experience for his children. He had been a military commander, he had contacts at the imperial court, he had been governor of the theme of Hellas and ended his career on his family estates near Larissa in Thessaly. He was well acquainted with Byzantine political life over the eleventh century. He was a pessimist; he clung to the old order, which he saw embodied in the imperial office. His affection for the old order only brought out the present shortcomings of imperial government more sharply. He attributed them to the personal failings of imperial officials and agents rather than as the breaking down of government and society. He was critical of the farming of taxes and of the imposition of surcharges, which gave imperial agents good opportunities to exploit the people of the provinces. He was contemptuous of those civil servants, little better than actors, who pulled the strings of power in Constantinople. In the prevailing uncertainty, when nobody, not even close relatives could be trusted, almost any course of action was full of danger. The only hope of security was to retreat within your household and immediate family and cultivate your garden. You should not allow outsiders to penetrate your home, for they came only to do you harm or make fun of you. If they were not able to seduce your wife, they might succeed with your daughter. Don't give hospitality, don't accept hospitality. It was a way of purchasing your favour. Don't accept gifts: 'I have seen many condemned to death through gifts',[7] commented Kekavmenos darkly. There is more than a tinge of paranoia, that may well be inseparable from the Byzantine character, but rarely is it quite so well developed as with Kekavmenos, who lived through difficult times: he reflects a society in a state of uncertainty and anxiety, where the village and the guild no longer gave the protection they once did and new forms of community, such as the town, were only just in the process of development. Instead there was intense competition to grab the opportunities which the breakdown of the old order offered.

NOTES

1. E Kurtz (ed.), *Die Gedichte des Christophoros Mitylenaios* (Leipzig, 1903), no. 134
2. *Ibid.,* no. 63
3. Michael Psellos (transl. by E R A Sewter), p. 170
4. *Ibid.,* p. 103
5. *Ibid.,* p. 338
6. *Ibid.,* p. 170
7. Kekavmenos, *Strategikon* (ed. Wassiliewsky–Jernstedt), p. 14; (ed. Litavrin), p. 146.

Chapter 5

INTELLECTUAL CURRENTS IN ELEVENTH-CENTURY BYZANTIUM

Kekavmenos's Greek may not be all that elegant and betrays his lack of higher education, but for a military man who ended his days on his estates far from Constantinople he displays surprising literary talents. It would be hard to imagine his equivalent in eleventh-century France even being able to put pen to paper. But that was a profound difference between Byzantium and the West at this time. Byzantium was a literate society, while in the West literacy was still very much the preserve of the clergy. To participate in public life in Byzantium at almost any level a man had to possess basic literacy. Kekavmenos was rather more accomplished than this, but he was aware how poor his command of the written word was. At the same time, he was suspicious of the highly educated. He did not approve of people who just dipped into books. Reading was a serious business. A book should be read from cover to cover. In his opinion 'it was the work of a babbler not to go right through the whole of a book, but just to choose a few passages to gossip about'.[1]

Pervading Kekavmenos's *Book of Advice* is a suspicion and a resentment of the highly educated élite of Constantinople. He suspected that its members were frivolous, impractical, and responsible for the deterioration he had witnessed in the condition of the Empire. Such resentment is only to be expected, because in the uncertain circumstances of the eleventh century there could be no better investment than a good education. It was the key to a successful career in the imperial administration; it brought social prestige; it was the badge of membership of the Constantinopolitan élite.

A basic education could be had in most parts of the Empire and was probably within the reach of a fair proportion of children. To take but a single example. St Lazaros of Galesion came from a poor peasant family living in western Asia Minor. Aged nine, he was sent for three years by an uncle, who was a monk, to a small town near by for his education at the hands of a notary. A basic education was one thing, higher education was another. It was to be found in Constantinople and perhaps a few of

76

the bigger cities, such as Thessalonica. It was expensive. Normally, it was only the children of the well-to-do who continued their education beyond the age of twelve or thereabouts. It was a great advantage to be born in Constantinople, simply because the opportunities for further education were so much greater. Its citizens were fully aware of this. Somebody, like Michael Psellos, who came from a guild background was able to go on with his education, which was to open up to him the path to the highest honours. It was still a hard decision for his family to make. There was a family council. His father and his uncles wanted him to enter a trade or profession, but his mother, fired by a vision of St John Chrysostom, was able to persuade them to allow him to continue his schooling. One suspects that many families from the Constantinopolitan middle class made sure that boys who showed aptitude were given the chance to finish their education and that as a result they provided the backbone of the Byzantine administration. Provincials came to Constantinople for their education; usually they were from families that were well connected, but occasionally they might be, like Michael Attaleiates, the historian, from a relatively humble background. In an autobiographical note he tells us that his beginnings were both humble and provincial. He gives effusive thanks to God for his education that enabled him to follow a successful administrative career. He was aware of how fortunate he had been.

The educational system and curriculum at Byzantium were very little changed from Hellenistic times and the basic aims remained the same. Its essence was rhetorical: to teach pupils to write and speak good Greek. The texts were the classics, to which were now added a few Christian writers. This stage of education would be completed when the pupil was sixteen or seventeen. It was possible to proceed beyond this point to a higher education, though comparatively few did. The content of this final stage varied, but to judge by the professorial chairs established by the Emperor Constantine VII Porphyrogenitus (945–59) it generally included rhetoric, philosophy, geometry, and astronomy. These professorial chairs were established with the express purpose of providing well-qualified recruits for the civil service, but it is not clear that these subjects had any sternly practical value, beyond that of providing intellectual discipline. They were almost certainly chosen because they had been taught in the great universities of late antiquity, such as Athens and Alexandria. They constituted solid bodies of knowledge to be passed on and textbooks were available. It remained a secular education; theology had no place in the curriculum and such philosophy as was taught was technical rather than speculative. There was little room within the educational system for speculation, philosophical or theological, which remained under normal circumstances a private affair.

The core of the educational system at Byzantium was the private school and schoolmaster. Occasionally an emperor or a great minister would interest himself in education. The Emperor Constantine Porphyrogenitus is just one example. His patronage did not lead to the creation of a university in the western medieval sense of a corporate body devoted to the furtherance of higher education. Nothing like this existed in Byzantium. All this emperor did was to support the work of some of the most prestigious scholars of his time by providing them with rooms and special funds. They became teachers by special appointment to the emperor. It was a personal initiative and the support lapsed with his death. More lasting was his reorganization of the private schools. He either brought them within the guild system of the capital or improved upon their existing arrangements by appointing a president of the guild of schoolmasters. This measure survived him into the eleventh century, and Michael Psellos's early schooldays.

Psellos claimed that before he burst on the scene the level of education and scholarship was low. It was perhaps more a question that with a warrior, like Basil II, on the throne they were not so highly regarded. The cultivation of the mind may not have offered much in the way of material reward, though there were educated men about Basil II, men like Nicephorus Ouranos, but the times dictated that he wrote military handbooks rather than philosophical treatises. The *synkellos* Stephen, the ex-metropolitan of Nicomedia, enjoyed a high reputation as a scholar, but much of his intellectual energy went into Basil II's pet project for an official canon of saints' lives. There did seem to be a dearth of masters capable of teaching at the highest level. Michael Psellos went in the end to John Mavropous, who was strictly an amateur of letters and instructed Psellos and his companions for the love of it. There is a strong impression that in the eleventh century there were more schools capable of teaching to a high standard than had existed in the tenth century, a sign perhaps of how much more important a good education became in the eleventh century. The schools which are mentioned are invariably attached to churches. As we have already seen, under Constantine Monomachos these schools were placed under the authority of the consul of the philosophers. His main responsibility seems to have been not anything to do with the teaching or curriculum but distributing sums of money among the different schoolmasters.

There were innovations in teaching methods. To the traditional exercises was added *schedographia*. This was a dictation. It might be composed by the teacher or it might be taken from some well-known piece of literature. The pupils would be expected to copy it down accurately, then it would be subjected to a grammatical, stylistic, and historical analysis. Why this kind of exercise was introduced in the eleventh century has been the object of a certain amount of speculation. The most popular view is that it was done to combat the growing gulf between the spoken and the learned language, but given that there had long been this gulf this does not seem a very convincing explanation. A better solution is perhaps that it was a more effective way of teaching growing numbers of pupils.

Michael Psellos claimed to have introduced the *schedographia*, but then he claimed to have introduced practically everything. Some of his pupils felt that he was a bit behind the times. They demanded to be taught the 'new rhetoric', by which the rhetoric of Hermogenes (second century AD) was apparently meant. He tried to convince them that Hermogenes was derivative and that the strength of his teaching was that it aimed at giving a rounded education. He also had to face criticism over the way he taught law from another student who thought that it was not done in sufficient depth. It would seem that there was a demand for greater specialization, whether in rhetoric or in law, and that Psellos's championing of a broad education in which most subjects were included – maths, philosophy, and law – was finding less favour.

Was it also a time of intellectual ferment? If you were to believe Michael Psellos, then it was. He claimed that single-handed he had revived the study of philosophy and to have rediscovered the teachings of Plato. He makes great play with his intimacy with the ancient philosophers. He writes to the Caesar John Doukas reminding him that Alexander had Aristotle, Dionysios of Syracuse had Plato, and he could have Psellos as his philosopher, though modestly suggesting that he was not quite the equal of the other two. His various writings are littered with references to Plato and Pythagoras. It was how Psellos saw himself – the philosopher who guided emperors. Modern historians have seen this as a pose and have been at pains to expose his claims to be a philosopher. By the most rigorous standards he was not a philosopher; his philosophical treatises were mere compilations, often from older compilations. He did not know Plato's works very well and preferred to approach them through the Neoplatonists, who had packaged Plato very conveniently. Psellos probably had a better grasp of the Neoplatonic writings than anybody since late antiquity. He used them not so much for purposes of speculation, but rather to embellish his rhetoric. They provided yet another quarry for fine phrases and apparently daring arguments. Rhetoric not philosophy was Psellos's forte. He was much in demand as a speech-maker, whether at court or at funerals. His letters were eagerly awaited and one of his patrons, the Caesar John Doukas, even made an edition of the letters he received from Psellos. One can understand why his rhetorical and literary talents were so highly appreciated. He was able to bring alive the arts of speech-making and letter-writing; he had mastered the conventions of antiquity and was able to inject into his speeches and his letters his own idiosyncrasies, experience, and views. Psellos was in such demand because he seemed to be original.

His originality hardly stemmed from his study of Plato, though he may have believed this to be the case. It lay in the study of human nature and the rules of conduct, rather than in metaphysical speculation. His ideas on character and conduct seemed to fill a gap in Christian teaching. The fathers of the church paid relatively little attention to questions of conduct. There was always the ascetic ideal, but this was hardly a practical guide to ordinary life. Psellos was scathing about the ascetic life. It was for supermen, not for the ordinary human being. The adept of asceticism seemed to scorn common humanity. Psellos insisted that he was a human being and as fallible as the next man: 'I confess to being human, a strange and fickle creature, a rational soul tainted by the body, a novel mixture of incongruous elements.'[2] Psellos was fascinated by human frailty and human variety. His fellow human beings were interesting for themselves, not merely because they had the capacity to search after the good. He argued that human life should be valued for its own sake and stressed the importance both of individuality and human relationships. There is undeniably a hedonistic, an epicurean strain to his views on human behaviour. Pleasure was to be sought, not shunned. His hedonism was simple and innocuous. The pleasures of family life meant much to him. He took great joy watching the progress of his only child, his daughter Styliane, and his grief at her death when only eight was deep, sincere, and bitter. The funeral speech he made on the death of his mother is filled with memories of a happy childhood and a strong affection for his mother and sisters. He made no secret of his disapproval of his mother's increasingly ascetic way of life after his father's death.

For Psellos the object of human life was not to lose yourself in the sterile ways of asceticism, but to fulfil yourself in a happy domestic life and, above all, in friendship. The idea of friendship was central to his view of human nature. Man was a social animal, whose nature was completed in friendship. In his letters Michael Psellos gave considerable attention to the nature of friendship. It was an affinity of souls, but all souls being of the same nature it might be supposed that friendship would be universal, which was clearly not the case. The soul was conditioned by the body and by upbringing. Education was therefore an important ingredient in friendship, because the souls of those with a similar education were more likely to be in harmony one with the other. He insists on how closely linked body and soul were, echoing the thoughts of one of his heroes, St Gregory of Nazianzus. For two souls united in friendship to be parted was physically painful, just like a body being cut in two. Friendship demanded physical contact. 'I carry your image in my soul and the folds of my soul absorb it intellectually. You are always with me in my memory, but I want to see you with my eyes and to hear your sweet voice in my ears.'[3] So Psellos wrote to one of his friends. Separation was, of course, inevitable; but the letter was some kind of substitute for physical presence. It kept memory alive rather better than a picture in Psellos's opinion: 'the letter reflected you, just as an icon reproduces through colours the living form of the prototype, but it was more than this: it was not composed of colours, but of thoughts, which are not synthetic, but provide the clearest idea of your intellect'.[4]

The letter was the medium of friendship. Of all genres of Byzantine rhetorical literature letters were perhaps the most popular and collections of letters survive in great numbers. They contain sentiments rather than concrete information, but they served a clear social purpose. They provided the means through which the educated élite at Byzantium could express their feelings of mutual interest and solidarity. They were the literary expression of the informal ties which held this élite together. Psellos exploited this network of self-interest in the most blatant way to further his own interests and those of his dependents and clients, but he also provided it with a rationale and a moral justification through his ideas on friendship. The possession of and struggle for power was transmuted by the spiritual beauty of friendship.

Friendship gave the educated élite the illusion of moral autonomy. It was a relationship between equals. It escaped subordination either to God or the emperor. It fitted with Psellos's conviction that man mattered for his own sake and not only because he was part of a divine or imperial scheme. 'I am an earthly being', Psellos proclaimed, 'made of flesh and blood, so that my illnesses seem to me to be illnesses, blows blows, joy joy, however much I may reject the well known saying that man is the measure of all things.'[5] It may be that he was protesting too much for he let drop the remark: 'It is not necessary for me to be measured by the hands of others: I am for myself both the measure and the norm.'[6] How better could he have expressed a belief in the autonomy of the individual! Man was to be studied for his own sake. He was not some two-dimensional creature at the mercy of Divine Providence, but a thoroughly complicated being, whose mood was constantly changing. 'Our lives take on many different shapes and our moods vary, sometimes being more sullen or more gay, as we struggle to outwit chance, or so Euripides says.'[7] That was the great thing for Psellos, 'to outwit chance': the ability to adapt to circumstances. But how this struggle went depended on a man's character. Man was a contradictory creature. There was always an inner struggle between the rational and irrational sides to his character. Reason ought to prevail, 'but residing in a body, which possesses its own rich variety, it is changed and transformed not only under the influence of a man's passions, but also under the pressure of external events'.[8]

History for Psellos was about the way people reacted to events. His *Chronographia* consists of a series of character studies, in which he attempts to follow the psychological development of a succession of emperors as they wrestled with the burdens and temptations of office. Some triumphed, but most were found wanting. Basil II was in his youth a dissipated seeker after pleasure, but, faced with a series of challenges that threatened to topple him from power, he became the iron-hearted puritan who held the Empire and himself in thrall. His brother Constantine VIII did not experience such a trial and remained an ineffectual ruler. Psellos's history is focused on human character and behaviour. How different this is from traditional Byzantine historiography, which is dominated by the action of Divine Providence! Psellos only brings in Divine Providence to explain the inexplicable, like George Maniakes's death in the hour of victory. Human affairs were almost autonomous, but not quite.

This is paralleled by his view of natural phenomena. He was intrigued by a whispering gallery that existed at Nicomedia. It was viewed by some as a marvel, for which there was no rational explanation. The more sceptical preferred to think that tubes had been built into the thicknesses of the wall. Psellos rejected both views and demonstrated that it was only a matter of the building's proportions. His conclusions were, he believed, in accord with scientific principles, as was his explanation for earthquakes. Their immediate cause was to be found in the emission of air from the bowels of the earth. He conceded that their ultimate cause might well have been the will of God, but this was beyond man's proper understanding. He preferred to treat the natural world as a distinct system that was amenable to scientific investigation. It was much the same with man. Ultimately, he was in God's power, but this did not stop him being a proper subject of study and interest in himself. This was the essence of Michael Psellos's humanism. He found it difficult to divorce himself from his natural surroundings, even in the face of death. Once when seriously ill he had to confess that 'he was not able to meditate on death. He could not become like unto God, for we are all part of the parts of nature and have not been set free from the harmony of nature.'⁹

From a modern standpoint Psellos's view of man, his delight in the variety of human experience, his pleasure in the oddities of human behaviour, his appreciation of the beauties of nature, all seem very attractive, but how influential was he? There is little doubt that as a young man he caught the mood of the times and helped to mould it. He has much in common with Christopher of Mitylene, whose poems reflect the outlook of that generation of clever young men to which Michael Psellos belonged. They were sincerely, if conventionally, Christian. Christopher of Mitylene was a follower of the monk Nicetas Synadenos. His words, he claimed, were food and drink to him. He composed a number of verses devoted to images. Psellos, too, has left a remarkably powerful description of the impression made upon him by an image of the Mother of God, which belonged to the monastery of Katharoi. It was as though she was completely transformed so that her beauty became God-like. The meaning of the icon could not be caught by mere visual perception; the onlooker had to absorb the message of the Mother of God's intervention for mankind. Less conventional areas of religion called forth Psellos's talent for mockery. He was much taken by the holy man Elias, who played the Fool for Christ's sake. The man had an encyclopaedic knowledge of Constantinople's low life. He was just as much at home in a brothel as he was in a monastery, by day giving himself to God and by night sharing himself with Satan. He was quite original, worshipping God and Mammon equally. Christopher of Mitylene's sense of humour was aroused by a relic collection put together by a monk called Andrew. It seemed to point to an excess of faith. There were ten hands of St Procopius, eight feet of St Nestor, and on and on the list goes. It all went to show that 'faith without the slightest discernment overturns nature and order'.[10]

This was a judgement which reflected an eminently sane attitude to life. Family life was appreciated. Christopher of Mitylene was close to his family. He composed a poem on the Zodiac for a female cousin. He grieved deeply at the death of his mother and wrote a poem to console his father for her loss. He has also left a series of poems on the death of his sister. Death is always close at hand. The pursuit of worldly success and wealth as an end in itself is pure vanity. Life is inconstant. He uses a game of backgammon as a metaphor for the ups and downs of life. Like a game of chance it ought to be enjoyed. Constantinople was full of diversions; there were friends and good company. There was much that was amusing. Sailing on the sea of Marmora he saw some fishermen casting their nets. He bought three draughts of fishes for 1 *nomisma*, hoping to get more than his money's worth. The first draught brought up stones, the second sand, and the third only water. Directed against others his humour was often more bitter. A man surnamed Choirinos, which can be roughly translated 'Porky', asked for copies of his works. He was told that 'a pig does not eat honey'.[11] Christopher assured an imperial official called Soloman that he was bound to inherit the kingdom of heaven, because despite his name he had less understanding than a little child.

Christopher of Mitylene and Michael Psellos belonged to a highly sophisticated society, conventional in its religion and in its devotion to family life, yet detached, sceptical, and irreverent. Its members felt no compunctions about exploring the legacy of classical antiquity. There was an appreciation of classical art for its own sake. Christopher of Mitylene felt that a bronze horse in the Hippodrome was almost alive, raising its front foot as though about to break into a gallop. There is none of that superstitious attitude towards antique statuary that had become normal in Byzantium. It still existed, of course, for when Michael Psellos was asked by the Emperor Constantine X Doukas for his opinion about an antique relief, he admitted that some might like to explain its meaning in a superstitious way. He preferred not to. Instead, he handled it in the most scholarly fashion. He starts by giving an exact description. On the right-hand side there was a figure seated on a throne and on the left-hand side a man with a sword in one hand and in the other something that it was difficult to make out, but the inscription underneath made it clear that it was the magical herb 'moly'. He therefore concluded that the man must be Odysseus and the figure on the throne Circe.

Psellos liked to see himself as an arbiter of taste. He wrote on literary style. He, of course, praised Plato. The other authors he singled out show the breadth of his tastes. Rather surprisingly the style of the tenth-century hagiographer Symeon Metaphrastes impressed him. It was simple, yet the author could bring alive a scene or a man's feelings. He also admired the sermons of Gregory of Nazianzus. Though steeped in Christian literature, he was able to appreciate Hellenistic romances, and their continuing popularity in Byzantium must have owed something to Psellos's advocacy. Even his interest in the popular language and popular idioms pointed the way forward to the creation of a literature in the popular language.

Psellos was undoubtedly influential, but his ascendancy was on the wane from the reign of Constantine X Doukas (1059–67). He seemed to be out of touch with the critical position in which the Empire found itself. He was criticized in his role as tutor to the future Emperor Michael VII Doukas (1071–78). His opponents maintained that far from turning him into a philosopher king, Psellos had rendered him unfit to rule. The failure of the Doukas regime did much to discredit Psellos's ideas. This is reflected in the work of Michael Attaleiates, who was of much the same age as Michael Psellos. He too was a scholarship boy who made a successful career in the administration. His rise to prominence was not as meteoric as that of Psellos. It was not until the late 1060s that he held any position of importance. He was a lawyer by training and inclination. His surviving legal treatise, the *Ponema nomikon*, was a reply to Psellos's *Synopsis legum*, a careless compilation, which must have irritated any professional lawyer, not merely for its lack of order, but also because of its presumption. Psellos suggested that lawyers lacked method and that he was recasting the laws along lines suggested by philosophy. Attaleiates's work is quite the opposite, just a clear and unpretentious exposition of the Basilics, since the late ninth century the main corpus of Byzantine law. Here is an example of the way Psellos's claim to pontificate on all matters because he was the 'Philosopher' was called into question and successfully countered.

Psellos's scientific interests seem to have left some mark on Attaleiates, to judge by the way he provides a more or less scientific explanation of the action of lightning. He rejected the superstitious view that it was a dragon-like creature as worthy only of the simple. But when Attaleiates came to consider the reasons for the Empire's failures his outlook was anything but scientific. This is in complete contrast to Michael Psellos, whose explanations were eminently rational. They are at several levels. We have seen how he analysed the psychological effects of office on different emperors. The burdens of empire usually found them wanting and exaggerated their faults. The emperors also failed to keep control over the system of government: excessive expenditure, the lavish distribution of honours all went to produce a bloated government machine, which could not be controlled and which was no longer effective. Psellos may not have provided a complete explanation but his approach is one that accords with that of most modern historians. Attaleiates is quite different. He is technically a very good historian. His treatment of individual episodes is clear and sane, but his general explanations are hackneyed: the Byzantines were being punished by God for their sins. His completely conventional approach is echoed in his will, where he explains that the monastery and almshouse that he is founding are an expression of gratitude for his success in life, which he attributes entirely to God. Success is conceived as a reward for a decent life; failure as the price of sin. There is no room for Psellos's insistence upon the importance of human efforts and human fallibility in the unfolding of events.

Psellos's stress on the primacy of human experience made him suspect. He seemed to be coming close to denying the importance of God in human affairs and, instead, to be exalting the power of human reason over revelation. On at least two occasions he was forced to make professions of faith in order to demonstrate the orthodoxy of his beliefs. He fell foul of his boyhood friend John Xiphilinos, who in 1064 became patriarch of Constantinople. He resented the imputations made against him. 'Plato is mine! I do not know how to bear the weight of this charge. Have I not in the past preferred the holy cross and now the monastic yoke?'[12] He had only accepted Plato's teachings in so far as they contributed to Christian dogmas. He had collated them with the scriptures in exactly the same way as the Cappadocian fathers had done. Indeed, he was claiming to belong to the same tradition as the fathers of the church, who had not disdained the use of reason nor rejected philosophy as an aid to the elucidation of the Christian faith. Xiphilinos, on the other hand, was an adept of mysticism, which Psellos opposed. He felt that it was arid, not to mention that it undermined that rational approach to christianity which he had espoused.

There had always been a strong mystical current in orthodoxy. Psellos did not dismiss it out of hand. He praised the mystical wisdom of some monks from Chios and asked that they pray for him. His concern was that mysticism was coming to dominate the church, leaving little room for his enlightened approach to christianity. Like his hero, St Gregory of Nazianzus, he believed that there was no single avenue to the mysteries of the church. The triumph of mysticism undermined the intellectual traditions of christianity. It made Psellos's opinions suspect, but in his view its deliberate cultivation of ignorance was harmful. Ignorance was a feeding ground for pride and self-conceit, which turned what seemed to be virtues into evil.

The sway of mysticism at this time is associated with St Symeon the 'New Theologian' (949–1022). In his lifetime he enjoyed a certain notoriety, but his ideas were relatively uninfluential. They only began to catch on in the 1040s and would therefore have seemed to have been an immediate challenge to Psellos's humanist views. In many ways Psellos was continuing the fight against Symeon, which had occurred in the lifetime of the saint, when his ideas were called in question by the patriarch and his administration.

Symeon came from a distinguished Paphlagonian family and was expected to have a successful career at the imperial court. He came, however, under the spell of a monk of the monastery of Stoudios, called Symeon Stylites. The young man's family thought this attachment was unhealthy and took him back to the family estates. His devotion to mysticism was there redoubled when he found a copy of that classic of mysticism, the *Ladder* of St John Climax. He hurried to return to Constantinople, became a novice, and was allowed to share a cell with his spiritual father, Symeon Stylites. This arrangement was soon frowned upon and they were both driven from the monastery. They found refuge in the suburban monastery of St Mamas, which was then run down and thoroughly corrupt. Symeon impressed through his way of life and his abilities as a preacher. When the abbot died, he succeeded. He did much to restore the monastery and to reform the life of the monks. He made the monastery the centre of the cult of his spiritual father Symeon Stylites who was now dead. There were great festivities which went on for several days and attracted a throng of people from all over the city. This was the cause of some concern to the patriarch of the day. He saw that there was a danger that a private cult would turn into a public one. If this were to happen, it would remove the process of canonization from the hands of the official church. The cult may have seemed all the more alarming for the reputation that Symeon was acquiring as a mystic and holy man. His teaching on the nature and practice of mysticism conformed to the orthodox tradition of mysticism, though he did not distinguish so clearly between the different stages that the mystic went through in his search for union with God.

It was not his mystical teaching as such that attracted the attention of the church authorities, but the claims he was making on behalf of the mystic. He insisted that only mysticism was the true end of a monastic vocation; that the wisdom attained through mystical illumination was superior to other forms of knowledge and that the spiritually enlightened formed an élite within the church. St Symeon prided himself on his lack of any higher education, but claimed that God being wisdom made him wiser than any sophist or orator, just as he had his disciples. The gifts of the spirit were not sent 'to those of little faith or too great ambition, nor to orators or philosophers, nor to those versed in Hellenic writings'[13] and on and on goes the list. Who had they been sent to and how could anybody tell? As far as St Symeon was concerned, the criteria were completely subjective. You knew of the presence within you of the Holy Spirit by a feeling of joy or by the shedding of tears, or by experiencing the divine light, which completely absorbed you and made you incorporeal. This produced a state of trance, where the mystic could hear God's voice from within the light. He possessed 'the understanding of the apostles, being moved by the Holy Spirit'.[14] It was thus still possible to live an apostolic life, to receive apostolic gifts, or, to put it another way, each generation of Christians possessed men who through the gifts of the Holy Spirit stood in the same relationship to Christ as the apostles had done. It was St Symeon's intuition that Christ's ministry was not set in the distant past, but was always present. It was the mystic who ensured that this was so. Consequently, the focus of the church should not be on the official hierarchy of patriarch, bishop, and priest, but upon the holy man.

There was only a single nearly objective criterion that Symeon produced for identifying those blessed with the gifts of the Holy Spirit: they should be bestowed by a spiritual father, himself renowned for his mystic powers. So Symeon Stylites filled his disciple Symeon with the power of the Holy Spirit, unworthy slave that he was, freely and without any effort. The disciple had a duty to submit himself entirely to his spiritual father: 'Not to submit to a spiritual father, in imitation of Him who obeyed His father as far as death on the cross, is tantamount to not being born spiritually', that was St Symeon's opinion.[15] One of the concrete signs of this submission was the daily confession that the disciple made to his spiritual father. St Symeon placed the greatest possible emphasis upon the importance of confession. The gift of the Holy Spirit was far more powerful than any ordination by the hand of man: 'He who has not seen its light remains in the shadow of death, be he emperor, patriarch, bishop, priest, in authority or under authority.'[16] St Symeon thus exalts the power attained through the Holy Spirit. It was people so blessed that had the power to bind and loose, to hear confessions, to celebrate the liturgy and to preach, not those who had been ordained by men. St Symeon insisted that to deny the existence of the gifts bestowed by the Holy Spirit was to deny Christ and to oppose the claims of mystics was a sin against the Holy Spirit. Such claims came close to subverting the traditional order of the church.

The challenge presented by Symeon was taken up at the beginning of the eleventh century by the patriarchal *synkellos* Stephen, a man with the highest reputation for piety and scholarship. He attacked the cult of Symeon Stylites that St Symeon was promoting. Symeon found the justification for his teachings in the life and cult of his spiritual father. If the cult was condoned then it would seem that Symeon's dangerous ideas had received official approval. If the cult could be suppressed, then his ideas would no longer have any acceptable justification. The case turned on the accusation that Symeon Stylites was a sinner, yet Symeon was celebrating him as a saint. Stephen won the day. An image of the disputed saint was brought before the patriarchal court and the title 'saint' was removed. Later the patriarch sent men to destroy all the images of this 'saint'. Symeon himself was condemned to a mild exile on the Asiatic shores of the sea of Marmora. Thanks to powerful friends, there was some partial rehabilitation, but Symeon preferred to remain in his place of exile, where he died in 1022, his influence reduced to almost nothing. The monastery of St Mamas passed under lay ownership.

He left behind a vast corpus of hymns and mystical writings. Shortly before his death he appointed a young monk called Nicetas Stethatos as his literary executor. Stethatos did very little to fulfil his responsibilities until prompted by a vision he had some thirteen years after the saint's death. He began in the mid-1030s to circulate his works. They produced a considerable volume of opposition. He was forced to pen a tract against the saint's detractors. It may be that he would have continued to fight a losing battle in his efforts to promote St Symeon's work and memory, had he not received the support of the Patriarch Michael Keroularios (1043–58). With his backing he was able to have Symeon's relics transferred to the capital in 1052 and then a few years later he composed a life of the saint. In this way he was able to provide a solid basis to the cult of St Symeon. Why the patriarch should have decided to support Nicetas Stethatos is something of a mystery. It seems to be unnecessary to search for Machiavellian motives. The patriarch had been a monk before ascending the patriarchal throne and is likely to have known about Nicetas Stethatos and his championing of the ideas of St Symeon. The saint's anti-intellectualism must have appealed to a patriarch who was notorious for his lack of learning.

Michael Psellos was scornful of the way the patriarch had become, as he put it, 'a devotee and initiate of the mysteries'.[17] He dismissed the patriarch's claims to learning as founded on no rational principles that he, Psellos, knew of. Perhaps the patriarch had been consulting the Holy Tablets, a jibe at his mystical pretensions. In this exchange the two main intellectual currents of eleventh-century Byzantium collided. Both had long antecedents reaching back to late antiquity, but it was only in the eleventh century that they took on a clear shape and came to constitute the predominant intellectual interests of the time. To a man such as Psellos who had a vested interest in humanism, mysticism seemed a threat. The pretensions of the holy man to wisdom through the path of ignorance were a challenge to the claims of the philosopher to act as the arbiter of society by virtue of his learning and power of reason.

There would have been relatively few among the educated who would have drawn quite so marked a distinction between mysticism and humanism. They existed side by side, each having its merits. This seems to be the conclusion to be drawn from the contents of the library of Eustathios Boilas, the Cappadocian landowner, who died *c.* 1059. It was quite a large collection numbering some eighty volumes. The majority were liturgical, patristic, or scriptural. He did, however, possess two manuscripts of St John Climax's *Ladder* – one which he had specially copied still survives. This was a classic of Byzantine mysticism and suggests that though living in the Anatolian borderlands he was not cut off from the mysticism then in vogue in the capital. Equally ownership of copies of the *Romance of Alexander* and Achilles Tatius's *Leucippe* suggests acquaintance with the literary tastes of the humanists of Constantinople. For the great majority of the educated mysticism and humanist interests were not mutually exclusive.

In themselves they were not necessarily dangerous. They helped to give Byzantine culture a greater breadth, but they also touched upon that most dangerous of questions: the purpose and value of human life. The answers they provided seemed to threaten the established order. Both Symeon and Psellos accepted the necessity of the existing imperial regime, but undermined its validity with their subversive ideas on the primacy of individual experience. Symeon thanked God 'for rescuing him by His ineffable decrees from emperors and *archontes*, who wished to use him, like some worthless implement, for the execution of their wishes'.[18] Imperial service was a negation of the one true end of human effort: the individual search for union with God. Psellos was concerned to relate man, not to God, but to his natural surroundings. The individual was capable of mastering his circumstances because of his rational faculty and his natural propensity for friendship. He was a social animal. Psellos tried to give back to man some of his autonomy both before God and before His representative upon earth, the emperor.

Both approaches could all too easily slip over into heresy. Many of the intuitions of St Symeon the 'New Theologian' intuitions smacked of heresy. His insistence on the gifts of the Holy Spirit might turn into the heresy of Messalianism, with its emphasis upon the primacy of possession. His ideas about the rejection of the corporeal aspects of the body and his emphasis on attaining a state of perfection came close to the teachings of the Bogomils, a dualist sect. Heresy had largely been a provincial phenomenon in the Byzantine Empire. This was the case in the eleventh century. In Paphlagonia there was a neo-Messalian community which developed around one Eleutherios, which was suppressed by the Patriarch Alexius Stoudites (1025–43). At the same time there was a Bogomil community in the theme of Opsikion, which went by the name of Phoundagitai. Heresy was part of provincial non-conformity. The change that would come about from the middle of the eleventh century was that it started to infiltrate the capital. In his indictment of the Patriarch Michael Keroularios drawn up in the autumn of 1058 Michael Psellos charged that the patriarch's patronage of the Chiot monks, Nicetas and John, was tantamount to heresy. They had come to the capital bringing with them a woman, Dosithea, who spoke in tongues. Keroularios, ever susceptible to the irrational, mystical side of christianity, fell under their spell. The charge may have been trumped up for political purposes, but this episode provides evidence of how easy it was for mystical practices to come under the suspicion of heresy. It was difficult to decide where mysticism ended and heresy began or whether a holy man was orthodox or heretical.

In similar fashion there was a danger that a humanist approach to christianity might also lead on to heresy. On at least two occasions

Michael Psellos was called upon to prove his orthodoxy, which he duly did. He was always much more interested in exposition than speculation. His pupil, John Italos was of a much more speculative disposition. He tried to apply the methods of philosophy to theology. He seemed to be proposing that human reason provided an instrument for the understanding of the mysteries of the faith on a par with revelation and the works of the fathers of the church. As we shall see, he came under grave suspicion of heresy.

By the time Alexius I Comnenus came to the throne in 1081 there seemed to be a serious problem of heresy in Constantinople. The alarm it caused reflected the feeling that traditional order was being undermined. This comes across from Kekavmenos's *Book of Advice*. What was needed was a reassertion of traditional order around the emperor. He was scathing about the sort of people that surrounded the emperor, worthless civil servants, mimes, and so-called philosophers. He warned too against having anything to do with holy fools.

The intellectual developments of the eleventh century had a disconcerting and disorientating effect on Byzantine society. They raised to prominence the holy man and the philosopher, the mystic and the humanist, who, in their different ways, underlined the importance of individual experience. Concern with the individual was a challenge to the traditional order with its emphasis upon imperial power and priestly authority. There was a change of perspective. The validity of the imperial and priestly offices may not have been questioned, but emperors and priests were left increasingly open to criticism for individual failings. If new concerns, new perspectives, and the resulting criticism seemed from an official point of view much like heresy, they also provided a cover and, to an extent, a justification for a new wave of heresy which began to infiltrate the capital. This only highlighted the disorientation which existed. The Empire had lost its sense of direction. To restore it was one of the essential tasks facing any emperor, but in the chaos which followed the defeat of Mantzikert this seemed nearly impossible.

NOTES

1. Kekavmenos, *Strategikon* (ed. Wassiliewsky–Jernstedt), p. 60; (ed. Litavrin), p. 240.
2. Sathas V, p. 506
3. Michael Psellos (ed. Kurtz–Drexl), II, no. 138
4. *Ibid.,* no. 159
5. Sathas V, p. 232
6. *Ibid.,* p. 220

7. Michael Psellos (ed. Kurtz–Drexl), II, no. 212
8. *Ibid.,* no. 136
9. *Ibid.,* no. 228
10. E Kurtz (ed.), *Die Gedichte des Christophoros Mitylenaios* (Leipzig, 1903), no. 114
11. *Ibid.,* no. 84
12. Sathas V, p. 444
13. I Hausherr, *Un grand mystique byzantin. Vie de Symeon le Nouveau Théologien (949–1022) par Nicétas Stéthatos* (Rome, 1928), p. lxiv
14. *Ibid.,* p. 97
15. Migne, PG, 120, c. 925
16. Hausherr, *op. cit.*, p. lxxvi
17. Sathas V, p. 505
18. Symeon le Nouveau Théologien, *Catachèses* (ed. and transl. by B Krivochéine and J Paramelle) (Paris, 1965), III, xxxvi, 32–5

Chapter 6

THE RISE OF THE HOUSE OF COMNENUS

During his brief reign Romanos Diogenes tried to build up a nucleus of loyal adherents. They included administrative and legal experts, such as the future historian, Michael Attaleiates, as well as members of some of the great families. The Comneni did very well under Romanos. Manuel Comnenus, the eldest son of John Comnenus, the brother of the Emperor Isaac, was raised to the rank of *protostrator* and in 1070 was placed in command of the Byzantine armies operating in Anatolia. The defeat of Romanos Diogenes at Mantzikert in the following year marked a real set-back to the fortunes of the Comneni. Power at Constantinople passed into the hands of the Caesar John Doukas and his followers. They imagined that Romanos had been killed on the field of battle, then came the news that he had survived the battle and was now intent on regaining his throne. His likely supporters in the capital were immediately objects of suspicion. His Empress Eudocia Makrembolitissa, was despatched to a convent, as soon as it was discovered that she was in correspondence with her husband. The acting head of the house of Comnenus, Anna Dalassena, the widow of John Comnenus, was hauled up on a charge of treasonable correspondence with Romanos. The trial was inconclusive. She was released, but with the possibility that the case against her might be reopened. Less than ten years later her sons Alexius and Isaac were in a position to seize the throne of Constantinople. In the intervening period the state of the Empire deteriorated out of all recognition, as different factions and families squabbled for control of the capital. Why the Comneni should have succeeded where others, equally well qualified, should have failed is the underlying theme of this chapter. The resourcefulness and ambition of Anna Dalassena may have been the decisive factor. Her husband's failure to press his claims to the imperial throne still rankled. It could be expunged through her sons.

THE CIVIL WARS

The Comneni played little active part in the civil wars which followed Mantzikert. Manuel Comnenus died just before the battle. Anna Dalassena sent his younger brother Alexius in his place, but Romanos made him go home again because he was still too young to campaign. Anna Dalassena and her sons could only wait on events. Romanos was released by the Seljuq sultan and soon gathered a force together from those units which had escaped from the defeat at Mantzikert. He made his base at Amaseia in north-eastern Anatolia. In the face of this challenge the Doukas faction showed extreme resolution. They despatched an army under the command of the Caesar John's younger son Constantine. It defeated Romanos's army, but he was rescued by the Armenian Katachour, the governor of Antioch. Romanos now made his base in Cilicia, which was already heavily settled with Armenians. Another army set out from Constantinople, this time under the command of the Caesar John's elder son Andronicus. Its most important contingent was a regiment of Franks. The fate of the Empire had passed in less than a year since the defeat at Mantzikert into the hands of Armenians and Franks. There was a battle near Tarsus and the Franks were victorious. Romanos escaped, but was soon handed over. He abdicated and became a monk, on condition that he would suffer no harm, but at Kotyaion on the way back to Constantinople he was blinded on orders from the government at Constantinople. It was done so savagely that he died little more than a month later on 4 August 1072.

The Caesar John Doukas seemed to be firmly in control, but this was an illusion. Events were going to show how little control the government at Constantinople possessed. It was apparent that it was more or less at the mercy of the troops and commanders that it employed. These were overwhelmingly foreign mercenaries. The Byzantine regiments which had formed the bulk of the troops got together for the Mantzikert campaign seemed to have vanished into thin air. This can scarcely be explained by huge casualties. It is more an indictment of Romanos's military measures, which were largely cosmetic; his theme armies just melted away. So poor was their organization that they could not even act as a home-guard to defend their districts against marauding Turks. In 1073 the central government sent out the young Isaac Comnenus with a force to counter these Turkish raids. It comprised in the main a body of Franks under the command of Russell Balliol. He knew of the phenomenal success of his fellow Normans in the south of Italy. It would have been obvious to him that the turmoil existing in Anatolia provided him with ideal opportunities to establish himself in command of the region. He deserted the Byzantine commander, who fell into the hands of the Turks. He made his way to Amaseia, which became his base. In very little time he had made himself the master of the old Armeniac theme, which very roughly covered the north-eastern rim of the Anatolian plateau. An army was scraped together and despatched against him under the command of the Caesar John Doukas. In the ensuing battle Russell Balliol was victorious thanks to the treachery of a Frankish contingent, which had been sent along with the Byzantine army. The Caesar John fell into the Norman's hands. The whole of northern Anatolia was now under his control. He advanced on Constantinople to extort recognition of his conquests from the Emperor Michael VII Doukas. The emperor refused his terms. He therefore had his prisoner, the Caesar John, proclaimed emperor. This was a direct challenge to the imperial dignity. The imperial government had no troops of its own to call upon. So it brought in a Turkish chieftain against the Norman upstart. Turkish cunning was more than a match for Norman *élan*. The westerners were defeated. Both Balliol and the Caesar John fell into the hands of the Turks. The emperor immediately ransomed the latter, who took the precaution of becoming a monk and going into retirement. It was not obvious that he had been proclaimed emperor entirely against his will, for he had fallen out with his nephew, the emperor, and had withdrawn from court some months before being sent against Balliol.

As for Balliol, he was ransomed by his wife and returned to Amaseia, where he soon recovered control over the region of the Armeniacs. He defended it stoutly against the Turks. The government at Constantinople continued to regard him as much more of a menace than any Turks. The young Alexius Comnenus was sent against him. It was his first major undertaking and he more than proved his worth. With the help of a Turkish chieftain he had Balliol seized and brought back to Constantinople. That done the imperial government was willing to leave Asia Minor to its fate.

THE FALL OF ANATOLIA

In the ten years which followed the defeat at Mantzikert the Turks established themselves in considerable numbers over large areas of Asia Minor, with the heaviest concentration around the north-western rim of the plateau. It is natural to see this Turkish settlement as a direct consequence of the battle of Mantzikert, even as directly connected with conditions existing in Anatolia before the battle. On closer inspection these assumptions do not seem to be very well founded. It is known, for instance, that the settlement of large numbers of Armenians in eastern Anatolia produced friction with the native inhabitants. In the years before Mantzikert this may have led to the alienation of the Armenians, but it is quite another thing to prove that this facilitated Turkish settlement. If anything, it worked in the opposite direction, since those areas heavily settled by Armenians were the last to succumb to the Turks. It is also argued that Anatolia's agriculture was in a bad way on the eve of the Turkish invasions and that this left the land open to Turkish penetration. It is enough to say that all the signs are that Anatolia was no less prosperous than it had been earlier, and probably more so. John Mavropous has left us a good description of the countryside around Euchaita, his bishopric in northern Anatolia. He begins by describing it as a treeless steppe, quite without charm, thus catching the drear winter face of the Anatolian plateau. He complains that it produced no wine nor olive oil nor any of the delicacies that an invalid or gourmet might expect. Spring was a different matter. The steppe bloomed, providing pasture for herds of sheep and cattle, and producing corn in abundance. The main towns of Anatolia were, as far as one can judge, in reasonably good shape. It was not a lack of prosperity which predisposed Anatolia to a Turkish conquest, but more the nature of the land. The Anatolian plateau has a climate and a flora not very different from the central Asian homelands of the Turks. It was well suited to the nomadic or at least pastoral way of life of the Turks. It is also true that control over Anatolia is always relatively fragile, because it depends upon holding a small number of key points. These are the towns, such as Dorylaion, Ankyra, Ikonion, Amaseia, Sebastea, and Cappadocian Caesarea, which dominate the main routes across the plateau. It is equally true that once control of these places is lost, Anatolia soon breaks up into its separate cantons, very roughly coinciding with the boundaries of the Byzantine themes.

This is exactly what happened in the chaos of Turkish raids and Byzantine civil wars, which followed the battle of Mantzikert. The government at Constantinople concentrated on eliminating local leaders, who might be a threat to the imperial throne, rather than combating Turkish chieftains, who were rather welcomed as potential allies. This apparent blindness to the nature and scale of the threat from the Turks on the part of the imperial government is easy enough to understand. The first priority was to establish the authority of the central government in the provinces. Then it would be easy enough to handle the Turks. At a time when the Byzantine military organization had more or less broken down, the Turks were looked upon as a valuable reservoir of troops. For the task of restoring imperial authority in Anatolia the Byzantine government ironically called in the Turks.

There was always the example of the Balkans to go on. The Petcheneks had been settled in the north-east of the peninsula and had been allowed to retain their tribal organization. The Byzantines nevertheless continued to control the frontier along the Danube. Much the same kind of thing was happening in Anatolia. Turkish tribes were dragged westwards through involvement in the Byzantine civil wars, but the old provincial governors, often Armenians, but not always, continued to hold the Euphrates provinces and recognized, at least nominally, the authority of the imperial government at Constantinople.

Where local Greek leaders were able to establish themselves, then there was always a chance that there would be successful resistance to the Turks. Trebizond is the obvious example. In 1075 the town of Trebizond fell to a Turkish chieftain. Theodore Gabras, the head of the most powerful family of the region, organized resistance, recovered Trebizond, and drove the Turks back beyond the Pontic Alps. The old theme organization was restored, providing Trebizond with an effective system of defence down to the fifteenth century. Trebizond was to prove quite exceptional. Very rarely did the great landowners stay to fight. Most of them had already transferred their main residence to the capital, to be nearer the centre of power. The historian Nicephorus Bryennios draws a moving picture of his father-in-law, Alexius Comnenus's reaction to the sight of the ancestral home at Kastamon, as he made his way back to Constantinople from Amaseia with his prisoner Russell Balliol. It was swarming with Turks. There was no lord to defend the place, because the Comneni had preferred residence in Constantinople to protecting their estates in Anatolia. Some families did stay on. The future Emperor Nicephorus Botaneiates resided on his estates in Phrygia from 1074 until 1077, providing, it must be assumed, the region with some defence. Even he finally decided that there was more to gain by rebellion against the government in Constantinople. The Empire could only be saved from the centre, not by local resistance. When he set out against Constantinople in the summer of 1077 he had a force of some 300 men. These would have been his retainers and relatives. To have any chance of taking Constantinople he had to take Turks into his service. Equally, to oppose his march on the capital the government of Michael VII turned to various Turkish chieftains. In this instance, the arbiter of Byzantium's fate turned out to be Suleiman, the son of Kutlumush, and he happened to be a member of the ruling Seljuq dynasty of Iran, despatched by the Seljuq sultan from Iran to establish some degree of order over the Turkish tribes rampaging through Anatolia.

It was not as though the Seljuqs of Iran planned the Turkish conquest of Anatolia. It occurred quite haphazardly, but once Turks began to settle in Anatolia and Turkish warrior chiefs began to make names for themselves, the Seljuq sultan wanted some degree of control over the conquest. He feared that otherwise it might produce some threat to his authority. Suleiman supported the rebel Nicephorus Botaneiates. He was allowed to leave Turkish garrisons in the numerous towns and cities of western Asia Minor, which opened their gates with such rejoicing to the rebel. Ostensibly, they were in the rebel's service; in reality, they were acting on their own account. The same pattern was repeated three years later when Nicephorus Melissenos rebelled. His base was the island of Cos. From there he made his way along the coastlands of western Asia Minor towards the capital. Once again he relied heavily on Turkish support and once again towns were surrendered to the Turks, so that by 1081 virtually the whole of central and western Asia Minor was controlled by Turkish chieftains. They held the main towns and fortresses, which would hardly have fallen so easily, had the Turks not been drawn into Byzantium's civil wars. Thus did the Byzantines surrender the keys to the control of Anatolia. The imperial government made things still worse by withdrawing what native troops it could from Asia Minor to Constantinople. The Chomatenoi, or soldiers from Choma, a place on the upper reaches of the Maiander in Phrygia, became one of the few Byzantine units in Michael VII Doukas's standing army, based in the capital. In 1081 Alexius I Comnenus was to set the seal on this process, when he withdrew the remaining Byzantine governors and their forces from the centre of Anatolia.

Asia Minor was lost to the Turks by default. Why should this have been, when the same provinces had put up such sustained and stubborn resistance to the Arabs? The Turks were perhaps a more formidable enemy than the Arabs. They were still a people on the move, seeking *Lebensraum,* while the Arabs sought booty, slaves, and occasionally martyrdom. Anatolia provided conditions that were well suited to the Turks' way of life, while the Arabs were discouraged by the harsh winter conditions of the Anatolian plateau. However, the argument that natural conditions disposed Anatolia to a Turkish rather than an Arab conquest only provides at the most a very partial explanation. The Arabs may have roamed at will across Anatolia, but they never secured permanent possession of the main towns, while the theme organization, more or less moribund in the eleventh century, then provided an effective sytem of local defence. In addition, the bulk of the population was able to retreat into the fastnesses in which the Anatolian plateau abounds especially along its rim. The Arabs rarely penetrated the western and northern rim of the plateau. It was here that there lay a series of bases from which it was possible for the Byzantines to strike back. Without the civil wars the Turks would not have been able to secure either the towns which controlled the routes across Anatolia, still less the northern and western fringes of the plateau. These were the areas of Asia Minor, which place-name evidence shows to have been earliest settled by the Turks. This band of early Turkish settlement stretching from the vicinity of Dorylaion to the mountains of Paphlagonia established a wedge between Constantinople and the rest of Anatolia. Behind it the process of symbiosis of Turk and Greek could go on, more or less unhindered. The loss of the towns of the coastal fringes of Anatolia meant that it would be many years before the Byzantines were in a position to undertake the conquest of Anatolia, and the longer this was delayed, the more thorough was the turkification of Anatolia. By 1097 when the first crusade crossed Anatolia, the westerners referred to the land as Turkey, which seemed to them the most obvious description. The Greeks who remained in Asia Minor either sought refuge in remote fastnesses or flocked to the safety of the towns. After an initial period of uncertainty they seem to have been content under Turkish rule. The local people lost the struggle for the countryside. Resistance was hopeless, with their lords gone and no form of defence. The Turkish freebooters plundered the land and stole their womenfolk, to be followed by the Turkish tribesmen, who came with their families and flocks and took possession of the land. This would hardly have been possible if the Turkish warrior chiefs had not been sucked into the civil wars which followed the defeat at Mantzikert.

NIKEPHORITZES

It would be easy to accuse Michael VII's government of criminal neglect of Asia Minor, though it was really a failure of judgement. Other issues and concerns were considered of more pressing importance. It was not as though the Turks were the only foe threatening the Empire. Conditions in the Balkans were also deteriorating. There was trouble from the Serbs and a Bulgarian rising in 1072 around Sardica and Nish, key positions on the great military road across the Balkans. Then the precarious foothold that the Byzantines still maintained along the Danube was threatened by the rebellion of Nestor in 1076. A native of the Balkans, perhaps a Vlach, he had been appointed imperial governor of the Danubian province, in the hope that, being a native, he would be able to bring the local people to heel. Instead he came to terms with the local chief and allied with the Petcheneks. With their combined support he crossed the Balkan mountains and marched on Constantinople. There was no Byzantine army capable of opposing him and the capital seemed to be at his mercy. The demands he made of the imperial government are at first sight surprising. He was not trying to extort recognition as an independent ruler of the Danubian lands. He sought only that the emperor should dismiss his chief minister Nikephoritzes. The emperor prevaricated; suspicions mounted between Nestor and his Petchenek allies, and he was forced to withdraw northwards across the Balkan mountains. The importance of this incident is twofold: Nestor's rebuff by the imperial government meant the end of any hope of holding on along the Danube; the region would now pass out of Byzantine control for some twenty years. This rebellion was more immediately a sign of the intense dissatisfaction produced by the ascendancy of Nikephoritzes.

Nikephoritzes was a eunuch, who came to prominence under Constantine X Doukas. That emperor appointed him duke of Antioch, both a recognition of his outstanding abilities and a means of removing an unsettling personality from court. To his enemies he was a 'great stirrer', but to Kekavmenos he was 'a man for all seasons: extremely able, exactly versed in both military and administrative matters, generous natured, even if he was a eunuch, with a penetrating mind, capable of thinking and speaking under pressure'.[1] Michael Psellos studiously avoids mentioning him in his *Chronographia,* surely because he had been outwitted by the eunuch. Caesar John Doukas brought him into the government, because he wanted an expert to run the administration. Once in charge of the machinery of central government, Nikephoritzes was able to oust the Caesar John, who retired to his estates in the autumn of 1073. Psellos stayed on at court only as tutor to the emperor without political influence. Nikephoritzes became the real ruler of the Empire, for Michael VII displayed neither an inclination nor an aptitude for rule. He was accused by his contemporaries of fickleness, but he stood by Nikephoritzes despite bitter criticism from many quarters. The ascendancy of the eunuch might have had something to do with the emperor's feeble character, but it cannot only have been that. The eunuch offered the illusion of imperial authority and escape from the family tutelage represented by the Caesar John Doukas. He also had plans for the restoration of the Empire, beginning with a reassertion of imperial authority.

The first step was to replenish the imperial treasury. This Nikephoritzes was able to do, even if it meant crushing taxation and the confiscation of church plate. His rule was harsh. There was no pretence even that it was beneficial to people of the capital. By the winter of 1076/77 the conditions in Constantinople were appalling. Refugees had been flocking in, bringing with them famine and a crime wave. There would probably have been some starvation in any case, but conditions were made still worse by measures taken by Nikephoritzes to impose central control over the corn trade. In normal circumstances, the provisioning of the capital was in private hands. Much of the food needed was forwarded through the small ports that dotted the coasts around Constantinople. These were largely in the hands of landowners, lay and ecclesiastical. Nikephoritzes confiscated them and placed them under state control. This upset the rhythm of local trade. Worse was to come with Nikephoritzes's establishment of a state monopoly of the corn trade of Thrace. He set up a special depot outside Raidestos, the main grain port on the Thracian shores of the sea of Marmora. Corn was no longer to be offered on the open market, but had to be sold to government officials at prices determined by the state. There were plenty of precedents for this kind of government intervention, but it meant that landowners were reluctant to sell to the government depot. This produced shortages, which allowed the government to sell at inflated prices. As the historian Michael Attaleiates noted, the rapid increase in the price of a leading commodity such as corn had disastrous repercussions throughout the economy. The expedient of a state corn monopoly was resented locally and was one of the main causes of a revolt which would break out in Thrace in 1077. One of the first things that the rebels did, once they had control of Raidestos, was to tear down the corn depot.

It would be vain to deny that Nikephoritzes's policies worsened the condition of the Byzantine Empire. His attempt to restore central authority only intensified inner divisions. Provincial landowners saw their position threatened without any obvious benefit to the well-being of the state. Only Nikephoritzes, it was supposed, benefited. Proof of this, if it were needed, was his receipt of rights of administration over the imperial complex at the Hebdomon, outside Constantinople. Nikephoritzes failed not because he was corrupt or preferred his own interest to that of the state, as his enemies suggested. It was much more that he followed the accepted civil service wisdom, that regeneration could only come from the centre through the restoration of central control. To this end he carried out some sensible military reforms, creating two new regiments of the Immortals and the Chomatenoi. The truth of the matter was that conventional solutions would no longer work and the civil service which for so long had been the real strength of the Byzantine Empire was no longer capable of its rescue.

Nikephoritzes was astute enough to realize that without the support of some of the great families his regime could not last. His ascendancy saw the Comneni as an increasingly important factor in the politics of the capital. He depended upon their loyalty, which was given because Anna Dalassena was so bitter an enemy of the Caesar John Doukas. As soon as Nikephoritzes secured control of the imperial government, her sons were given important military commands. Her eldest surviving son, Isaac, was sent out as governor of Antioch, seen by the Byzantine government as the key to the situation in Asia Minor. As long as it remained in Byzantine hands, there was every chance that Asia Minor would eventually be recovered from the Turks. The importance of the appointment was underlined by the marriage of Isaac to a cousin of the Empress Mary of Alania. Isaac arrived in Antioch to find that conditions were desperate. Not only was the city hard pressed by the Turks, but there was an anti-imperial faction led by the Patriarch Aimilianos, an enemy of Nikephoritzes from the time that he had been duke of Antioch. Isaac managed to spirit him off to Constantinople, where, it was hoped, mistakenly, that he would be less of a nuisance. The departure of the patriarch did little to calm the city down. The people rose in revolt and pinned the governor down in the citadel. With the help of reinforcements from the surrounding towns and fortresses Isaac put the rebellion down with great loss of life. There may have been an element of social discontent in this uprising. It is recorded that the rebels plundered the houses of the nobility, but there is also a more straightforward explanation. There were still governors appointed by Romanos Diogenes holding sway in the Euphrates lands, notably the Armenian Philaretos. The troubles in Antioch should probably be seen as a continuation of the civil wars. Antioch would fall to Philaretos in 1078. Before this Isaac Comnenus had been captured in battle by the Turks. He was ransomed at great expense by the citizens of Antioch and returned to Constantinople. Isaac's defeat meant that Antioch passed out of the direct control of the imperial government. Nikephoritzes's Anatolian strategy, such as it was, lay in ruins.

In Constantinople opposition was mounting against his rule. The moving spirit was the patriarch of Antioch, Aimilianos. His support came from a group of bishops and from the guilds. Why the guilds should have come out against Nikephoritzes can only be a matter for conjecture. In the light of the very generous treatment they received when Nicephorus Botaneiates came to power, it is possible that Nikephoritzes attempted in some way to restrict their privileges. The opposition of the bishops to the eunuch was more straightforward. They had been forced by conditions in the provinces to seek refuge in the capital, but they remained spokesmen for their dioceses. It was quite clear that Nikephoritzes was sacrificing the provinces while he endeavoured to build up central power. Only a change of regime offered any hope that his policies would be reversed. The leader of one group of bishops opposed to Nikephoritzes was the metropolitan of Ikonion, which lay close to Nicephorus Botaneiates's centre of power.

On the day after Epiphany 1078 they organized an assembly in St Sophia, where Nicephorus Botaneiates was proclaimed emperor. Botaneiates had begun his bid for the imperial throne in the previous summer, but had achieved little positive success. His move had sparked off a counter-rebellion in Thrace under Nicephorus Bryennios, the head of the greatest family of Adrianople. His supporters and relatives soon brought the remaining towns of Thrace over to his side. Bryennios then marched on Constantinople in the autumn of 1077. Knowing the opposition that existed in Constantinople to Nikephoritzes's regime, he had high hopes that the capital would be betrayed from within. But support within the capital evaporated once Bryennios's troops pillaged and burnt the suburban estates belonging to rich and influential citizens of Constantinople. In the face of the approaching winter the rebel army was obliged to retreat to Adrianople. Even so, the position of the imperial government in the early months of 1078 seemed untenable. There was a rebel army at Adrianople, while in the capital there was a disaffected group of bishops who had openly proclaimed another rebel emperor. Nikephoritzes met the challenge by dragging the bishops out of St Sophia where they had sought sanctuary. This brought the ban of the patriarch down on those responsible, which weakened Nikephoritzes's position still further. Alexius Comnenus remained loyal and urged the use of military force against opponents of the regime within the capital. Rather than resort to such a measure Michael VII preferred to abdicate in favour of Botaneiates. This occurred on 31 March 1078, while the latter was still at Nicaea. It was not until 3 April that he entered Constantinople. Nikephoritzes tried to flee from the capital, but was brought back and tortured to death, in an effort to discover where he had hidden the treasure he was supposed to have accumulated.

ALEXIUS COMNENUS'S COUP

Botaneiates was an old man. He came to rescue the Empire. The first step was to heal the divisions caused by Nikephoritzes's harsh policies. Debts owing to the state were cancelled. The small ports around Constantinople which had been confiscated were returned to their original owners. The new emperor was excessively generous. Ranks and pensions were doled out with scarcely a thought to the people and senators of Constantinople. He was purchasing the favour of the capital. He placated senatorial opinion by legislating ostensibly with the consent of the senate. He won over the palace by marrying Mary of Alania, the wife of the Emperor Michael VII, who had become a monk. He did not even proceed against supporters of the previous regime, such as the members of the Comnenus family. The very reverse: they were kept at court and Alexius Comnenus was to receive promotion, being appointed commander-in-chief of the western armies. It may well have been that the Comneni were now so well entrenched at court and in the capital that the new emperor dare not proceed against them openly. Early in 1078 Alexius Comnenus married Eirene Doukaina, the granddaughter of the Caesar John Doukas. This went some way towards healing the vendetta that had existed between the Comneni and the Caesar John's family. It also gave further protection to Alexius Comnenus, because the new emperor was beholden to the Caesar John, for the way he had forced Michael VII to become a monk and had stagemanaged Botaneiates's marriage to Mary of Alania.

Alexius Comnenus's reputation as a skilful commander was enhanced by the way he suppressed Nicephorus Bryennios's rebellion and then put down another uprising, this time led by the governor of Dyrrakhion, Basilakes. These successes allowed Alexius to reassert some measure of control over leaders of local unrest in other parts of the Balkans. Here was a pointer to the future. There was still a possibility of recovering control over the Balkan provinces of the Empire, providing the will was there. Anatolia was a different matter. Botaneiates had to come to terms with the real cost of the support given to him by the Turks. Suleiman's intentions became clear when he seized the strongly fortified city of Nicaea, soon after Botaneiates's entry into Constantinople. This blocked any advance into the interior of Anatolia and commanded the whole region opposite Constantinople. Botaneiates sent a series of expeditions to win back the city, but they achieved nothing. He had been counting on a quick success. Without it the true weakness of the Empire was soon revealed. The state was literally bankrupt.The gold coinage was so debased that it stood at no more than eight carats fineness. Even so the state could not pay its debts. Nicephorus Botaneiates had to suspend the payment of pensions and salaries to the holders of offices and court dignities. The general opinion was that Botaneiates was too old for the job: the difficulties besetting the Empire were too serious to be left to a man now in his eighties. This opened up once again the question of succession. The Empress Mary of Alania intended that her Porphyrogenite son Constantine Doukas should succeed. She had married Botaneiates, as a way of protecting her son's rights to the throne. Anna Dalassena had hopes that her sons might come into the reckoning by virtue of their connection with the Emperor Isaac Comnenus. Botaneiates preferred to groom one of his relatives to succeed him.

This threw Mary of Alania and the Comneni together. They entered into what can only be described as a conspiracy to defend the rights of Constantine Doukas. Mary of Alania even adopted Alexius as her son, in order to strengthen the ties between them. Such an understanding could hardly have been kept secret and Nicephorus Botaneiates's henchmen, Boril and Germanos, determined to move against Alexius Comnenus and his brother Isaac. Alexius won over to his cause the commanders of two regiments stationed in the Thracian countryside. His plans have an air of desperation about them. He hurriedly left Constantinople on 14 February 1081. His mother and the rest of his womenfolk had to seek refuge in St Sophia. His brother-in-law George Palaiologos was only persuaded to join the conspiracy at the last moment. The Caesar John Doukas was out of Constantinople residing on his Thracian estates. He must have been aware of Alexius's difficulties at court, but he does not seem to have been consulted about the timing of his flight from Constantinople, still less can he have stagemanaged the coup. News of Alexius's rebellion startled him: 'Oh, the pity of it' was his immediate reaction, but he decided to put his full weight and experience behind Alexius. There was little else he could do. The fortunes of the Doukas family rested with the young man, whom the Caesar John had deliberately chosen as his family's protector. He was an old man and could not be expected to live for many years longer. His elder son Andronicus died in 1077 and his younger son Constantine three years earlier. He judged that his family would be best served by marrying his eldest granddaughter Eirene to the most promising young man at the Byzantine court.

The Caesar John's help was invaluable. He started by relieving a tax-collector of his takings and thus putting the coup on a sound financial basis. His opinion was decisive when it came to the question of which of the Comneni brothers, Alexius or Isaac, should be acclaimed emperor.

Isaac was the elder, but he stood down because Alexius had the stronger backing. It was the Caesar John who organized their entry into Constantinople on 1 April 1081 by bribing the commander of the German mercenaries, who were guarding a section of the walls. His friendship with the Patriarch Cosmas was instrumental in persuading Nicephorus Botaneiates to abdicate rather than oppose the Comneni. The old emperor still had his household troops and there was a very strong possibility that they would have been able to mop up the Comnenian troops who had spread through the city looting. Their activities meant that the mood of the city was already beginning to turn against the Comneni.

The Caesar John backed Alexius because he could see no other way of protecting his family, while Alexius was using the Caesar as a means to an end. Once he had obtained possession of the palace and the imperial office, the support of the Doukas faction seemed less valuable. Eirene Doukaina was not allowed into the imperial palace. Instead, Alexius kept state with his adoptive mother, the Empress Mary of Alania. There were rumours that he was considering getting rid of Eirene and with her the inconvenient Doukas connection and marrying Mary of Alania. What is certain is that Alexius was crowned alone by the Patriarch Cosmas. The Comneni were to be out-manœuvred all the same by the Caesar John. He gauged quite rightly that Mary of Alania and the Patriarch Cosmas were Alexius's weak points. Mary of Alania was in his debt for the way he had protected her and her son when Botaneiates came to power. He induced her to leave the palace after securing safeguards from Alexius Comnenus for her son's imperial rights. The Patriarch Cosmas was closely connected with the Caesar John. The Comneni wished to get rid of him and put their own nominee on the patriarchal throne. The Caesar John fixed the price for his abdication. 'By Cosmas', the patriarch is supposed to have exclaimed, 'if Eirene is not crowned by my own hands, I shall never resign the patriarchal throne.'[2] And so it was. The deal was struck and Eirene was crowned empress. The wary alliance of the Doukas and Comnenus houses was sealed.

The Caesar John could retire once more to his estates satisfied. He is a baffling figure; intervening decisively in the affairs of the day, apparently in control of events at one moment and then all too ready to retire to his estates. His biographer, D I Polemis, thought that this contradiction might be explained by the way he combined wealth and high social position with a distinct lack of ability or inclination for government. 'In vain one looks for any constructive element in the policies which he had inspired.'[3] This is to miss the point. Caesar John was not interested in policies; he was interested in his family. He was at his best when his family was in danger. In one battle he saw his elder son Andronicus, unhorsed, lying seriously wounded on the ground. He rushed into the fray and threw himself across his son to save his life. He was in good aristocratic fashion capable of a heroism that belied the epicureanism which Michael Psellos wished upon him. In other less dramatic ways, too, the Caesar John strove to protect his family. In this he was entirely consistent. If his touch at times seems to have been far from sure, it was because much of Byzantine politics continued to turn on the public interest. His career nevertheless marks the way dynastic concerns were becoming increasingly decisive in Byzantine political life.

This was confirmed by Alexius Comnenus's coup and the events which followed it. Alexius clearly hoped that he would be able to seize power for himself. We have seen how he occupied the imperial palace and tried to rid himself of his young wife, Eirene Doukaina. This was not just a threat to the Caesar John and his family, but also to George Palaiologos, who was married to Eirene's sister Anna. He was astute enough to secure possession of the imperial squadron of ships. He refused to allow the sailors to acclaim Alexius Comnenus alone: 'It was not for your sake', he cried, when asked to explain his action, 'that I won so great a victory, but for Eirene.'[4] Even at this stage in his career Alexius showed himself an exponent of the art of the possible. He needed George Palaiologos and the fleet, because they prevented Alexius's rival for the imperial dignity, Nicephorus Melissenos, from crossing over the Bosporus to Constantinople. Melissenos was yet another of Alexius's brothers-in-law. Once he saw that Alexius was firmly in control of the capital, he came to terms with him. He gave up his imperial claims, accepted the rank of Caesar, and was granted the city of Thessalonica as an apanage.

The character of the regime brought into being by Alexius Comnenus's coup was becoming clear. Power was now in the hands of an alliance of aristocratic families, all united by close marriage ties. They were the Comneni, the Doukai, the Palaiologoi, and the Melissenoi. The architect of this alliance was the Caesar John Doukas, but it was kept together by his bitter enemy, Anna Dalassena. Her skill in arranging marriages for her offspring ensured that the Comneni would stand close to the centre of any alliance of aristocratic families. She brought to the capital the assumptions and methods of the great families of Anatolia, where power depended very heavily on carefully arranged marriage alliances. Her influence was to be all the more potent because one of Alexius's first acts was to appoint her to run the administration. In this way the dynastic principle was introduced into the sanctum of the civil service. It was also introduced into the ordering of the imperial court. The hierarchy of the Byzantine court consisted of a series of ranks. Some of them went back to the late Roman Empire and others were added over the course of the centuries without there ever being any radical overhaul. This was becoming more and more essential because of the inflation of honours which had been a feature of court life during the eleventh century. Right at the beginning of his reign Alexius Comnenus swept away the highest ranks of the court hierarchy, with the exception of that of Caesar which he had granted to Nicephorus Melissenos. He created a new ranking system based on the title *sebastos.* This was an imperial epithet, equivalent to the Latin Augustus. It had only been granted out sparingly before Alexius came to the throne. Alexius had been one of the few recipients. He created the title of *sebastokrator,* a conflation of *sebastos* and *autokrator* (or autocrat, one of the imperial titles), for his brother Isaac and placed him at the top of the court hierarchy. Another brother was made *protosebastos.* Generally speaking the title *sebastos* was given to all those connected by blood or marriage to the emperor and it placed them in a class by themselves at the top of the court hierarchy. Anna Comnena singled this out as one of the most important of her father's reforms. She was quite right. The emperor's family in its widest sense had never previously enjoyed any special position in the court hierarchy. Now the highest ranks at court were reserved exclusively for them. It conformed to an aristocratic assumption about power and privilege belonging to the family as well as being vested in an office or a rank.

As we shall see, Alexius I Comnenus was faced for nearly twenty years with overwhelming dangers. He did not always deal with them wisely. He suffered reverses which would have led to the overthrow of earlier emperors, but he overcame them and remained emperor because he had the support, almost always whole-hearted, of the aristocratic families, who had come to power with him.

THE NORMAN THREAT

Having secured the imperial throne, Alexius Comnenus considered the condition of the Empire. It was not encouraging. Anatolia, including those parts closest to Constantinople, was to all intents and purposes lost to the Turks. The northern Balkans were in the hands of the Petcheneks and other local leaders, while Robert Guiscard, the Norman conqueror of southern Italy, was preparing to invade the Albanian provinces of the Byzantine Empire. He claimed to be upholding the rights of the former Emperor Michael VII Doukas and even kept a man in his camp who claimed to be that emperor. Michael VII had entered into an alliance with Robert Guiscard in 1074. This had been sealed by the betrothal of Guiscard's young daughter and Michael's infant son, Constantine Doukas. This marriage alliance lasted only briefly. It was brought to an end when Botaneiates overthrew Michael VII. Guiscard used this as a pretext to mount an invasion of Albania. It was almost devoid of troops following the rebellions of Nicephorus Bryennios and Basilakes, both of whom had been governors of Dyrrakhion, the main town of the region. Alexius protested to Robert Guiscard in vain that he should desist. The Norman was hardly likely to be impressed by Alexius's claim that now he had overthrown the usurper Norman intervention was no longer necessary.

However spurious it may have seemed, Guiscard's claim to be championing the rights of the ex-Emperor Michael VII was deeply disturbing to Alexius Comnenus. He had enemies at home who might be willing enough to accept the Norman ruler's claims. This was one reason why Alexius Comnenus should have singled out Robert Guiscard as his main opponent. Other enemies, such as the Turks and Petcheneks, might seem to present a much more pressing threat than the Norman, but they were not a challenge to the imperial office. A victory over Guiscard would unite Byzantine society behind Alexius in a way that could not happen if he concentrated on the Petcheneks and Turks, the more so because of the papal blessing which the Norman's venture had received. Alexius could play on Byzantine distaste for the papacy.

There was a quite different reason why Alexius should have considered the challenge from Robert Guiscard to be the most serious facing him, one that must have assumed increasing prominence as the campaigns against the Normans progressed. Albania would provide the Normans with a bridgehead from which they could stir up trouble in the Balkans. Guiscard was in the process of establishing some measure of suzerainty over the Serbian chiefs. Once across the Albanian mountains the Normans threatened Thessalonica and the rich lands of southern Macedonia. If they chose, they could move southwards from Albania through Kastoria and Ioannina and they would have Thessaly and the Greek lands at their mercy. The loss of the Greek provinces would have had the most serious consequences for the Byzantine emperor, because it was only here that the administrative system continued to function effectively. These lands must have been supplying Alexius Comnenus with a very substantial proportion of his revenues. It is hardly an exaggeration to say that, should the Greek lands be lost to the Normans, there could be no hope of restoring the Byzantine Empire.

To meet so pressing a danger Alexius adopted a strategy of stark simplicity. He would catch the Normans while they were still besieging Dyrrakhion, before they had time to establish a secure bridgehead. Their reliance on sea communications made their position vulnerable. Alexius was able to engage the services of the Venetian fleet against the promise of concessions on customs duty. The Venetian fleet defeated the Normans and so brought a measure of relief to the Byzantine garrison at Dyrrakhion, commanded by George Palaiologos. It gave Alexius time to get his forces together. By October 1081 his army was closing in on Dyrrakhion, which was still hard pressed by the Normans. After some hesitation Alexius decided that he had to risk a battle against the Normans, as the only way of relieving the city. The Byzantines were totally defeated. Many Byzantine commanders were killed, which presumably means that there were heavy casualties among their soldiers. The Varangian Guard was almost wiped out; even if, in this instance, their commander survived. The emperor himself only escaped thanks to the swiftness of his horse. Dyrrakhion fell almost immediately. The Normans then moved on to occupy Ioannina and Glabinitza, thus securing the key points for an advance into Greece. Many of the local Byzantine governors went over to the Normans, considering that the position was hopeless.

Alexius tried to create a diversion by bringing the German Emperor Henry IV down into Italy at the cost of huge sums of money. Guiscard hurried back to Italy, but it made little difference because he left his eldest son Bohemund in command of his new conquests. Bohemund threatened to break out to the south into the Greek lands. In May 1082 Alexius set out from Constantinople in a desperate effort to prevent this. He engaged Bohemund, but once again suffered defeat. He fled north to Ohrid, one of the key positions on the Via Egnatia, linking Dyrrakhion to Thessalonica. He gathered another army and was again defeated. The people of Ohrid surrendered their town to Bohemund, though in the castle a garrison loyal to Alexius continued to hold out. The network of fortresses protecting the approaches to Thessalonica defied Bohemund's probing and he decided to turn southwards against Larissa, the key to control of Thessaly. It was commanded by Leo Kephalas, the son of a family servant of the Comneni. He held out for six months, giving Alexius time to collect new forces.

At last in the late summer of 1083 Alexius arrived in Thessaly. He skirted round Larissa and made his way to Trikalla, which commanded the Normans' main line of retreat northwards. Alexius had learnt from his previous encounters with the Normans that the Byzantine troops were no match for them in the open field. He adopted tactics borrowed from the Turks, who were masters of the ambush and knew how to deploy archers to bring down the Norman chargers. In the confused fighting that followed the Normans had the worse of the encounter. They abandoned the siege of Larissa and retired to Kastoria. A year's indecisive campaigning in the mountains of northern Greece left the Norman commanders discontented and Bohemund found it difficult to keep their loyalty. In the late autumn of 1083 Alexius had little difficulty in capturing Kastoria. Most of the Norman garrison went over to him and entered his service.

The danger from the Normans was still not over, but by the end of 1083 Alexius had much to be pleased about. He had prevented the Normans from penetrating the plains of Macedonia and Thessaly. The richest provinces of his Empire had not been lost. He had learnt the tactics needed to neutralize the Normans' superiority in the open field. The resilience of the Byzantines was amazing. In large measure it must be attributed to Alexius's leadership. He never despaired, when he had every reason to. The regular Byzantine military forces, so carefully reformed by Nikephoritzes, were more or less destroyed at the battle outside Dyrrakhion. Yet Alexius continued to raise new armies. Where did his troops come from? He relied heavily on mercenaries. Many were Franks, but there were also Turks. He could also make use of the military retinues of the great aristocratic families, as well as his own family's retainers. It was only a scratch force, just capable of stemming the Norman advance, but hardly strong enough to drive the Normans out of their bases in Albania. In 1084 Robert Guiscard was once more ready to invade the Byzantine Empire. The Byzantines used the Venetians to try and prevent his crossing over to Albania, but the Normans finally prevailed in a series of sea battles with the Venetians. With control of the sea secured, Guiscard prepared to seize the island of Cephalonia, which would provide him with an excellent base for the conquest of Greece and the Peloponnese, but before he could complete his schemes, he died of fever on 17 July 1085. His death was followed by civil war in southern Italy. The Normans evacuated Byzantine soil. Dyrrakhion was surrendered to Alexius by a faction of its inhabitants. It was a fortunate outcome, but it seemed to justify Alexius's strategy and the great sacrifices that he had demanded of his people. His prestige was immeasurably increased.

THE PETCHENEKS

Thus did Alexius succeed in rescuing the Greek lands, but the remainder of the Balkans was in a turmoil. Power at the local level had passed into the hands of various chieftains. Alexius was brought face to face with the true nature of affairs in the course of the Norman wars. In his search for troops he recruited a force of nearly 3,000 from the heretical Paulicians. They were renowned for their martial qualities and had been settled around Philippopolis since the tenth century. They formed part of the army defeated in October 1081 outside the walls of Dyrrakhion. Thereafter they made vague promises of help, but never fulfilled them. Alexius became more and more suspicious of their intentions. They were in a position to cut his communications with the capital. He gathered them together, as though to review them and register them for military service, but it was a trap. He had them arrested; their chiefs were exiled; their property confiscated, and the community scattered. The remnants were gathered together by Travlos, a Paulician who had served in Alexius's household. He established a new centre in the Balkan mountains. He turned for help to the Petcheneks, who had been living reasonably peacefully in north-eastern Bulgaria. Like other local leaders, their chiefs felt that Alexius's treatment of the Paulicians was the first step in a concerted effort to restore Byzantine rule in the northern Balkans. They went on to the offensive.

The first Petchenek attack on Thrace was contained with some ease by the Byzantine armies. In 1087 Alexius decided to deal with the Petcheneks once and for all. It was the only way he could recover control over the Danube frontier, where the towns and fortresses had passed under the control of local magnates. The key was the town of Dristra, now ruled by a native, probably Vlach, chieftain called Tatos. Alexius sent his fleet to the Danube, while he advanced with his army over the passes of the Balkan mountains. It was an impressive display of force and the Petcheneks were inclined to come to terms. Alexius moved on to secure possession of Dristra. Its two citadels, however, held out against him. This left him in a dangerous position. He was in hostile countryside, hundreds of miles from the safety of Thrace, and his line of retreat over the Balkan mountains was threatened. He decided that rather than face harassment and almost certain defeat by the Petcheneks and their Vlach allies as he retreated, he would attack the Petcheneks head on. It was a piece of foolhardiness typical of his early years. The Byzantine army was once again completely defeated and Alexius and many of his commanders only escaped from the rout with great difficulty.

The Petcheneks were not able to follow up their great victory. They were attacked and defeated by the Cumans, yet another Turkic people who had been shunted across the Russian steppe to the plains north of the Danube. The Byzantines were thus given some respite, but it had nothing to do with Alexius. The Cumans were acting on their own account, not for a Byzantine paymaster. In the aftermath of their victory over the Petcheneks the Cumans offered their services to Alexius, but the emperor preferred to come to terms with the Petcheneks. This did not prevent a series of Petchenek raids into Thrace over the next three years. Once again the Byzantine armies proved capable of a holding action, but the constant warfare took its toll. By the winter of 1090/91 Alexius Comnenus was finding it more and more difficult to get together sufficient troops to counter the Petcheneks. He tried recruiting among the Bulgarians and the Vlachs.

It was not as though the Petcheneks were his only enemy. Just as alarming was the way control of the sea was passing into the hands of the Turks. The Turkish emir of Smyrna, Tzachas, had constructed a fleet and was systematically seizing control of the Aegean islands. He entered into negotiations with the Petcheneks. He wanted them to seize Gallipoli. This would interrupt communications between Constantinople and the Aegean and allow Tzachas a free hand in the Aegean. Alexius reacted with his usual resolution and daring. He singled out the port of Ainos at the mouth of the river Maritsa as the key point. If the Byzantines could hold this, they would be able to prevent any effective cooperation between Tzachas and the Petcheneks. His calculations were upset by the arrival of a large army of Cumans. There had been negotiations with them more than a year earlier, but the Cumans had not come at the emperor's beckoning. Their appearance had nothing to do with diplomatic sleight of hand. Alexius was desperately afraid that the Cumans might decide to join forces with the Petcheneks, in which case his position would have been untenable. He had to win over the Cuman chiefs. They received gifts, but it seems to have been a splendid banquet which finally won their support. They sealed their pact with oaths and gave hostages as pledges of their good faith. After three days of preliminary skirmishing battle was joined at the foot of Mount Levounion on 29 April 1091. The Petcheneks were overwhelmed. As the Byzantine rhyme had it: 'All because of one day the Scythians never saw May.' It was a decisive victory. The Petcheneks were a broken people. Their remnants were settled at Moglena in the Vardar valley, guarding the approaches to Thessalonica. They were in future to provide Alexius with an important body of light-armed cavalry. The Cumans remained a problem. After the battle of Mount Levounion they retired with their spoils back over the Danube, but they returned three years later. Alexius had to take their invasion very seriously because they were backing a pretender, who claimed to be Leo, the son of the Emperor Romanos Diogenes. They had no difficulty in occupying the Danubian fortresses. Byzantine control in the Balkans remained very superficial. Local people were ready to help the Cumans. The Vlachs guided them through the passes over the Balkan mountains. The people of the towns drove out their Byzantine garrisons, welcomed the Cumans, and acclaimed the pretender. The emperor made Ankhialos on the Black Sea coast his base. He refused to be drawn into battle against the Cumans; and they preferred to go off to attack the city of Adrianople with equally inconclusive results. They broke up into raiding parties, which Alexius was able to harry and finally defeat. With this victory over the Cumans in 1094 Alexius finally recovered control over the Balkans as far as the Danube. Even the traditionally recalcitrant Serbs came to terms with Alexius.

Byzantine rule in the Balkans was harsh. It had many of the characteristics of a military occupation. Theophylact of Bulgaria, who was made archbishop of Ohrid in *c.* 1090, paints a sombre picture of conditions in the countryside around Ohrid in the ensuing years. The imperial administration was rapacious. Peasants fled to the forests to escape the tax farmers, the only people who seemed to profit. Peasants were rounded up to serve in the Byzantine armies. Theophylact protested that the region was being denuded of population and that agriculture was suffering as a result. Not much attention was paid to further protests made by the archbishop about the way the privileges of his church were being ignored and estates being confiscated. The local governors were hard men, a surprising proportion of them belonging to the imperial family. They were there to hold the country down from their strongpoints.

ALEXIUS I COMNENUS AND ASIA MINOR

Now that the Balkans were coming under effective Byzantine administration Alexius was free to turn to the problem of Asia Minor. For more than ten years all he had been able to do was to maintain a foothold on the shores opposite Constantinople. The position was almost irretrievable. We have already seen how he withdrew what garrisons he had from the interior of Anatolia at the very beginning of his reign, as he scraped around for troops with which to oppose the Norman invasion. There were still places nominally subject to the Byzantine emperor in the Euphrates lands, but one by one they were lost. Antioch which was the key to the region fell to the Turks at the end of 1084. Edessa would succumb soon afterwards and Melitene as well. Trebizond continued to hold out in the far north-east of Anatolia, but it was virtually a 'fief' of the Gabras family.

Alexius came to terms with the Seljuq ruler of Nicaea, Suleiman, in June 1081, thereby recognizing that he had no effective control over Asia Minor, but he gained a very useful ally. In 1083 Suleiman sent a force of 7,000 troops at Alexius's request to help him against the Normans. Other Turkish chiefs took service with Alexius; some were converted to christianity. Abul-Kasim who succeeded Suleiman at Nicaea even received the title of *sebastos* and with it honorary membership of the imperial family. Alexius might have felt that he had established an acceptable *modus vivendi* with the Turks.

Any such comforting thoughts were to be destroyed by the career of Tzachas, the Turkish emir of Smyrna. He took to the sea and threatened the Byzantine hold on the Aegean. This created the spectre of Turkish raids on the Greek mainland. It was something Alexius could not afford, seeing how heavily he relied on these provinces for his revenues. A tremendous effort was necessary because the Byzantine navy had been allowed to run down. A new fleet had to be commissioned. This was ready by the beginning of 1092 and was put under the command of the emperor's brother-in-law, John Doukas. He succeeded in wresting the islands of Mitylene and Chios from Tzachas and forced him back to Smyrna. He was then able to suppress rebellions that had been simmering in Crete and Cyprus, thus assuring the Empire of control over the Aegean. The Turkish threat was being contained.

By 1095 there seemed at long last to be nothing to divert Alexius from the reconquest of Asia Minor. He began by establishing a bridgehead around Nicomedia. The scale of the project can be judged from his ambitious plan to reopen Justinian's famous canal linking the river Sangarios and the gulf of Nicomedia. This, it was hoped, would provide a barrier against Turkish raids and secure a base from which to conquer Nicaea. These plans had suddenly to be shelved, as news reached Constantinople that hordes of westerners were making their way eastwards. For the next year and more Alexius's energies would be devoted to supervising the passage of the first crusade through his territories. A new chapter in Byzantine history was just beginning.

NOTES

1. Kekavmenos, *Strategikon* (ed. Wassiliewsky–Jernstedt), p. 73; (ed. Litavrin), p. 266
2. *Alexiad* (transl. by E R A Sewter), p. 109
3. D I Polemis, *The Doukai* (London, 1968), p. 40
4. *Alexiad* (transl. by E R A Sewter), p. 106

Chapter 7

ALEXIUS I COMNENUS AND THE RESTORATION OF THE EMPIRE

How daunting a challenge Alexius Comnenus found the passage of the first crusade emerges from the pages of the *Alexiad*, Anna Comnena's history of her father's reign. If Alexius was able to handle it effectively, this was very much because by the autumn of 1096, when the crusaders began to gather about Constantinople, the Empire was in a much healthier condition than it had been even five or six years earlier.

The nadir of Alexius's reign was reached in the winter of 1090/91. The patriarch of Antioch, John the Oxite, addressed two biting speeches to the emperor at that time. It was now nearly ten years since Alexius had come to the throne. Things had gone from bad to worse: 'the frontiers of the Byzantine Empire had been reduced in the East to the Acropolis of Byzantium and in the West to the Golden Gate'.[1] The patriarch was suggesting with pardonable exaggeration that the Empire was limited to Constantinople alone. He noted the disillusion and weariness that existed among the bulk of the population. No longer would they accept the old explanation that disaster and misery were punishments for sin. To many it seemed that God's guiding hand had been removed and that the disasters of the previous years were the results of sheer chance. God's order was taken for granted by the Byzantines, but it seemed to have been replaced by chaos. All suffered, the people, the church. The prosperous had become poor and the poor were either beginning to die from hunger or forced to become refugees and vagabonds, as they sought refuge from the barbarians. Only the emperor's relatives prospered in the midst of this misery, with their palaces and their retinues. 'In very truth,' the patriarch intoned, 'your relatives, O Emperor, have become the greatest pest upon the Empire and upon all of us.'[2]

Alexius had to thank the support of a close-knit network of relatives for his survival during the difficult opening years of his reign. They saw a series of failures and miscalculations which would have brought down a lesser man. It was not just defeat on the field of battle that Alexius had to contend with. The political difficulties which had beset the Empire with

114

increasing force since the middle of the eleventh century did not miraculously disappear the moment that Alexius secured the throne. The internal condition of the Empire continued to deteriorate. To master the discontent that this produced he instituted as harsh and as oppressive and as unjust a regime as Byzantium had ever known. It was observed that he ruled not as a trustee for his people, but as the head of an aristocratic family. 'He thought of and called the imperial palace his own house':[3] that is how the historian Zonaras summed up Alexius's attitude towards imperial authority. This made him all the more tenacious of power and less inclined than perhaps previous emperors had been to heed public opinion. His chief duty was to his family, whereas emperors normally put their responsibilities to their people first.

He could not ignore public opinion completely. Right at the very beginning of his reign there was intense hostility against him in Constantinople provoked by the brutality with which he had seized the imperial throne. To placate public opinion he went to the Patriarch Cosmas as a suppliant and confessed his guilt. He was condemned along with his relatives to perform penance and thus purge their offence. Then after his defeat outside the walls of Dyrrakhion in October 1081 he was desperately short of money. He proceeded to seize treasures belonging to the church. He claimed to be acting out of dire necessity, but was forced to promise in a solemn Golden Bull that he would never repeat such an action. Thereafter he showed a much less tender regard for public opinion. The decisive event was without doubt John Italos's trial and conviction on charges of heresy.

JOHN ITALOS

John Italos was of southern Italian origin. He came to Constantinople and was a pupil of Michael Psellos, who admitted that, 'if he was not in everything excellent, he was a master of his craft', which was oratory. 'His speech did not bring joy to the soul, but compelled one to ponder over what had been said .... It might not fascinate through its beauty, but subdued through the force of argument.'[4] Italos was to succeed his master as consul of the philosophers in the course of Michael VII's reign. His main responsibility was for higher education, but he was a man of some political influence. He was given responsibility for the emperor's policy of *rapprochement* with the Normans. He enjoyed the favour of the Emperor Michael VII and his brothers and exercised an intellectual ascendancy over the Doukas court. He seemed to the young to have more to offer than Michael Psellos in the way of teaching philosophy. Psellos's approach was, as we have seen, distinctly rhetorical. He might claim to have rediscovered the philosophy of Plato, but it was John Italos who initiated its serious study. He was venturing into dangerous territory, because he was not attracted to the study of philosophy for technical reasons, but for its metaphysical content. He was blurring the dividing line between theology and philosophy, between the 'Inner' and the 'Outer' Wisdom.

How dangerous this was is apparent from the experience of Michael Psellos. Even if his claim to be a philosopher was not much more than a pose, it brought him under grave suspicion of heresy, and temporary excommunication by his old friend, the Patriarch John Xiphilinos (1064–75). He defended himself and his use of rational enquiry towards theological ends very cleverly. He claimed to be shaking with wrath at the patriarch's charge that he was predisposed to the teaching of Chrysippos and the Stoics: 'to have always worked for Christ, then to be accused of intimacy with Chrysippos, and to be aware that I have been separated from God by you, who was both my friend and judge, and that I have been consigned to Plato and the Academy! I do not know how I have endured it so long'.[5] He claimed to 'have disproved almost, but not quite all of Plato's opinions, since not all of them are worthless, for his teachings on justice and the immortality of the soul have become for our people the origin of like dogmas'.[6] Thus he drew attention to the value for the Christian of the study of Plato and he went on to insist that theology demanded a logical approach, 'for the use of rational argument is not contrary to the teaching of the church, nor a principal alien to philosophy, but the only instrument of truth and means of finding the thing which we are seeking'.[7] Psellos had little difficulty in showing that he was working in the same tradition as great fathers of the church, such as St Basil and St Gregory Nazianzus, and even Maximus the Confessor. He begged the patriarch's forgiveness and was restored to communion with the church.

John Italos was less wary, less of a politician. His willingness to treat theology as a branch of philosophy gave his enemies a hostage to fortune. He discussed a variety of heretical opinions. Naturally he insisted on their impiety, but his disclaimers seemed to belie the enthusiasm with which they were discussed, while his conclusions seemed to point to their possible validity. It was soon being said that his teaching was corrupting the young. The Emperor Michael VII Doukas advised him to submit various of his propositions to the patriarch anonymously. This he did and they were found to be heretical. Though he had not been condemned by name, he thought it prudent to submit a personal profession of faith to the Patriarch Cosmas for approval. The patriarch studiously ignored it. Italos's orthodoxy remained in doubt. The Patriarch Cosmas's abdication soon after Alexius Comnenus's coup provided Italos with a chance to reopen the affair. The new Patriarch Eustratios Garidas was attracted by Italos and his teaching. Rumour even suggested that he was almost becoming 'his dedicated pupil'. At a preliminary hearing the new patriarch subjected those propositions of Italos which had earlier been condemned to the most superficial of examinations. The next day the patriarchal synod met in full session to consider Italos's submission. Italos was there surrounded by his following. He had an array of books in front of him to help him with his case. He was confident that his profession of faith would be found to be orthodox. Before the synod could give its verdict, the mob burst into the chamber in the gallery of St Sophia, where the meeting was being held. They would have thrown Italos from the gallery to his death on the floor of the nave below, but he managed to get out on to the roof of the church and found a hiding place there. Thus constrained the patriarch handed the matter over to the emperor.

In March 1082 Alexius I Comnenus accordingly assembled a special convocation consisting of prelates and senators to consider the matter. They found Italos's profession of faith unsatisfactory on several counts. Particularly culpable was his treatment of the relation of God the Father and God the Son. It was easy to detect the influence of those 'professors of perdition',[8] the Neoplatonists Proclus and Iamblichus, who taught that all created matter will eventually return to the One God. Italos could therefore be accused of ranging God the Son with creation. His profession of faith was duly condemned, and Italos retracted his views. Alexius remained suspicious. He ordered that Italos should now recant his teachings before the patriarch and synod, but not just Italos, his pupils too. They were to be condemned along with their master to permanent exile. Alexius had yet another surprise in store. Just before the convocation broke up, he produced another ten propositions culled from Italos's writings. They were allegedly 'crammed with Hellenic ungodliness'.[9] John Italos stood by the first nine, which had already been considered in 1076, but rejected the tenth, implicating him in iconoclast views, which was concocted by Alexius and his advisers. The patriarch was to condemn the first nine and examine the tenth.

This duly occurred on the Feast of Orthodoxy, 13 March 1082, when John Italos abjured his beliefs before emperor, patriarch, and synod, and was condemned to a monastery. This was not quite the end of the affair, because the emperor wanted Italos's pupils condemned. There was serious criticism of the emperor's handling of the case against John Italos, among the bishops and the clergy of St Sophia. On 21 March 1082 the patriarch had to threaten those involved with anathema. The grumbling against the emperor clearly had some effect, because five deacons of St Sophia in danger of being banned from teaching because they had been pupils of John Italos were cleared of sharing his heretical opinions. That is not to say that other pupils of Italos did not suffer this ban.

It is difficult to fathom exactly why Alexius should have so desired the condemnation of John Italos and his pupils. Was it for political advantage pure and simple? To be sure it was a way of distracting attention from his seizure of church treasures to pay for the war against the Normans; a way too of discrediting several influential senators or their children, who had been pupils of John Italos and were suspected of sharing their master's condemned beliefs. Yet it was more than this. It can be no coincidence that the condemnation of John Italos should have occurred on the Feast of Orthodoxy. On this day, one of the most solemn in the calendar of the Orthodox church, the victory over Iconoclasm was celebrated. The Synodikon of Orthodoxy was read out. This consisted of a long series of anathemas against heterodox beliefs and teachings. When Alexius Comnenus came to power, this was still more or less in its original form. Iconoclasm was the last heresy anathematized. Under Alexius new anathemas were added, beginning with those against the impious teachings of John Italos. There are grounds for believing that Alexius deliberately timed his attack on John Italos to culminate in his condemnation on the Feast of Orthodoxy, 1082. To the charges against Italos Alexius added a crude accusation of Iconoclasm. The purpose can only have been to signal the true nature of Italos's teachings: his use of Hellenic sophistries and impieties constituted in the same way as Iconoclasm a breaking of the image of the faith. Each year as the Synodikon of Orthodoxy was read out, the faithful would be reminded of Alexius's defence of orthodoxy against this new 'Iconoclasm'.

Italos was so closely connected with the Doukas regime that Alexius would have been well aware that there were political advantages to be gained from his condemnation, but these were incidental to his main purpose: to proclaim that he came to restore the Empire. This could only be achieved if he swept away the impurities which had disfigured the Empire. Italos's teachings were but one manifestation of a corrupt regime. The imperial palace had become an Augean stable of vice. According to Anna Comnena the women's quarters had been the scene of awful depravities since the time of Constantine Monomachos. Alexius's mother, Anna Dalassena, set about cleansing them. Thenceforward there was to be decorum and discipline. She instituted a regular routine, with a special time set aside for religious services. In the words of her granddaughter, 'the palace assumed the appearance rather of a monastery'.[10] Under the influence of Anna Dalassena the Commeni went to great lengths to present themselves as thoroughly devout. It was a necessary part of their programme, which stressed that they came to protect orthodoxy, and to ensure the well-being of the church and society. In this there was a very high propaganda content, which left many contemporaries unimpressed. Its concrete results were not of the same order as Alexius's more practical measures, but it deserves attention because it was an essential part of the business of government.

HERESY

Alexius added to his reputation as the defender of orthodoxy by a steady stream of heresy trials. Most of these involved relatively harmless 'holy men', who had become fashionable in the capital and had attracted a following, but to the theologically suspicious their teachings shaded into heresy. Such men were Nilos of Calabria and Theodore Blachernites. In other times they might well have escaped detection. The Bogomils were a different matter. They appeared to constitute a real threat to orthodoxy not only because of their dualist beliefs, but also because they were in the process of creating their own ecclesiastical organization. The date of their trial can be established with reasonable accuracy. It cannot be much later than 1100, since the emperor's brother Isaac took an active part in the proceedings and he retired from public life soon after that date. The historian Zonaras places the trial immediately after the passage of the first crusade in 1097. Such a date is supported by the following words of Anna Comnena, with which she prefaces her father's attack on the Bogomils: 'He had recently freed himself of most of his cares in east and west, and was now turning his attention to things more spiritual.'[11]

In a totalitarian state, such as Byzantium was, heresy is often only a figment of official paranoia. Was this true of the Bogomils? It seems not. Alexius Comnenus commissioned a refutation of their doctrines. This was not some concoction based on condemnations of ancient heresies, as was so often the case. The details given show that Alexius was dealing with a living heresy. The starting point of Bogomil beliefs was the fall of Satanael, whom they identified with the elder son of God. He fell to earth which was still covered with waters. He divided the waters and made the earth habitable. He created the sky, 'a second heaven'. He tried to create man, but could not give him a soul, which he stole from God. To protect his creation, God sent Jesus Christ; according to the Bogomils, his second son. He brought with him the possibility of salvation. The Bogomils therefore saw man as a battleground between Good and Evil, between Satanael and Christ. They rejected the material world as the realm of evil and with it the teaching and sacraments of the church. Christ did not partake of the material world, he was not man, incarnate of the Virgin Mary. He was the Word of God and only appeared to take on human form. The Bogomils therefore set little store by his death and resurrection. Man was not to be redeemed through Christ's sufferings, because he had not in any sense suffered. It was his teaching, which aimed at liberating the soul from the body, which offered the hope of redemption. The Bogomils accepted no priesthood, only an elect. It was popularly believed that these *perfecti* did not die, but were carried up to heaven in a slumber.

These beliefs, though differing in detail, bear a marked resemblance to those of the Bulgarian Bogomils in the tenth century. It therefore seems likely that Bogomilism seeped into the capital from this source. The leader of the sect in Constantinople at the end of the eleventh century was a Byzantine doctor called Basil. He had been active for some fifteen years, and attracted a considerable following, thanks to his reputation for holiness. There was outwardly little to distinguish him from other holy men. He took care not to betray his real teachings. It would be difficult to distinguish his rejection of the material world from extreme asceticism, but it would have been extremely attractive in the late 1080s when there was an atmosphere of despair in many circles of the capital. It was being suggested in the midst of so many disasters that God had 'abandoned the things of the world to be borne along by chance'.[12] Unlike most holy men Basil actively sought converts. He created his own organization around twelve apostles, who were sent out to evangelize. He is alleged to have boasted that in fifty-two years almost the whole world would be converted to his teaching.

Getting wind of Basil's activities Alexius and his brother Isaac cross-examined him in private; they pretended to be captivated by his personality and interested in his teachings. Basil was lured into confessing his beliefs, which a stenographer happily concealed behind a curtain busily took down. Alexius then had these teachings condemned by a specially summoned convocation. Basil refused to abjure his beliefs and even declared himself ready to die for them at the stake. Alexius had his followers rounded up. They, together with their leader, were condemned to be burnt. In the end the emperor relented and only Basil was burnt on a huge pyre in the Hippodrome. His followers were imprisoned. Alexius stagemanaged the affair so that it had the maximum publicity. It bears some of the features of a show trial. He may have derived some political advantages from it, but these would only have been incidental. His main purpose was to show once again that he had purged the Empire of an evil. It was a convenient pendant to his political successes.

ALEXIUS AND THE CHURCH

Alexius could pose with some authority as a champion of orthodoxy, but its well-being went beyond the suppression of heresy. One particular problem caught the emperor's attention. It concerned the institution of *kharistike* or the temporary transfer of the administration of monastic properties to a lay patron. This was a well-established practice. There had been complaints in the past about various abuses which had come about. Generally speaking, though, it worked well and to the mutual benefit of both parties. Alexius might have been expected to give it his blessing because his relatives apparently stood to gain by it, now that Alexius was in power. The initial impetus for reform certainly did not come from him, but from the Patriarch Nicholas Grammatikos (1084–1111) right at the beginning of his reign. His main motive seems to have been to protect episcopal interests. Bishops found it difficult to keep track of monasteries which should have been under their control, once they had been granted out in *kharistike*. They lost revenues due to them and some 'were in danger of suffering complete desolation'.[13] The bishop of Kyzikos was so destitute that he could not pay for the lighting of his church or conduct proper church services.

The attack was then taken up by John, patriarch of Antioch. He was one of the emperor's bitterest critics. He deplored the effect which lay patronage was having on the spiritual life of monasteries. There was increasing secularization. The lay patron could foist on a monastery a number of lay brothers, who had nothing to do with the spiritual life of the monastery, but just consumed the monastery's wealth. All kinds of irregularities were creeping in: monks were getting involved in business; abbots were being pressurized by lay patrons into waiving the three-year probationary period that monks had to serve. These charges were not lost on Alexius. He had a duty to check the spiritual failings of the monasteries. He set an example by acting as a patron of holy men, such as St Cyril Phileotes, St Meletios the Younger, and, above all, of the founder of the monastery of St John on the island of Patmos, St Christodoulos. The Comneni themselves were great founders or refounders of monasteries, which they generously endowed. This gave them a different perspective on the institution of *kharistike*, which comes out in the tortured phraseology of the foundation charter which the historian Michael Attaleiates drew up for his own monastic institution in 1077. It drips with his agony lest it pass out of the hands of his family and under the control of an interloping *kharistikarios*. Family interest may therefore have been an added reason why Alexius cooperated whole-heartedly in the patriarch's concerted effort to check the main abuses in the system of lay patronage of monasteries. The measures he took were administrative in design: the essential was that all transactions in monastic property were to be registered in the patriarchal archives. The clear intention was to strengthen patriarchal control over monastic property and monasteries generally. Thenceforward more and more monasteries were designated patriarchal and imperial monasteries, which meant that they came under the direct protection of the patriarch and emperor. The main effect of the campaign against *kharistike* may well have been to give the emperor and patriarch a greater hold over the monasteries.

Alexius was accepting one of the major changes which had come about in the course of the eleventh century: the growth of patriarchal authority. The removal of Michael Keroularios by Isaac Comnenus had seemed to be a victory for imperial power, but it was a Pyrrhic one.

Patriarchal authority was already too solidly based. The architect was not so much Michael Keroularios as his predecessor Alexius Stoudites. It was his work that the Patriarch Nicholas Grammatikos took up, even down to the attack on *kharistike*, a problem which had attracted the Patriarch Alexius's attention. He also defended ecclesiastical jurisdiction from encroachment by the secular authorities and regularized the payment of *kanonikon*, a tax due to the church from all communities. These measures received imperial confirmation.

Alexius Comnenus had, however, grasped a vital point. Patriarchal authority rested upon the patriarchal synod and the patriarchal administration, which was staffed by the clergy of St Sophia. Alexius did all that he could to forge an alliance with the clergy of the patriarchal church. He supported them in a series of disputes they had over control of the administration with the metropolitan bishops. The episcopal spokesman was Nicetas, bishop of Ankyra. He was involved in what seemed a relatively minor matter about one of his suffragan bishoprics. It had been raised to metropolitan status by the Emperor Constantine X Doukas. He demanded that it should return to its former dependence on his church. This was opposed by the patriarchal clergy, because they had acquired effective rights of appointment to the see – a state of affairs which would come to an end if Nicetas had his way. For the patriarchal clergy control of such appointments was essential for representation upon the patriarchal synod. Control of the synod was the real point at issue. Nicetas was alarmed at the way the character of the synod was changing. It was coming to concentrate on the day-to-day administration of the church, rather than on matters of dogma and canon law. It was vital for metropolitans to be present, but their domestic concerns often made this difficult, leaving the possibility that the synod would come under the sway of the patriarchal clergy. The bishops protested at the right accorded to the *chartophylax* of St Sophia to preside over the synod in the absence of the patriarch. This was a clear indication of the pretensions of the patriarchal clergy. Alexius Comnenus intervened in the interests of 'ecclesiastical decorum'[14] to protect the position of the *chartophylax*. He confirmed that he was the patriarch's deputy.

A measure of Alexius Comnenus's increasing influence within the church was that in June 1107 he could proceed to a general reform of the clergy. He believed that 'Christian society was exposed to danger because of the way the condition of the ecclesiastical hierarchy was day by day deteriorating'.[15] The word of God was not being preached. He had to remind bishops that they had a duty to preach throughout their dioceses. It was for this reason that they received *kanonikon*. They were to leave the capital and return to their sees. Alexius perceived that in addition there was a need for an order of preachers. They might be either priests or deacons, the priests being paid slightly more 'out of a sense of respect' for their rank. In the first instance, they were to work among the neighbourhoods of the capital, where they would not only preach the word of God, but would also act as a moral police force. They were to check the activities of wandering monks and holy men, who were often wolves in sheep's clothing. The emperor hoped that these measures would also be extended to the provinces. It may be that the whole scheme was abortive, since it is almost impossible to find any trace of these preachers. All that may have come out of it was the creation of a series of teaching posts attached to the church of St Sophia. These went to strengthen the intellectual ascendancy of the patriarchal clergy.

Alexius's reform of the clergy had propaganda value. It was proof that the emperor had the welfare of Christian society at heart. This was also to be seen, in a more practical form, in his charitable work. The influx of refugees into the capital created terrible problems. Alexius dealt with them in traditional style. By 1096 he had refounded the orphanage of St Paul's on the acropolis of Constantinople. Anna Comnena describes it as a city within a city. Here were concentrated all aspects of social welfare. The intention was worthy and no doubt some basic education was provided for the young, but reading between the lines of Anna Comnena's enthusiastic account it does sound as though the housing provided was cheap and the purpose somewhat restrictive. Into it were swept the unwanted of the capital.

THE DEFUSION OF INTERNAL OPPOSITION

Alexius's attack on heresy and his measures for ecclesiastical reform and social welfare form an essential part of his handling of government. Their practical importance is often hard to gauge; their propaganda content was clearly high. They were designed to hammer home the message that Alexius was worthy of the imperial throne and were a reply to criticism of his rule, which reached a peak in the winter of 1090/1091, and then began to subside. The main burden of this criticism was that he ruled not as a steward for his people, but as though the Empire was his private property. He imposed crushing taxes, which impoverished most sections of society. Only his relatives prospered. 'He provided his relatives and some of his retainers with cartloads of public moneys and distributed generous allowances to them, so that they abounded in wealth and had retinues which were fit for emperors rather than private citizens. Their dwellings were in size comparable to cities and in luxury not dissimilar from imperial palaces.'[16] That is how the historian Zonaras put it. He notes that the emperor did not treat the rest of the

123

nobility with the same generosity, and that he discriminated against the senate, which represented the old ascendancy. It consisted of members of old families and influentual office-holders. Civilian and Constantinopolitan interests predominated. It reached a peak of influence in the reign of Nicephorus Botaneiates, who sought its approval for his legislative measures.

Alexius signalled his intentions towards the senate from the outset. Several of its number were assaulted by his troops during his seizure of power. Opposition to the Comneni on the part of the senate remained low key. It can be detected in the storm which broke out in the summer of 1082 over Alexius's seizure of church property. In the next year there was a conspiracy against the emperor, in which senators were implicated, but it was widely believed that many were falsely accused. They were nevertheless deprived of their property, a lesson which would not have been lost on other senators. There was no other conspiracy involving the senate until around the year 1100. It originated in a circle of discontented army commanders, but the figure-head was John Soloman, the president of the senate, and other leading senators were drawn into it. It was betrayed to the emperor. John Soloman was induced to confess his part and to implicate the other conspirators. He was condemned to imprisonment. The other conspirators, including their ringleader Michael Anemas, were paraded shaven-headed through the streets of Constantinople to the jeers of the populace. They were to be blinded, but this was commuted to imprisonment thanks to the prayers of the young Anna Comnena.

The quiescence of the senate is not altogether surprising. Its prestige stemmed from a nostalgia for Imperial Rome, while its power depended in the end on imperial favour. It was composed of men who preferred to work within government rather than against it. They were not disposed to refuse what Alexius offered them: positions of secondary importance within the government. It was part of the ascendancy which the emperor quickly established over his capital. How exactly he achieved this remains mysterious. It reversed the trend of Byzantine politics, which ever since 1042 and the overthrow of Michael V had seen the people of the capital exercise growing political power. The mob ceased to be the force it once was and scarcely makes an appearance on the political scene under Alexius. It had a part to play at the trial of John Italos in 1082, but it was then clearly acting in the emperor's interest. Later Alexius was able to direct the passions of the populace against the Bogomils. It might tentatively be suggested that he was able to use his attacks upon heresy as a way of capturing public opinion in the capital.

A great many 'undesirables' must have been swept out of the porticoes that lined the main streets of the capital and into the welfare complex that Alexius created at St Paul's. Even before he came to the throne their presence had become irksome. They preyed on office-holders, who, receiving promotion, were traditionally expected to entertain them and give them alms. Michael Attaleiates records that with the excessive number of promotions that occurred under Nicephorus Botaneiates they did so well for themselves that they found it too exhausting to pick up all their perks. The honours system was breaking down, with consequences that permeated down through society. A man's standing in Constantinopolitan society depended on his rank at court and the clientele that his largesse secured. Almsgiving and charity were equivalent in modern terms to nursing a constituency. The change that seems to have occurred over the eleventh century was that patrons no longer exercised effective control over the masses, but were increasingly at their mercy. But the more anarchic a society becomes, the more susceptible it is to strong government.

Does this apply to the guilds, too? Until Alexius's accession they were a force to be reckoned with, but they then more or less disappear from view. How can one explain the sudden eclipse of the guilds? There is only a single text which sheds much light on the matter. It is the record of an apparently inconsequential lawsuit over some property. The parties involved were the widow of a businessman and her maternal uncles. The case was to be settled by the administration of oaths and it turned on how the uncles would give their oaths, whether in private or publicly. They claimed that as senators, which they were, they had the right to take their oaths privately; their niece insisted that as businessmen, which they equally were, they had to take their oaths in public. The matter was deemed important enough to go before the emperor in June 1090. The verdict he gave was to have general effect. It went as follows: 'Only those senators, who are not in any way enrolled in a guild subject to the prefect of the city, but have preserved the dignity of their rank, have the right of having the oath administered to them in private; members of guilds and those in business do not enjoy this privilege.'[17] The effect of this ruling was to re-establish in at least one particular the legal distinction that had formerly existed between senator and guildsman. It would be attributing too much importance to a single document, if it were suggested that Alexius Comnenus was following some carefully thought out programme. His main priority was to ensure the ascendancy of his own family. If anything was decisive in his taming of Constantinople, it was the way he concentrated power in his own family. This done, measures designed to re-establish social discipline in the capital would have had a greater chance of success. The turbulence of the capital in the eleventh century stemmed from the breakdown of a reasonably clear-cut social order. This was a periodic feature of Constantinopolitan life, but was normally of short duration, in contrast to what happened in the eleventh century, when it seemed that the capital might evolve a different kind of society. As hierarchical distinctions weakened, so informal social ties strengthened. Power resided not only in position at court, but also in the family, the household, the retinue, and the clientele. The Comneni proved best able to master this social flux, but to guarantee their own position they needed to reimpose the old barriers, separating senator and guildsman, patron and client.

ADMINISTRATIVE REFORMS

We have seen how right at the beginning of his reign Alexius Comnenus created a new hierarchy of court titles for his immediate family. This theoretically turned the imperial family into a new order imposed on the top of Byzantine society. It is one thing to give precedence at court, another real power. Alexius ensured that the honorific prestige accorded to his relatives was not empty show. They were granted great estates, but according to a new principle, which showed that their share in the imperial honour was not just a matter of form. They received the administration of different parts of the Empire and drew the revenues that would normally have gone to the state. These were temporary grants and could be rescinded at the emperor's will. The name given to these grants was *pronoia*. The origin of such grants can perhaps be traced back to similar grants made in the mid-eleventh century from the imperial demesne. There was, though, an important difference. The grants made by Alexius came not from the imperial demesne, but from the public lands belonging to the state. A rough equivalent would be the apanages of medieval France. The Caesar Nicephorus Melissenos was granted Thessalonica; Alexius's brothers Adrian and Nicephorus received *pronoiai* in neighbouring Khalkidike. Nicephorus Diogenes, the son of the Emperor Romanos, whom Alexius treated like his own son, was given the island of Crete. These grants marked a break with one of the principles of Byzantine government: that the public lands of the state were to be directly administered by the imperial administration. Instead, they might be granted out to individuals at the emperor's pleasure. Alexius created a new form of property right. At the beginning of his reign this was an expedient which did not go beyond his immediate family, but it was full of possibilities.

In the course of the twelfth century it would come to be used to support the troops of the Byzantine Empire. The soldier would receive a temporary grant from the state of various revenues, in return for which he served in the Byzantine armies. The *pronoia* was evolving into something not unlike the western fief. Alexius must be given the credit for this innovation, but it was done very tentatively and on no great scale. It was one more expedient to place beside the others he had tried in the course of his reign, as he sought desperately to keep his armies in the field. It turned out to be a reasonable solution to the problems involved in paying his troops. Although no positive proof can be adduced, it does seem likely that it was the emperor's knowledge of western practice which suggested this adaptation of the *pronoia* to his military needs.

MILITARY ORGANIZATION

When Alexius came to power he had the makings of a reasonably effective army, thanks to the work of Nikephoritzes. There were some Guards regiments, such as the Varangians, the Excubitae, the 'Immortals', and the Vestiaritai. There were troops recruited in the Balkans from the Paulicians and the Vardariot Turks. There were even native regiments raised in Macedonia and Thessaly, remnants of the old theme organization. There were also various foreign mercenaries. This army was lost outside the walls of Dyrrakhion in October 1081. Thereafter, for many years Alexius raised his armies as best he could. He made as much use as he was able of foreign mercenaries. The Turks provided him with a reservoir of troops. The contingent of Flemings engaged through the good offices of Robert, count of Flanders, in 1089 was invaluable, though numbering no more than 500 knights. Often Alexius was reduced to rounding up peasants from the Balkans. Adrianople seems to have been the key to this local recruiting. The Byzantine battle array at Dristra in 1087 suggests a very different sort of army to that which had fought at Dyrrakhion. The emperor positioned himself in the centre, surrounded by his personal bodyguard and various relatives, including his brother Adrian who had a force of Latin mercenaries with him. The Caesar Nicephorus Melissenos had command of the left wing and on the right were stationed various Turkic mercenaries. It was very much a scratch force composed of family retainers, mercenaries, and perhaps some peasant levies. Alexius lost the battle and with it another army. He sought to plug the gaps by creating a corps some 2,000 strong called the *archontopouloi*. This was recruited from the sons of soldiers killed in battle. They were young and inexperienced, some were scarcely more than children. In their first encounter with the Petcheneks in 1089 they were caught in an ambush and suffered heavy casualties. By the winter of 1090 as Alexius prepared to face yet another Petchenek onslaught, the condition of his army was pitiful. He got together his garrison troops and all the new recruits he could muster. These numbered no more than 500 all told. These almost certainly represented what might be termed the standing army. He then sent out a summons to 'his kinsmen by birth or marriage and all nobles enrolled in the army' ordering them to join up with him. This was the army that was going to fight at Levounion in April 1091. It might loosely be described as a feudal army with a strong admixture of mercenaries gathered from almost all points of the compass. Eloquent testimony of their diverse origins comes from monastic privileges of the time with their long lists of foreign mercenaries from which the monasteries were to be protected. The battle of Mount Levounion added a new source of troops, the defeated Petcheneks. Once their remnants had been settled, they contributed a valuable contingent of troops, who played an important role escorting the various crusader groups through the Balkans and on through Anatolia.

With the passage of the first crusade a new chapter begins. Byzantine forces were engaged on many fronts. The emperor's brother-in-law, the Grand Duke John Doukas undertook the reconquest of western Asia Minor from the Turks. Another Byzantine force was operating under the command of the first recorded Cantacuzenus in Cilicia and northern Syria. The novelty was that they were in command of both naval and military forces. This was a temporary expedient designed to meet the needs of the moment. It did not amount to any permanent reorganization. This seems only to have come in 1107 in the face of Bohemund's threatened invasion. Alexius then got together an élite corps of 300 young commanders. He trained them himself. They formed part of his household. The best of them were despatched as battalion commanders to hold the passes through the Albanian mountains against the Normans. The discipline of the Byzantine forces in their encounter with the Normans on this occasion would seem to be proof of the success of the measures taken by Alexius. They are not likely to have much altered the motley character of the Byzantine armies. They were designed to improve the system of command and make it more amenable to imperial control. It is more than likely that it was the members of Alexius's officer corps that were the first to receive military *pronoiai*. They were in a sense an extension of his family.

Alexius's approach to military organization was typical of his approach to administration generally. He lurched from expedient to expedient, until he was able to evolve reasonably satisfactory solutions to the problems he faced. The result was often radical change. This was not deliberately sought. In the case of the army he would no doubt have preferred the organization he inherited, but this he destroyed through his own rashness. He had to improvise. His great concern was to ensure that those in command were loyal to him. His first Grand Domestic, or commander-in-chief, was Gregory Pakourianos, whose support had been so vital to the success of his coup. When he died in battle against the Petcheneks in 1086, he was succeeded by the emperor's brother Adrian. At the very beginning of his reign the emperor appointed another of his brothers, Nicephorus, Grand *Droungarios* of the fleet, giving him command of the imperial flotilla based on Constantinople. A brother-in-law Michael Doukas held the rank of *protostrator* or second-in-command of the armed forces. For another brother-in-law John Doukas the office of Grand Duke of the fleet was specially created in 1092. It gave him overall command of combined forces in the Aegean. His activities in this region continued over several years, in the course of which the Grand Duke evolved an administrative competence. He came to be responsible for most of the naval organization and since this was heavily concentrated in the Aegean region he was given overriding responsibility for the provinces of Hellas and the Peloponnese and of Crete.

PROVINCIAL ADMINISTRATION

The theme of Hellas and the Peloponnese was an exception inasmuch that it retained some of the characteristic features of eleventh-century provincial administration. It continued to have a civilian governor, the *praitor*. Elsewhere civilian governors disappeared and were replaced by military governors who bore the title of duke or *katepano*. Hellas and the Peloponnese was more or less the only part of the Empire untouched by war or foreign invasion. In other parts of the Empire the establishment of a military administration was part of the restoration of order in the Balkan provinces and of reconquest in western Asia Minor. The first stage was the establishment of garrisons in the towns and major fortresses and then these would be grouped together as a theme under a military governor.

Was the restoration of military administration to the themes accompanied by the re-creation of the theme armies? The evidence does not favour such an idea. An essential step would have been, of necessity, the revival of the old system of military holdings. This would not have been impossible, since its vestiges still remained, administered by the department of the military *logothete* or auditor. Instead of widening its competence, Alexius soon wound up the department, sufficient proof that he had no intention of reviving the theme armies in their ancient form. The garrisons that held down the provinces were detachments from his main forces, a practice which had been followed in the case of the frontier provinces of the Empire since the middle of the tenth century. A great many, probably the majority, of military governors recorded in Alexius's reign were army commanders. They were quartered out in the provinces with their units ready to move on to their next assignment. They were very much an army of occupation, designed to keep the local people in order, as much as defend the area from foreign attack. There is plenty of evidence from both the Balkans and Asia Minor that the loyalties of local townspeople to the Empire were scarcely even lukewarm. Occasionally, local opinion was so powerful that it had to be consulted, as happened in 1094 at Ankhialos on the Black Sea coast during the Cuman war. Alexius was using it as his main base and his position was uncertain. Other towns in the area had gone over to the enemy. So, he called a general council of war, to which the leading citizens of the town were invited. Local interests were more often ignored. Military governors instituted a regime that was harsh in the extreme. They were interested in securing supplies for their own men and to do so terrorized the surrounding countryside. They were also there to back up the activities of the tax-collectors. The passage of tax-collectors at this time was little different from that of an invading army, perhaps worse because they plundered more systematically.

As was to be expected, the emperor entrusted members of his own family with important provincial governorships. Dyrrakhion was the key to Albania and the wars against the Normans. After it was recovered from the Normans in 1085 it was entrusted successively to Alexius's brother-in-law John Doukas, then to his nephew John Comnenus, and then to the latter's brother Alexius. Another brother was governor of Verroia, which commanded the approaches to Thessalonica. A different strategy had to be adopted in Adrianople, the key to Thrace. It was still dominated by the two great local clans of Bryennios and Tarchaneiotes. During the Cuman war of 1094 Alexius Comnenus summoned their chiefs at the head of the leading citizens of the town to a conference. This was done to secure their loyalty against the promise of fitting rewards. Nicephorus Bryennios was given overriding authority within Adrianople. Alexius was bowing before the realities of local power. The support of the Bryennioi was of such importance that two years later he married his daughter, the historian Anna Comnena, to Bryennios's son, also called Nicephorus. In this way, the Bryennioi were drawn within the Comneni family network, and past enmities between the two families were forgotten. Alexius tried to do much the same with the Gabras family, who controlled Trebizond, the key to the Pontus region. He appointed Theodore Gabras, who had wrested the town from the Turks, duke of Trebizond, thus confirming his hold on the place. Unsure of his loyalty, he kept the latter's son Gregory a virtual hostage at the imperial court. The pretext was that he was to be married first to a daughter of the *Sebastokrator* Isaac Comnenus and then to a daughter of the emperor himself. This was the cause of some friction and various attempts were made by Theodore Gabras to rescue his son from Constantinople. In 1103, some years after his father's death, Gregory was made duke of Trebizond. Once again Alexius had to bow before the realities of local power. Gregory rebelled, but was finally brought to heel by one of the emperor's nephews and brought back to Constantinople. But before the end of Alexius's reign Trebizond returned once again to the Gabras family, when Gregory's brother Constantine was appointed duke. He was among the most successful of the commanders who came to prominence in the later part of Alexius's reign.

Alexius was enough of a realist to accept that in certain areas it was necessary to work through local families. Where practical he preferred to use his own family, in its broadest sense. So, in 1082 in the face of the Normans he sent Leo Kephalas to hold Larissa. This man was the son of a servant of his father, as was Tatikios, another of his trusted commanders. The family almost became a principle of government at all levels of the administration. Provincial governors made full use of their retinues. The first duke of Crete appointed after its reconquest by the Grand Duke John Doukas in 1093 was an officer of his household and remained in his service. Some twenty years later we find the governor of Crete in the service of the new Grand Duke Eumathios Philokales.

CENTRAL ADMINISTRATION

This principle applied with equal force in the central administration. Nothing bears out Zonaras's dictum that Alexius acted like the head of an aristocratic family than his decision taken within a few days of securing power to hand over control of the machinery of government to his mother Anna Dalassena. That was all too often how aristocratic households worked. She continued to run the government until shortly before her death, *c*. 1102. Her rule was harsh and she was blamed for the oppressive regime the Comneni instituted. The debt of the Comneni to their mother was immense: not only did she dominate government, she also ensured family unity. One incident will illustrate the ascendancy she had over her family. Alexius suspected the loyalties of his nephew John Comnenus, the son of the *Sebastokrator* Isaac. A bitter family quarrel ensued. The *sebastokrator* was resentful. The affair was patched up and the brothers reconciled; with Alexius telling Isaac, 'Go in peace now to Constantinople and tell our mother what has passed between us.'[18]

Anna Dalassena was more interested in control than in reform. Such reform as there was aimed at securing more effective control over the machinery of government. As soon as her son appointed her viceroy, a new *logothete* was appointed to assist her. He was the *logothete* of the *sekreta*. Its holder was to supervise and coordinate the functions of the different bureaux of the civil service. Lack of coordination, duplication of effort, demarcation disputes, these had been some of the weaknesses of the Byzantine civil service. The creation of this new post was intended to counter these defects. But, more than this, it would allow a greater measure of control over an institution that was likely to be hostile to the Comneni. The new officer was not in any sense a policy-maker. This guarded against the perennial danger that the emperor would become little more than a mouthpiece for the civil service. In a sense he acted as a buffer between the imperial family and the civil service.

FINANCES

As foreigners and Byzantines alike were inclined to remark, the great strength of the Byzantine emperor was his ability to lay his hands on ready money. Alexius was no exception. Even at the darkest times of his reign he seems to have been able to get hold of cash. The methods used were oppressive and arbitrary: surcharges were piled on to the basic tax and new exactions devised. In desperation, as we have seen, he might simply confiscate church treasure. There seems to have been no semblance of order in his financial organization until 1094 at the earliest, when a new official the Grand Logariast of the *sekreta* makes his appearance. His function was analogous to that of the *logothete* of the *sekreta*, that is to say it was his job to coordinate and supervise the activities of the financial bureaux of the central government. In 1099 another new financial office appears for the first time: that of the Grand Logariast of the *euage sekreta*, that is the imperial demesne, which still retained a separate identity.

The next step was to reform the system of taxation, which was not just oppressive, but had become completely chaotic. Outside Greece it must have been impossible to keep the tax registers up to date, but the problem went far deeper than this. The existing tax assessments were calculated according to the old full-value coinage, but now with the continuous debasement of the coinage a vast number of different issues of widely varying fineness were in circulation. In what coins was tax to be paid? How were the devalued coins to be related to the old full-value coins? There were splendid opportunities for tax evasion or, more realistically, for tax-collectors to line their pockets. Until order was returned to the monetary system, taxation would continue to be in a chaotic state. Conversely, until the system of taxation was reorganized, it was unlikely that the emperor would have enough money at his disposal to renew the coinage.

For many years the condition of the Empire was far too serious for Alexius to think in terms of a reform of the currency. He followed an irresponsible monetary policy, continuing to debase the gold coinage. Some of the issues at the beginning of his reign contained no more than two carats of gold. Only after the Petcheneks had been defeated once and for all in 1091 was Alexius in a position to start upon a combined reform of the monetary and taxation system. In 1092 on the occasion of his new-born son John's coronation, he issued a full-value gold *nomisma*. If this was intended as a prelude to the return to the full gold standard, it was a failure. Debased coins continued to circulate in profusion. Various expedients were tried for relating the different issues but with little success. It was not until 1109 that a satisfactory rate was established. The basic taxation was to be collected in *nomisma* of eight carats, one-third of the fineness of the full-value *nomisma*. Any fractions of a *nomisma*, always an important part of the revenue, were to be collected in copper currency, the old equivalence between gold and copper coinage having been very roughly restored. The minting of the new full-value *nomisma*, or *hyperpyron*, as it became known, does not at this point seem to have had much practical value, except perhaps as a standard against which to relate other coins in circulation.

Nothing could have been more important for the internal strength of the Byzantine Empire than its monetary system and its tax system. By bringing some kind of order to the monetary system, he succeeded in making the system of taxation work more effectively. There is no sign that he undertook any major reform of the fiscal system. The basic taxes remained the same: peasants without holdings paid a hearth-tax; those with holdings paid a combined hearth- and land-tax, which varied with the size of property and the number of plough teams. In addition there were a multiplicity of dues and various surcharges. Alexius was not interested in reform; he wanted to make the existing system work. It was very much a matter of trial and error. His reform of the coinage was more a series of expedients, which at long last produced a satisfactory solution, satisfactory in the sense that the existing fiscal machinery was able to function reasonably effectively.

CONCLUSION

There is no point in talking about a Comnenian 'revolution in government'. By and large Alexius remained true to the system of government he inherited. He patched it up and made it work, but he made it work for him and his family. This was the great change which he brought about. It provided some kind of a resolution to that often disguised struggle between aristocracy and autocracy about which so much of the politics of the eleventh century revolved. The aristocratic principle triumphed with Alexius Comnenus. He did everything to root the aristocracy in the foundations of the state and thus transform it. His reform of the honours system meant that their position at the apex of society was enshrined in the court hierarchy. It was further strengthened by the way the offices of the imperial household were from Alexius's reign onwards given to members of the aristocracy. They had previously been the preserve of eunuchs, the staunchest upholders of Byzantine autocracy. Above all, Alexius created in the *pronoia* a new kind of property right to bolster the position of the aristocracy.

Alexius's accession to power produced a new and clearer definition of aristocracy. It was seen to coincide with the imperial family in its widest sense. The civil service élite was demoted to a position of second rank. Many of the great noble families of the eleventh century, who failed to break into the charmed Comnenian circle, gravitated to the ranks of the civil service. Some, like the Bryennioi and the Gabrades, retained local power. Some received military command and hovered on the fringes of the imperial aristocracy. They constituted a disaffected element about the emperor and were a frequent source of plots against him. With the accession to power of Alexius Comnenus the *ethos* of Byzantine court society changed. It was not just that Anna Dalassena put an end to the frivolous goings-on which had characterized life at the Byzantine court since the days of Constantine Monomachos. This was coupled with a renewal of martial pride. Anna Comnena's accounts of the wars fought by her father are tinged with a Homeric complexion. War was no longer the business of armchair strategists, but of heroes. Anna catches the atmosphere of the time in one of her footnotes. She recounts that the son of one of Alexius's commanders was killed in an engagement with the Petcheneks. The man could not endure the thought of his son's death. For three days and nights he beat his breast in grief with a huge stone until he finally killed himself. Mingling with Homeric reminiscences was a new interest in military prowess, best caught in Anna Comnena's description of her future brother-in-law: 'Nicephorus was an expert with the lance and knew how to protect himself with a shield. On horseback he gave the impression that he was not a Byzantine at all, but a native of Normandy.'[19]

The Byzantines knew the Normans well. They had fought against them in southern Italy and Albania and Norman mercenaries had taken service in the Byzantine armies. The Byzantines could not help despising them as barbarians, but they admired their martial qualities. In many ways, they conformed better than the Byzantines to that ideal of aristocratic prowess which was coming into vogue at the Comnenian court. Even before the first crusade set out, the Byzantines were filled with that ambivalent attitude towards the West and westerners that would characterize their relations throughout the twelfth century.

NOTES

1. P Gautier, 'Diatribes de Jean l'Oxite contre Alexis 1er Comnène', *Revue des Etudes Byzantines,* 28 (1970), p. 35
2. *Ibid.,* p. 41
3. John Zonaras, *Epitomac Historiarum Libri XIII–XVIII,* III (Bonn, 1897), p. 766
4. Michael Psellos (ed. Kurtz–Drexl), I, p. 53
5. Sathas V, pp. 445–6
6. *Ibid.,* pp. 444–5
7. *Ibid.,* p. 447
8. Th I Uspenskij, 'Deloproizvodstovo po obvineniju Ioanna Itala v eresi', in *Izvestija Russkago arkheologitcheskago Instituta v Konstantinopole,* 2 (1897), p. 46
9. *Ibid.,* p. 59
10. *Alexiad* (transl. by E R A Sewter), p. 120

11. *Ibid.*, pp. 496–7
12. Gautier, *art. cit.*, p. 23
13. Th I Uspenskij, 'Mnenija i postanovlenija Konstantinopol'skikh pomestnykh soborov XI i XII vv. o razdatche tserkovnykh imushchestv', in *Izvestija Russkago arkheologitcheskago Instituta v Konstantinopole,* 5 (1900), p. 17
14. Zepos, *Jus*, I, p. 359
15. *Ibid.*, p. 351
16. Zonaras, *op. cit.*, III, p. 767
17. Zepos, *Jus*, I, p. 645
18. *Alexiad* (transl. by E R A Sewter), p. 265
19. Ibid., p. 301

Chapter 8

ALEXIUS I COMNENUS AND THE WEST

Alexius was 'blooded' as a military commander in the decade following the defeat of Mantizkert in 1071. He understood from his own experience what the collapse of the Empire's frontiers meant. Once on the throne he would leave domestic affairs to his mother, while he concentrated on restoring the frontiers. Anna Comnena catches an echo of her father's aims, when she tells us that he 'manœuvred round Byzantium, the centre of his circle, as it were, and proceeded to broaden the Empire: on the west the frontier became the Adriatic Sea, on the east the Euphrates and Tigris'.[1]

By 1095 Alexius had succeeded in restoring the frontiers of the Empire in Europe to the Danube and the Adriatic. His eyes then turned eastwards to Anatolia and the distant Euphrates. His daughter's addition of the Tigris may be the hyperbole of disappointed hopes, but the Euphrates was another matter. At the beginning of his reign there were still some local rulers along the Euphrates who were nominally subjects of the Byzantine Empire. The conquest of Anatolia and the restoration of the Euphrates frontier were immense tasks, but the political situation gave hope of success. Seljuq power was collapsing in the civil wars which followed the deaths in quick succession in 1092 of the great Seljuq vizier Nizam al-Mulk and his master, the Sultan Malik Shah. To grasp the opportunities presented Alexius needed all the troops he could get, troops, moreover, who would be capable of matching the Turks. The Franks were the obvious source of supply. They were already serving in considerable numbers in the Byzantine armies and had acquitted themselves well against the Turks in one or two encounters.

Anna Comnena singles out the contingent of Flemish knights, some 500 strong, who took service with her father in 1089. This was the result of an agreement he had made with Robert I, count of Flanders. He had met the count in the autumn of 1087, when the latter was returning through the Balkans from a pilgrimage to Jerusalem. He agreed to supply the emperor with a force of knights, sealing the pact in western style by taking an oath of loyalty to the Byzantine emperor.

Alexius derived solid benefits from this meeting with the count of Flanders; more important for the future were the insights he gained into western institutions and mentality. It can only have reinforced Byzantine awareness of how much the pilgrimage to the Holy Sepulchre meant to western knights. At about the same time as the meeting was taking place between Alexius and the count of Flanders, Pope Victor III (1086–87) was writing to the emperor's mother, Anna Dalassena, requesting that the Byzantine tolls on pilgrims to the Holy Land should be lifted. The Byzantines did not just exploit the pilgrim traffic; there are also examples of hostels being constructed for pilgrims along the routes they followed across the Balkans, as acts of charity.

Alexius's willingness to accept a western oath of loyalty from the count of Flanders is at first sight surprising. It must mean that the Byzantines were beginning to comprehend the importance in the western world of feudal ties. However much they may have appreciated the martial qualities of the Franks, they were difficult to deal with. Their loyalties were so often suspect. The employment of a western form of oath seemed an effective way of binding them in loyalty to the Byzantine emperor. It also opened up new possibilities of recruitment. In the past, Frankish mercenaries had made their own way to Byzantium to take service in the imperial armies, and, very occasionally, Byzantine recruiting sergeants may have been sent to the West. Now direct negotiations with western leaders seemed to offer a more satisfactory alternative.

In 1091 or 1092 Alexius is supposed to have written to Robert, count of Flanders, asking for new troops. As it stands, Alexius's letter is certainly a forgery, but it may be based on a genuine document. It contains a description of conditions in Anatolia and the Aegean which fits the early 1090s quite uncannily. It mentions the recent loss of Mitylene and Chios, which did indeed fall to Tzachas, the Turkish emir of Smyrna, in 1090. The letter ends with this appeal: 'Act fast, lest you lose the kingdom of the Christians, and worse, the Lord's Sepulchre.'[2] It was in much the same terms that the Byzantine agents were to appeal in 1095 to the council of Piacenza and Pope Urban II was to make his momentous plea to christendom in November 1095 at the council of Clermont, thus launching the first crusade. What was Alexius's part in this? Did he, as a thirteenth-century Byzantine chronicler suggested, deliberately emphasize the threat to the Holy Sepulchre in order to elicit western sympathy for Byzantium and thus obtain the military assistance he needed?

What is absolutely certain is that neither Alexius, nor for that matter Urban II, could have been aware of the depths of the response touched off by the appeal made at Clermont. It had to do with changes occurring in western Europe; to put it as briefly as possible, rapid development in many fields, economic, intellectual, ideological, and political, had created a society ill at ease with itself. The framework of social explanation largely elaborated in the Carolingian period no longer provided satisfactory answers. The delivery of the Holy Places would provide not only a sense of mission but also a common purpose out of which a new sense of identity might be fashioned. It gave hope of the creation of an ideal order with peace at home and the Holy Places wrested from the infidel.

In all this Alexius was the unwitting agent who brought together the ingredients of the crusade: papacy, Holy Sepulchre, and the church militant. Like most Byzantine emperors before him his Italian policy had to take into account the papacy, while his knowledge of western knights led him to stress the importance of the Holy Sepulchre. Alexius experienced the full force of the church militant at the beginning of his reign in the shape of Robert Guiscard. His campaign against the Byzantine Empire had the full blessing of the Roman church. He received a banner from Pope Gregory VII. He came allegedly to restore to the Byzantine throne Michael VII Doukas who had been unlawfully set aside. The threat from the Normans was linked in Alexius's mind to backing from the papacy. An understanding with the papacy might help to neutralize the danger from the Normans.

He therefore welcomed the overtures made to him by Pope Urban II in 1089. Faced with the challenge of an anti-pope, Urban II found the restoration of friendly relations with Byzantium an attractive proposition. He wanted the Latin churches in Constantinople to be reopened and his name restored to the diptychs of the Byzantine church. Alexius was all in favour of accepting this request, which would mean that formally the churches of Rome and Constantinople were once more in communion. Alexius was reviving a line of policy followed by the Emperor Michael VII Doukas. He presumably knew of Pope Gregory VII's bombastic announcement made at that time to the effect that he would attend a general council of the church at Constantinople and with an army at his back rescue eastern christendom. The idea of a pope leading an army to Constantinople might not have been very attractive, but it did suggest that the pope was capable of raising an army.

Alexius went to considerable efforts to try and win over the Byzantine church to the idea of a reunion of churches. He used the rhetorical skills of Theophylact of Bulgaria to play down the differences between the two churches. Theophylact produced a tract which shifted much of the blame for the break between them on to the Byzantines. The Byzantines had treated the Latins with arrogance, when they should have shown more tolerance of Latin practices. The azymes, for instance, were not a sufficient cause for a schism. The addition of the *filioque* to the creed was the only serious Latin error and this was done out of ignorance, not malice. The patriarchal synod was not so convinced that the Latins were blameless. Its members listened to the emperor's arguments that the pope's name should immediately be restored to the diptychs, but they insisted that before this could happen the pope must send a statement of belief; and the Patriarch Nicholas wrote in September 1089 to Urban II to this effect. It never came and negotiations between the two churches were for the time being at an end. There is a tantalizing reference in the *Alexiad* which suggests that there may have been more to this set of negotiations than just the restoration of communion between the churches. In the winter of 1090/91 Alexius delayed coming to grips with the Petcheneks as long as he could because he was expecting troops to reach him from Rome. There is nothing to suggest that, in fact, supply of troops was tied to the reunion of churches, but it does mean that Alexius saw Rome as a potential source of troops. The request for military aid for eastern christendom delivered by imperial plenipotentiaries to the council of Piacenza should not be seen as some kind of accident, but as the logical development of earlier negotiations.

The appeal was couched in terms that were expected to be attractive to the papacy and the western church. Its results were all the same not quite what Alexius had anticipated. The approach of a horde of pilgrims under Peter the Hermit and Walter the Penniless was most alarming. Rumour suggested that it was nothing less than a mass-migration. They were 'more numerous than the grains of sand on the seashore or all the stars of heaven'.[3] Alexius dealt with them as best he could. He had them ferried across to Asia Minor, where many of them were killed by the Turks. In their wake came the more disciplined knightly contingents under great lords. This was what Alexius had been hoping for. He dealt with them very efficiently. They were escorted across the Balkans and their leaders were brought to Constantinople, where almost all of them were persuaded to take an oath of loyalty in the western manner to the Byzantine emperor. He was following the procedure which had worked so effectively with Robert, count of Flanders. The two leaders who gave him most difficulty were Raymond of St Gilles, count of Toulouse, who had some claim to be considered the military chief of the crusade, and Bohemund, the Norman ruler of southern Italy, and in the past a redoubtable adversary. Raymond refused to take an oath of loyalty to the Byzantine emperor. His objection was almost certainly that such an oath was not current in Languedoc. He did not owe fealty to any superior for his lands and was reluctant to become the liegeman of the Byzantine emperor. A compromise was finally reached on 26 April 1097, when Raymond agreed to respect the life and honour of Alexius. It was a formula which satisfied both parties. Raymond did not admit the overlordship of the emperor, while the latter had an undertaking that Raymond would uphold Byzantine interests. Raymond would remain completely loyal to his compact with Alexius, which is more than can be said of Bohemund. There was from the beginning mutual suspicion. Bohemund took an oath of loyalty to Alexius, but when he requested that he be made Domestic of the East, Alexius refused. He feared that Bohemund would use such a position to assert his authority over the crusade and direct it towards his own ends. It was considered opinion at the Byzantine court that the leaders of the crusade were exploiting the naïve piety of the pilgrims with the intention of overthrowing the Byzantine Empire. Anna Comnena puts it well: 'To all appearances they were on pilgrimage to Jerusalem; in reality they planned to dethrone Alexius and seize the capital.'[4]

The Byzantines were probably exaggerating the danger from the crusade, but Alexius could still congratulate himself on the way he had secured the loyalty of the leaders of the crusade by his use of the western oath. He became their overlord. He offered to provide them with the aid they needed, be it money, food, or military support. In return, the crusader leaders agreed to return to Alexius any places they captured which had formerly belonged to the Byzantine Empire.

By the spring of 1097 the crusaders were ready to cross over to Anatolia. In May a joint force of Byzantines and crusaders laid siege to the key point of Nicaea, the Seljuq capital in Anatolia. After a siege of seven weeks the city surrendered, thanks mainly to the persistence of the crusaders. From Nicaea they set off on the main road across Anatolia. The plans the crusaders had are not clear. They must have relied upon advice from Alexius. He put at least one of the crusader leaders in touch with Christian Armenians who might prove useful. He also provided the crusaders with a small force under his trusted commander Tatikios. He was to guide the crusaders across Anatolia and to see that they fulfilled their promise to return Byzantine territories. This all suggests that Alexius was hoping to use the crusaders to recover control over the Euphrates frontier together with Cilicia, where the Armenians remained very powerful. The key to a permanent restoration of Byzantine authority in this region was Antioch, and its conquest must have been for Alexius the main objective of the crusade.

The crusaders wound their way up on to the Anatolian plateau. On 30 June the vanguard of the crusading armies under Bohemund began arriving in the plain of Dorylaion. It was a region that was already heavily settled by Turks. Enormous numbers of Turks from all over Anatolia had gathered to oppose the crusaders' passage across the Anatolian plateau. The Turks came to grips with the crusader vanguard. By luck or good management the crusaders were able to outmanœuvre the Turks, who had not counted on the swift arrival of the other crusader contingents. The crusaders won a complete victory and the Turks melted away. The road across Anatolia was open. The crusaders met very little opposition. By the autumn the bulk of the crusading armies was down in northern Syria laying siege to Antioch, while the first steps were being taken to secure control over the various Armenian principalities in Cilicia and the Taurus mountains. To the east of the Euphrates Baldwin of Boulogne had made himself master of Edessa and the surrounding territory, welcomed with open arms by the local Armenians.

There seems to have been no question of surrendering Edessa to the

Byzantines, even though it might well have been argued that it was still nominally subject to the Byzantine Empire at the beginning of Alexius's reign. Antioch was an even greater prize, and it was not one that the Byzantines would happily relinquish to the crusaders, for the simple reason that their whole strategy turned on that city. With the crusaders was the small Byzantine force under Tatikios. With hopes of a crusader success dwindling, Tatikios made his excuses and abandoned the siege in February 1098, claiming that he was going for reinforcements, which was indeed the case. In the early summer of 1098 Alexius Comnenus set out with the bulk of his forces to rescue the crusaders, who were now trapped within the city. He reached Philomelion within striking range of Ikonion, the main obstacle on the road to Antioch. Here his nerve failed him. He was told by three crusader leaders, who had escaped from the beleaguered city, that the crusaders could at best only hold out for a few more days and were contemplating flight. There was still more disturbing news that a Seljuq army had been despatched with orders to prevent Alexius breaking through to Antioch.

Alexius turned back. In the past rash decisions to press forward to the frontiers of the Empire had cost him the loss of two armies. It was the sensible decision, but the wrong one. The crusaders defeated the Seljuq army sent against them on 28 June 1098 and secured possession of Antioch. Properly it should have been surrendered to the Byzantines, but there were no Byzantines to surrender it to. Bohemund argued that the Byzantine emperor had in any case forfeited it, because he had failed to fulfil his obligations as a lord: he had not come to the aid of his vassals at a time of the direst emergency. It was a point of view disputed by another crusader leader, Raymond of Toulouse, who also had designs on Antioch, but he was outmanœuvred by Bohemund, who made sure that his men held the citadel and most of the city.

Raymond then led the crusaders on to Jerusalem. He expected to be made king of Jerusalem, but once again he was to be disappointed. The best he could do was to cooperate with the Byzantine forces operating along the Syrian coast. The emperor invited him to Constantinople in June 1100 almost certainly to help with the passage of a new crusade which was awaited. The crusaders began arriving in Constantinople at the end of 1100. One group composed of Normans and Lombards insisted on following the northern route across Anatolia passing through Ankyra. Their intention may have been to rescue Bohemund who was languishing in a Turkish gaol. This did not please Alexius who was negotiating for Bohemund's release on his own account. Not being able to dissuade the crusaders, he put Raymond at their head. They set off across northern Anatolia. They got as far as Amaseia, where they found it impossible to break through the Turkish cordon. They were severely mauled as they retreated northwards to the Black Sea coast. Raymond managed to get back to Constantinople and proceeded by sea to the Holy Land, his understanding with the Byzantine emperor still intact. Another group of crusaders, mostly Burgundians and Aquitanians, decided to take the southern route across the peninsula. They were completely defeated as they were approaching the passes through the Taurus mountains to Cilicia. Somebody had to be blamed and Alexius was the obvious scapegoat. Once again he and his officers had apparently failed to help the crusaders, when support was necessary.

The crusaders were coming to regard the Byzantines as enemies rather than as allies. They were at odds over Antioch. About March 1099 Alexius formally called upon Bohemund to give up the city, which he refused to do. A Byzantine force from Cyprus was despatched to secure the ports of Cilicia and northern Syria. Laodicea (or Lattakieh) was the most important. Possession of this port would go far towards isolating the crusaders in Antioch. Crusader resentment became the more bitter because the next year Bohemund fell into the hands of the Turks. His nephew Tancred was left to defend Antioch. He proved more than a match for the Byzantines, finally in 1103 driving them from Laodicea. The prize was too valuable to be lightly abandoned. In the next year another Byzantine expeditionary force was despatched to northern Syria. After a long struggle the Byzantines secured control once again of Laodicea.

Bohemund had by now been released from captivity. He saw that the Byzantines were slowly gaining the upper hand. He decided to leave the defence of Antioch to Tancred, while he slipped back to the West in order to prepare an invasion of Byzantine Albania. He intended to harness crusading enthusiasm against Byzantium, putting it about that the Byzantine emperor was a traitor to christendom and that it was therefore a holy undertaking to overthrow him. He launched a virulent propaganda campaign against Byzantium, which set the western stereotype of the Byzantines as effete, treacherous, and schismatic. Pope Paschal II gave his blessing to his invasion of the Byzantine Empire. He even vested Bohemund with powers of a papal legate to help him recruit troops from France for his war against the Byzantines.

In 1107 Bohemund crossed over to Albania, secured the port of Avlona, and then moved against Dyrrakhion. He failed to take the city. The Byzantine fleet cut off his communications with southern Italy. His forces could not break out of the Albanian plain because the Byzantines held the passes through the mountains. Even more unsettling was the presence in Alexius's camp of many Norman princes and barons, who were opposed to Bohemund. He knew that he was trapped and he sued for peace. Alexius was able to dictate terms. Peace was made at Devol in September 1108. The treaty was in the form of an imperial chrysobull. Bohemund was to keep Antioch, but only on condition that he remained the emperor's liegeman and also swore allegiance to the emperor's son and heir, John Comnenus. Bohemund had to promise to provide military service whenever the emperor might request it. On paper

Alexius seemed to have all he wished. The ruler of Antioch recognized that he was a vassal of the Empire. The threat to the European provinces of the Empire from the Normans of southern Italy was for the time being at an end. Bohemund had, however, gained one important objective. To meet his invasion Alexius had recalled his best troops from Cilicia and northern Syria, thus relieving the pressure that had been building up on Antioch. Tancred had been able to recover the Byzantine strongholds. There was no compelling reason why he should honour his uncle's undertakings to the Byzantine emperor. The outcome was that Alexius had established a claim to suzerainty over Antioch, but not effective authority there. Alexius looked to the Seljuqs for help. In 1111 he sent an embassy to the Seljuq sultan at Baghdad proposing an alliance against the crusaders. It came to nothing but it confirmed all the worst suspicions stirred up by Bohemund's propaganda against the Byzantines.

Alexius's entanglement with Antioch cost the Empire dear. The outcome constituted perhaps the worst set-back of his reign. It disrupted his understanding with the crusaders, on which his eastern strategy was based. It diverted Byzantine troops to Cilicia and northern Syria, when they could have been used to reinforce Alexius's efforts to wrest Anatolia from the Turks. In the wake of the passage of the first crusade his commanders succeeded in recovering the western coastlands of Asia Minor from the Turks, but the Byzantine hold remained precarious because Alexius's forces were not able to establish themselves on the Anatolian plateau in strength. Alexius's preoccupation with Antioch allowed the Turks to consolidate their position in Anatolia. In 1116 Alexius made one last attempt to reassert Byzantine authority in the interior of Anatolia. He occupied the plain of Dorylaion and pushed on southwards to Polybotos in the hope of occupying Ikonion, which was fast becoming the main centre of Seljuq power in Anatolia. At the approach of the Byzantine armies Shahanshah, the Seljuq ruler, came out with his emirs to meet the Byzantine emperor. Some agreement was reached. The Seljuq ruler became a federate of the Byzantine emperor while Alexius agreed to evacuate the Greek population of central Asia Minor. His solution was to recognize the authority of the Seljuqs in the hope that this would guarantee the safety of the western coastlands of Asia Minor. The murder of Shahanshah a little more than a year later by a stepbrother only underlined the fallibility of this solution. As with the rulers of Antioch, so with the Seljuqs of Anatolia he was left with a claim to suzerainty, which he handed on to his heirs. It would turn out to be a dubious legacy.

In terms of territory recovered Alexius gained much less than he hoped from the first crusade, no more than the western coastlands of Asia Minor, which he could have reasonably expected to reconquer without crusader help. The hopes he had of the crusade turned to ashes. It should have been his masterstroke. He handled its passage with such finesse. The way appeared open to the restoration of Byzantine power in the East.

The crusaders made a deep impression upon the Byzantines. They seemed to epitomize the martial virtues that christianity required. Anna Comnena catches this in an apocryphal story she included in her history about the count of Flanders. Just before the crucial battle for Antioch on 28 June 1098 he begged to be allowed to go out against the infidel with only three companions. He implored God for help. Then with the shout of 'God with us' he and his companions charged and shattered the opposing forces. Anna felt that 'a divine power was manifestly aiding the Christians'.[5] To her father the crusader knights 'in the prime of their life, at the height of their strength, of noble lineage, seemed to rival the heroes of old'.[6] These are the echoes of the optimism that reigned at the Byzantine court at the time of the first crusade. It would soon be turned into a much more sombre assessment of the crusaders and their intentions. This is best approached through the pages of the *Alexiad*. Anna Comnena was putting the finishing touches to her history in 1148, half a century after the passage of the first crusade, when news was coming of the approach of another crusade. This is unlikely to have coloured her account of the first crusade. What did were her father's later difficulties with Bohemund. These convinced her that the crusade was a conspiracy against Byzantium led by unscrupulous Franks, who remained what they had always been: covetous, vainglorious, and inconstant. The crusade brought these qualities into clearer focus and gave westerners a more precise identity in Byzantine eyes. They were Latins distinguished not only by their barbarous natures, but also by their allegiance to the papacy. At first, the Byzantines seem to have found it difficult to see a clear connection between the crusade and the papacy. Anna Comnena did not present the first crusade as papally inspired. For her the initiator of the enterprise was Peter the Hermit. This almost defies explanation, since she is likely to have known of her father's negotiations with the papacy, which led up to Urban II's call for a crusade. She even records that Hugh of Vermandois, the French king's brother, had received the banner of St Peter at Rome to take with him on crusade. Perhaps she was trying to protect her father's reputation, but it is more likely that first impressions of the crusade would have minimized the role of the papacy and emphasized the part played by Peter the Hermit; the element of pilgrimage being most in evidence.

The part played by the papacy began to dawn upon Anna Comnena at the time of Bohemund's invasion of the Byzantine Empire. Its justification rested upon two things: papal approval and the idea of the just war. Pope Paschal II's willingness to back Bohemund confirmed Anna's suspicions of the papacy. Earlier in her history she indicts Pope Gregory VII for making war on the German Emperor Henry IV. This she took to be proof of the way the western church was being perverted. This could hardly be more graphically demonstrated than in the conduct of western priests: 'He will communicate the Body and the Blood of the Deity and meanwhile gaze on bloodshed and become himself "a man of Blood" (as David says in the Psalm). Thus the race is no less devoted to religion than to war.'[7] Such was Anna Comnena's opinion. It helped to justify her more or less unprecedented claim that the church of Constantinople not only enjoyed a primacy of honour within the Christian church, but also exercised jurisdiction over 'all dioceses throughout the Oikoumene'.[8] There was the hint that the papacy would use the crusade against Byzantium to assert its own unjustified claims to primacy. Here were the germs of an interpretation of the role of the papacy which would harden in the later twelfth century and apparently receive confirmation in the events of the fourth crusade.

In the early twelfth century these suspicions were only just beginning to be formulated. Byzantine propagandists were still not sure as to the exact nature of the claims being made for papal authority. Alexius himself wished to play down the differences between the two churches because he still hoped to come to terms with Western christendom in the wake of his victory over Bohemund. He even tentatively put himself forward as a possible protector of Pope Paschal II, who had fallen into the hands of the German Emperor Henry V. In 1112 he wrote to the citizens of Rome, sympathizing with the plight of the pope and suggesting that with their consent he might receive the imperial crown from the papacy. He was soon negotiating with Paschal II over a reunion of the churches. Even Alexius's propagandists found it difficult to accept the precondition put forward by the pope for the settlement of differences between the two churches: that 'from the outset the members must adhere to the head'.[9] In other words, the union of the churches necessitated the recognition of papal primacy by the Byzantines. This demand puzzled the Byzantine propagandists. Did it mean that the papacy was claiming 'the good coinage'[10] of imperial authority? In that case there was no possibility of any understanding between the two churches. The papal claim that Constantinople should recognize the authority of Rome, the mother church, was equally absurd, because Constantinople represented a new dispensation. The gulf separating Byzantium and the papacy became clearer slowly and painfully. It would increasingly revolve around the question of papal primacy. It was also becoming harder to tolerate differences of practice, as more and more westerners penetrated Byzantine territory. A Byzantine theologian happened to be staying in Rhodes in 1099, when Pisans and Venetians coming to the help of the crusaders wintered on the island. He was horrified at the way the simpler spirits began to adopt western practices in the matter of the azymes.

The presence of Italians reminds us how many strands there were to the crusade. Each had to be re-evaluated. Before the crusades the West scarcely impinged upon Byzantium. The papacy had occasionally to be taken into consideration; there were Italian merchants in the ports of the

Empire and Frankish mercenaries serving in Byzantine armies, but they could all be considered separately and dismissed as of relatively little importance. The crusade created an awareness in Byzantium of the West as a distinct entity, which was a threat at many different levels.

There must always have been large numbers of Italians at Constantinople. They came in the main from the cities of southern Italy, such as Bari and Amalfi. The merchants of the northern Italian cities of Pisa and Genoa are unlikely to have been found in the ports of the Byzantine Empire much before the crusades, simply because it was only in the middle of the eleventh century that those two cities acquired any role in the trade of the Mediterranean and then it was more or less limited to the western Mediterranean. Venice was a different matter. It had already been granted trading privileges by Basil II in 992, which meant a reduction in the tolls payable on each Venetian ship as it entered the Hellespont at Abydos. This no doubt gave some limited encouragement to Venetian enterprise, but the Venetian commercial documents of the time do not seem to show that before Alexius came to power the Venetians had acquired any dominant role in the commerce of the Byzantine Empire. The foundation of their commercial ascendancy was the chrysobull that Alexius granted to the Venetians in May 1082. By it they were totally exempted from the payment of customs duties and other harbour tolls. They were allowed free access to nearly all the ports of the Empire, only the Black Sea, Crete, and Cyprus being placed out of bounds. In Constantinople they were granted quays along the Golden Horn and other property there, which would form the nucleus of a 'factory'. The doge received the title of *protosebastos* and with it honorific membership of the imperial family, while the Venetian patriarch of Grado was given the ecclesiastical dignity of *hypertimos*. Alexius was in this way clearly trying to bind Venice more closely to the Empire. By the terms of the treaty Venetians also had to promise that they would be loyal subjects of the emperor. Some modern historians have bitterly criticized Alexius for the concessions he made to the Venetians, on the grounds that he was surrendering control over the Byzantine economy to the Venetians and thus paving the way for the decline of the Empire. Other historians have suggested almost the reverse. Alexius made these concessions in order to renew the economic foundations of the Empire. The guild system of Constantinople with its restrictive practices would, it is argued, be swept away, because the guildsmen would not be able to compete with the Venetians. This would mean that a regulated economy would give way to a market economy, leading to the possibilities of economic growth.

Both these points of view have something to recommend them, in the sense that Alexius's concessions to the Venetians touched off long-term changes for good and ill, but it is scarcely probable that Alexius would have pondered such distant possibilities. He was in desperate need of an ally in his war against the Normans. He had lost one army the previous autumn; Dyrrakhion had just surrendered to the Normans; there was every chance that the Normans would be able to break through to Thessalonica. Alexius was therefore willing to promise almost anything to the Venetians, who were in a position to harry the Normans and cut their lines of communication. The Venetians provided Alexius with quite invaluable aid, proving at least in the short term the wisdom of his policy.

In the years leading up to the first crusade the Venetians began to capitalize on their privileged position in the trade of the Empire. They made Corinth into a centre of operations, but the money they had at their disposal was limited – a share in a ship's anchor still represented considerable capital. Trade was very largely in the hands of a few noble families, who did have the liquid wealth to invest in Byzantine goods. Their stake in the Byzantine Empire was not of such importance that the Venetians were willing to forgo the opportunities offered by the crusade. By the summer of 1100 a Venetian fleet was operating off Jaffa and negotiations were in progress over the grant of trading privileges in the fledgling kingdom of Jerusalem. The Genoese and the Pisans were there before them. The Genoese insisted that their privileges should be inscribed in gold in the church of the Holy Sepulchre at Jerusalem.

The Venetians may have been disturbed at the way the crusade had dragged these potential competitors eastwards in its wake. The Byzantines certainly were. The Pisan fleet going to the help of the crusaders in 1099 was severely mauled by the Byzantines and prisoners taken were slaughtered. This treatment contrasted with the relatively warm welcome that the crusaders had received in Constantinople some two years earlier. It reflects how Antioch had embittered relations between Byzantium and the West. Thenceforward the cities of Pisa and Genoa were to be a force in the Aegean and eastern Mediterranean; and Alexius tried to come to terms with them. Faced with the threat of invasion from Bohemund Alexius wrote to Pisa and Genoa, along with Venice, trying to keep them out of the Norman camp. This did not prevent a great fleet composed of Genoese, Pisan, and southern Italian ships setting out against the Byzantine Empire in 1111. It was probably done at the instigation of Tancred, by now ruler of Antioch. There was probably another motive behind this expedition: a desire to break into the potentially lucrative trade of the Byzantine Empire. It failed to force a passage through the Hellespont. Negotiations began and in October 1111 Alexius reached an agreement with the Pisans. The Pisans agreed in future to respect the frontiers of the Byzantine Empire and to avoid any alliance with enemies of the Empire. In return they were to have free access to Byzantine markets, paying only 4 per cent customs duty instead of the usual 10 per cent. They received their own quarter in Constantinople and, as a mark of special honour, seats were reserved for them in the Hippodrome and in St Sophia. They were thus gathered into the embrace of Byzantine ceremonial. The Pisans were to remain among the Empire's most loyal allies. Yet another potential threat to the Empire was neutralized. Alexius may at the same time have entered into negotiations with the Genoese, but there is no record of any treaty having been concluded. The Genoese were perhaps unwilling to compromise their position in the Holy Land by coming to an understanding with the Byzantine emperor.

As a result of Alexius's perseverance Byzantine prestige and power were restored. Byzantium was once again the dominant power in the Near East and the Balkans, but there is no disguising that the foundations of this power were very different from those of the Empire of Basil II. Alexius may have hoped to restore clearly defined frontiers and frontier regions of the sort that had characterized the Byzantine Empire under Basil II. Outside a relatively restricted circle of lands around the Aegean Alexius's authority was personal in character. The crusader leaders were his lieges; the Seljuq emirs his federates; the Venetians his servants. This gave him some claim to moral authority, but it was no substitute for the strong administrative system which had held together the Byzantine Empire under Basil II. Even in those areas where a regular provincial administration existed, it was increasingly permeated by private interests. At home and abroad imperial authority rested on much flimsier foundations. If Alexius had restored the appearance of power, rather than the substance, his work gave his heirs hope that a full restoration of Byzantine authority was still possible. His solutions may have compromised the old Byzantine concept of imperial sovereignty, but there were benefits to be gained. They suited conditions in a world which was changing rapidly. The circumstances of Alexius's reign strained that marvellous ability to adapt which Byzantium displayed throughout its long history. The crusade created an entirely new set of conditions within which Byzantium had to work. It focused western Europe's expanding energies on Byzantium and created a dilemma which its emperors never properly resolved, how to harness the energies and resources of a power which was potentially hostile. The regeneration of Byzantium required western cooperation. The result was the interpenetration of Byzantium and the West in a way which had never happened before. Byzantium's frontiers became increasingly permeable as westerners established themselves in various capacities on Byzantine soil, while Byzantine influence spread outwards into the western lands and the crusader states. The opportunities seemed limitless. History may judge that it was all a mirage, but at the time Alexius seemed to have opened up a new chapter of Byzantine ascendancy.

NOTES

1. *Alexiad* (transl. by E R A Sewter), p. 206
2. E Joranson, 'The Problem of the Spurious Letter of Emperor Alexius to the Count of Flanders', *American Historial Review,* 55 (1949–50), p. 815
3. *Alexiad* (transl. by E R A Sewter), p. 309
4. *Ibid.,* p. 319
5. *Ibid.,* pp. 351–2
6. *Ibid.,* p. 353
7. *Ibid.,* p. 317, n. 37
8. *Ibid.,* p. 63
9. P Jaffé, *Regesta Pontificum Romanorum,* i (Leipzig, 1885), p. 748
10. J Darrouzès, 'Les documents byzantins du XIIe siècle sur la primauté romaine', *Revue des Etudes Byzantines,* 23 (1965), p. 58

Chapter 9

JOHN II COMNENUS (1118–1143)

Alexius could exclaim with pride to his son John, 'What daring knight is there, out of some western land, overconfident in his prowess and oversure of his great strength, what tribe is there, surrounding us in its tens of thousands, which has not yielded to me, has not cowered before me, and has not shrunk from my presence, defeated and utterly undone?'[1] He was aware though of the dangers that he was bequeathing to his son. He urged him to 'use all his ingenuity to turn aside the commotion coming from the West, lest time and necessity conspire to test and humiliate the high majesty of the New Rome and the prestige of the imperial throne'.[2] This advice comes from the political testament that Alexius composed during his last illness for his beloved son John – 'a father's prayers brought to perfect fruition'.[3]

Once again all Alexius's steadfastness was needed, if he was to ensure his son's succession. His health had been bad, ever since his return from his last campaign against the Turks in 1116. The doctors tried to cure him with a regime of purgatives. Now they advised the desperate remedy of cauterizing his stomach. All the while his Empress Eirene Doukaina and his daughter Anna were nagging him to alter the succession in favour of Anna's husband, the Caesar Nicephorus Bryennios. In the last years of Alexius's reign his empress became an increasingly powerful figure. The emperor was 'inhibited by her formidable presence, for she possessed a sharp tongue and was quick to reprimand the slightest insolence'.[4] She used her ascendancy over her husband to oppose the succession of their son John. Her motives are difficult to fathom. Perhaps she still clung to a belief that the imperial dignity properly belonged to her family, the Doukas, and considered that her daughter Anna had a better claim to the throne than her son. That was certainly how Anna felt.

Alexius's apparent lack of grasp in his last years is revealed by his handling of the trial of Eustratios, bishop of Nicaea, who was accused of heresy. The bishop was a pupil of John Italos. He escaped condemnation in 1082 and later came back into favour at the imperial court. During Eirene's ascendancy he became the emperor's chief religious adviser. He was a spokesman in debates with the Latins in 1112 and later with the Paulicians and the Armenians. He composed two tracts against the Armenians and committed himself to views that brought down upon him the charge of heresy. His opponents extracted twenty-four propositions that they considered heretical. He was supposed to have advanced the unlikely view that 'Christ reasoned in the manner of Aristotle'.[5] His opponents singled this out to bring home the fact that Eustratios was using philosophical methods in the same way as his master John Italos. They charged that 'he believed that he would be able to escape condemnation, as he had formerly avoided condemnation with John Italos'.[6] Like his master, Eustratios was opening up some of the great questions of dogma, which had apparently been settled once and for all by the fathers of the church; for instance, the relationship of the human and the divine in Christ. He advanced the proposition that 'the humanity of our Saviour Christ adores the inaccessible Godhead, not only on earth, but also in heaven'.[7] This left him open to the charge that he was devaluing Christ's humanity. From a theological point of view the interest of Eustratios's trial lies in the way it showed that the problems and approaches pioneered by John Italos continued to have their fascination for Byzantine theologians. If Eustratios was condemned for heresy and driven from his see, the questions he raised would come up again under Manuel I Comnenus (1143–80) and be the cause of bitter controversy.

From a political point of view the affair underlined Alexius's apparent loss of touch. In much the same way as Michael VII Doukas persuaded John Italos to submit a profession of faith to the patriarch of the day, Alexius got Eustratios to submit his errors to the synod, to abjure them, and to plead that his tracts against the Armenians, which contained them, had been circulated without his knowledge. When the synod met on 26 April 1117, the patriarch counselled acceptance of Eustratios's plea. The vote went against the patriarch and Eustratios would be condemned as a heretic to lose his see. The emperor and the patriarch only made a feeble effort to sway opinion in the synod in favour of Eustratios. The emperor did little more than canvass the vote of the bishop of Corinth while the patriarch obtained undertakings from the bishops of Sardis and Naupaktos that they would support his proposal. Earlier in his reign the emperor would have been more forceful.

Eustratios's trial was perhaps the most important event of the closing years of Alexius's reign. Yet Anna Comnena makes no mention of it. She refers coyly to Eustratios as 'more confident in his powers of rhetoric than philosophers of the Stoa and Academy',[8] but conceals how close their ties were. She was his patron and he dedicated his commentaries on the *Nicomachean Ethics* of Aristotle to her. Rather than being a set-back for Alexius Comnenus the condemnation of

Eustratios is more likely to have been a defeat for the Empress Eirene and her daughter Anna in their struggle with John Comnenus.

John Comnenus outmanœuvred his mother and sister. As soon as he saw that his father would not live out the night, he stole in and took the signet ring from his finger and, using this as proof of his father's wishes, assembled his supporters. They seized the Great Palace of the Emperors and the gates of the city. By the time the emperor died on 15 August 1118 John Comnenus was firmly in control. Anna Comnena refused to accept this rebuff to her imperial ambitions and almost immediately began to plot the overthrow of her brother. She was to fail because, to her intense disgust, her husband refused at the last moment to commit himself to the plot. The conspirators were rounded up. They were treated leniently. Anna Comnena was first deprived of her property, but this was soon restored to her, but she was kept in semi-confinement with her mother in the nunnery of Our Lady of Grace. Her husband continued to serve the new emperor faithfully down to his death in 1139.

In his bid for the throne John Comnenus relied heavily on the support of his brother Isaac, but the brothers were soon to become estranged. In 1130 Isaac had to flee the land. He sought refuge in various eastern courts, where he hoped to find support for his ambition to seize the throne of Constantinople. These family quarrels would become a constant feature of life at the Comnenian court. They first come out into the open during Alexius's last illness. They seem to have been sparked off by the sibling rivalry of John and Anna, which went back to the cradle. To this may have been added the Empress Eirene's resentment at the eclipse of the Doukas family. But it went deeper than this. Alexius's political testament presents a rather traditional view of imperial authority as the fount of justice and piety, while for practical purposes his rule was built on the support of his family. There was a conflict of interests. In theory, imperial authority was to foster the public good; in practice, the Empire was run for the benefit of the imperial family. It was a dilemma that John was left to solve. He was unwilling to tolerate any great degree of family interference in the running of the Empire. He turned for support to his father's personal servants, men, such as Eustathios Kamytzes, Michaelitzes Styppeiotes, and George Dekanos, who had been forced into the background during Eirene's ascendancy.

His most trusted servant was John Axoukh. He was of Turkish origin. He was captured as a child and given to the Emperor Alexius who decided that he would make an ideal companion for his son. John Comnenus raised him to the rank of Grand Domestic or commander-in-chief of the Byzantine armies. Such was his power that members of the imperial family were expected to dismount and make obeisance to him, when they met him. This was symptomatic of the new emperor's attitude towards the members of the imperial dynasty. Axoukh was aware of the resentment that his promotion produced among the imperial family. It is possible that Anna Comnena's conspiracy was directed as much against his ascendancy as against her brother. After its detection, John Comnenus wished to hand over her property to his favourite, but Axoukh shrewdly declined the offer, indicating that this would make him still more unpopular and would hurt the emperor's reputation, for it would seem that he had no respect for family ties. This was no doubt the impression that he had been giving.

Thanks to John Axoukh the new emperor dealt with the first difficulties of his reign admirably. He succeeded in asserting his dominance over the imperial dynasty, without alienating them completely. Even allowing for his later estrangement from his brother Isaac Comnenus he retained a remarkable ascendancy over the court and capital, which allowed him to concentrate on foreign policy almost to the exclusion of anything else. At first sight, his one real task was to pick up the pieces of his father's Anatolian strategy. With the evacuation of much of the Greek population in 1116 the conquest of Anatolia seemed to have been shelved. The Byzantines were again on the defensive. As a result, Turkish pressure on the coastlands of western Asia Minor began to build up and some important places such as Laodicea in the upper Maiander valley were lost and the Turks threatened to occupy the whole Maiander valley. Campaigns in 1119 and 1120 did something to restore the situation in this area. Sozopolis which commanded the route leading from the Maiander valley up on to the Anatolian plateau was recovered and once again the Byzantines had secured the initiative against the Turks, but nothing could be done immediately to exploit this success, because the European frontiers which had seemed secure suddenly gave way and John Comnenus found himself struggling to retain his father's gains in the Balkans.

In 1122 the nomads of the Russian steppes broke through the Danube defences. They are described as Petcheneks, but the majority are likely to have been Cumans. John Comnenus lulled them into a sense of false security by giving their chiefs presents, distributing largesse, and entering into treaties. He then made a surprise attack on their main laager, which was near Beroia, the modern Stara Zagora, just to the south of the Balkan range. It was a closely fought battle, but due to the bravery of the Varangians who hewed a way through the circle of wagons the Byzantines were finally victorious. The survivors were settled and enrolled in the Byzantine army. This victory was followed by a punitive raid against the Serbs, who were always restless. Many were rounded up and shipped across to Nicomedia in north-western Asia Minor, where they were settled as military colonists, to strengthen the Byzantine defences against the Turks. This raid against the Serbs brought the Byzantines into direct contact with the Hungarians, who were competitors for influence in the north-western Balkans. Ever since the marriage of John Comnenus to a Hungarian princess ties between the Byzantine and Hungarian courts had been reasonably close. Byzantine control along the middle reaches of the Danube rested on an understanding with Hungary. This was undermined by the Byzantine practice of giving refuge to various dissident Hungarian princes and nobles, who were settled in Macedonia. For the Byzantines it seemed to be a convenient form of blackmail. In 1128 the Hungarians attacked the Byzantine outpost on the Danube, Branitshevo, where there had been clashes between Hungarian merchants and the local inhabitants. The Hungarian forces swarmed through the Balkans down the Great Military Road, penetrating to the outskirts of Philippopolis. John Comnenus had to fight two hard campaigns to restore the frontier with Hungary. The Serbs took the opportunity to recover their independence, but, all in all, John Comnenus had succeeded in preserving Byzantine influence in the Balkans and in holding on to the Danube frontier.

He had been less successful in his dealings with the Venetians. At the beginning of his reign, when his attention was focused on the problems of Anatolia, he had refused to ratify the privileges granted by his father to the Venetians. His reasons for doing so have nothing to do with economic considerations. Byzantine foreign policy was motivated by reasons of state, a mixture of ideology and legal rights. The privileges of the Venetians placed them outside the direct control of the Byzantine authorities. This made them supercilious in their dealings with the native people. It led in the end to an incident where one of the great officers of state, a member of the imperial family, was abused by the Venetians. This was a challenge to imperial authority. It had to be rebuffed. It showed that the Venetians were failing to honour their undertaking to be loyal servants of the Empire. Now that Sicily no longer seemed to be any sort of menace to the Byzantine Empire, the services of the Venetian fleet ceased to be so important. The Venetians, for their part, found themselves preoccupied with the crusader states. In 1119 there had been an appeal for help from Baldwin II, king of Jerusalem, following the defeat and death of Roger, prince of Antioch, at the battle of the Field of Blood. Baldwin II was anxious to round off the conquest of the Holy Land by the capture of Tyre, but this could only be done with the help of Italian sea power. Venice was able to extract a great deal in return for its aid in the undertaking. When Tyre surrendered on 7 July 1124, the Venetians took possession of a third of the city. The Venetians thus obtained a solid foothold in the crusader states. That accomplished, they could return to their difficulties in the Byzantine Empire. On the way home the Venetian fleet stopped at Rhodes and ravaged it. The Venetians then made the island of Chios their base and terrorized the coastlands and islands of the Aegean. In March 1125 the Venetians sailed away making for home, but they were back the next year, attacking the island of Cephalonia. All the Byzantines could do was to burn the Venetian quarter in Constantinople. John Comnenus decided that he must come to terms and in August 1126 he ratified the Venetian privileges. The war with the

Venetians interfered with his plans for the reconquest of Anatolia. The only way he could hope to defeat the Venetians was by diverting money to the construction of new fleets, but this would have detracted from the military capability of the Empire. Byzantium could not fight both a land war and a sea war. It was much more convenient to allow Venice its privileged position, even if this did seem to infringe Byzantine sovereignty, and in return receive naval assistance. It would allow Byzantium the free hand it needed for the conquest of Anatolia.

Western preoccupations therefore meant that John Comnenus was not in a position to devote his full energies to the reconquest of Anatolia until 1130. Like his father, he had two goals: to recover Antioch and restore the Euphrates frontier and to re-establish some measure of Byzantine control over the interior of Anatolia. This was divided between the Seljuqs who ruled the southern part of the central plateau from Ikonion, or Konya, and the Danishmends who controlled the northern half. In 1130 the Danishmends were in the ascendancy. In 1124 they seized Melitene and looked poised to extend their authority southwards into the Euphrates lands. In pursuit of this goal they defeated and killed the prince of Antioch, Bohemund II. They also extended their power northwards to the shores of the Black Sea. In recognition of their successes the caliph of Baghdad was in the process of granting the title of Malik or king to their chief Gümüshtegin. This was a direct challenge to the rights of overlordship claimed by the Byzantine emperor over the lands of Anatolia. Add to this the fact that John's brother Isaac sought refuge at the Danishmend court and it is clear that this dynasty was seen as a formidable threat to Byzantine pretensions.

The key to any advance against the Danishmends was the castle of Kastamonu, the ancestral home of the Comneni. Progress was slow because this was a region of heavy Turkish settlement. It only fell to the armies of John Comnenus in 1132 at the end of a third campaign. This victory was celebrated by a triumphal procession through the streets of Constantinople. The celebrations were premature, because at almost the same time the Danishmends succeeded in recovering the fortress. John Comnenus persevered. In 1135 he failed in a bid to capture Gangra, some 50 miles to the south of Kastamonu, but the next year both places were reduced by the Byzantine armies thanks to the efficiency of the Byzantine artillery. Gangra soon returned to the Turks; it was too exposed for the Byzantines to defend it effectively. The returns for six years hard campaigning were meagre. It meant that the emperor had neither the time nor energy to look to his interests in other parts of Asia Minor.

The towns and strongholds that the Byzantines held in Cilicia had fallen piecemeal to the Latins of Antioch and various Armenian princes. The most powerful of these was Leo from the Roupenid family. About the year 1136 he besieged Seleucia, the Byzantine strongpoint which commanded the coast road into Cilicia from southern Anatolia. John II

Comnenus decided that he had gained what he could for the time being in the north of the peninsula and that the time was ripe to make good the claims he had on the Armenians of Cilicia and the Latins of Antioch. The treaty of Devol (1108) made it abundantly clear that both Antioch and Cilicia came under the overlordship of the emperor of Constantinople. The chief places of Cilicia were recovered with surprising ease. John Comnenus then advanced on Antioch which was the most important goal of his expedition. In 1137 the prince of Antioch was Raymond of Poitiers. He held the principality in the right of his wife, the daughter of Bohemund II. The marriage had only been celebrated in the previous year and Raymond was still not securely in control of Antioch. When John Comnenus appeared before the gates of Antioch in 1137 the crusader princes were in no position to put up serious resistance. They were hard pressed by Zengi, the atabeg of Mosul, who had just killed Pons, the count of Tripoli, and had defeated Fulk of Anjou, the king of Jerusalem. Raymond went to the Byzantine camp and there did homage to the Byzantine emperor for Antioch. He agreed to ally with his suzerain against the Muslims and, should they capture Aleppo and the surrounding region, to hand over Antioch to the emperor in return for Aleppo. John Comnenus was also given the right to enter Antioch, a right which for the moment he declined to exercise. This done the Byzantine emperor departed with his armies for winter quarters in Cilicia.

In the spring of 1138 the Byzantines joined up with the Latin forces. The Byzantine army with its fearsome siege train mightily impressed the Muslims of Syria, but apart from taking one or two small fortresses achieved precious little. The defences of Aleppo, the main prize, were reconnoitred and it was decided that they were too strong. The allied forces moved on to Shaizar on the Orontes. Its conquest would have opened up the way to Hama, which lay a few miles downstream. The siege was pressed with great vigour and the lower town was taken, but the citadel continued to hold out. With news coming that Zengi was gathering his forces, John Comnenus decided that he was in too exposed a position to prosecute the siege any further. The ruler of Shaizar offered to pay an indemnity and the allied forces withdrew. It was a demonstration of Byzantine military power that was long remembered, but the concrete results were negligible. John Comnenus returned to Antioch with Raymond of Poitiers and with Joscelin of Courtenay, the count of Edessa. He made his solemn entry into the city of Antioch with these two Latin princes acting as his grooms. He installed himself in the palace and demanded that the citadel should be handed over to him. Joscelin of Courtenay was able to raise up a tumult in the streets of the city. John Comnenus found himself besieged in the palace. He agreed to leave the city and diplomatically accepted Raymond of Poitiers and Joscelin of Courtenay's protestations that they had nothing to do with the uprising. They claimed it was entirely spontaneous. John Comnenus had been away for two campaigning seasons. His army was beginning to get restive. It was time for him to be going home. He despatched a detachment of his army on punitive raids against the Seljuqs of Rum, who had been harassing his lines of communication. As he was passing through Seljuq territory, his brother Isaac came to meet him and threw himself on the emperor's mercy and they were reconciled.

The emperor had been away for more than two years. In that time Turkish pressure on the Sangarios frontier had reached such a pitch that the mountainous region around Mount Olympus was in danger of being lost. John Comnenus refortified two of the key points in this area, Lopadion and Akhyraous, while he waited for the stragglers from his Syrian campaigns to catch up with him. Having secured the Sangarios frontier, his energies were turned towards the recovery of north-eastern Anatolia. There was still the problem of the Danishmends, while Trebizond and the Pontus had been more or less independent for some fourteen years under Constantine Gabras. A display of force was enough to overawe Gabras. This was followed by the siege of Neokaisareia or Niksar, a Danishmend strongpoint, controlling the routes from the Black Sea coast into the interior. The expedition took place in the autumn of 1140. The weather was very bad and the Byzantine army soon found itself without horses or provisions. The emperor was forced to raise the siege and make his way back to Constantinople, which he reached in the middle of January 1141.

The rest of the year was spent with his army at his training camp on the river Rhyndakos (Orhaneli), beneath the slopes of Bithynian Olympus. His army needed a rest before embarking on the next undertaking, which was the conquest of Cilicia and Antioch. This would require at least two campaigns. He first secured his lines of communication from the Maiander valley to his base at Attaleia. Then he moved with a speed that took the Latins by surprise into northern Syria. He forced Joscelin of Courtenay, the count of Edessa, to give hostages for his good behaviour. He then advanced on Antioch and demanded that the prince, Raymond of Poitiers, should surrender the city and the citadel. Raymond played for time by calling a general assembly. He placed before them the ultimatum of the Byzantine emperor. They rejected the Byzantine demand. It was late in the year and John Comnenus decided that he could wait. He retreated to winter quarters in Cilicia.

There in the spring of 1143 he met with a hunting accident. He apparently grazed his thumb on a poisoned arrow. He paid little attention to the wound, but before long the poison had spread through his body and he was beyond the help of his doctors. There is absolutely nothing in the sources to suggest that it was anything but an accident. It was, however, extremely convenient for the Latins of the crusader states, who would have found it difficult to resist further pressure from John Comnenus. It also turned out to be of advantage to the emperor's youngest son Manuel. He was with his father on campaign, while his elder brother Isaac was back in Constantinople. As John Comnenus lay on his death-bed, he decided that his youngest son should succeed to the throne, even though this went against usual practice. He formally invested him with the imperial regalia on Easter Monday 1143. Manuel had already begun to distinguish himself as a soldier and seemed more capable than his elder brother of carrying his grandfather's and father's work through to a successful conclusion.

There would, of course, be no successful conclusion. With the benefit of hindsight it is easy to detect signs of this ultimate failure. There were few solid gains to show for years of hard campaigning: it is not even certain that the Byzantines held on to Kastamonu for any length of time. The local people, even the Greeks who were still left in the interior of Anatolia, were reluctant to accept Byzantine rule. The Greeks living on the islands in Lake Beyshehir had to be reduced by force before they would accept Byzantine rule. They much preferred the overlordship of the Seljuqs of Konya, who left them to their own devices. They regarded the Byzantines as enemies. 'Thus,' in the words of Nicetas Choniates, 'custom strengthened by time is stronger than race or religion.'[9] This might have been true of the Greeks of Anatolia, but not of the Turks. They were conscious that Byzantium represented an alien people, religion, and culture and, though always quarrelling among themselves, would unite in the face of Byzantine aggression. The same is equally true of the Latins.

The Byzantine reading of the situation would have been quite different. At the time of John Comnenus's death the twin goals of Byzantine foreign policy, the restoration of the Euphrates frontier and the recovery of control over central Anatolia seemed within grasp. The Turks had been overawed; the route to Attaleia on the south coast of Asia Minor, the key to communications by land and sea to Cilicia and Syria, was safely in Byzantine hands; and Cilicia and Antioch were at last coming within the Byzantine sphere of influence. There was talk of John Comnenus turning Cilicia and Antioch together with Attaleia and the island of Cyprus into an apanage for his youngest son, Manuel. It had the merits of being an attractive solution, which might appeal to the Latins of Antioch, who clearly opposed direct Byzantine rule. John Comnenus was at pains to conciliate the Latins of the crusader states. He wrote in the last months of his life to Fulk of Anjou, king of Jerusalem, proposing that he should come to the Holy Land to help drive out the infidels and to visit the Holy Places. Fulk wrote back in guarded terms, welcoming a pilgrimage, but not a military expedition. John Comnenus seems to have been trying to present himself, how sincerely it is impossible to tell, as sharing the ideals of the crusaders. In the death-bed speech which Nicetas Choniates put into his mouth, he talked of his desire to visit Palestine 'to ascend the mountain of the Lord, as the Psalmist puts it, and to stand in His holy place; justified by the law of war to drive away the encircling enemy, who have often seized the Sepulchre of our Lord, just as in former times the gentiles took the ark by force of arms'.[10] As an earnest of his desire to visit the Holy Places he had already had a huge lamp of gold made, which he hoped to present to the church of the Holy Sepulchre. He may even have made some claim to the guardianship of the Holy Sepulchre.

Such a claim was only likely to have deepened the suspicions of the Franks of Outremer, but it was symptomatic of the central place which the West was assuming in Byzantine foreign policy in the last years of John Comnenus's reign. He would have preferred to ignore it, but this became impossible once Roger II of Sicily restored Norman power. By 1130 he had recovered southern Italy and had assumed the title of king, which the Byzantines saw as a direct challenge to their continuing claims over Sicily and southern Italy. To neutralize the potential danger of a Norman invasion of Albania, John Comnenus turned to the German emperors, who also saw the Normans as competitors. The German emperor Lothair had Byzantine backing for his expedition of 1136 which reached as far south as Bari. Lothair was succeeded in 1138 by Conrad III. A Byzantine embassy was despatched in 1140 to treat about a marriage between the Emperor John's youngest son Manuel and a German princess as a way of cementing the alliance of the two Empires. The bride chosen for Manuel was Bertha of Sulzbach, a sister-in-law of the German emperor. She arrived in Constantinople in the summer of 1142. The German alliance marked a decisive shift in Byzantine foreign policy. It was left to the new emperor, Manuel Comnenus, to deal with its consequences. It seemed to open up the possibility of intervening in western Europe. Byzantine foreign policy became increasingly grandiose. The key to success in the Balkans and Anatolia appeared to be the exercise of influence in the circle of lands surrounding these regions from France through Russia to the lands of the Caliphate and Egypt. It was a chimera, but for a time Byzantium seemed to be the most powerful force on the international stage.

NOTES

1. P Maas, 'Die Musen des Kaisers Alexios I', *Byzantinische Zeitschrift*, 22 (1913), p. 352
2. *Ibid.*, pp. 357–8
3. *Ibid.*, p. 361
4. John Zonaras, *Epitomae Historiarum Libri XIII–XVIII* III (Bonn, 1897), p. 766
5. P Joannou, 'Eustrate de Nicée. Trois pièces inédites de son procès (1117)', *Revue des Etudes Byzantines*, 10 (1943), p. 34

The Byzantine Empire

6.   J Darrouzès, *Documents inédits d'ecclésiologie byzantine*, (Paris, 1966), p. 304
7.   Joannou, *art. cit.*, p. 32
8.   *Alexiad* (transl. by E R A Sewter), p. 466
9.   Nicetas Choniates (ed. by Van Dieten), p. 37
10.   *Ibid.*, p. 42

Chapter 10

THE FOREIGN POLICY OF MANUEL I COMNENUS (1143–1180)

Manuel Comnenus was left in a difficult position. He was proclaimed emperor in distant Cilicia, while his elder brother Isaac, who had every reason to expect to succeed his father, held the imperial palace at Constantinople. How anomalous Manuel's position was at the beginning of his reign is underlined by a story preserved by the historian Nicetas Choniates. On his way back to Constantinople he stopped at Chonai to pray at its famed church of the Archangel and to receive the blessing of its saintly bishop, who was incidentally the historian's godfather. The clergy of the town were amazed at the emperor's youth and doubted whether he was capable of enduring the burdens of office. They wondered whether he might not have to overthrow his brother Isaac, whom they considered to have a better claim to the throne. Such speculation turned out to be unnecessary. Manuel sent John Axoukh on ahead of him to secure the capital. The faithful Grand Domestic performed the task admirably. He had Isaac Comnenus confined in the monastery of the Pantokrator and snuffed out a plot by the Norman, John Roger, who was married to one of John Comnenus's daughters. The clergy of St Sophia were won over by generous grants of money.

Manuel arrived to find Constantinople his. He appointed a new patriarch, since the patriarchal throne was vacant. The first act of the new patriarch was the coronation of the emperor. It was done with all due solemnity. A contemporary stresses the parallel with the anointing of David: 'If in those days the horn and the chrism and Samuel adorned the head of David, so too with us were none of the old customs neglected, for the horn represents influence and power from above and Samuel the holy patriarch ... while the imperial chrism is none other than the oil of good tidings.'[1] The question of exactly when anointing was introduced into the Byzantine coronation office remains unanswered. This passage suggests that anointing is still to be understood figuratively. The choice of phraseology is nevertheless revealing. The twelfth-century canonist Theodore Balsamon made plain that in the case of usurpation anointing by the patriarch wiped away the stain of the crime.

Coronation set the final seal on Manuel's legitimacy. His position was secure enough for him to allow his brother Isaac and his uncle of the same name out of confinement. He could now turn to the problems of Anatolia. If his father's and grandfather's aims were still not achieved, they seemed to be within grasp. He despatched a joint naval and military force against Cilicia and Antioch, in order to preserve the gains that his father had made. Raymond of Poitiers, the prince of Antioch, attacked the Byzantine army and was heavily defeated. The coastlands of his principality were ravaged by the Byzantine fleet. This set-back for the Franks of Outremer was followed at the end of 1144 by the fall of Edessa to Zengi, the atabeg of Mosul. The principality of Antioch was now fully exposed to Muslim attack. Raymond therefore went to Constantinople as a suppliant. Manuel at first made a show of ignoring him, but then accepted his homage and promised him help. It all seemed to show how heavily the crusader states, and especially Antioch, now relied on Byzantine support. The emperor could therefore concentrate on strengthening his frontier against the Turks. By 1146 he was ready to mount a punitive expedition against Masud, the Seljuq sultan of Konya, now the strongest of the Turkish rulers in Anatolia. The historian Cinnamus has preserved the letters exchanged between the emperor and the sultan. The emperor demanded that the sultan recognize his overlordship; the sultan felt himself strong enough to resist such a demand and challenged the emperor to battle. The Byzantines advanced down the road from Dorylaion, swept aside Turkish resistance at Akrounos, and seized Philomelion, where the sultan had established his headquarters. Manuel was able to release a great many Byzantines who had been captured by the Turks in their razzias into Byzantine territory. Earlier Byzantine expeditions rarely penetrated beyond Philomelion, but borne along by success Manuel pressed on to Konya, which he half-heartedly put under siege. His intention was almost certainly to demonstrate the might of the Byzantine Empire and to force the sultan to come to terms. Manuel had not come prepared for a long siege and therefore decided to withdraw, intending to come back the following year. There was a rumour that the nations to the west, 'rebelling by ancestral custom',[2] were about to invade the Byzantine Empire in full force. It was an intimation that the French were preparing a new crusade to avenge the loss of Edessa. It was essential that he get back to his capital.

He took the quickest, if not the most direct route, back, which led from the headwaters of the Maiander, down the Maiander valley to the coastal route through Asia Minor. The retreat proved to be difficult. The Byzantines were harried all the way by the Turks. Manuel was able to extricate himself and his army largely thanks to the heroism he displayed. He was spurred on by the knowledge that it was apparently a western custom to celebrate one's marriage by feats of bravery on the battlefield. Just before setting out on his campaign against the Turks, Manuel had finally married his German bride, Bertha of Sulzbach, who took the name Eirene. She arrived in Constantinople in 1142. Manuel had therefore displayed a marked reluctance to go through with the marriage. It may partly have been that she was rather too stolid, pious, and obstinate for his taste. It was a matter of jest at the Byzantine court that she had no time for rouge, eye-liner, and other cosmetics. There were other considerations which are likely to have been more important. The marriage should have sealed an alliance between Germany and Byzantium against Roger II of Sicily. The Byzantines were reassessing the danger from this quarter. There seemed little harm in exploring the possibility of a *rapprochement* with the Normans. While talks were going on, there could be no question of proceeding with a German marriage. In the end, nothing came of these negotiations. There is every reason to suspect that the enemies of Roger of Sicily at the Byzantine court, mostly Norman refugees, were able to persuade Manuel against coming to terms with the Norman king. At the end of 1144 a Byzantine diplomat left for the German court. His task was to renew the understanding which had existed with the previous German Emperor Lothair II, and at the same time to obtain better terms over the marriage. Bertha of Sulzbach was not of imperial blood. The Emperor Conrad was outraged at the idea that she might therefore be rejected as a bride for the Byzantine emperor. It would infringe the dignity due to his rank. The Byzantine envoy finally agreed that the marriage would go ahead, but linked with this was a request for 500 knights. Conrad willingly agreed, offering 2,000 or 3,000, if need be. He even expressed his readiness to come with the full strength of his realm to the aid of the Byzantine emperor. This sounded like pure rhetoric, but turned out to be uncomfortably near the truth.

A German bishop returned with the Byzantine envoy to Constantinople to ensure that the Byzantines were as good as their word, which they were not thought to be. The marriage was duly celebrated and Manuel could be satisfied. The German alliance effectively neutralized the threat from Norman Sicily and he could concentrate on the restoration of Byzantine overlordship in Anatolia. He was not to know that just before his marriage Pope Eugenius III had issued his crusading bull and that the first steps were being taken to launch the second crusade. A new crusade was cause for trepidation. There were people connected with the court who could remember the passage of the first crusade; the emperor's aunt, Anna Comnena, for instance. She was just at that moment putting the finishing touches to her history of her father's reign, in which the first crusade was presented as the climax of his achievements. It seemed with the passage of time a daunting challenge which Alexius I had managed to surmount thanks to his skill and forbearance. If the pages of the *Alexiad* are to be trusted, opinion at the Byzantine court was that the true aim of the first crusade was the conquest of Constantinople. It was natural to assume that the second crusade would have the same goal.

THE SECOND CRUSADE

Manuel Comnenus let himself be guided by the example of his grandfather. In August 1146 he wrote to Pope Eugenius III thanking him for news of the proposed crusade. He promised to support the crusaders, as long as they showed him the same honour that the soldiers of the first crusade had given to Alexius I Comnenus. He proposed that the crusaders should hand over to him any conquests they might make of territories formerly belonging to the Byzantine Empire. At the same time he replied to the French king, Louis VII, whose court was the centre of preparations for the new crusade. He professed to be delighted that the king was about to set out against the infidels and promised to provide him with the necessary supplies, asking in return that the old pacts that existed in his grandfather's time were renewed. He must have meant by this that the leaders of the crusade should take an oath of homage to him.

The great fear must have been that the French king would cooperate with Roger II of Sicily, who would be able to manipulate the crusade for his own ends, like another Bohemund. Louis VII indeed wrote to Roger asking for his aid, and Roger had written back in the most enthusiastic way promising not only help with provisions and transport, but also that either he or his son would take the cross. A meeting was held at Etampes in February 1147; the French king turned down Roger's offer and accepted instead that the army should travel through Byzantine territory along the route followed by the bulk of the first crusade, the route, it was fondly believed, trodden by Charlemagne on his legendary journey to Jerusalem. It may have been respect for tradition that decided the French king to go through the Byzantine Empire. It may also have been that in the meantime the German Emperor Conrad and many of his magnates had also taken the cross and were preparing to march through the Byzantine Empire.

A German emperor taking the cross was not something the Byzantines had anticipated. The first crusade had been a Frankish undertaking and the crusader states were French in speech and Frankish in character. Conrad was immediately suspected of using the crusade as a cover for his imperial claims. In the letter which Conrad had sent to Manuel over the question of his marriage to Bertha of Sulzbach, he had entitled himself August Emperor of the Romans, while addressing Manuel slightingly as illustrious and famous king of the Greeks. It was clear that he vaunted his claim to the imperial title, while dismissing that of the Byzantine emperor. Byzantine suspicions were therefore concentrated on the Germans, while their attitude towards the French was more affable.

The speed of the German approach and the size of their army took the Byzantines by surprise. Emissaries hurried northwards in the summer of

1147 when it was known that they were already close to the Byzantine frontier. The Germans gave pledges on oath that they were not coming to harm the Empire. In return the emperor's representatives were able to promise that the Germans would find markets as they crossed the Byzantine Empire. Somehow the huge straggling army made its way across the Balkans. There were incidents along the way, but rarely was there a danger of conflict on any scale. The Byzantine escorts carried out their task very effectively. The Byzantine emperor hoped to keep the Germans away from Constantinople. He tried to persuade them to by-pass Constantinople and to cross the straits of Gallipoli to Abydos and thence through western Asia Minor to the Holy Land. It was the most sensible route to take and the one that the Byzantines increasingly used for their Anatolian campaigns, but the Germans would not be persuaded. They advanced to Constantinople. Conrad proposed that Manuel should come out and meet him, a proposal which the Byzantine emperor rejected as unworthy of his office. Rebuffed in this way Conrad proceeded to establish himself across the Golden Horn at a place called Pikridion which was opposite the imperial palace of the Blakhernai. There is no way of knowing what Conrad's intentions were. Manuel was determined to get the Germans across the Bosporus. He deliberately provoked a section of the German army. In the battle which followed the Germans suffered heavy casualties. It was this which persuaded Conrad to cross with the bulk of his force to Damalis on the other side of the Bosporus. Manuel was now ready to negotiate. Amidst the rhetoric of the communications exchanged between Manuel and Conrad, it seems that on the Byzantine side the stumbling block was the German refusal to return to the Byzantines any lands they might win from the Turks. On the German side there was a reluctance to make any concessions that might be interpreted as a recognition of Byzantine superiority. Manuel offered Conrad an alliance which he rejected. Therewith the Germans set out across Asia Minor on the road which leads to Philomelion. The march was a disaster. The Germans failed to equip themselves with sufficient food for the journey. They hoped to live off the countryside, which with winter coming on was improvident. They were unable to break through the Turkish cordon they met once they reached Dorylaion. Dispirited and starving they turned back to Nicaea, where they met the French and other contingents, including the Bohemians, under their king, Vladislav.

The passage of the French had so far been much smoother. The Byzantines were less suspicious of their intentions. Byzantine emissaries extracted pledges before they entered Byzantine territory that they would do no harm and in return the Byzantines agreed to supply them with provisions. The question of what would happen to any conquests that the Franks might make in former Byzantine territory was to be left to a meeting of the French king with the Byzantine emperor. The Franks had little to complain about as they made their way through the

Balkans; most of their grumbles were directed at the Germans who had preceded them. There seem to have been few difficulties with the Greeks, except over the rate of exchange for their coins. King Louis was received with due honour by the Byzantine emperor. He was even allowed to sit in the presence of the emperor. Manuel also gave the French king a guided tour round his capital and then treated him to a state banquet. Since the feast-day of St Denis, the French patron saint, fell while the French were still waiting outside Constantinople for other contingents to join them, the Byzantine emperor mounted a lavish celebration, which mightily impressed the French. Manuel's generosity baffled Odo of Deuil, the French chronicler of the second crusade, who was almost invariably hostile towards the Greeks. He decided that 'no one could understand the Greeks without having had experience of them or without being endowed with prophetic inspiration'.[3]

The French then crossed over the Bosporus. Manuel made known his terms for his continuing aid. According to Odo of Deuil these were: 'a kinswoman of the king's who accompanied the queen, as a wife for one of his nephews, and the homage of the barons for himself'.[4] He also held out the prospect of appropriate gifts for the king and his barons. Surprisingly, the proposed marriage seems to have caused the greatest resentment among those involved, almost certainly because they feared the obligations that such a marriage might produce. It was agreed that the barons should do homage to the Byzantine emperor, since this was held not to infringe their primary loyalty to the French king. They probably became liegemen of the Byzantine emperor, in the same way as Vladislav of Bohemia, who passed through Constantinople at the same time as the French armies.

The experience of the Germans showed that the direct route across Asia Minor was not practical. So, joining up with the remnants of the German armies the crusaders made their way through the coastlands of western Asia Minor. The rains of autumn made the route difficult and the crusaders were thankful to stop in Ephesus and the surrounding plains for Christmas. The French then pressed on down the Maiander valley on the road to Attaleia, which they reached after many difficulties, being harried the whole way by the Turks. At Attaleia Louis VII arranged with a Byzantine admiral for shipping to take him to Antioch. The Byzantines were able to provide enough ships to take the king and most of his barons to Antioch, but the rank and file of the army were left to make their way along the coastal road to Tarsus. Few if any got through.

Conrad did not accompany Louis VII. Instead, he preferred to return to Constantinople with his magnates. He was magnificently received by Manuel Comnenus, who even tended him when he fell ill. Some agreement was reached, sealed by the betrothal of Conrad's brother, Henry of Austria, to Manuel's niece, Theodora. Manuel provided the Germans with subsidies and a fleet, which brought them safely to harbour at Acre. It might have been better if they had never arrived. The crusaders' attack on the city of Damascus was a fiasco. The great German historian Otto of Freising took part in the second crusade, but it was such a dispiriting experience that he passes it over in almost complete silence. He says only that, 'if it brought no worldly success, it was good for the salvation of many souls'.[5]

Conrad escaped from the Holy Land as soon as he could. The squadron of Byzantine ships took him to Thessalonica where Manuel was waiting to meet him. There on Christmas Day 1148 the two emperors allied against Roger of Sicily. They agreed on a joint campaign against the king of Sicily for the coming year. Conrad pledged himself to hand over southern Italy to the Byzantines as a dowry for Manuel's empress. The alliance was sealed by the marriage of Henry of Austria to Theodora Comnena. For Manuel Comnenus it seemed a very satisfactory outcome to the episode. He could congratulate himself that he had handled the passage of the second crusade as skilfully as his grandfather had that of the first; perhaps even more so, for Alexius I had not had to contend with a Norman invasion. Roger of Sicily exploited the passage of the second crusade to plunder the cities of Thebes, Corinth, and Athens and to conquer the island of Corfu. With a treaty concluded with the German emperor and another made with the Venetians Manuel was now in a position to take the offensive against the Normans.

The experience of the second crusade re-affirmed for the moment that Byzantine sense of their superiority which had been challenged by the Latins. Western armies might be much larger, but the Byzantine army was superior in military science and discipline. It was this which explained the defeat of a much larger force of Germans by the Byzantines outside the walls of Constantinople. Manuel Comnenus was at pains to rub in this fact in a letter he wrote to the German emperor soon afterwards: 'One must distinguish contestants in war not by number, but by their excellence and exercises and skill therein.'[6] No effort was made to chasten the French in this way. The dignity of imperial ceremonial and the splendours of Constantinople were sufficient, it was fondly believed, to convince them of Byzantine superiority. The Byzantines took great pleasure in the obvious enmity which existed between the Franks and the Germans. Here was plenty of scope for the age-old tactic of 'Divide and Rule'.

Until the passage of the second crusade Byzantine foreign policy had been directed to limited objectives, pursued in piecemeal fashion. There were possibilities of more grandiose schemes, but these were usually ignored. True to this tradition Manuel Comnenus concentrated in the first years of his reign in securing his frontiers with the Turks and preserving his rights over Cilicia and Antioch. The passage of the second crusade cast doubt on the efficacy of such a careful approach, because it taught that it was not possible to separate the different aspects of his foreign policy. They all interlocked. Constantinople was the fulcrum around which the forces of East and West revolved. It opened up the possibility of an alternative strategy. Its essentials are caught by an orator of the Comnenian court: Manuel 'was able to deal with his enemies with enviable skill, playing off one against the other with the aim of bringing about peace and tranquillity. He spilt as little of his own subjects' blood as he could, but roused up his enemies against one another. Thus by creating wars among foreign peoples, he hoped to obtain the greatest possible success, increasing the strength of the Empire and exhausting that of his opponents.'[7] This was certainly Manuel's intention. His panegyricist has assumed that intention automatically became fact. Whether it did remains to be seen. Manuel could not attain his ends by diplomacy alone. He hoped to use it to create conditions in the circle of lands beyond the Balkans and Asia Minor which would allow him to exercise effective control in those traditional areas of Byzantine rule, but even here he seems to have been content with overlordship rather than direct rule. The emphasis was on the prestige of the Byzantine emperor, which would allow him to overawe other rulers. Foreign princes who came to Constantinople were treated magnificently, but to the Byzantines it was proof of their client status. They would be expected to provide the Byzantine emperor with troops. Contingents furnished by client rulers, as the Byzantines regarded them, formed a significant part of Manuel's armies. The trappings of power were thus accompanied by some of its substance.

If Manuel Comnenus strove to attain the ends of his foreign policy by indirect means, the underlying principles remained within a distinctly Byzantine tradition. The French chronicler Odo of Deuil noted perceptively that the Greeks 'are of the opinion that anything which is done for the Sacred Empire cannot be judged treachery'.[8] Reason of state was still the controlling principle of Byzantine foreign policy. This only underlined the gulf that existed between Byzantine and western political ideals. It helped to reinforce that strong body of opinion in the West which held Manuel responsible for the abject failure of the crusade. According to the historian of Outremer, William of Tyre, the Byzantine emperor envied the success of the Latins, 'for it is well known that the Greeks have always looked with distrust on all increase of power by the western nations (as they still do)'.[9]

Surprisingly this charge is supported by the Byzantine historian Nicetas Choniates. To his mind, Manuel exploited the crusaders shamefully. He allowed chalk to be mixed with the flour sold to them. He had a special debased coinage minted for transactions with them, and finally he encouraged Turkish chieftains to attack the crusaders as they attempted to cross Asia Minor. Nicetas's sympathy for the crusaders is expressed in the long speech which he puts in the mouth of the French King Louis VII, as his army prepared to force a crossing of the river Maiander in the face of the Turks. 'If Christ died on our behalf,' the French king urged his knights, 'with how much greater justice should we be killed for Him? Let the reward of this pious journey be at last to die in battle.'[10] It is an impressive attempt by a Byzantine to penetrate the crusading mentality. It might be argued that Nicetas's perspective has been blurred by the disasters which overtook the Byzantine Empire in the last decades of the twelfth century. He was able to see that the second crusade contributed to that alienation of the West from Byzantium, which led to the disaster of 1204. He was therefore inclined to blame Manuel Comnenus for his handling of the passage of the second crusade. The truth is that the Byzantine emperor was indifferent to its fate. His main purpose was to vindicate Byzantine superiority and extract what advantage he could. To the westerners at the time and to a Byzantine writing half a century later it looked like betrayal.

The fate of the second crusade confirmed the worst prejudices that westerners had about the Byzantines. They were malicious and hypocritical, to which were added religious differences. Odo of Deuil complained bitterly of how the Byzantines forced Latins who married Byzantines to renew their baptism. If the Latins used a Greek church to celebrate the mass, the Byzantines then purified the altar before they were willing to use it again. There was a strong feeling among the French crusaders that the Byzantines hardly counted as Christians and could therefore be killed with an easy conscience. There was a party around the French king that urged an alliance with the Normans and an attack upon Constantinople. Louis VII had little difficulty during the crusade in dismissing such advice as near lunacy, but it was a different matter once the crusade had ended in disaster. Byzantium seemed more clearly an enemy. This is apparent in the changing attitude of Peter the Venerable, abbot of Cluny. Before the second crusade he saw the Byzantine Empire as the bulwark of christendom. He described the role of Constantinople in a way which would have appealed to any Byzantine statesman. 'Standing at the mid-point of east, west, and north, it overawed the east, subdued the north, and defended the west.'[11] After the failure of the second crusade Peter wrote to Roger II of Sicily. The theme of the letter was the treachery of the Byzantines and the purpose to urge the Norman king to take vengeance upon them.

THE NORMANS OF SICILY

Plans were being laid for another crusade to avenge the failure of the second crusade. They centred on Roger II of Sicily. This was in itself reason for alarm on the part of the Byzantines, because the Normans of Sicily had already shown in the course of the second crusade how vulnerable the Byzantine Empire was. In the summer of 1147, while Manuel Comenus was busy supervising the passage of the second crusade, a Norman fleet had seized the island of Corfu. Then, after an unsuccessful foray into the Aegean, where Monemvasia proved too strong for them, they struck into the Gulf of Corinth. Meeting no opposition they landed and plundered the richest territories of the Empire. The city of Thebes fell to them. The wealthiest inhabitants were forced to make a statement of their property, which was then seized. Many people were herded off into captivity, particularly women chosen either for their beauty or for their weaving skills. It was Corinth's turn next. The inhabitants took refuge in the nigh impregnable Acrocorinth, but its commander surrendered it with scarcely a fight. The Normans sailed away; their ships loaded down to the gunnels with booty and captives. It was a piece of opportunism pure and simple. The Normans held on to Corfu. It had considerable strategic value with its command of the entrance to the Adriatic. It might also be turned into a base from which to menace Byzantium's Greek provinces.

Its recovery would go some way towards restoring Byzantine prestige. But for such an undertaking, Manuel needed Venetian help. In October 1147, while the Norman raid was still going on, he confirmed the Venetians' privileges, which he had so far failed to do, and in March of the following year he granted the Venetians an extension of their factory at Constantinople. In return they agreed to serve against the Normans until the end of September. The Venetians saw Norman occupation of Corfu as a potential threat to their control of the Adriatic, but they were only too happy to win advantage for themselves from Byzantium's misfortune. Manuel Comnenus hoped that the campaign against Corfu would be over and done with by the autumn of 1148. His plans did not go as expected. His own fleet did not reach Corfu until towards the end of the year and the Venetians were held back by the death of the doge. Manuel himself was diverted by news of a Cuman invasion of the Balkans. This occupied him until the autumn. He made a spectacular raid north of the Danube, which achieved very little. The winter was spent in the company of the German emperor, Conrad. As we have seen, Manuel was able to persuade him into an alliance against the Normans of Sicily. A joint expedition was envisaged for either 1149 or 1150.

The siege of Corfu begun in the emperor's absence was not going well. The Grand Duke Stephen Kontostephanos who was directing operations was mortally wounded by the Norman artillery. Worse was to follow. The Byzantines came to blows with their Venetian allies and this turned into a full-scale battle, in which the Venetians were worsted. They sailed away and plundered Byzantine shipping. They even seized the imperial barge. The emperor was not aboard, but the Venetians found imperial vestments. They dressed up a Moor as emperor and acclaimed him. They were mocking Manuel's swarthy appearance. For the time being Manuel showed great forbearance. The essential was to restore harmony between the allies and to press on with the siege. He succeeded in this and the siege was intensified. Roger II tried to distract the besiegers by sending a fleet into the Aegean, which had the impudence to sail on through the straits of Gallipoli and even penetrate the Golden Horn. As it returned it was caught by a squadron of Byzantine and Venetian ships which had been detached from the siege. The Norman fleet was heavily defeated. The Norman garrison at Corfu lost heart. There seemed to be little prospect of relief. In the summer of 1149 the garrison commander surrendered to Manuel and with several of his officers entered Byzantine service. Manuel followed up this victory by launching punitive expeditions against the Hungarians and Serbs, who had been induced by Roger II of Sicily to invade Byzantine territory. The Hungarians and the Serbs were suitably chastised and when Manuel returned to his capital on Christmas Day 1149 there was great rejoicing. The emperor celebrated his successes with a triumphal procession through the city.

'The Sicilian Dragon' had been humbled, but he was still dangerous, as long as there were plans to launch another crusade. Manuel had thought after the recovery of Corfu to mount an expedition against the Normans in Italy. He may even have contemplated leading it in person, but in the end gave the command to his Grand Domestic John Axoukh. He was instructed to make the city of Ancona his base. Bad weather and Venetian advice combined to put an end to this project. Manuel continued to put pressure on the Emperor Conrad to fulfil his promise of a joint expedition against the Normans, but this may only have been a way of countering the plans there still were for a crusade. With the death of Eugenius III in 1153, followed in quick succession by that of Roger II of Sicily in February 1154, the danger from Sicily subsided.

Roger II had been a strong, successful king. His long rule had created resentments, which broke out on his death. The leader of the opposition was a nephew of his, Robert of Bassonville, count of Loritello. He turned for support first to Frederick Barbarossa, who had succeeded his uncle Conrad as ruler of Germany in 1152. He received more positive encouragement from Alexander, count of Gravina, a Norman exile, who had served at both the Byzantine and the German courts. He put him in touch with Michael Palaiologos and John Doukas, two high-ranking Byzantine agents, who had been sent to Italy to stir up trouble. They had orders to cooperate, if they could, with Frederick Barbarossa. They went to his camp. He claimed in a letter to Otto of Freising that he would have liked to have accepted their proposal for an expedition against Sicily, but his army was tired of campaigning, and so he headed for home. The Byzantine agents took his attitude to mean that he would approve an attack upon the Normans. They used the large sums of money they had to raise troops locally. This force went to back opponents of William I, the new king of Sicily.

They were able to recover much of Apulia. For the Byzantines the great success was the surrender of Bari towards the end of 1155. This was won over by Byzantine gold, but there was also resentment among the citizens at Norman rule. They tore down the donjon which was the symbol of Norman overlordship. Other of the coastal cities came over once Bari had surrendered. Manuel sent reinforcements. The phenomenal success of the Byzantines was only possible because of local support, but there were soon signs that this would evaporate. The Byzantine commanders told Robert of Bassonville that they had not been sent to fight for him, but to conquer on their own account. When Bassonville asked for a loan of money from Michael Palaiologos, he was refused, though the Byzantine commander was willing to make him a gift of money. It was Bassonville's turn to refuse. It would have made it seem that he was just a hired mercenary in Byzantine service. Palaiologos died soon afterwards and the affair was patched up. The combined forces pressed south towards Brindisi, which was the key to the conquest of Apulia. On 15 April 1156 the siege began. The lower town soon capitulated, but the garrison held out in the citadel. The assaults on the citadel became more and more furious as news came that William I was marching to the rescue with a vast army. The Byzantines failed to take the citadel. Robert of Bassonville abandoned the siege, while the Italian mercenaries demanded that their pay should be doubled, and when this was refused they too departed. Only a very small Byzantine force, composed largely of Cuman, Alan, and Georgian auxiliaries, was left to face the Norman army. Battle was joined on 28 May 1156. The Byzantines were defeated and their commanders fell into the victors' hands. The rebels came to terms or took to the hills and the cities were quick to open their gates to the royal army. Byzantine success in southern Italy had proved ephemeral.

Had Manuel Comnenus seriously aimed at the conquest of southern Italy? In his negotiations first with Conrad and then with Frederick Barbarossa, he seems to have been at pains to obtain recognition of Byzantine rights to southern Italy. On the other hand, he never provided his commanders in southern Italy with any worthwhile forces. On any realistic assessment the conquest of southern Italy was out of the question, but it was less impractical to think in terms of bringing Apulia within the Byzantine sphere of influence. The main towns could be brought under Byzantine protection in the same way as the city of Ancona had been. That this was Manuel's aim is suggested by the proposal he made to Pope Hadrian IV at the beginning of the Italian campaign. In return for cooperation against William I, he asked for three Apulian ports; these presumably to include Bari and Brindisi. These would strengthen Byzantine defences in the Adriatic and would weaken Sicilian sea power, which had proved so dangerous to the Byzantine Empire. Insistence upon rights did not mean conquest. Much of Comnenian foreign policy revolved around the acquisition and preservation of rights. In the case of southern Italy these were especially important because of the numbers of Norman refugees at the Byzantine court. For them Manuel's claim to southern Italy was an earnest that they might one day return and reclaim their lands. The restoration of the Norman exiles would weaken the Sicilian monarchy and ensure that the initiative along the Adriatic passed into the hands of the Byzantines. These aims hardly amount to delusions of grandeur on a Justinianic scale, which is the charge sometimes laid against Manuel for his Italian involvement.

The campaign of 1155–56 at least exposed the vulnerability of the Norman kingdom to Byzantine pressure. Manuel hoped to salvage some advantages. In the summer of 1157 he despatched Alexius Axoukh, the son of the Grand Domestic, to Ancona. His instructions were to embarrass William I by raising troops to help his opponents. The true aim seems to have been to secure a favourable bargaining position. Alexius had a fair measure of success. He recruited troops and induced a number of cities to recognize some degree of Byzantine overlordship. Even the citizens of Rome flew the emperor's banner to the embarrassment of the pope. Norman exiles were able to break into southern Italy and one of them completely defeated a royal army sent against him near Monte Cassino. Under cover of these manœuvres negotiations had already begun between Manuel I and the Sicilian court. By the spring of 1158 a treaty had been agreed. There was to be an exchange of prisoners of war, though the people carried off from Thebes and Corinth in 1147 were not returned. Manuel agreed to recognize the Norman ruler's royal title, thereby giving up his claim on southern Italy. Why should Manuel have been willing to concede so much? The answer almost certainly lies in William's undertaking that he would be his ally in the west. This alliance was directed against Frederick Barbarossa. He had been disturbed by Byzantine successes in Italy. In particular, the city of Ravenna seemed willing to accept some measure of Byzantine suzerainty. Early in the spring of 1158 a German force approached Ravenna and brought it back to its old allegiance. It then proceeded to Ancona, from which it ejected Alexius Axoukh, thus depriving the Byzantines of a strong bargaining counter in their negotiations with William I of Sicily.

HUNGARY, SERBIA, AND RUSSIA

The treaty of 1158 between Byzantium and Norman Sicily marks a break in Byzantine foreign policy. For more than twenty years it had rested on an understanding with the German emperor, cemented in 1148 by the treaty of Thessalonica. It provided Byzantium with the conditions it needed to get to grips with the Normans of Sicily, whose sea power threatened its Greek lands. With the thirty-year truce negotiated in 1158 Manuel Comnenus secured one basic objective – the neutralization of this threat, even if he had failed in his more ambitious aim of turning Norman Sicily into a client state.

The *entente* with the German emperor gave Manuel Comnenus something far more important than support against the Normans of Sicily: a free hand in Hungary. While the Byzantine historians pay relatively little attention to Manuel Comnenus's involvement in Italy, they devote more space to Hungary than to any other aspect of Byzantine foreign policy. This is not just a reflection of Byzantine successes in this area, but a measure of the importance that Hungary possessed for the Byzantine Empire. Between 1151 and 1167 no less than thirteen expeditions were despatched against the Hungarians, some of which the emperor commanded himself. In no other area did Manuel make quite such a concerted effort.

Why was Hungary so important at this time? It was, first and foremost, a serious competitor for influence in the Balkans. It controlled Dalmatia, Bosnia, and Croatia, and it looked as though the Serbs were passing under its hegemony. The Serbs were still very largely a pastoral people. They herded their flocks of sheep and cattle in the mountains and forests of the western Balkans. It was more or less impossible to penetrate their fastnesses. The late autumn was considered to be the best time to campaign against them because the forests were bare and they were thus deprived of some of their cover. Like all highland peoples they pressed down towards the more fertile lowlands. The Serbs presented the Byzantines with something of the same problem as the Turkish nomads in Asia Minor. They were a threat to the *pax byzantina* which prevailed in the lowlands. The Serbs were particularly dangerous because they menaced the two great arteries of communication across the Balkans upon which Byzantine hegemony depended: the Via Egnatia from Dyrrakhion to Thessalonica and the Military Road leading from Belgrade and the Danube frontier through Nish and Sardica to Adrianople and Constantinople. Hungarian interference in Serbia therefore threatened Byzantine control of the Balkans. Hungary was also a competitor in another area. There seemed to be a real danger that the Russian principalities, including Kiev, might be drawn into its sphere of influence, thus undermining Byzantine prestige in the Black Sea area. Just as with Norman Sicily, so with Hungary Manuel aimed at neutralizing a threat to areas of vital interest to Byzantium and, if possible, to guarantee this state of affairs by turning it into a harmless client state. A subsidiary consideration was almost certainly the booty, especially prisoners of war and slaves, that were to be gained.

Large numbers of Serbs were rounded up during the raids which Manuel mounted against them in the late summer and autumn of 1149. They were then settled around Sardica and in other provinces of the Empire. These raids failed to break Serbian resistance. Their chieftain, the Grand Župan, continued to rely on the promise of Hungarian aid. The next year Manuel launched a full-scale punitive expedition. A Hungarian force coming to the aid of the Serbs was defeated, the emperor playing a notable part. He got the better of their leader in single combat. This was enough to persuade the Grand Župan to throw himself on the emperor's mercy. He became once again a client of the Empire and agreed to supply the Byzantine emperor with 2,000 men, when he was campaigning in Europe and 500 in Asia Minor. It seems also to have been agreed that in future the emperor had the right to confirm the Grand Župan in office.

The stage was now set for a direct attack upon Hungary. The time was well chosen, because the Hungarian King Geza II (1141–62) was preoccupied with the Russian principalities. He had gone to the aid of his son-in-law, Izjaslav, the prince of Kiev, threatened by the princes of Suzdal' and Galicia, who were allies and clients of the Byzantine emperor. Izjaslav was already suspect in Byzantine eyes. In 1147 he imposed his nominee as metropolitan on the Russian church, which at the very least showed a lack of respect for the rights of the patriarch of Constantinople, who normally appointed the Russian metropolitan. At the worst, it could be construed as an attack upon any remaining links with Byzantium, and a desire to align the Russian lands more closely with the West. The Hungarian king reckoned that he had more to gain from rescuing his son-in-law than in supervising the defence of his kingdom in the face of the expected Byzantine invasion. The result was that the Hungarian lands suffered at the hands of the Byzantine forces during the campaign of 1151. In the following year Geza came to terms with the Byzantine emperor. The vast numbers of prisoners driven off by the Byzantines in the previous year were returned and the Hungarian king acknowledged his client status. This only brought a temporary lull along the Danube frontier. Geza was encouraged by Manuel's cousin and rival Andronicus Comnenus to back him in a bid for the Byzantine throne. He attacked the Byzantine fortresses along the Danube in 1155. The Hungarians were held with some difficulty, but a demonstration in the following year was enough to bring Geza once more to heel.

Manuel Comnenus had more or less achieved what he wanted. Hungary was quiescent. Kiev had returned to the Byzantine sphere of influence when Izjaslav died in 1154 and the ecclesiastical schism came to an end. The Serbs, as a token of their loyalty, dutifully submitted their dynastic squabbles to imperial arbitration. The death of Geza II in March 1162 brought this highly satisfactory state of affairs to an end. Geza's son Stephen III was immediately crowned king. This went against traditional practice, which favoured the succession of the dead king's eldest surviving brother. Geza's brothers had sought refuge at the Byzantine court. Manuel pressed the claims of one of them, also named Stephen. The Hungarians rejected him decisively. They suspected, in the words of Nicetas Choniates, that if they 'were ruled by him, he would be under the sway of the Byzantine emperor'.[12] Having failed to secure the Hungarian crown, he sought refuge in the Danubian fortress of Zemun. Here he was trapped by his rival Stephen III. The young Hungarian king could not afford a long siege, because it would only be a matter of time before a Byzantine army was sent to the rescue. He therefore had the elder Stephen assassinated. One of his servants was bribed to commit the deed. He opened up a vein in his master's arm and rubbed in a poisoned salve. The Borgias could hardly have done better. His death encompassed in this way in April 1165, the garrison of Zemun surrendered and the fortress returned to the Hungarians.

The failure of the Byzantines to secure the crown of St Stephen for their puppet was having serious consequences for their position along the Danube. Particularly worrying was the support that the young Hungarian king had from the Germans and Czechs. He was being drawn ever more closely within the German orbit. This had repercussions in Serbia and in the Russian lands. The Serbs were becoming restive once again. Manuel tried to counter this by appointing a new Grand Župan, Dessa, but his demand that in return the Serb should surrender the fertile tract of land he held to the west of Nish only left him resentful. Hungarian success encouraged him to seek their help. There were rumours at the Byzantine court that he was negotiating for a marriage with a German princess. He was playing a dangerous game. In 1165 Manuel Comnenus turned aside from his march to the Danube frontier and brought Dessa to book. He was unwilling to trust his protestations of loyalty and had him taken away to Constantinople, where he was confined in the imperial palace. For the moment, Manuel had managed to isolate the Serbs from the Hungarians.

The Russians too were drawing dangerously close to Hungary. Yaroslav, the new prince of Galicia, reversed his father's policy of friendship with the Byzantine Empire. He supplied Stephen III with troops. Their alliance was to be sealed by the marriage of his daughter to the Hungarian king. Even more disturbing in its way was the stance taken by Rostislav, the new prince of Kiev. In 1164 he publicly challenged Byzantine ascendancy over the Russian church, refusing to accept a metropolitan appointed by the patriarch of Constantinople. The disaffection of the Russian princes was such that Manuel's cousin and rival Andronicus Comnenus was encouraged to escape from the imperial palace and seek refuge in Galicia (1165). Manuel Comnenus despatched a member of the imperial family to make the rounds of the Russian courts to restore the situation and negotiate the return of his dangerous cousin. His mission was a success. Andronicus was handed over. The prince of Galicia was persuaded to give up the idea of a marriage alliance with Hungary and the prince of Kiev to accept the patriarch's nominee as metropolitan of the Russian church. The subtlety of a Byzantine diplomat cannot be the sole explanation of this success.

The balance of power along the Danube was shifting once again in favour of Byzantium. In 1165 the Byzantines were able to recover the fortress of Zemun and Stephen III was forced to recognize Byzantine claims to the region between the river Save and the Danube, an area now known as Fruška Gora. He had also to accept as a *fait accompli* the Byzantine conquest of Dalmatia. The next year one Byzantine army broke through the Transylvanian Alps and another attacked through the Carpathians from the direction of Galicia. The Hungarians had not anticipated invasion from these directions and their lands suffered. These were punitive raids, in retaliation for a Hungarian victory over a Byzantine force earlier in the year. In 1167 Manuel Comnenus got together a vast army with the intention of breaking Hungarian resistance. He entrusted command of the army to his nephew Andronicus Kontostephanos. The Hungarians trusting in their earlier victory over the Byzantines came out to meet the new army near Zemun. Battle was engaged on St Procopius's day (8 July). The Byzantines won a complete victory. The Hungarians made peace on Byzantine terms. They had to accept Byzantine control of Dalmatia and Croatia, as well as the Fruška Gora; they agreed to provide hostages for good behaviour; to pay Byzantium a tribute and supply troops.

There was a further stipulation, which suggested that the Byzantine emperor aimed at something more than the humiliation of Hungary. It was laid down that the Hungarian church should come under the sceptre of the Byzantine emperor 'so that the royal crown of the Hungarian ruler remains subject to [the emperor's] sovereignty'.[13] There is no question here of the Hungarian church being subordinated to the patriarch of Constantinople. It was a political arrangement, pure and simple. The royal crown of Hungary was the symbol of its ruler's legitimacy. It was originally presented by the Emperor Michael VII Doukas (1071–78) to the Hungarian King Geza I (1074–77). It is in the shape of a diadem and is studded with enamels. Their iconography proclaims the theory of the Byzantine family of kings and illustrates the subjection of the Hungarian king to the power of the Byzantine emperor. Manuel was reclaiming the traditional rights of the Byzantine emperor over the crown, which was tantamount to a claim to suzerainty over the king of Hungary. Whoever disposed of the crown, controlled the succession to the Hungarian throne. The claim of the Byzantine emperor was almost certainly directed against Lukacs, the archbishop of Esztergom, who had used his control of the crown to become the arbiter of Hungarian politics. He was consistently hostile to the Byzantines, resentful of the presence within Hungary of a strong orthodox community. He was held to have master-minded the removal of pretenders to the Hungarian crown who relied on Byzantine backing. As it was picturesquely put at the time, 'they were killed by the breath of his head'.[14]

Manuel Comnenus had to establish his rights over the 'Holy Crown of Hungary' because he was at that time contemplating nothing less than the union of the Byzantine Empire and Hungary. This was to be effected by the marriage of Manuel's only surviving child of his first marriage, his daughter the Porphyrogenite Maria, to Stephen III's younger brother and heir, Bela. Their engagement was celebrated probably in the year 1163. Bela was raised to the new position of despot, which placed him at the head of the Byzantine court hierarchy. It was roughly equivalent to the position of *Urum* at the Hungarian court, which was given to the heir apparent. Such a plan was upset by the birth in September 1169 of a son, Alexius, to Manuel's second wife. In March 1171 he was formally recognized as heir apparent to the Byzantine throne. Bela was demoted to the rank of Caesar and the engagement to Maria was broken off, but he remained at the Byzantine court. In March 1172 Stephen III of Hungary died unexpectedly. A deputation of Hungarian magnates came to the Byzantine emperor, requesting that Bela should be sent to them as king. Manuel complied and exercising his rights as suzerain had Bela acclaimed king, but only after he had taken an oath to uphold the interests of the Byzantine emperor. Bela was as good as his word and remained a loyal ally of the Byzantine Empire.

The accession of Bela to the Hungarian throne coincided with Manuel Comnenus's final triumph over Stefan Nemanja, the real founder of the medieval Serbian kingdom. Unable to resist a punitive raid which Manuel unleashed against Serbia in 1172 he came to the emperor as a suppliant, bareheaded and barefooted, with a halter around his neck and a sword in his hand. He threw himself on the emperor's mercy. He was taken off to Constantinople, where he figured in a triumphal procession through the streets of Constantinople. The Serbs made no more trouble for the remainder of Manuel's reign. Manuel had achieved his major aims. The western Balkans were now under Byzantine control and Hungary had become a client state.

THE GERMAN EMPIRE AND PAPACY

From his accession the German Emperor Frederick I Barbarossa (1152–89) cast his shadow over Manuel's Hungarian policy, as he did over almost all aspects of Byzantine foreign policy. At the time of Geza II's death in 1162, when the succession to the Hungarian crown was disputed, rumours were rife at the Byzantine court that Frederick was about to invade the Byzantine Empire with his whole 'nation'. They proved to be quite without foundation. At the beginning of his reign Frederick may have entertained the idea of bringing Hungary under his sway, but he was soon disabused of the notion by his princes. He took little direct interest in Hungarian affairs, preferring to leave matters in the hands of Henry Jasomirgott and Vladislav of Bohemia. The former he made duke of Austria in 1156 and the latter he raised to the rank of king in the same year. Neither was consistently hostile to Byzantium. Henry was the stepbrother of the Emperor Conrad and had married a Byzantine princess. He was inclined to continue a policy of *entente* with Byzantium. Vladislav had taken an oath of allegiance to Manuel at the time of the second crusade. Nor were they urged on by Frederick to take a strong line against Byzantine intervention in Hungary. The emperor almost always advocated making concessions.

Suspicion of the German emperor's intentions nevertheless persisted at Byzantium. It remained almost an article of faith in court circles that Frederick's ultimate ambition was to invade the Byzantine Empire. At first sight, this preoccupation with the threat posed by the Germans is difficult to understand. It is true that at the beginning of his reign Frederick made it clear that he would not be bound by the treaty of Thessalonica, then seen as a cornerstone of Byzantine foreign policy. This did not prevent him from trying to re-establish an understanding with the Byzantine Empire, if perhaps one that was less weighted in its favour. Embassies were even exchanged over his possible marriage to a Byzantine princess. These came to an end with the Byzantine intervention in southern Italy in 1155. Frederick objected to this infringement of the 'honour' of his Empire. He insisted that southern Italy properly belonged within the Western Empire. Byzantine success, as we have seen, was shortlived. After their withdrawal in 1158 it should have been possible to effect an amicable, if informal division of power – Hungary to the Byzantine sphere of influence; Italy to the German. Instead tension increased and mutual suspicions were heightened. Why should this have been?

On the surface it seems to have been nothing so much as an empty dispute over the imperial title. The Byzantine emperor jealously guarded his claim to be the one Emperor of the Romans and Constantinople's as the seat of empire. To be addressed as king of the Greeks by the German ruler was an affront. Quarrels over titles are not always unimportant, especially if prestige is at stake; and the prestige of the imperial office was vital to both emperors. It was not just that the imperial office was their very being; it was also a matter of power. Both rulers faced conditions of great political fragmentation, where any clear order had apparently been lost. The emperor had a duty to restore order, which offered the hope that this might lead to the restoration of effective imperial authority. It did not matter that the power obtained might be largely indirect in character: the power to arbitrate, though also the power to appoint or confirm appointments. Such considerations did not necessarily create an insuperable barrier to *entente* between the two empires. The Emperor Conrad was particularly sensitive about his imperial claims, yet these did not prevent him from reaching an understanding with both John II Comnenus and his son Manuel.

In the conflict between Manuel and Frederick something more than a question of titles was involved, nothing less than the whole nature of imperial authority. This was opened up by Frederick Barbarossa's quarrel with the papacy. He claimed that the imperial title was his by virtue of his election, not by virtue of his coronation by the pope. Successive popes, for their part, insisted that the imperial dignity was in their gift. The break came in 1159, when there was a disputed election for the chair of St Peter. Frederick supported one candidate, Victor IV, against another, Alexander III, which led to a schism within the western church.

Manuel Comnenus could easily have held aloof from this quarrel. He chose not to, almost certainly because it seemed an opportunity, too good to be missed, to increase his influence in the West. But why should Manuel have been interested in interfering in the West, if his basic objectives remained those of his father and grandfather: to ensure Byzantine control over its traditional territories in the Balkans and Anatolia? Because he could not and did not want to escape his grandfather's legacy, which tied the fate of Byzantium to the West. Latins were settled in considerable numbers in Byzantine territory, above all at Constantinople. Whether as merchants or as soldiers they had become a vital element in the functioning of the Byzantine state. It was only politic for the Byzantine emperor to maintain diplomatic contacts with the rulers of the West and especially the city states of northern Italy from which the bulk of the Latins settled in the Byzantine Empire came. The West was not only a potential source of strength to the Byzantine Empire; roused to communal action in the shape of the crusade it was also a potential threat. The papacy seemed to hold the key. The crusade came under papal auspices. With papal support the crusade might cease to be a threat; indeed might be turned to Byzantium's advantage. Intervention on the side of the papacy seemed to offer much and the risks seemed negligible: it was already clear that there was little if anything to be gained from courting the German emperor.

There was, however, a serious stumbling block. The Greek and Roman churches were not in a state of full communion. Until the differences separating the two churches were settled, there seemed little likelihood of active cooperation between the Byzantine emperor and the papacy. There had been intermittent negotiations over the question of the reunion of churches. Their tone had been polite and tolerant, but the question of papal primacy proved too much for the Byzantine side. As one Byzantine theologian put it in the course of a debate in 1136, 'the Roman Pontiff is not called the Prince of Priests nor the supreme priest nor anything of the sort, but is merely the bishop of the leading See'.[15] The Byzantines were still willing to accord the bishop of Rome a primacy of honour, but not of jurisdiction. By January 1156 when Manuel Comnenus had a letter drafted on his behalf to Pope Hadrian IV, Byzantine opinion seemed to be hardening even on this point. There was no recognition of any primacy of honour due to Rome. It was instead strongly implied, that 'the throne of Constantinople is greater than that of Rome',[16] to quote the title later given to the letter.

The schism within the western church created a set of political circumstances that seemed to alter the terms of the theological debate. The initiative came from Pope Alexander III. He made some offer to Manuel Comnenus in 1161. A source close to Frederick Barbarossa records cryptically that Alexander III promised the Byzantine emperor 'the vanities of vanities, which he had not expected'.[17] At about the same time a cardinal was writing to Manuel Comnenus in the warmest possible terms, assuring the emperor that he was held in the highest regard at Rome. He openly hinted that the papacy wished for his protection against the German 'tyrant', recalling the harm 'inflicted on our church by the tyranny of the barbarians, from the moment they are known to have usurped the imperial name'.[18] Those 'vanities of vanities' may well have been some offer by Alexander III to recognize the Byzantine emperor as the one legitimate emperor. This would have been a return to the conditions existing at the turn of the fifth century, when there was one emperor at Constantinople, exercising some degree of authority over the 'barbarian' kings of the West. This was very much in line with ideas then current at the Byzantine court. The imperial titulature that Manuel adopted at exactly this time was deliberately reminiscent of that employed by Justinian with its series of triumphal epithets.

The pope was angling for Byzantine participation in an alliance with France and Sicily against Frederick Barbarossa. He chose his bait skilfully. Nothing was to come of this scheme, but the offer, open or veiled, caught Manuel's imagination. He now claimed to be 'the heir of the crown of Constantine the Great and in his spirit holding sway over all his rightful possessions, even if some have broken away from our Empire'.[19] It was the expression of extravagant hopes nurtured by the papal overtures.

All the ingenuity of Byzantine diplomacy was brought into play. Manuel had first to convince the curia of his sincerity. He tried to do this by clamping down on the anti-Latin agitation there then was in Constantinople. This stemmed from a theological controversy centring on Christ's words: 'For my Father is greater than I' (John 14: 28). This opened up the question of the relationship of God the Father and God the Son. It was started around the year 1160 by a Byzantine diplomat, who had been involved in a similar dispute while on a mission to Germany. He considered heretical the Latin teaching that Christ was both 'inferior and equal to the God that begat Him'.[20] His criticism of the Latins soon won him a large following, not only among the monks and people, but also among the bishops and patriarchal clergy. The emperor intervened; he called together a meeting in the imperial palace, to which he summoned Hugh Eteriano, a Latin theologian from Pisa, who had settled at Constantinople. The emperor requested tha the set forth Latin teaching on the matter. This he did, convincing the emperor of its orthodoxy. The example of the emperor was followed by leading members of the court, but outside there remained a vociferous opposition. Manuel asked Eteriano to put his views down on paper to serve him as a guide in this dispute, which in March 1166 was brought before a synod. The proceedings were carefully organized by the emperor, who framed the final declaration, which all had to sign: 'I agree with the teaching of the divinely inspired Fathers of the Church about "My father is greater than I" and I acknowledge that this was said with His created and suffering flesh in mind.'[21] It was a clever formula designed to conciliate Byzantine opinion, while demonstrating his sympathy for Latin theology.

Manuel's support for the papacy was shown in more practical ways. In his struggle with Frederick Barbarossa, Alexander III looked for help from the Lombard cities, who were disturbed by the prospect of German intervention. The fall of Milan in 1162 to Frederick Barbarossa had been a terrible warning. In 1165 Manuel despatched one of his most experienced men, Nicephorus Khalouphes, to Venice in order to stiffen the resistance of the Lombard cities to the German emperor. Out of this initiative came the League of Verona, for which the Byzantine emperor at first acted as paymaster. This intervention in Italy was coupled with new initiatives in Sicily. In 1166 its king, William I, died, leaving his young son William II to succeed him. Manuel immediately offered a marriage alliance. The young king was to marry his daughter and heiress, Maria, which would lead to a union of the crowns of Byzantium and Sicily. Given that Maria had only a little while earlier been offered to Bela, the heir to the Hungarian throne on much the same terms, it is difficult to know how seriously this overture to Sicily was meant. The line of Byzantine policy is, however, quite unmistakable: support throughout Italy was necessary if negotiations with the papacy over the imperial office were to have any chance of success.

By 1167 negotiations had reached the point where a delegation of three cardinals was despatched to Constantinople. They came to discuss the question of the Byzantine emperor's authority over 'Old Rome and the whole of Italy'. Questioned more closely by the emperor the cardinals agreed that they were willing to offer the submission of their land to the emperor in return for protection against Frederick Barbarossa, always assuming that agreement could be reached over the differences separating the two churches. In the dialogue that followed doctrinal differences were diplomatically avoided. Manuel Comnenus strove to find common ground in the figure of St Peter, who, he argued, was the teacher of the whole church, not just of Rome. He also gave his partial blessing to the Donation of Constantine, interpreting it in a way that upheld imperial authority: 'the bishop of a church inherits honour and precedence over all other churches by virtue of imperial authority.

Do we not learn that such precedence was finally and more fully granted to the pope by Constantine the Great in that edict he had promulgated, when he transferred the insignia of Empire from the city of Rome to this great city that bears his name.'[22] In this way he accepted Rome's primacy, without abandoning Constantinople's claim to be the true seat of empire. The emperor's views seem to have satisfied the cardinals. Drafts were exchanged of a treaty, whereby in exchange for recognition of papal primacy Manuel was to be accepted as emperor in the West. At the last moment Alexander III refused to go through with it because he claimed that he would be accused of simony. The truth was that he no longer needed Byzantine protection. Frederick Barbarossa's army was ravaged by plague which broke out in the summer of 1167 and the German emperor was forced to retreat from Italy.

Manuel nevertheless persisted in his line of policy. He was again making overtures to Alexander III in 1169, and in the following year a marriage was arranged between one of the emperor's nieces and Otto Frangipani, the pope's most influential backer in Rome. At the end of the year a German embassy led by as imposing a figure as the imperial chancellor, Christian of Mainz, arrived at Constantinople in the hope of detaching Manuel from his papal alliance. It achieved very little. The coolness of its reception by the Byzantine emperor hardly prepares us for the volte-face that was to take place in 1172. The occasion was the visit of Henry the Lion, the duke of Saxony, to Constantinople, while on his way to Jerusalem on pilgrimage. This was timed to coincide with the official German embassy to the Byzantine court. Henry succeeded in reconciling the two emperors. Exactly what he had to offer remains mysterious. It is likely that he was able to hold out to the Byzantine emperor the prospect of a free hand in Hungary. Stephen III of Hungary died just as Henry was passing through the country and it was vital that the Byzantines should place their candidate, Bela, on the throne of Hungary. Henry may also have hinted that the treaty of Thessalonica might be reactivated. This would have been an attractive proposal, coming at a time when Manuel must have begun to realize that his pro-papal stance was unlikely to produce any immediate dividends.

Manuel found that he had been duped. Frederick Barbarossa had no intention of coming to terms with the Byzantine emperor. In 1173 his forces with Venetian support attacked Ancona, Byzantium's foothold in Italy. He even began to negotiate for an alliance against Manuel with the Seljuq sultan, Kilidj Arslan. Manuel's western policy was in tatters. He found himself more or less isolated. When Frederick invaded Italy in 1176 he could discount the possibility of any Byzantine intervention against him. Frederick's army was, of course, decisively defeated in 1176 by the forces of the Lombard league at the battle of Legnano. This prepared the way for a reconciliation of German emperor and pope enacted in the following year in the treaty of Venice.

This was the cause of a surprising bitterness at the Byzantine court. It was the bitterness of the outmanœuvred. Alexander III's recognition of Frederick Barbarossa as emperor was a joke, 'a shabby and servile trick'. The pope had, it was felt at the Byzantine court, 'in the fashion of a time server adapted to the changes of fortune'.[23] His claim to transfer empires was shrilly denounced and Constantinople's status as the one and only capital of the Roman Empire was as insistently affirmed.

Manuel Comnenus had been guilty of making compromising concessions in these areas, which had brought the Byzantine Empire humiliation. This outcome should not have been a surprise to deep-thinking Byzantine diplomats. Byzantine ideas about empire – embodied in the person of the emperor and in the fabric of Constantinople – were quite incompatible with papal claims to supervise the transmission of the imperial office. It seems unlikely that so clever a man as the Emperor Manuel Comnenus was unaware of this. He probably calculated that short-term advantages would outweigh any long-term deterioration in Byzantine relations with the West. Failure brought with it his isolation from the West. This turned out to be a more serious matter than he perhaps imagined, because so much of the strength he relied on for the restoration of his Empire was provided by westerners. It became a race against time. Would Manuel be able to exploit the opportunities provided by his overtures to the papacy before the inevitable reaction in the West to Byzantine meddling set in? In Hungary Manuel was successful and the Byzantine hold on the Balkans seemed to have been secured. This was at best only a very indirect offshoot of his overtures to the papacy, which were much more directly concerned with the crusader states. Manuel hoped to use *entente* with the papacy in the short-term to take the initiative along Byzantium's eastern frontier by bringing the crusader states more closely within the Byzantine orbit.

BYZANTIUM AND THE CRUSADER STATES

It seemed at one point in the mid-1150s that Manuel Comnenus was no longer interested in preserving any real Byzantine influence in Cilicia and northern Syria. His efforts at intervention had been tentative and unsuccessful. In 1150 he bought at some cost the remains of the country of Edessa, which amounted to a handful of fortresses close to the Euphrates. They were lost to the Muslim ruler of Aleppo, Nur ed-Din, within a year. Soon afterwards he despatched his cousin Andronicus Comnenus to restore Byzantine influence in Cilicia by bringing the Armenian ruler Thoros to heel; all to no avail. Equally unsuccessful was his bid to find a suitable husband for Constance, regent of Antioch since the death of her husband Raymond of Poitiers in 1149. She turned down his candidate as too old and married instead Reginald of Châtillon, a glamorous knight who had come out from France with the second crusade. The new prince of Antioch soon quarrelled with the Byzantine emperor, alleging that he had not been properly rewarded for an attack upon the Armenian Prince Thoros. In 1156 he equipped a fleet and ravaged the Byzantine island of Cyprus. He defeated and captured the Byzantine commanders and took away much plunder. There was nothing Manuel Comnenus could for the moment do.

To those more perspicacious than Reginald of Châtillon this humiliation of the Byzantine emperor boded ill for the Franks of Outremer. In 1154 Damascus finally fell to Nur ed-Din. Without any Byzantine cover the northern frontiers of the crusader states were now exposed to the full force of Nur ed-Din's power. It would take all the military resources of the crusader states to hold the frontiers. This would mean that the Franks would hardly be able to exploit the opportunities for plunder and expansion which were opening up at that very moment in Egypt. The young king of Jerusalem, Baldwin III, was now of marriageable age. The High Court of the kingdom decided that overtures should be made to Manuel Comnenus over the possibility of a Byzantine bride for their king. It accordingly despatched envoys to Constantinople in the summer of 1157. At first, Manuel Comnenus was not very enthusiastic and the negotiations dragged on for nearly a year. Finally in September 1158 the emperor's niece Theodora Comnena arrived at Tyre as a bride for the king of Jerusalem. But before the marriage took place she was crowned queen, no doubt as a precaution that the Franks would honour their undertakings.

At much the same time, Manuel was finishing his preparations for a descent upon Cilicia. The swiftness of his approach took the Armenian Prince Thoros by surprise and the main fortresses of the Cilician plain were soon back in Byzantine hands. Thoros came to the emperor and made his submission, as did Reginald of Châtillon, who expected the emperor to take his revenge for the attack on Cyprus. He preferred to throw himself on the emperor's mercy, rather than to wait for the king of Jerusalem to intervene on his behalf. He probably calculated that he could expect little real support from the king now that he had married a Byzantine princess. The king sent to the emperor asking whether he was expected to appear before him. The emperor insisted that 'as a beloved son of the empire'[24] he should not delay his coming. His marriage brought with it a certain obligation before the Byzantine emperor. He was received with fitting honour by the emperor, even if his throne was rather lower than the emperor's. None of this settled the delicate matter of the position of Antioch. Baldwin III hoped to be recognized as lord of the principality. To counter this Reginald professed to accept not only the suzerainty of the Byzantine emperor, but also agreed to surrender the citadel of the city to the Byzantines, to accept in the city a Greek patriarch, and to provide the Byzantine emperor with a large contingent of knights. The king intervened to reduce the number of knights that

Antioch was to provide the Byzantine emperor. The question of a Greek patriarch was shelved and the citadel was not handed over to the emperor. Manuel Comnenus came away from his Cilician expedition with relatively little in the way of concrete gains, but with his prestige enhanced by the magnificent ceremonial of his entry into Antioch at Easter 1159. He rode in triumph through the streets of Antioch to the cathedral of St Peter. Reginald of Châtillon and the nobility of Antioch acted as his grooms, accompanying him on foot. Baldwin followed behind on horseback at a becoming distance without his royal insignia. The emperor then spent eight days in the prince's palace, even dispensing justice to the people of Antioch. This was rounded off by a tournament in which the emperor demonstrated to the Franks his knightly prowess.

This ceremonial was no petty charade. It sealed the alliance between Manuel and the Franks of Outremer, spelling out both obligations and rights. Manuel Comnenus preserved his rights of overlordship over Antioch, but there was no further question of annexation. Instead, he would receive in proper western fashion a quota of knights from his vassal. The tournament emphasized that Manuel understood his duties as overlord in western and not in Byzantine terms. The presence of the king of Jerusalem in the cavalcade was an admission of the emperor's pre-eminent rights over Antioch.

How highly Manuel valued his alliance with the Franks of Outremer is evident from the way he turned to the king of Jerusalem when he was looking for a new bride after the death of his first empress in 1160. The two most eligible crusader princesses were Melissende of Tripoli and Maria of Antioch. The emperor was happy to leave the final choice to the king of Jerusalem. He decided in favour of Melissende. In the meantime, Reginald of Châtillon, the acting prince of Antioch, had fallen into the hands of the Muslims. The Byzantines deemed that in the circumstances much more was to be gained from a marriage between Manuel and Maria of Antioch. The king of Jerusalem had every reason to be deeply offended at the way he had been treated. He nevertheless saw to the arrangements for the new marriage, which was finally celebrated at Constantinople in the church of the Holy Wisdom on Christmas Day 1161. The alliance was too valuable to be undermined by a personal slight.

During the negotiations the king of Jerusalem made no objections when a Byzantine general came to Syria to demand the contingent of troops owed by the principality of Antioch. He even supplied a further body of troops which he had agreed to furnish. These soldiers were needed for a campaign that the emperor was mounting against the Seljuqs of Anatolia. As they were marching through Anatolia late in 1161, they were caught by the Turks. Though taken by surprise, they won a complete victory. The Seljuq sultan immediately came to terms with Manuel. He could not sustain a war against Byzantium on two separate fronts. There could have been no better demonstration of the value of the alliance to the Byzantine emperor.

Its value to the crusaders was just as clearly demonstrated after the very serious defeat they suffered in 1164 at Harim just outside Antioch. Bohemund III, the prince of Antioch, fell into the hands of Nur ed-Din along with many other great barons. The new king of Jerusalem, Amalric, was away campaigning in Egypt. There seemed every chance that Antioch would fall to the Muslims. Manuel immediately despatched a large force to Cilicia under the command of one of his most trusted generals, Alexius Axoukh. Nur ed-Din relaxed his grip on Antioch. The Byzantine emperor also arranged for the prince of Antioch's ransom to be paid. After his release the prince came to Constantinople. He was honourably received as was befitting the emperor's brother-in-law and richly rewarded, but he had to accept the installation of a Greek patriarch in Antioch and the expulsion of the Latin.

Manuel was not willing to renounce the traditional role of the Byzantine emperor as the protector of the Orthodox church in the Holy Land. He used the ascendancy he had in the crusader states to promote its welfare. He was even able briefly in the 1170s to negotiate the return of an orthodox patriarch to Jerusalem. He was a generous patron of the orthodox monasteries that continued to exist in the Judaean hills and along the river Jordan. Thanks to him many of them were rebuilt after the terrible earthquake of 1157. His largesse was not limited to the orthodox community alone. He took an interest in the main shrines of the Holy Land, even if they were in Latin hands. He helped with the repairs and embellishing of the church of the Holy Sepulchre at Jerusalem and he paid for the decoration of the church of the Nativity at Bethlehem. He was presenting himself as the protector of the Holy Places, even if in purely military terms this was a task that belonged to the king of Jerusalem, who 'with royal arm and sinews opens up deep sepulchres for any unbeliever who dares attack the Holy Sepulchre'.[25]

The stance taken by Manuel Comnenus was the cause of some resentment among the Franks. There was general rejoicing in Antioch when the Greek patriarch was killed in an earthquake which brought down his church on top of him and the Latin patriarch returned in triumph. On the political plane the Byzantine alliance was too important to allow such considerations much weight. The new king of Jerusalem, Amalric, turned, like his brother Baldwin III before him, to Constantinople in search of a bride. A Byzantine princess duly arrived in August 1167. She too was crowned queen before the marriage ceremony was carried out. This marriage was linked with the most ambitious joint undertaking, nothing less than an assault on Egypt. The germs of the idea almost certainly came from Amalric, but he was probably seeking for some indirect participation on the part of the Byzantines. The

Byzantine court considered the proposal very carefully and decided to assume a major role. The Byzantine historians, Nicetas Choniates and John Cinnamus, both indicate that the Byzantine emperor now took the initiative. He sent envoys to Egypt claiming tribute. The demand seems to have been framed in terms of the corn-tribute which Egypt had given Constantinople before the conquests of Islam. Nicetas Choniates saw Manuel attempting to emulate earlier emperors whose territories 'stretched from the frontiers of the Orient to the pillars of the West'.[26] Could Manuel have so lost his sense of the possible to dream of restoring the Empire of Justinian?

It seems unlikely. Byzantine foreign policy was worked out with great care. To westerners of the time the shrewdness of the Greeks was proverbial. Otto of Freising noted that 'they undertake no important matter without frequent and prolonged deliberations'.[27] What most recommended an attack upon Egypt was that it would bind the crusader states still more closely to the Byzantine Empire. This made an undertaking not directly in Byzantium's interests worthwhile. King Amalric found the Byzantine offer of cooperation in this venture decidedly embarrassing. Having recently wedded a Byzantine princess he could hardly turn down their overtures. But it seemed that conditions in Egypt were now such that the country was ready to fall to the Franks of Outremer. Without waiting for the conclusion of negotiations he attacked Egypt in the autumn of 1168. He reached Cairo, but allowed himself to be bought off. He then agreed to invade Egypt in concert with the Byzantines the following year. The Byzantine fleet set out from Constantinople in July 1169. It was an imposing force. The Greek sources suggest that it consisted of nearly 300 sail. William of Tyre estimated it at just over 200. He was much impressed by the sixty horse-transports and the huge dromons which acted as transport vessels. The Byzantines came, however, with only sufficient provisions for three months. This suggests that their primary objective was not the conquest of Egypt, but the establishment of a bridgehead at the mouth of the Nile. From the outset Amalric prevaricated. His fear was that the Byzantines might well get more than their fair share of the booty and of any conquests that were made. The combined forces did not arrive before the Nile port of Damietta until the end of October, just when the Byzantine provisions were beginning to give out. The siege was a fiasco. The Byzantine commander was under instructions from Manuel Comnenus not to act without Amalric's consent. The king of Jerusalem allowed the siege to drag on much longer than it should. The Byzantine commander lost patience and finally ordered his troops to begin the assault. Amalric was in the meantime negotiating a peaceful surrender of the town and the assault was called off. The Byzantine troops were starving and nothing would keep them in Egypt. They scrambled to get aboard the ships to take them home. Much of the Byzantine fleet was lost through storms on the return journey. William of Tyre is not quite able to conceal how badly the Franks had behaved towards their allies throughout the whole enterprise.

Surprisingly, this did not put an end to the alliance of Byzantium with the crusader states. The outcome was improved by the appearance at the Byzantine court of envoys from Egypt bringing gifts and suing for peace. Amalric, conscious that he had been at fault, went in 1171 to Constantinople, where he was magnificently entertained. Manuel listened favourably to his proposals for another expedition against Egypt, and a treaty was drawn up. The historian John Cinnamus pays little attention to Amalric's visit except to insist that he became the emperor's vassal. It may not have been quite so specific a subordination to the Byzantine emperor that was established, but some degree of Byzantine overlordship was surely recognized. Manuel took his duties towards the crusader states seriously. In 1177 a Byzantine fleet of 150 sail appeared off Acre. It had arrived to implement the agreement between Manuel and the late King Amalric for a joint invasion of Egypt, an agreement which had been ratified by Amalric's son and heir, Baldwin IV. The arrival of the Byzantine fleet was timed to coincide with the crusade of Philip, count of Flanders, but the count was adamant that he would take no part in any expedition against Egypt. Thus ended hopes of mounting another joint invasion of Egypt.

It marked the complete collapse of Manuel's most ambitious project, which was nothing less than harnessing the crusade to further Byzantine interests. In 1175 he wrote to Pope Alexander III with news that he had restored the town of Dorylaion, the key to control of the routes across the Anatolian plateau. He claimed that the route to the Holy Sepulchre had been rendered safe for both Latins and Greeks. It was his firm intention to wage war against the infidel and he turned to the pope for help. The pope, for his part, proclaimed a crusade to 'promote his pious proposal'.[28] Manuel Comnenus was interested in the first instance in asserting control over Anatolia, but he hoped to be able to cover his rear by promoting a crusade, which would have the additional value of strengthening his alliance with the crusader states. These hopes came tumbling to the ground with his defeat by the Seljuqs at Myriokephalon in 1176.

The importance of the crusader states in Manuel Comnenus's foreign policy is amply demonstrated by the closeness of the dynastic contacts. It was quite unprecedented. Members of the nobility of both Antioch and Jerusalem could expect a warm and generous welcome at the Byzantine court. Several served Manuel, Baldwin of Antioch rising to be one of his trusted commanders. The alliance with the crusader states seemed to offer Manuel several advantages. It helped to check the Seljuqs of Anatolia, hemming them in to the south. It added to the emperor's prestige as protector of the Holy Places, but, above all, it gave the emperor a window to the West. He could show his benevolence towards western christendom and hope to turn suspicion into friendship, the better to tap western strength and energy. Manuel was not being totally unrealistic, but in the interests of this alliance he committed himself to projects which upset the balance of Byzantine foreign policy. They suggested that it was being run more for Byzantium's allies than for Byzantium itself.

BYZANTIUM AND THE SELJUQS

Manuel's original intention was to use his alliance with the Franks of Outremer as a balance against the Seljuqs of Anatolia. There is a clear parallel with his policy in the Balkans, where he used the ascendancy he gained over Hungary as a way of controlling the anarchy of the Balkans. Just as in the Balkans the Byzantines had to accept the depredations of Serb, Vlach, and Albanian herdsmen as a necessary evil, so in Anatolia they had to come to terms with the Turcoman nomads who were settled in large numbers along the western fringes of the central plateau and kept pressing down towards the valleys of the coastlands. The best they could do was to refortify the frontier areas, and to re-create local military forces capable of defending the region. This Manuel did in the 1160s around Pergamon when he created the new theme of Neokastra. The historian Nicetas Choniates hailed this as one of Manuel's most useful achievements. It restored prosperity to a region which had suffered at the hands of marauding Turks.

Byzantine authors never have a good word to say about the Turcoman nomads. They were cruel, untrustworthy robbers. It was generally recognized that the Seljuq sultan of Ikonion had little control over them. Byzantine hostility towards them was not carried over to the Seljuqs. They could hardly be considered as aliens. There was a great deal of interpenetration. Turks served in the Byzantine armies; some of them were converted to christianity and rose to the highest positions. The Axoukh family were of Seljuq origin. Alexius Axoukh seems to have retained some sense of affinity with the Seljuq ruling family. He decorated one of his palaces with scenes celebrating the martial achievements of the Seljuq sultan, with whom he was supposed to have a treasonable understanding. It may have been nothing more than the fact that, just as there was a pro-Latin clique at the Byzantine court, so Axoukh was the leader of a pro-Seljuq group. He was the loser in a bout of court intrigue and was forced to go into a monastery. At the Seljuq court at Konya there were many Byzantine exiles. The most notable were members of the Gabras family and a cousin of Manuel Comnenus, who apostasized to Islam. Manuel Comnenus concerned himself with the problem of apostasy and the conversion of Muslims to christianity. He tried to make it easier to become a Christian. He removed the anathema which any convert had to pronounce against the God of Mohammed. This was done on the request of Iktiyar ad-Din Hasan ibn Gabras, later to be Kilidj Arslan's Grand Vizier, who considered converting to christianity but was deterred by the requirement to abjure the God of Mohammed. Manuel's intention was in this way to strengthen the hold of christianity in the Seljuq territories and at the Seljuq court, where there were Christians in influential positions. He was willing to tolerate a large measure of political devolution, but it was to be counterbalanced by the continuing influence of the Orthodox church.

Such a policy would only work if the sultan was brought firmly within the Byzantine orbit. This Manuel achieved by 1162. He undertook a whole series of campaigns against the Seljuq frontiers from 1158 until 1161. As we have seen, it was a victory by a force of Franks under the Byzantine general, John Kontostephanos, at the end of 1161, which seems to have decided the Seljuq sultan, Kilidj Arslan, that he would have to come to terms with Manuel. He came in the spring of 1162 as a suppliant to Constantinople. He was entertained with great magnificence. He became a client of the emperor, promising to furnish him with troops. He received a great amount of treasure in return and the promise of further subsidies. In return, he bound himself to hand over to the Byzantines the town of Sivas (Sebastea) and the surrounding region. Byzantine bishops were allowed to return to their sees.

It seemed to be an ideal state of affairs. Why did Manuel not allow it to continue? The overthrow of Alexius Axoukh in 1167 meant that the pro-Latin party was in the ascendant at the Byzantine court. There was no longer a strong body of opinion to urge the advantages of *entente* with the Seljuqs. Instead, it seemed that all the benefits of *entente* lay with the Seljuq sultan. He used it to extend his authority over most of the Danishmend territories along the northern and eastern edges of the Anatolian plateau. Nor did he show any sign of honouring his pledge to return a number of cities to the Byzantine emperor, including Sivas. The only check he encountered was the ruler of Aleppo, Nur ed-Din, who took the surviving Danishmend emirs under his protection, but he died in 1174. Now there was nothing to prevent Kilidj Arslan from seeking to emancipate himself from his tutelage to the Byzantine emperor. Both sides were eager for war and they were not willing to use any diplomatic means to prevent it.

Manuel was intent on nothing less than the capture of Konya. It would increase his prestige enormously and it would place the route to the Holy Land under his control. He prepared his campaign with great thoroughness. He began by reoccupying Dorylaion. This had been deserted and the region had become one of the most important centres for the nomads in the north-western corner of the Anatolian plateau. He was able to beat off their attacks and construct a fortress, which dominated the approach to Konya from the north. He then moved on at the end of 1175 to the Phrygian uplands and the sources of the river Maiander. There he fortified the site of Soublaion or Khoma, as it was more usually known. This commanded the approach to Ikonion from the west. At roughly the same time he tried to secure the northern town of Amaseia, which would have threatened the Seljuq hold over the territories they had acquired at the expense of the Danishmends. This attempt failed, but he then sent another force to seize Niksar (Neokaisareia), some 60 miles to the east, in the hope of creating a diversion, while he attacked Konya.

In the summer of 1176 Manuel collected together his army. He decided to attack Konya via the Maiander valley. It provided the shortest route through Turkish territory, even if through difficult country. He made his way to his base at Soublaion. Kilidj Arslan was expecting reinforcements from eastern Anatolia and he tried to stall the Byzantine invasion by making overtures of peace. Manuel rejected these. He advanced out of Soublaion towards the deserted fortress of Myriokephalon. He kept good order, but progress was very slow, because of the vast baggage train. The sultan decided to wait for the Byzantines at the pass known as Tzivritze, which lay beyond Myriokephalon. The Byzantine column which stretched for several miles was drawn up in the following order. There was a vanguard and a rearguard. The most vulnerable section was the baggage train. The emperor was escorting it, covered by bodies of troops on his right and left wings. The vanguard screened by infantry had no difficulty forcing its way through the pass to open ground at the further end, where its commanders ordered a halt. The main weight of the Turkish attack then fell on the right wing of the escorting troops. These were under the command of Baldwin of Antioch. The terrain was against them. They found themselves pinned against the steep slopes on the southern side of the pass with little hope of manœuvring against the Turks. Baldwin was killed and his troops suffered heavy casualties. Their defeat allowed the Turks to block the centre of the pass. This produced complete confusion. The baggage train was brought to a standstill, able neither to advance nor retire. The emperor gave up and decided to fight his way out, hoping to get through to the vanguard. It was a very close thing. Uncharacteristically, he was close to despair and thought of abandoning his army altogether. He was dissuaded by Andronicus Kontostephanos, the commander of the rear guard. He had been able to get through with little difficulty and with his support Manuel managed to join up with the vanguard. The army was more or less intact. Only the right wing under Baldwin of Antioch and the troops escorting the baggage train had suffered heavy casualties, but as soon as Kilidj Arslan offered terms the emperor took them. He had lost his siege train, which put paid to any realistic hope of conquering Konya, but by all accounts he had also lost something more precious: his nerve. 'Never again did he exhibit the gaiety of spirit which had been so characteristic of him. ... Never again did he enjoy the good health which he had possessed to such a remarkable degree. In short, the ever-present memory of that defeat so oppressed him that never again did he enjoy peace of mind or his usual tranquility of spirit.'[29] That was the opinion of the historian William of Tyre. It was an impression gained at first hand while on a mission to the Byzantine court in 1179.

The terms offered by Kilidj Arslan were reasonable in the extreme. Manuel was to be allowed to retreat in peace. He was able to ransom a reliquary containing a splinter of the True Cross. He only had to agree to pull down the fortifications he had so recently erected at Dorylaion and Soublaion. Those of Soublaion he destroyed as he retreated, but once safely back on Byzantine territory he thought better of destroying Dorylaion. The sultan remonstrated, but the emperor refused to be bound by a concession made under duress. The sultan countered by sending an army to invade the Maiander valley. It was completely defeated by the Byzantine force sent against it. This was followed up by some punitive expeditions against the Turcoman nomads settled in the region around the upper Maiander valley. Manuel's last campaign undertaken in the winter of 1179–80 was to relieve the fortress of Klaudiopolis, the modern Bolu. The Turks melted away in the face of the emperor's swift advance.

The defeat at Myriokephalon therefore appears not to have been a major disaster. It seems little different from Manuel's 1146 campaign against Konya, when it was only with difficulty that he managed to extricate his army from the Anatolian plateau. Almost nothing was lost and the Byzantines proved quite capable of meeting Turkish pressure on their Anatolian frontiers. Modern historians have nevertheless seen the defeat at Myriokephalon as a watershed. They reflect opinion at the time. Even Manuel in a letter to the people of Constantinople compared his defeat to that suffered at Mantzikert by Romanos Diogenes, but insisted that he had been able to make peace on his own terms.

There are obvious if superficial parallels between the defeats at Mantzikert and at Myriokephalon. They both seemed to open the way to the disintegration of the political and social fabric of the Empire. On closer inspection it becomes clear that this was not a direct consequence of defeat. It was much more that pressures were building up, that might possibly have been diffused by military success, always a desperate course of action, which the Byzantines were normally loath to pursue; battle being such a chancy affair. Romanos Diogenes and Manuel Comnenus were risking battle for different ends: Romanos to strengthen his control over the Empire. This was not a problem for Manuel, few Byzantine emperors ever sat so securely on their throne. Instead, he needed a great victory to validate a foreign policy, which seemed increasingly unrealistic. The direct gains that the Byzantines might expect from the conquest of Konya were small. Its main value would have been to secure the land route across Anatolia to the crusader states.

It would revive the prestige of the Byzantine emperor in the West, where, as we have seen, he had become almost completely isolated. Defeat merely confirmed this fact. The papacy took great pleasure in his discomfiture and at the treaty of Venice in 1177 between the pope and the Emperor Frederick Barbarossa, the Byzantine emperor was not even mentioned as a possible ally of either partner. His shadow had hung over Italian politics for thirty years or more, now he was more or less irrelevant. Byzantium and its emperor were to be patronized. In the opening address of the Third Lateran Council of 1179 there was an unequivocal claim to papal supremacy over the church of Constantinople, while in the same year Frederick Barbarossa wrote in the most insulting terms to Manuel addressing him as king of the Greeks. He was called upon to recognize Barbarossa's authority and to submit to the pope.

Manuel Comnenus's foreign policy has been condemned as overambitious. This is what it became, but its underlying concept was extremely perceptive. Manuel understood the possibilities that his grandfather had opened up for the restoration of the Byzantine Empire. He grasped the lesson that influence and indirect authority counted for almost as much as direct rule. His original intention was to use the influence he gained in the Latin lands to ensure Byzantine ascendancy in the Balkans and Anatolia. This would protect the inner core of the Byzantine Empire around the sea of Marmora and the Aegean. It would have the additional advantage of attracting Latins to take up service in the Byzantine Empire. Manuel was counting on their military and commercial skills to provide his Empire with a new source of strength. His foreign policy became distorted once he saw influence among the Latins as more important than the immediate interests of the Empire. It began to involve him in chancy ventures, such as the attack on Egypt in 1169 and the invasion of the Seljuq territories in Anatolia in 1176. These were proof of how unrealistic his foreign policy was becoming. At the same time, as we shall see, he was beginning to discover that there were difficulties attached to the settlement of Latins in his Empire, while the favoured position they enjoyed at his court was cause of much resentment.

NOTES

1. Michel Italikos, *Lettres et Discours* (ed. by P Gautier) (Paris, 1972), p. 292
2. Cinnamus (transl. by C M Brand), p. 43
3. Odo of Deuil (ed. and transl. by V G Berry), p. 68
4. *Ibid.*, p. 76
5. Otto of Freising, *The Deeds of Frederick Barbarossa*, p. 106

6.   Cinnamus (transl. by C M Brand), p. 66
7.   Eustathius, *Opuscula* (ed. by T L F Tafel) (Frankfurt, 1832), p. 199
8.   Odo of Deuil (ed. and transl. by V G Berry), p. 56
9.   William of Tyre (transl. by E A Babcock and A C Krey), II, p. 170
10.   Nicetas Choniates (ed. by Van Dieten), p. 69
11.   Peter the Venerable, *Letters* (ed. by G Constable) (Cambridge, Mass., 1967), I, p. 208
12.   Nicetas Choniates (ed. by Van Dieten), p. 127
13.   R Browning, *Studies on Byzantine History, Literature and Education* (London, 1977), no. IV, p. 203
14.   Quoted in G Moravcsik, *Byzantium and the Magyars* (Amsterdam, 1970) p. 83
15.   Migne, PL, 188, c. 1218
16.   Georges et Dèmètrios Tornikès, *Lettres et Discours*, p. 325
17.   F Güterbock, 'Le lettere del notaio imperiale Burcardo intorno alla politica del Barbarossa nello scisma ed alla distruzione di Milano', *Bullettino dell'Istituto storico italiano per il Medio Evo,* 61 (1949), p. 57
18.   *Recueil des Historiens des Gaules et de la France,* XVI (Paris, 1878), p. 15
19.   Zepos, *Jus,* I, p. 410
20.   Cinnamus (transl. by C M Brand), p. 189
21.   Zepos, *Jus,* I, p. 414
22.   J Darrouzès, 'Les documents byzantins du XIIe siècle sur la primauté romaine', *Revue des Etudes Byzantines,* 23 (1965), p. 76
23.   Cinnamus (transl. by C M Brand), p. 167
24.   William of Tyre (transl. by E A Babcock and A C Krey), II, p. 277
25.   W Regel, *Fontes rerum byzantinarum,* I (St Petersburg, 1892), p. 39
26.   Nicetas Choniates (ed. Van Dieten), p. 160
27.   Otto of Freising, *The Deeds of Frederick Barbarossa,* p. 66
28.   P Jaffé, *Regesta Pontificum Romanorum,* II (Leipzig, 1888), no. 12684
29.   William of Tyre (transl. by E A Babcock and A C Krey), II, p. 415

Chapter 11

MANUEL COMNENUS AND THE LATINS

THE VENETIANS AT CONSTANTINOPLE

In the course of the twelfth century Latins began to settle in increasing numbers at Constantinople, even if the scale was not perhaps as massive as is sometimes suggested. Not too much trust should be placed on the figures given by contemporaries. It is difficult to believe that there were upwards of 10,000 Venetians in the Empire in 1171, let alone that there were 60,000 Latins settled in Constantinople in 1182, even allowing for a floating population of Latin merchants and mercenaries, adventurers, drifters, and pilgrims. The Latin pilgrim was a byword for poverty in twelfth-century Constantinople.[1] The numbers of Latins permanently resident in Constantinople should probably be reckoned in thousands rather than tens of thousands. There is just one accurate figure to play with. Only seventy-four Genoese claimed that they had been injured, when in 1162 the Venetians and the Pisans sacked the newly established Genoese factory in Constantinople. The Genoese authorities reckoned that damage to Genoese property amounted to 30,000 *hyperpyra*. We do not know the amount of damages claimed by the Venetians for the loss of property suffered in 1171, when Manuel Comnenus had all the Venetians in the Empire arrested, but reparations were fixed at slightly less than four times the amount of the Genoese figure. These figures are far from being strictly comparable, but, making due allowances, they invite caution about the numbers of Venetians settled in the Byzantine Empire in the mid-years of Manuel's reign.

The Genoese were relative newcomers to Constantinople. The bulk of their commercial interests in the Levant were concentrated in the ports of the Holy Land. The Venetians and Pisans, in contrast, were long established in the Byzantine Empire. The Venetians had had a factory at Constantinople since 1082 and the Pisans since 1111. The Pisans had a large stake in the foreign trade of the Byzantine Empire, but we know next to nothing about their commercial activities. We are, on the other hand, very well informed about the Venetians. Several hundred commercial documents survive from the twelfth century which allow us to plot the pattern of Venetian involvement in the trade and economic life of the Byzantine Empire.

Venetian trade in the Byzantine Empire seems only to have taken off after the renewal of their privileges by John II Comnenus (1118–43). The Venetians secured two valuable new concessions. They were allowed to trade in Crete and Cyprus which had previously been forbidden to their merchants. This favoured Venetian participation in the lucrative trade between the Byzantine Empire and the ports of the Holy Land and the Nile delta. It was further agreed that in future Byzantines would not have to pay any duties on transactions with Venetians, thus removing a significant barrier to the development of Venetian trade with the native population. In the past, doing business with the Venetians cannot have held out many attractions to the Byzantines, since they would have had to bear the various charges due to the state. In the early twelfth century Venetian involvement in Byzantine trade seems to have taken the form of sporadic ventures to Constantinople and various provincial centres. The sums invested were not all that large and normally in currency in use at Venice. Only from the 1130s do Venetians begin to invest considerable capital in their Byzantine ventures, in some cases reaching 1,000 *hyperpyra* or more, and it became usual to work with Byzantine rather than Italian currency. It was one sign of the way they were beginning to infiltrate the Byzantine economy. Another was the rising curve of Venetian contracts concluded in either Constantinople or some provincial Byzantine town. These reached their peak in the 1160s. Further expansion was cut short by the expulsion of the Venetians from the Empire in 1171. Ensuing lawsuits about debts contracted in the Byzantine Empire before this bear witness to the dislocation it caused to the Venetian economy.

One of the heroes of the hour was a Venetian sea-captain called Romano Mairano. He was the master of a massive three-masted cog. He used it to rescue many Venetians from Constantinople and to bear them safely to Acre in the Holy Land. Constantinople had been his main centre of operations since the early 1150s. His career is exceptionally well documented and it gives a good impression of the activities of a Venetian sea-captain operating out of Constantinople, even if he was rather more successful than most. He started at Constantinople in partnership with his brother Samuel and acted as an agent for his brother-in-law back in Venice. It was a typical family business arrangement. By 1156 he was sufficiently well established in Constantinople to lease out property there. His interest in shipping went back to the previous year when in partnership with another Venetian he acquired a quarter share in a ship bound for Venice. He returned on the same ship with a cargo of wood for Constantinople. He then acquired a ship of his own and with his brother concentrated on the run down the western coast of Asia Minor to Smyrna. These ventures seem to have provided them with the capital to break into the trade between the Byzantine Empire and the ports of the Holy Land and Egypt. They still kept their main interests at Constantinople, where in 1169 they acquired a wharf on a six-year lease. This was part of a deal with the Venetian patriarch of Grado, which cost them the substantial sum of £500 veronese.

If Romano worked out of Constantinople, other Venetian merchants and sea-captains preferred to make provincial towns their centre of operations. From the 1130s the Venetians began acquiring property in different towns. It would be grouped around a monastery or a church which had come into Venetian possession. Venetian monasteries and churches are attested in the following places in the Byzantine Empire during the twelfth century: Adrianople, Raidestos, Halmyros, Corinth, Thebes, Sparta, Dyrrakhion, even on the island of Lemnos. These churches and their priests had an invaluable role to play; they kept the weights and measures that were to be used by the Venetians in their transactions; they acted as depositories for valuables and documents, and the priest often served as notary to the local Venetian community. Many of these churches were acquired in the 1130s, when the Venetians were exploring the possibilities of local trade within the Byzantine Empire. A place, such as Lemnos, never acquired any importance as a trading post, while towns, such as Adrianople and Raidestos, proved disappointing. Nor do Romano and Samuel Mairano's voyages to Smyrna seem to have led to a permanent Venetian presence in the ports of western Asia Minor. There are precious few indications of Venetian interest in Thessalonica, despite its famed fair of St Demetrius. The Venetians concentrated their activities on the Greek towns of Corinth, Sparta, Thebes, and Halmyros. They dealt mostly in olive oil and other agricultural products, including linen and cotton. With the exception of Thebes these places were all ports in the middle ages. Thebes was the main centre of the region, the seat of the governor of the theme of Hellas and the Peloponnese, and it lay within easy reach of the gulf of Corinth. There are some signs that on the eve of the Venetian expulsion from the Empire Venetian merchants operating from Thebes were trying to break into the overland trade of the Greek provinces, but it was the sea which gave the Venetians their main advantage. It perhaps helps to explain their concentration on bulk goods. The sea was the only practical route for such commodities over any distance. The cost of transporting them by land was crippling. The profits to be made from carrying them by sea were probably not very high, but the Venetians were in the enviable position of not having to pay any customs duties. For luxuries, such as the silks produced at Thebes, the costs of transport were less of a problem. The profits to be made were sufficiently high for transport costs and customs duties to be less of an obstacle than with bulk goods. The Venetians had no clear advantage in the field of luxury goods.

Although they were strongly entrenched at Thebes, there is no sign that they were interested in breaking into its silk trade.

These considerations suggest a substantial role for the Venetians in the economy of the Byzantine Empire rather than the overwhelming domination that is sometimes attributed to them. They clearly controlled, as one would expect, most of the commerce between the Byzantine Empire and Venice; they probably had the major share of the trade between Constantinople and the ports of the Holy Land and the Nile delta, and they well-nigh monopolized the export of agricultural products from the Greek lands. It would be an exaggeration to suggest that they had a stranglehold over the internal trade of the Empire. Outside Constantinople and the Greek lands they can only have had the most tenuous foothold. From an economic point of view, the activities of the Venetians were largely beneficial to the Byzantine Empire. Byzantine shipping may have suffered, but against this the Byzantines stood to gain as agents, brokers, changers, bankers, and ships' chandlers.

The Venetians contributed a great deal towards the commercial prosperity of the Byzantine Empire in the middle years of the twelfth century. It has always seemed that Manuel was therefore acting against the best interests of the Empire, when on 12 March 1171 he ordered the arrest of all Venetians in the Empire and the confiscation of their property. This action constituted a turning point in the history of the Byzantine Empire. The reasonably amicable relations between the Empire and the maritime republics of Italy were replaced by suspicion and often open hostility, as Byzantine emperors tried to play off one republic against another. In such circumstances it became almost impossible to control the Italians. The arrest of the Venetians in 1171 was a pointer to the future disintegration of the Empire in much the same way as the defeat at Myriokephalon was to be.

It remains something of a mystery why Manuel Comnenus should have taken this action against the Venetians. The historian Nicetas Choniates is most unforthcoming. It is hard to believe his suggestion that Manuel was motivated by the bitter memory of the insulting charade put on by the Venetians at his expense during the siege of Corfu more than twenty years earlier. He hints that the emperor had got wind of some even worse piece of mischief on the part of the Venetians, but he gives no indication as to its nature. John Cinnamus is more helpful. There was friction over the exact status of those Venetians who had settled permanently in the Empire. The emperor objected to the way they had begun to establish themselves outside their factory in Constantinople. They took Byzantine brides and it was difficult to distinguish them from the general run of Byzantine citizens.

That was the problem, for the Venetians were able to claim privileged status, which placed them beyond the control of the Byzantine authorities. They were not only exempted from the payment of customs duties and sales taxes. The chrysobull of Alexius Comnenus also made it clear that no Byzantine official from the prefect of the city downwards had any jurisdiction over them. This was bound to be cause of friction, the more so because commissions began to come out from Venice to hear disputes that arose within the Venetian communities settled in the Byzantine Empire. They deliberately instilled a respect for 'the honour of their *patria*'[1A] into their fellow citizens. Their activities underlined the independence of the Venetians within the Empire, which was all the more frustrating for the Byzantine authorities now that the Venetians were beginning to spread out among the native population. Manuel's solution was to separate the Venetians permanently settled in the Byzantine Empire from those only temporarily resident. The latter were presumably to continue enjoying the special fiscal and judicial status, as laid down in the chrysobull of 1148; the former were to become imperial burgesses. The creation of this order was an experiment that failed. Little is known about their exact status. They seem to have been the commercial counterparts of the imperial liege knights created by Manuel Comnenus. These were western knights directly bound in homage to the Byzantine emperor. The imperial burgesses were therefore presumably exempted from the payment of customs duties and sales taxes, but instead of being subjects of some Italian republic were directly answerable to the emperor. In this way, the emperor hoped to avail himself of the commercial talents of the Italians.

The difficulty is to know when Manuel Comnenus attempted to impose this solution. Cinnamus places it shortly before the Venetians of Constantinople attacked the Genoese quarter in 1170, which was the immediate cause of Manuel's decision to expel the Venetians from his Empire. He demanded that the Venetians pay for the damage, which they refused to do and instead made threats about a punitive expedition like that undertaken in John II Comnenus's reign. The Venetian sources provide a variant on this. Manuel seized Venetian property. The Doge Vitale Michiel replied by placing an embargo on trade with the Byzantine Empire. Manuel saw that this was harming the prosperity of the Empire. He accordingly offered the doge a commercial monopoly in the Empire if he allowed his merchants to return. The doge immediately licensed huge numbers of merchants – 20,000 is the figure given – to trade in the Byzantine Empire. They brought with them rich merchandise, which the crafty emperor then seized. The thrust of the Venetian story is that Manuel deliberately lured Venetians to the Byzantine Empire so that he could plunder their wealth.

If the Venetian embargo was in response to the measures taken by Manuel after the Venetian assault on the Genoese quarter in 1170, then not much trust can be placed in this story. The attack cannot have taken place until after May 1170, when the Genoese formally took possession of their quarter. The Venetians would have had to reach Constantinople before early March 1171, when the arrest occurred. Since it is most unlikely that they would have sailed during the winter months, the mass emigration of Venetian merchants would have had to take place before October at the latest. There hardly seems to be enough time to fit in all the events mentioned in the Venetian account.

It is suspiciously reminiscent of the embargo on trade with the Byzantine Empire, which the Doge Vitale Michiel is supposed to have imposed in 1166–67. This was in response to the overtures made by the Byzantine emperor to the Sicilians over the possibility of a marriage between their new King William II and his daughter the Porphyrogenite Maria. Such a marriage might have harmed Venetian interests in the Adriatic. This was a climax of a period of strained relations between the Venetians and the Byzantine Empire, which began with a joint attack by the Pisans and the Venetians on the Genoese quarter in 1162. The embargo of 1166–67 does not seem to have been very effective, since Venetians continued to trade in the Byzantine Empire. On 10 December 1167 Byzantine emissaries arrived at Venice, requesting that the doge should provide Byzantium with the customary naval support. This suggests that the differences had now been patched up. It is reasonable to suppose that, if there is anything in the Venetian tradition of a mass exodus of Venetian merchants to the Byzantine Empire, it occurred at this time. To judge by the commercial documents that have survived, Venetian activity in the Byzantine Empire was at its height between 1167 and 1170. The detail that the Venetians were offered a commercial monopoly at this time may have some foundation, for Manuel neglected to renew the commercial privileges of the Pisans and the Genoese and refused to allow them to return to their factories in Constantinople. This was in retaliation for the 1162 incident, when the Venetians and the Pisans attacked the Genoese quarter. The Venetians, in contrast, were restored to imperial favour.

The Genoese made repeated attempts to recover their position at Constantinople from 1164 onwards, but it was only in May 1170 that their privileges were renewed and the factory restored. Manuel Comnenus followed this up in July by renewing the privileges of the Pisans. Why was the Byzantine emperor willing to risk the good relations he had built up with the Venetians by coming to terms with their rivals? The wording of the imperial chrysobulls to Pisa and Genoa suggests that Manuel was seeking their help against Frederick Barbarossa. It can hardly be a coincidence that in 1170 the same Byzantine embassy dealt with both Pope Alexander III, Barbarossa's doughtiest opponent, and the Republic of Genoa. Whatever Manuel's motives may have been, the Venetians only saw a threat to their position at Constantinople. The return of the Genoese seemed very much like an act of betrayal on the part of the Byzantine emperor. Venetian anger exploded in an attack upon the Genoese quarter. It was both an affront to imperial authority and an example of the way one strand of Manuel's foreign policy snagged against another. The prestige of the emperor demanded that he keep order among his clients, whence Manuel's action against the Venetians in March 1171.

The Venetians repeated the tactics that had worked so successfully in the reign of John II Comnenus. They sent a fleet to the Aegean. It besieged the town of Eurippos, the capital of the island of Euboea. The Venetians were able to burn down a few houses, but then sailed away to Chios which they made their base for the winter of 1171/72. They were plagued with disease; they were not able to withstand the Byzantine fleet despatched against them. Without a battle being fought they were chased out of the Aegean. It was as great a humiliation as the Venetians ever suffered at the hands of the Byzantines. The Doge Vitale Michiel, who had commanded the expedition, was murdered once he got back to Venice. His successor mounted an attack in the following year against the city of Ancona, which was a Byzantine protectorate. This too was a failure. But the treaty they concluded with the king of Sicily in September 1175 alarmed Manuel Comnenus. He put out feelers and soon afterwards the Venetians accepted their old status within the Empire and reparations were fixed at 1,500 lb of gold for the property lost in 1171. The final details may not have been completed at the time of the emperor's death, since negotiations continued later under Andronicus I and Isaac II.

The Venetians were chastened and the outcome might seem to be a success for Manuel Comnenus. The turn of events, after Manuel's death, indicated otherwise. His foreign policy not only left Byzantium isolated; it also produced at the very heart of the Empire an embittered and alienated people, the Venetians. Only after Manuel's death did it become apparent what damage they could do to the Empire. But already the attitude of the Byzantines towards the Venetians was beginning to harden.

Before the end of the eleventh century the Byzantines paid very little attention to the Venetians. They feature in a posthumous miracle of St Symeon the 'New Theologian'. A slave runs off with a valuable icon of the saint and sells it to some Venetians. This incident belongs to the middle years of the eleventh century. There is no comment on the Venetians, good or bad. They were not yet people exciting much interest in Byzantium. A century later some Venetians acquired an icon of St Stephen quite legally from the sacristan of a church in Constantinople. This incident was cause for moral indignation on the part of a member of the patriarchal clergy. He did not blame the Venetians. It was more a reflection on the Byzantines themselves: they were 'willing to sell anything for gold'.[2] The Venetians were less interested in gold and more in the *philotimo*, in the modern Greek sense of prestige, which possession of such an icon brought. The Byzantines were now uncomfortably aware of the Venetians who dwelt among them. They could not really be dismissed as the historian Nicetas Choniates tried to do as 'men of a crafty disposition, who gained their livelihood in the manner of

Phoenicians by roaming the seas'.[3] They may have been crude, vigorous people, who in John Cinnamus's words were 'filled with sailors' vulgarity',[4] but they also revealed the inadequacies of the Byzantines themselves, and this was hard to forgive.

BYZANTIUM AND THE LATINS

Such ambivalence was part of the general attitude of Byzantines to westerners. The old-fashioned contempt for the barbarian continued, but it was an inadequate response to people who were in some ways their superiors. The crusades gave to the collection of barbarian tribes and people of the West a collective identity, which they had not previously enjoyed in Byzantine eyes. United under the crusading banner they were to be feared. From the reign of Manuel Comnenus the Byzantine intelligentsia began to reassess their own identity in the face of the Latin threat. In order to emphasize that 'vast chasm of discord'[5] which existed between Byzantine and Latin, they began to refer to themselves as Hellenes, forgetting the pejorative associations this usage had with paganism. The favour enjoyed at the court of Manuel Comnenus by Latins was cause for resentment on the part of highly educated Byzantines who saw preferment going to 'barbarians' hardly able to speak Greek properly. This comes out with vivid force in a letter written in the mid-1150s by a Byzantine bishop, who was trying to get his uncle a job at court: 'I can't believe that a Philhellene and lover of freedom would docket a Hellene with barbarians nor a free man with people who are slaves by nature. I can't abide the sort of people who use the barbarian tongue, nor, if I may speak my mind, those apparent servants of Mars. They are the kind of people who are on such good terms with barbarians that they prefer the barbarian to the Hellene, alleging against the Hellene, though a hero, a lover of the Muses and Hermes, that of the two he is the inferior.'[6] He urges that in the face of Latin infiltration Byzantines must stick together. He quotes Proverbs 17: 17: 'A friend loveth at all times, and a brother is born for adversity.'

This line of criticism is taken up by the historian Nicetas Choniates, when he comes to assess Manuel Comnenus's reign. Latins, he claimed, flocked to the Byzantine court and were so favoured that they received huge sums of money from the emperor. He had such trust in them that not only did they receive high commands, they were also put in charge of the law courts, which in the past had required men skilled in the law. They were also involved in the assessing and raising of taxes, with the result that the fiscal administration became oppressive and corrupt.

Choniates's criticism may contain an element of exaggeration, but not unduly so. There were many Latins at Manuel's court. He used them extensively in missions to western and crusader courts. Some, such as the Norman exile, the count of Gravina, seem to have become permanently domiciled in the Byzantine Empire. Others were only temporarily in the emperor's service; for instance, the Byzantine mission of 1163 to the French court included the Venetian abbot of St Mary's, Adrianople, and the prior of the hospital of St John at Constantinople. It was an example of the way the emperor made use of those Latins resident on Byzantine soil. In religious matters, he seems to have relied heavily on the Pisan theologian Hugh Eteriano, whom he commissioned among other things to draw up a dossier on the dogma of the Procession of the Holy Spirit.

In 1177 Hugh Eteriano got caught up with Manuel Comnenus's financial expert, Astaforte, a Jew of western origin. Manuel gave him the task of finding ways of extracting money from the imperial burgesses. Astaforte laid it down that a burgess was 'to be compelled to surrender [to the state] one third of all property acquired or rendered through the judgement of a court'.[7] It was a clever way round their exemption from taxes. Eteriano was one of the executors of the will of the Pisan Signoretto, who had become an imperial burgess. Astaforte was informed that he had died intestate and claimed his property for the state. Eteriano tried to rescue his property, but was imprisoned for his pains. Only the intervention of his brother Leo, an imperial interpreter, with the emperor saved him and the case was dropped. If Astaforte's activities were directed against Latins rather than Byzantines, they do show that Manuel was happy to use westerners in the shadier reaches of his fiscal administration.

There is less evidence for Latins playing much part in the administration proper. Nicetas Choniates may have been thinking rather of second- or third generation Latins, men such as Alexius Giphardos (Gifford), who held high military command as well as being governor of the theme of Thrakesion, or Isaac Aaron, the commander of the Varangian Guard. Aaron was born at Corinth, but had been carried away as a child into captivity in Sicily, where he learnt the Latin tongue. He became the spokesman for the Latins at the Byzantine court and was responsible for denouncing Alexius Axoukh in 1167. He himself was overthrown not long afterwards. He abused his position as go-between in negotiations between the emperor and western envoys. He was able to tamper with proposals they brought, so that they fitted better with what he took to be the emperor's wishes. He hoped in this way to gain both the emperor's favour and the westerners' gratitude. There was undoubtedly a strong pro-Latin 'lobby' at the imperial court. It almost certainly had the ear of the emperor. This was cause for deep resentment on the part of the Byzantine bureaucrat, who was conscious that the bureaucracy no longer exercised its traditional ascendancy over the emperor.

It found expression in widespread criticism of Manuel's foreign policy. It was said that Manuel 'nourished inordinate desires out of self-regard, turning his gaze to the ends of the earth. However enthusiastically and boldly he may have carried out his policies, he strayed from the precepts laid down by former emperors, wasting to no good purpose the money he collected from his subjects.'[8] Nicetas Choniates who retails this criticism was inclined to exonerate the emperor. Manuel was terrified that his Empire would be overwhelmed by the unmatched strength of the Latins. His ambitious foreign policy was designed to pre-empt any western attack, by creating, just like 'the best of landowners'.[9] a firebreak around his domain. Nicetas Choniates believed that the disasters that followed his death were adequate proof of the effectiveness of his foreign policy. This conclusion avoids coming to grips with the dilemmas of Manuel's foreign policy, which otherwise Nicetas Choniates has illuminated with the skill and clear-sightedness to be expected from a man who was to become chief minister. To check the Latins Manuel set about winning the initiative beyond the frontiers of the Empire, but this ambitious undertaking depended upon exploiting the skills and goodwill of potential enemies. As diplomacy became the centre of the emperor's concerns, so Latins became more and more prominent at court. This was to store up trouble among the bureaucracy and church, the traditional props of imperial power. Abroad his manœuvring was eyed with suspicion and eventually left him more or less isolated. At home, there was growing alienation and anti-Latin feeling. The combination was lethal, made worse by the measures Manuel took on his death-bed to secure the succession of his young son Alexius. He made his clients, the kings of Hungary and Jerusalem and the prince of Antioch, together with the Seljuq sultan, guarantors of the succession.

THE LATINS AND MANUEL COMNENUS

Manuel was much admired in the West, becoming something of a legend for his generosity. The crusader historian William of Tyre, who had dealings with him on a number of occasions, described him as 'a great-souled man of incomparable energy'.[10] Rather more surprising are the contents of a letter which Bernard of Clairvaux had drafted in the most respectful terms to the Byzantine emperor. He was seeking his favour for a son of the count of Blois, who wished to enter his service. The abbot was sure that it would provide the young man with 'the dignity of military discipline'. He asked the emperor 'to administer the vows of knighthood and gird him with a sword against the enemies of the cross of Christ'.[11] St Bernard may have been labouring under certain misapprehensions about the Byzantine court, but his letter is clear evidence that in the West the Emperor Manuel had a reputation as a patron of chivalry.

For his part Manuel was much attracted by the prowess of western knights and sought to outdo them. His German empress was constrained in full senate to admit 'that she drew her descent from a great and warlike race, but out of all of them she had never heard of any who boasted so many feats in a single year'[12] as her husband. Manuel insisted on using 'a lance incomparable in length and size', customarily known as an 'eight-footer'.[13] He showed it to that paladin, Raymond, prince of Antioch, who was apparently most impressed. It is easy to detect in this incident a spirit of adolescent emulation, but it also reveals Manuel's appreciation of western chivalry. This would be translated into the trust he placed in the Latins at his court.

'He relied so implicitly on the fidelity and ability of the Latins that he passed over the Greeks as soft and effeminate and entrusted important affairs to the Latins alone.'[14] With these words William of Tyre catches the Latin view that Manuel was a ruler who was too good for the Greeks. Western sources are nearly unanimous in their condemnation of the Greeks for their treachery and their lack of warlike qualities. Writing at the court of Henry II Plantagenet (1154–89) Walter Map rather charmingly attributed the decline of Greece to exhaustion brought about by the Trojan War. Since then 'there is nowhere to be found among the Greeks aught lofty or eminent; to such an extent have they declined that they have become the hateful refuse of all peoples and castaways of every commonwealth'.[15] Walter Map catches the essence of the charge against the Greeks. They had degenerated and had no right to the wealth and power that they still possessed.

Mingled with contempt was a deal of envy, for the image of Byzantium fascinated the West. Its fairy-tale quality made it the background for the *romans d'antiquité*, then in vogue in the courts of France. The ceremonial of the Byzantine court was much admired in the West, and its robes of honour were copied in the courts of Jerusalem, Palermo, and Venice. In Sicily Byzantine mosaicists produced works designed to present the Norman king of Sicily in the image of a Byzantine sovereign. The works of Byzantine artists were prized in the West and in the crusader states and were a source for new artistic developments. A bishop of Cahors in the south-west of France visited the eastern Mediterranean in 1112 and was so impressed by Byzantine architecture that he had his cathedral rebuilt in the Byzantine style. It enjoyed some local success and a number of domed churches were put up in the south-west of France in the first half of the twelfth century. It was in the twelfth century that western scholars began to discover the riches that were stored up in Byzantium. A number of western clerks gravitated to the Comnenian court in the course of the twelfth century. They learnt Greek and made translations into Latin. Some might seem to be of little weight. Apart from medical works there were books on dreams and other lore, dealing with the virtues of animals, stones, plants, herbs, and planets. There was an insatiable appetite for marvels in the West, which Byzantium could feed. There is little sign of interest in Greek philosophy. James of Venice is known to have translated the *Posterior Analytics* of Aristotle, while at Constantinople, but it was so obscurely done that it was almost impossible to use and had little or no impact on the West. Undoubtedly, the most important theological work translated was St John of Damascus's *De fide orthodoxa*. A part of the text was first translated in Hungary and then *c*. 1153 the whole was translated at Constantinople by Burgundio of Pisa. It was to be an important source of Peter the Lombard's *Libri Sententiarum* which were finished some four years later. Peter plundered the *De fide orthodoxa* to support his dogmatic contentions, but on the question of the Trinity he preferred to follow St Augustine, an indication that the Greek theologian was not a formative influence on his thought, just a useful source. Byzantium was a convenient quarry. Its influences did not go deep and were soon swallowed up.

Burgundio of Pisa was the most prolific of the Latin translators working at Constantinople. His work was undertaken either with western patrons in mind or at their specific request. So Pope Eugenius III got him to translate some of the homilies of St John Chrysostom, the pope even going to the trouble of acquiring a manuscript from Antioch. Hugh Eteriano, whose learning was so respected by the Emperor Manuel Comnenus, remained on very close terms with western theologians. He may have been deeply versed in Greek patristics, but his sympathies were consistently Latin. Although called in by Manuel to advise on the theological controversy over Christ's words: 'My Father is greater than I', he was not impressed by the outcome: 'a superfluous controversy, quite useless', was his final comment.[16] His main work was undertaken at the request of Manuel Comnenus on the question of the Procession of the Holy Spirit. He was to compile a selection of patristic authorities bearing on the problem. Pope Alexander III was delighted and urged him to carry out the task. His purpose was to get to grips with the arguments of Byzantine theologians and use the Greek fathers to support the Latin teaching on the Procession of the Holy Spirit. He found very little and in those few instances when there seemed to be some support for the Latin position he was almost always guilty of doctoring the texts. His researches into Greek patristics did not force him to alter his position one iota. He even resorted to the argument that in the end the pope had the right 'to confirm the brethren, issue decrees, and set forth interpretations in cases of obscurity'[17] in order to justify the addition of the *filioque* to the creed at the instance of the papacy. Pope Lucius III was delighted with the result and in 1182 made him a cardinal. He died a few months later. There was no meeting of minds.

Hugh Eteriano might allow that 'Greece is intellectually accomplished',[18] while a German acquaintance of his went still further.

He deliberately contrived to get sent to Constantinople at the very end of Manuel's reign so that he might be better acquainted with Greek theology. 'Seeing that all the doctrines of the Latins issue forth from Greek sources, I included in my prayers the hope that with God's help I should acquire through incontrovertible authorities, if at all possible, the wisdom of Greece in order then to reach a decision on our dissensions.'[19] At Constantinople he sought out Hugh Eteriano to provide him with information about the teaching of the Greek fathers on the Trinity. Hugh provided the necessary extracts from St Basil and St Gregory Nazianzus. He added his own treatise on the Procession of the Holy Spirit, which was directed against 'the opinion of the modern Greeks' in conformity 'with the writings of the ancient doctors of Greece',[20] by which he meant the Greek fathers. There is a nice distinction here. There was much to be gained from the Greek fathers, but the 'modern Greeks' were in error. They were degenerate and schismatic, yet they still controlled a wealth of learning, not to mention a vast mass of relics, none of which they deserved. They even had the effrontery to demand that a Latin marrying a Greek woman should abandon the rites of his church; they scrubbed clean altars which had been used for mass by a Latin priest. Latin resentment and envy was reciprocated by the Byzantines. They found Latin presumption hard to swallow. During the theological dispute over 'My Father is greater than I' dislike of the Latins took on a decidedly religious complexion. Hugh Eteriano relates that Latins were then 'pointed out in the streets of the capital as objects of hatred and detestation'.[21]

Manuel Comnenus was only too well aware of the dilemma created. He wished to find a way of settling the religious differences separating the two churches. He told Hugh Eteriano that 'if you could eradicate them, then every Latin would reach a secure and peaceful harbour throughout the confines of our Empire',[22] but he confessed that he thought this an impossibility because of differences on the question of the Procession of the Holy Spirit. At this point, theology touched upon the internal politics of the Empire, for Manuel had come to rely heavily upon the Latins in his service. Their support was vital to his ascendancy over court and government. Their unpopularity on religious grounds therefore threatened the stability of imperial government. But the truth of this would only become apparent after his death in 1180.

NOTES

1. *Poèmes prodromiques en Grec vulgaire* (ed. by D C Hesseling and H Pernot) (Amsterdam, 1910), pp. 36, 54
1A. A. Lombardo and R. Morozzo della Rocca, *Nuovi documenti del commercio veneto dei secoli XI–XIII* (Venice, 1955), no. 8

2. Michel Italikos, *Lettres et Discours* (ed. by P Gautier) (Paris, 1972), p. 235
3. Nicetas Choniates (ed. Van Dieten), p. 171
4. Cinnamus (transl. by C M Brand), p. 210
5. Nicetas Choniates (ed. Van Dieten), p. 301
6. Georges et Dèmètrios Tornikès, *Lettres et Discours*, p. 129
7. G Müller, *Documenti sulle relazioni delle città Toscane coll'Oriente Cristiano e coi Turchi* (Florence, 1879), p. 12
8. Nicetas Choniates (ed. Van Dieten), p. 203
9. *Ibid.*
10. William of Tyre (translated by E A Babcock and A C Krey), II, p. 461
11. Migne, PL, 182, c. 672–3
12. Cinnamus (transl. by C M Brand), p. 81
13. *Ibid.*, p. 99
14. William of Tyre (transl. by E A Babcock and A C Krey), II, p. 461
15. Walter Map, *De Nugis Curialium* (ed. by M R James) (Oxford, 1914), p. 87
16. P Classen, 'Das Konzil von Konstantinopel 1166 und die Lateiner', *Byzantinische Zeitschrift*, 48 (1955), p. 365
17. Migne, P L, 202, 375
18. A. Dondaine, 'Hugues Ethérien et le concile de Constantinople de 1166', *Historisches Jahrbuch*, 77 (1958), p. 483
19. C H Haskins, *Studies in the History of Mediaeval Science*, (Cambridge, Mass., 1924), p. 210
20. *Ibid.*
21. A Dondaine, 'Hugues Ethérien et le concile de Constantinople de 1166', *Historisches Jahrbuch*, 77 (1958), p. 481
22. A. Dondaine, 'Hughes Ethérien et Léon Toscan', *Archives d'histoire doctrinale et littéraire du moyen âge,* 19 (1952), p. 126

Chapter 12

THE GOVERNMENT OF MANUEL I COMNENUS (1143–1180): COURT, CHURCH, AND POLITICS

The prominence of the Latins under Manuel Comnenus has something to do with the very nature of Byzantine autocracy. Like Basil II before him, Manuel needed foreigners to help him in his bid to establish a personal ascendancy over Byzantine government and society. He was, as we have seen, attracted by the Latin ethos with its emphasis on prowess and loyalty. These were exactly the qualities he was looking for in the members of his entourage, who were to serve as the agents of his personal authority. He attached to his personal service a cadre of imperial liege knights. They were recruited from the West and were bound to the emperor by the ties of liege homage.

Manuel needed to build up his personal authority, if he was to escape from the dilemma which faced the emperors of Byzantium from the twelfth century onwards. They were caught between their traditional responsibilities to their church and people and their dynastic obligations, for they were at one and the same time God's vice-gerent on Earth and the head of the most powerful aristocratic family. Before the Comneni came to power emperors scarcely regarded their family connections and responsibilities. Rarely did they share their power with members of their family, other than their sons. Under the Comneni the claims made by the imperial family for a share in government could easily impair the emperor's effective authority.

Manuel sought to dominate both his family and the traditional apparatus of government. Only in this way would he be able to draw strength from both the traditional and dynastic sides of his office, rather than being ground between them. It would take more than half of his reign to achieve this end. That he succeeded was largely due to the skilful way he was able to balance the different aspects of imperial authority. He made great play with the traditional virtues and responsibilities of the Byzantine autocrat. Scarcely ever were these more assiduously celebrated than by the orators of his court. Yet Manuel never forgot that he was a Comnenus.

There was no apparent contradiction, in part because Manuel saw to it that each side of the imperial office had its special setting. His personal rule received its clearest expression in the life of the great military camps, where he was at his happiest. While in Constantinople he divided his time between the Great Palace of the Emperors and the Blakhernai Palace. The former was the seat of empire; the latter 'the imperial residence of his ancestors'.[1] The Great Palace remained a symbol of power; and for any aspirant to the imperial throne the first place to seize. Manuel Comnenus's first concern as emperor was to eject his elder brother Isaac from the Great Palace, for 'not only were there piles of money stored there, but also the imperial insignia'.[2] It remained incidentally the site of the imperial mint. Manuel emphasized the continuing importance of the Great Palace by adding to it. He built a new throne room, looking out over the sea. He had it decorated with mosaics celebrating his victories. The Great Palace was mainly used for official business and ceremonial. It was here that Manuel displayed the traditional face of imperial authority.

He preferred to reside at the Blakhernai on the Golden Horn, which he did much to improve and embellish. Odo of Deuil who visited it in 1147 was mightily impressed by its 'excellent construction and elegance'.[3] Manuel also took pains to strengthen its defences, turning it into a veritable fortress. It became a dynastic stronghold. Here Manuel was the imperious and demanding head of a great family, organizing things on the spur of the moment. On one occasion he wanted a marriage feast to take place there and then in the palace of the Blakhernai. It was Lent and it was the middle of the night. His servants wondered where they could possibly get together all that was necessary to satisfy the emperor. They thought of the nearby monastery of St John the Baptist of Petra. They woke the abbot up and he, happily, was able to provide all that they needed; red and black caviare included.[4]

Contemporaries took the dynastic side of imperial authority for granted. The littérateur John Tzetzes has left us details of a quarrel involving Manuel Comnenus. He lets drop what the emperor's opponents were saying and what his own thoughts on the matter were: 'It is their opinion that it is hard to get the Comneni to change their mind, once they have made a decision, but not being well acquainted with the Comneni they delude themselves, for the Comneni will not easily undo what is good, but will strive to put right what they know to be mistaken and wrong.'[5] It is a muted appeal to the emperor couched in terms of family honour and virtue. Membership of the Comneni family demanded certain moral qualities. This was the essence of aristocracy, in which other families might share: the Kontostephanoi, for example. Tzetzes's remarks about the Comneni are not very different from the plea made by a bishop to his local governor, who came from the Kontostephanos family: 'I beg and pray, your excellency, to desist from such practices, for I cannot bear the thought that by tolerating them you are in danger of soiling your imperial blood and sullying the good name of the Kontostephanoi, who are renowned for their justice and piety.'[6] The Kontostephanoi were an ancient family which came into renewed prominence under Manuel Comnenus. They married into the imperial family and provided a series of military and naval commanders. Aristocracy derived from the imperial blood, but it also inhered in individual families.

THE COURT ARISTOCRACY

The historian Nicetas Choniates divided up Comnenian court society into 'those renowned by virtue of their imperial blood, those senators holding civil offices, those distinguished by rank, and those whose position rests on imperial favour'.[7] The highest ranks at court belonged to the imperial family. Precedence depended upon the exact relationship to the reigning emperor. Alexius I Comnenus's order of ranks was refined and elaborated. At the top of the court hierarchy came the *sebastokratores*, the brothers and the paternal uncles of the reigning emperor, then came his brothers-in-law and his nephews and cousins, and finally there were the *sebastoi*, who were more distant relatives of the reigning emperor or simply honorary members of the imperial family. The emperor selected many of his naval and military commanders, as well as his provincial governors, from close relatives. This was the core of the aristocracy proper. It consisted of the direct descendants of Alexius Comnenus and members of families, such as the Kontostephanoi and the Palaiologoi, who were allied to the imperial house. These were old families long prominent in the affairs of state, but, as Manuel's reign wore on, they were joined within the charmed imperial circle by others of less renowned lineage, such as the Angeloi, Cantacuzeni, and the Batatzes. It was part of a process that did not become fully clear until after the death of Manuel Comnenus: the house of Comnenus was losing its cohesion and was being replaced by a series of aristocratic families, each with its own identity and interests.

Beneath the aristocracy came the civil servants and other functionaries with their own special orders of rank, *nobelissimoi, kouropalatai, proedroi*. The division between the two groups was not absolute. There were civil service families, such as the Kamateroi, which were allied to the imperial house, and members of the imperial aristocracy who held positions in the civil service, but this blurring at the edges was only to be expected. Again there were the beginnings under Manuel Comnenus of a development that only took positive shape after his death: the emergence of a series of civil service dynasties.

The most difficult group to place in the hierarchical scheme of the

Byzantine court is the last on Choniates's list – 'those whose position rests on imperial favour'. They sound as though they were courtiers without any established rank, or the personal servants of the emperor. One of the criticisms that Nicetas Choniates made of Manuel Comnenus was that he was too ready to shower his personal servants with favours. Some were eunuchs, others not even Byzantine. The career of the eunuch Thomas would seem to bear out some of these strictures. Nothing is known of his background, except that he came from the island of Lesbos. At some stage he settled in the capital and made a living blood-letting. His skill gained him entry into the imperial palace where he made his fortune. The Emperor Manuel took him into his personal service. His success was probably something of an exception, because eunuchs did not play as prominent a role at court under the Comneni as they had done in the eleventh century. The core of the emperor's entourage was made up of men who distinguished themselves as soldiers. They were not necessarily of high birth. Such a man was Basil Tzintziloukes, who held the position of *chartoularios* at the beginning of Manuel's reign. The *chartoularios* was an officer of the emperor's entourage, as were the imperial *vestiaritai*. Some of them are named in a list of 1166. Two of them, Alexius Petraliphas and Andronicus Lampardas, are known from other sources to have been military commanders of note. Lampardas was one of the heroes of the great Byzantine victory over the Hungarians in 1167. These *vestiaritai* along with other officers of the imperial entourage held the rank of *sebastos* and were treated as honorary members of the imperial family, ranking above the holders of the great civil offices. The personal service of the emperor therefore provided an avenue into the upper ranks of court society. The Petraliphas family is a case in point. By the end of the twelfth century it had become one of the great families of the Empire. Its origins can be traced back to a Norman adventurer who took service under Alexius Comnenus. His immediate descendants lived out their lives in the provincial obscurity of Didymoteichos in Thrace. It was only Alexius Petraliphas's successful career in imperial service that opened up the path to the family's future greatness.

THE ARISTOCRATIC CONNECTION

Byzantine society under the Comneni was dominated by a series of interlocking aristocratic connections, which came together in the imperial court. They reproduced many of the features of the emperor's personal rule. If the emperor had *vestiaritai* in his entourage, so too did the great men of his court. The best example is Manuel's uncle, the

Sebastokrator Isaac. When he founded a monastery in 1152, he settled his *vestiaritai* on lands he had given to his new foundation. They were to provide a garrison for the fortress he had built to protect the monastery. They were in this way to perform for the monastery the duties they had formerly acquitted for their master. Isaac surrounded himself with a court that reproduced many of the features of the imperial household, if on a far less lavish scale. Like the emperor he had his *protovestiarios* or comptroller of the household. He had his *pinkernes* or butler and he possessed a secretary; not to mention a military retinue. The aristocratic household also provided administrators and overseers for the family estates. Manuel's sister Mary sent her bailiff (*baioulos*) to supervise the handing over of some property she had gifted to an Athonite monastery.

Service in an aristocratic household was an accepted way of beginning a career. It was particularly attractive to young men without strong family connections, though the experience of John Tzetzes was a warning for the unwary. His desperate search for aristocratic origins betrays that his family no longer counted for much. He found a position as secretary to a member of the imperial aristocracy, who had been made governor of Verroia. To his dismay Tzetzes was summarily dismissed and sent back to Constantinople. He blamed his master's wife. He was condemned to abject poverty and his career never truly recovered from this early set-back. Demetrios Tornikes was luckier. He came from an ancient family, whose fortunes had been eclipsed. It had gravitated away from Constantinople to the city of Thebes. He was brought up in the household of Anna Comnena, as a companion for one of her grandsons. He remained in her service, and this was the first step of a career which would culminate in the office of the logothete of the drome, effectively foreign minister of the Empire.

It was to just such a young man starting out on a career that the poem, known as *Spaneas*, was addressed. It provided sound advice on how to conduct yourself. If you went into aristocratic service, 'then honour your lords and love them like your parents; show a fitting humility and readiness to please'.[8] The author of the poem regarded service in an aristocratic household and obedience to a lord as something quite normal, but they seem to have alarmed Manuel Comnenus. He legislated against the practice of taking service with a lord. He expressed himself horrified that 'some even of the well born ... serve for hire those in superior positions and ranks'.[9] Still worse was the way that some lords treated their servants as though they were slaves and refused to allow them to leave their service. It is more than likely that what really worried the emperor was the permanence of the relationships that were being established. Purely informal ties seemed about to acquire legal force. There was an element of legal conservatism involved, but a more pressing consideration may have been the desire to limit competition from and among the grandees of the court.

The author of *Spaneas* also enjoined his protégé to 'love your friends so that you will always have them'.[10] Friendship remained as in the eleventh century another important informal tie, uniting in mutual obligation men of roughly equal social status. Such informal relationships provided, as it were, much of the cement of aristocratic society, though their very informality makes their character hard to catch. Their workings are glimpsed in the literary circles that were a feature of Comnenian court society. One such circle was connected with the convent of Our Lady of Grace, which was founded by Eirene Doukaina, Alexius I Comnenus's empress. She retired there after her husband's death and her daughter Anna had apartments just outside its walls, overlooking the garden of the monastery of Philanthropos. Eirene Doukaina stipulated that her residence would pass after her death to Anna, and then to Anna's daughter, Eirene, as would the lay patronage of the convent. Eirene's literary tastes were for the Fathers. Her *theatron* or literary circle probably reflected such tastes. Her daughter Anna Comnena was more profoundly intellectual. She encouraged Michael of Ephesus to complete his commentaries on Aristotle – the first since the seventh century. He complained of her zeal in the matter: he had ruined his eyes working by candlelight to meet her deadlines. She was also a patron of Eustratios of Nicaea, who equally worked on Aristotle. Her interest and support therefore played a vital part in the revival of a systematic study of Aristotle in Byzantium.

It is more than likely that this literary activity was some compensation for her exclusion from public life. It gave Anna Comnena a stage for her undoubted intellectual abilities. One of the members of her circle, George Tornikes, the future bishop of Ephesus, remarked that 'she often displayed the power of her intellect, eagerly attacking the views of the philosophers'.[11] In the *Alexiad* she shows a marked sympathy for Michael Psellos and his cultivation of philosophy. The admiration may only have been for his intellect and learning – prized commodities in Byzantium, which brought with them prestige and a modicum of power. In the past they had been the preserve of men, such as Psellos, who had exploited them to strengthen their social and political position. In much the same way, Anna's intellectual and literary activities shed glory on her branch of the imperial house and, more to the point, attracted to her interest potential publicists, thus ensuring that she was not entirely isolated from the life of the court and the capital.

Another literary patroness was the Comnenian princess known to history as the *sebastokratorissa*. She was Eirene, the widow of Manuel Comnenus's brother, the *Sebastokrator* Andronicus. Her origins remain something of a mystery. It is only a guess that she came from the West. She collected around her an impressive array of literary talent. Theodore Prodromos claimed about the year 1152 that he had been her servant for twelve years. He composed for her poems celebrating the birth of her son Alexius and lamenting the death of her husband. Constantine Manasses belonged to her circle and composed his world chronicle in verse for her. John Tzetzes was another member of the circle. His *Theogonia* was dedicated to her. This was an attempt to provide a compendium of classical mythology for the beginner. He claimed a shade dishonestly that the only patron he wished for was the *sebastokratorissa*. He had every reason to be grateful to her. She rescued him from the near penury which his peremptory dismissal from aristocractic service brought. The interests of this group seem to have been philological more than anything else. Tzetzes was famed for his commentaries and allegories on Homer. He was thoroughly indignant when he learnt that another member of the circle was pirating some portions of his commentaries and passing them off as his own. Like Anna Comnena the *sebastokratorissa* would fall foul of the reigning emperor. Early in the reign of Manuel Comnenus she was gaoled in the imperial palace. Released, she was again imprisoned, this time at the Blakhernai. She was then confined in the monastery of the Pantokrator. Theodore Prodromos wrote to the emperor pleading her cause. She would be released, but hardly because of Prodromos's advocacy, rather because her son John became the emperor's most trusted confidant.

Literati sought patronage to further their own interests rather than those of their patrons. Michael Italikos, the future bishop of Philippopolis, belonged to the circle of Eirene Doukaina, extemporizing on one occasion a very pretty eulogy of the old empress. He wrote to her later: he did not want her to think that philosophy disqualified him from undertaking tasks of practical importance. If she would only let him descend from the stars, he would be able to show her that he possessed all the practical skills necessary for an administrator. He was looking to her for support in the opening stages of his career. She had procured him a position as professor of medicine, but he did not consider the pay good enough. Theodore Prodromos, on the other hand, was nearing the end of his career and what he demanded of his patrons was the security of repose in a monastery as a lay brother. John Tzetzes also sought security – the security of a steady income. He was overjoyed when the city prefect promised him an official salary and the rents from three perfumery shops.

It is rather harder to see exactly what practical benefits patrons derived. There was perhaps some prestige and influence to be gained if protégés reached high office in church or administration, but it was not as though they attached themselves to a single patron or that a patron's favour was the sole means of livelihood. Literati sought patrons where they could. If they did not make their way into the civil service or the church, they usually taught as a way of making ends meet. In a poem addressed to the Emperor Manuel Comnenus, Theodore Prodromos claimed that unlike others he had not been 'the servant of many lords ... but from his earliest youth to have recognized but a single court and a single lord'.[12] He was not being strictly honest. He worked for many patrons; he was a professional man of letters, but it is probably true that his loyalty was given to only one or two, whom he would recognize as his lord.

These literati lived on the fringe of aristocratic society and much of their work was produced for aristocratic patrons and can therefore be assumed to reflect something of aristocratic tastes. There is no doubt that the literature produced was rich and various, if often tiresome. One can only assume that Tzetzes's patrons were entranced by his disquisitions on Homer and Greek mythology. There is little doubt that Theodore Prodromos's poetry, especially that which glorified his patrons, was very much to aristocratic taste. Prodromos could turn his hand to almost anything – commentaries on the scriptures, a saint's life, a commentary on Aristotle's *Posterior Analytics*, an animal fable. He also produced a romance, *Rhodanthe and Dosikles*, in the Hellenistic manner. This was a new departure. He was followed by others who were connected with Comnenian court circles. Does this renewal of the Hellenistic romance in the mid-years of the twelfth century reflect the aristocratic taste of the time? There is nothing to prove conclusively that they were written for aristocratic patrons, though both Theodore Prodromos and the author of another of these romances, Constantine Manasses, belonged to the circle of the *sebastokratorissa*. Another author, Nicetas Eugeneianos, was a friend and possibly a pupil of Theodore Prodromos. He was also attached to the service of the *Sebastos* Stephen Comnenus. The fourth member of this group of authors, Eumathios Makrembolites, came from a rather more distinguished background. He belonged to a civil service dynasty and he may even have held the post of prefect of Constantinople. It does seem safe to conclude that the new vogue for romance reflects the tastes of the Byzantine court under Manuel Comnenus.

This revival of the Hellenistic romance at the court of the Comneni was a natural progression from the interest shown in the Hellenistic romance in the eleventh century. These novels were previously condemned by a Christian society as scandalously erotic, but they were beginning to be seen as possibly possessing redeeming features. Michael Psellos approved of their style and structure, but what about the content? This was the object of a discourse attributed to this period. What moral value did Heliodorus's *Ethiopian Tale* possess? That was the question put by an imperial secretary. The answer he got was that it was like Circe's draught: it turned the unworthy into pigs, but raised others to higher things. For them it was edifying, 'mixing the wine of contemplation with the water of narrative'.[13] It presented a 'paradigm' (*archetypos pinax*) of the four cardinal virtues. Thus, it was possible to disinfect the romance of its pagan and erotic elements and to open up the way to a revival of the genre. It has recently been suggested that the novel became the edifying literature of the Comnenian court, ousting the lives of the saints. It is an attractive idea. The *risqué* packaged as edification must have appealed in the pleasure-loving atmosphere of

Manuel Comnenus's court. It condoned the pursuit of love. The novels would be used to pay tribute to the beauty of the ladies of the court. It is their heroines who catch the eye; the heroes are wishy-washy, hardly conforming to the military ideals of the Comnenian court. There are striking parallels with western courtly romances which owed their inspiration to female patronage, but there is no need to posit western influence to explain the appearance of these Byzantine romances. Their elevated style militates against this. They are pastiches of the Hellenistic novel. As Elizabeth Jeffreys has shown, if anything, it is the other way round: the Byzantine example may have inspired the western romance.[14]

This does not mean that there were no western influences at work in the Byzantine court. At the very least, Manuel Comnenus and his aristocracy were motivated by a desire to emulate and outdo western champions some of whom, such as Raymond of Poitiers, were well known at the imperial court. That western tastes may have seeped in is suggested by a poem that Theodore Prodromos addressed to the Emperor Manuel Comnenus. The poet foresees the possibility that the emperor might be tempted to replace him with a bard. The word used is *zouglos*,[15] which must derive from the French *jongleur*. It seems rather a remote possibility that the Byzantine emperor would have had a Frankish *jongleur* to entertain him at court. But there is a clue to the meaning of Prodromos's jibe. He was writing this poem not in the learned language that he used for most of his work, but in the popular language. It is perhaps the most striking feature of Byzantine literature of the Comnenian period that the vernacular begins to be used for literary purposes. The demand for such literature was not popular in origin, but came from within the court; perhaps even from the emperor himself, given that so much of the earliest literature in the vernacular is addressed to the emperor in person. We are told of the pleasure he took 'in those extemporizing to the lyre and harp'.[16] The thrust of Prodromos's poem suggests that he regarded such '*jongleurs*' as his chief competitors for the emperor's favour. Their renditions would have been in the popular language. Therefore in order to keep the emperor's attention Prodromos used the vernacular for some of his occasional poetry, especially when asking for favours.

In one of his poems in the vernacular addressed to the Emperor Manuel Comnenus Theodore Prodromos makes a passing reference to the Akritic cycle of poems. He calls the emperor a 'New Akrites' and laments, 'O, that another Akrites had then been there, to pin on his cloak and pick up his mace ...'.[17] These are the first clear references to the Byzantine hero Digenes Akrites, a legendary figure around which a series of popular poems accumulated. The material from which they were fashioned relates to the eastern frontiers of the Byzantine Empire in the ninth and tenth centuries. They circulated orally, but at some stage they would be given literary form and the vernacular would be heavily influenced by the learned language. The shape the poems took was very close to the romances which were in vogue at the Comnenian court. The content, form, and language of the poem of *Digenes Akrites* seem to chart the transformation of families with their roots in the eastern provinces into a court aristocracy. Such considerations all point to the reign of Manuel Comnenus as the time when the cycle of *Digenes Akrites* was given clear literary form.

At the very least, the poem of *Digenes Akrites* will tell us a little about the literary tastes of Manuel Comnenus's court and the atmosphere that prevailed there. It may even enlighten us about the preoccupations and values of the court aristocracy. The poem was intended as entertainment. It is divided into two parts. The first deals with the marriage of the hero's parents. They were an unlikely match – a renegade Muslim emir and a daughter of the noble house of Doukas. This part of the poem is handled quite realistically and has a solid basis in fact. The second part is devoted to the hero's life and adventures, ending with his death from a chill – a reminder of how much the author was indebted to the *Romance of Alexander*. The element of romance is much stronger than in the first part. The hero is allowed a series of amorous adventures, the most spectacular with the Amazon Maximo. He met her in single combat, overcame her, and allowed himself to be seduced by her. Then in a fit of remorse for betraying his young wife, he murdered her, consoling himself with the thought that she was an adulteress. The introduction of an Amazon may have had something to do with the impression made on the Byzantines by the ladies who accompanied the second crusade. They rode into the capital astride their horses, which was thought less than ladylike. They were reckoned 'to outamazon the Amazons'.[18] Be that as it may, the presence of an Amazon adds to the unreality of the setting for Digenes Akrites's adventures, which are supposed to take place along the eastern frontier of the Empire. He struggles with bandits and brigands until he finally brings peace to the borderlands. The climax of the poem is his meeting with the Emperor Basil, who comes out to the borders especially to meet him, such is his fame. Digenes makes obeisance to the emperor, who urges him to speak his mind. He recalls the traditional responsibilities of an emperor, 'to love obedience, pity the poor, deliver from injustice the oppressed, accord forgiveness to unwilling faults, not to heed slanders, accept no injustice, scatter the heretics, confirm the orthodox'.[19] Digenes is acting very much as the emperor's conscience. The emperor grants him power over the frontiers by a chrysobull. Digenes then moved with his wife to the banks of the Euphrates where he built himself a magnificent palace.

It is the individualism of the hero which comes across most forcefully. He is involved in innumerable feats of arms but always on his own account. He subdues the borders single-handed or so it seems. His dealings with the emperor are on an individual basis and on terms of near equality. His reward is his own palace set 'amid a wondrous pleasant paradise',[20] in other words miles from anywhere, beyond the reach of the emperor. There was without doubt a very large element of wishful thinking, a desire to escape from the all-pervading imperial presence. It presented an ideal of aristocratic independence which may not have counted for very much at Manuel Comnenus's court, but would be increasingly in evidence after his death.

ANDRONICUS COMNENUS AND THE POLITICS OF THE COMNENIAN COURT

Power was concentrated at the Comnenian court in the hands of the emperor and a tight circle of relatives. Politics were kept as far as possible within the family circle. The Comnenian court therefore often erupted in scenes of violence. On one occasion, early in Manuel's reign his brother Isaac started to needle him, insisting that his achievements were much inferior to those of their father. Another member of the Comnenian clan leapt to the emperor's defence and insulted Isaac, who tried to decapitate him. Only the prompt intervention of a further member of the imperial clan prevented murder. The emperor got caught in the mêlée and bore a scar on his wrist for the rest of his life as a memento of this incident. Politics, thus, often took the form of family squabbles as different branches of the imperial house sought to protect their honour and interests. We have already seen how the emperor's most dangerous rivals were disappointed siblings, like John II Comnenus's brother Isaac. He was forced into exile, touring various oriental courts in the hope of winning support against his brother. The task proved hopeless and he was reconciled with John II Comnenus in 1138; he did not easily give up his dreams of empire, but 'like an ancestral inheritance passed them on to his children'.[21]

His younger son Andronicus would fulfil his hopes, becoming emperor three years after Manuel Comnĕnus's death. His life reads like one of those romances that were so popular at the Comnenian court – imprisonment, escape, exile. He was built on a heroic scale, being well over six feet tall. Like another Akrites, he took pride in his martial prowess and in his skill in hunting and delighted in the pursuit of women. Once just hearing of the beauty of a crusader princess, he fell in love with her, abandoned his command in mid-campaign, and set off to Antioch to court her; with gratifying results. The Emperor Manuel was not amused and Andronicus moved on to the court of Jerusalem, where he was consoled by the widowed queen.

The historian Nicetas Choniates dismisses these escapades: Andronicus was just a 'woman-mad stallion'.[22] That was only one side of the story. They were also part of his rivalry with his cousin, the Emperor Manuel Comnenus. The crusader princess was a sister of the emperor's new consort, Maria of Antioch, while the widowed queen was one of Manuel's nieces. It was a liaison which would have brought to mind Andronicus's biting jibe at the expense of the emperor, when taken to task for his own affair with a distant cousin: at least, 'he wasn't like the emperor who slept with his niece'.[23]

This rivalry went back to boyhood. Andronicus was brought up with Manuel. They raced and wrestled together. In the early part of Manuel's reign Andronicus was high in the emperor's favour. He was made governor of Cilicia and then appointed to the Danube frontier, where he was entrusted with delicate negotiations with the Hungarian king. It was then that he apparently came to a tacit understanding with the Hungarians that he would receive their backing for a bid against the throne of Constantinople. Andronicus returned to the capital in 1154 with his mission, it would seem, successfully completed. Then in the following winter Manuel was to have him arrested and imprisoned in the Great Palace of the Emperors at Constantinople. Treasonable contacts with a foreign power may only have been an excuse. Even his apparent attempt to assassinate Manuel Comnenus may have been trumped up. Underlying this episode there was a struggle for power between Andronicus and his many enemies at court. His main opponent was John Comnenus, the eldest son of the *sebastokratorissa*. He was offended by Andronicus's open liaison with his widowed sister, but this masked the political rivalry between the two men. Both sought the chief position at court now that the Grand Domestic John Axoukh, the dominant personality at court in the early years of Manuel's reign, was dead. John Comnenus was raised by the emperor to the rank of *protovestiarios* and *protosebastos*. This put him in charge of the imperial household and gave him precedence at court. The historian John Cinnamus singles this promotion out as the real cause of Andronicus's disaffection.

Andronicus made repeated attempts to escape from his confinement in the Great Palace. Once he managed to get away as far as Melangeia on the main road into Anatolia. At last, in 1165 with the aid of accomplices he got clean away. He reached the Russian principality of Galicia, where he was cordially received and given some villages by the prince. But the latter was soon under pressure from the Byzantine government to give up his dangerous guest. Andronicus was handed over but this time Manuel did not return him to captivity. The two men were reconciled. Andronicus even received a military command in the ensuing campaign against Hungary. This reconciliation did not last long. The two men were soon at loggerheads, this time over the oath which Manuel required from all his subjects: that they would support the succession of his daughter Mary and her fiancé Bela of Hungary in the absence of any male heirs. Andronicus objected that Manuel might have sons by his new Empress Maria of Antioch, but, more than this, he could not bear the idea of a foreigner lording it over Byzantines as emperor. His stance won him many supporters. To isolate him Manuel sent him out, once again, as governor of Cilicia. Rather than carry out his duties properly, he preferred, as we have already seen, to woo a crusader princess. This was the beginning of a new and truly extraordinary chapter in his life. He wandered the East, moving from court to court, finally finding refuge with the Turkish emir of Koloneia. Manuel was reconciled with him for the last time some three months before his death in September 1180. He hoped in this way to smooth the accession of his young son Alexius. The irony was that Andronicus would overthrow the young Alexius and seize the throne.

As emperor, Andronicus stood for a set of policies that went directly counter to those favoured by Manuel Comnenus. He was anti-Latin, where Manuel had been well disposed to the Latins; he sought support among the bureaucrats, to which Manuel had been indifferent. In this he was exploiting the frustrations felt by many at Manuel's court. His opposition to Manuel clearly struck a chord. This is to be seen in the support that he received, when he opposed Manuel's plan to impose a foreigner as the next Byzantine emperor. He was not without friends. He was helped on his way to Galicia by an old retainer of the Grand Domestic John Axoukh. It looks as though Andronicus was able to count on some support from the Axoukh connection. Its head was now Alexius Axoukh, the son of the Grand Domestic. He was one of Manuel's most accomplished commanders, acquitting himself well in Italy in 1157–58. He too would come under suspicion in 1166 immediately after Andronicus's defection.

He was arrested at Easter 1167. There were a variety of charges. It was alleged that he had recruited a body of Cuman mercenaries for a coup against the emperor. He was supposed to have been in treasonable correspondence with the Seljuq sultan and the decoration of his palace was held to be proof of this, for it apparently celebrated the sultan's martial deeds. Nearer the mark was the accusation that Axoukh employed magic to prevent the birth of a son to the emperor. Manuel remarried in 1161, but it was not until 1169 that his new bride presented him with a child, his son Alexius. Axoukh was therefore almost certainly caught up in the question of the succession, in the same way as Andronicus had been. We have seen how the emperor's nomination of the Hungarian Bela as his successor divided the court along pro- and anti-Latin lines. Axoukh's Seljuq connections would have singled him out as an opponent of the proposed succession. Nicetas Choniates suggests that the accusations against him were trumped up and singles out the Latinophile Isaac Aaron as the main instigator of the charges against him.

After the birth of a son to Manuel and his new Empress Maria of Antioch the succession ceased to be such a divisive issue at court. Aaron, who was the commander of the Varangian Guard, was in his turn arraigned on a charge of treason in 1172. He was accused of aiding the Venetians, who had just raided the Aegean, and of tampering with official correspondence with western powers. The then nigh obligatory charge of magic was also included. The Empress Maria seems to have been the moving force behind his arrest and condemnation. It marks her appearance on the political stage, as a personality to be reckoned with.

THE STYPPEIOTES AFFAIR

Under the Comneni bureacrats were rarely figures of political importance. They were expected to be experts in their field. Such a man was John of Poutzes, who held the office of Grand Logariast and controlled the fiscal organization under John Comnenus and in the early years of Manuel's reign. He was efficient; he made a great deal of money and married an aristocratic bride. He managed to remain aloof from the bureaucratic jealousies, which were the usual form that politics took in the civil service. His colleague John Hagiotheodorites was less fortunate. He was the victim of the intrigues of his subordinate Theodore Styppeiotes, who was raised in the early 1150s to the position of *epi tou kanikleiou* or keeper of the imperial inkstand. He was in effect the emperor's chief secretary, but he became more like a first minister, as the emperor entrusted him with more and more of the affairs of state. His downfall was to be encompassed through the machinations of a rival, John Kamateros, the logothete of the drome, but more seems to have been involved than petty jealousy. It was an event which made an impression far beyond the frontiers of Byzantium. It was even noted by the continuator of Otto of Freising's *Deeds of Frederick Barbarossa*. He has Styppeiotes plotting in 1159 the murder of the emperor, who was away at Antioch. Manuel's empress, the German Bertha, got wind of the plan and had him arrested. John Cinnamus agrees on the occasion of the arrest, but Styppeiotes's offence was to have prophesied that the 'span of the emperor's life was measured out'.[24] In his place the senate should elect an *archon* capable of directing the state's business as in a democracy. Such utterances would most certainly have been treasonable: democracy was anathema in Byzantium.

Nicetas Choniates has a quite different version of Styppeiotes's downfall. He puts the blame squarely on John Kamateros, who spread rumours of the most vicious kind about Styppeiotes. In 1159 Manuel called upon him to substantiate them. He could only claim rather lamely that Styppeiotes had not carried out the emperor's instructions over Sicily to the letter. The emperor's suspicions were aroused, but for the moment he took no further action. Some six years later John Kamateros's professional jealousy of his colleague quickened still more when the latter administered the oaths taken to Bela and the Porphyrogenite Maria. This was a task that properly belonged to Kamateros as logothete of the drome. It was then that Kamateros forged a letter purporting to be from Styppeiotes to the king of Sicily and had it concealed in his rival's papers. He persuaded Manuel to send agents to look through them. The treasonable document was found and Styppeiotes was condemned to be blinded.

This version of the story is much the most detailed and circumstantially convincing, but John Cinnamus's account cannot be dismissed out of hand, for by 1165 he was a member of the emperor's entourage and ought to have been well informed. Nicetas Choniates, in contrast, can only have been relying on civil service gossip, because he did not enter the administration until the very end of Manuel's reign and then in a minor capacity. The likelihood is that each account contains a fragment of the truth. The evidence for such a conclusion comes from an examination of the imperial chrysobull, which Styppeiotes had drawn up in November 1158. Manuel Comnenus had already left the capital and was campaigning in Cilicia. The chrysobull laid it down that any action or order of the emperor contrary to equity and the law was to be considered null and void. 'In the common interest'[25] it was to be given greater force by being registered in the patriarchal archives. It was clearly designed to meet criticism of Manuel Comnenus's rule, while he was away from the capital. However well intentioned it may have been, the chrysobull could easily have been presented as an attack upon the emperor's authority and the first step down the slippery path to democracy. It would have been all the more alarming because its promulgation more or less coincided with Andronicus Comnenus's first escape from gaol. News of this event brought Manuel hurrying back from Antioch to his capital. In such circumstances, it is easy to see the emperor relieving his minister of office and ordering some drastic punishment, which may or may not have been carried out.

There is a chance that Styppeiotes's disgrace was short-lived, for the chrysobull in question was to be formally registered in the state archives in August 1159. This must mean that it finally received imperial approval and suggests that Styppeiotes was, at least, partially rehabilitated. If he recovered the office of keeper of the imperial inkstand, he never fully regained the trust of the emperor. Manuel would have been sensitive to any accusations made against Styppeiotes over Sicily, because his Sicilian venture had drawn a great deal of criticism. The costs were enormous. By 1157 they already amounted to 30,000 lb of gold. Such a waste must have alarmed any conscientious civil servant and have been a constant reproach to the emperor. Manuel was not likely to show any mercy to a minister accused, however falsely, of treasonable correspondence with the king of Sicily.

THE BUSINESS OF GOVERNMENT

The government of Manuel Comnenus is perhaps best approached through the criticism made of it by Nicetas Choniates. 'Money expended for no useful purpose' headed his list of criticisms. 'The revenues collected in tax were not so much stored away in vaults or hidden in the bowels of the earth. They were rather recklessly disgorged and doled out to monasteries, churches, and to Byzantines of the inferior sort, though the greater part went to foreign riff-raff, most especially to the Latin peoples.'[26] These are the words of a cautious civil servant, who would have preferred the emperor to keep a healthy reserve in hand so as to meet any eventualities. The dangers proved to be less financial embarrassment – Manuel Comnenus never seems to have had much difficulty in raising cash for his various undertakings. Rather did his demands begin to undermine the soundness of the fiscal system, and this was to be a legacy to his successors. The tax farmers regarded their commissions as a licence for extortion, or, as Choniates put it, like 'fallow land to furrow with their own ploughs'.[27] Even worse, in Choniates's opinion, was the way the task of carrying out tax assessments was given to foreigners. They would have the assistance of some Byzantine who was capable of the technical work involved. Choniates thought that the evident lack of trust displayed by the emperor in the native Byzantines undermined their honesty and efficiency. It was all too easy to blame foreigners and Latins, in particular, for the perennial failings of the Byzantine administration. Should Choniates's criticisms therefore be dismissed out of hand? Perhaps not. He was, after all, the chief minister of the Empire at the turn of the century and presided over the disintegration of the Comnenian system of government. He is almost certainly right to trace the beginnings of this process to the reign of Manuel Comnenus. His foreign policy placed a terrific strain on the Empire's resources. The role of foreigners is more problematical. We have seen how Manuel employed a Jew of western origin as a financial adviser. His shady activities were directed against the Latins settled in the Empire rather than against the Byzantines themselves, but they point to Manuel's search for new sources of revenue towards the end of his reign.

Just as disastrous, in Choniates's opinion, as Manuel Comnenus's financial administration was his reform of army finance. In the past, only a few élite units had enjoyed the privilege of *pronoiai*. In other words, their members had drawn their revenues direct from the peasantry of a particular district or village and had enjoyed rights of administration. The majority of the troops enrolled in the Byzantine army received wages in the normal way. Manuel Comnenus decided to extend grants of *pronoiai* to most of the troops in the Byzantine army. Choniates considered that this undermined the morale of the crack

225

troops, who saw their privileged position disappearing. He was also
offended by the social origins of those who took up the new grants of
pronoiai. Manuel seemed to be enrolling anybody into his army: 'tailors
who made a miserable living, grooms, bricklayers, and coppersmiths'.[28]
And not just Byzantines, even 'semi-barbarian runts': a claim that is
amply confirmed by a grant made towards the end of Manuel's reign of
pronoiai to sixteen Cuman soldiers in the theme of Moglena near
Thessalonica. Nicetas Choniates's testimony is not to be dismissed
lightly.

There is independent evidence that Manuel carried out some far-
reaching military reorganization. At the beginning of his reign he
became concerned to improve the armament and expertise of his
cavalry. He rearmed them and retrained them on western lines. This
meant abandoning the relatively inexpensive bow and arrow and small
circular shield, which had been the traditional Byzantine equipment. He
substituted the western lance and the large triangular shield which
covered most of the body. Though nothing is said specifically, it seems
likely that heavy western armour was also introduced. Training took the
form of tournaments according to western fashion. The costs involved
would have been formidable and Nicetas Choniates makes it clear that
the soldiers were expected to bear the cost of the initial outlay. Artisans
from the towns would have been one group who would have been able to
put up the money needed, if not for themselves, then for their children.
They would have been attracted by the social status that went with
military service under the Comneni. To judge by one piece of legislation
from Manuel Comnenus's reign, enrolment in the army was only a little
inferior to membership of the senate. It established that imperial grants
of real estate could only be alienated to persons belonging either to the
senate or the army. Any infringement would mean its return to the state.
It is not impossible that this piece of legislation referred to *pronoiai*.

It would seem that Manuel Comnenus proceeded to an ambitious
reorganization of his army which necessitated a large-scale extension of
the *pronoia* system to finance it. This is the view of G Ostrogorsky,[29] but
it has not received unanimous approval, very largely because there are
so few traces of the *pronoia* in twelfth-century sources. In many parts of
the Empire the growth of the military *pronoia* seems to have come after
1204 rather than before. This is true of the region around Smyrna and of
Epiros, while there is no clear evidence for the existence of *pronoiai* in the
Peloponnese before the Frankish conquest. In the case of the
Peloponnese it was almost certainly because it came under the
supervision of the Grand Duke, who was responsible for the naval
administration of the Empire. Epiros and Smyrna were in the twelfth
century rather distant from the main centres of military organization.
These were the great military camps created by John and Manuel
Comnenus. The chief camp in Anatolia was sited on the Rhyndakos
plain near Lopadion, not far from the shores of the sea of Marmora.

Three camps are mentioned in the Balkans. There was one at Pelagonia to the west of Thessalonica on the Via Egnatia, another at Sofia on the great Military Road across the Balkans. The third was at Kypsella in Thrace near the mouth of the Maritsa, which served as a transit camp for moving units from Europe to Asia Minor. It was around these military centres that Manuel Comnenus was likely to create *pronoiai*, not in distant Smyrna or the Peloponnese. There was also plenty of spare land available in the southern Balkans out of which to create *pronoiai*. The relatively little evidence that exists on the *pronoia* in the twelfth century would seem to bear this out.

The extension of the *pronoia* brought complications. As Nicetas Choniates put it, 'the inhabitants of the provinces, who had previously only had the state as their lord, now suffered dreadfully at the hands of greedy soldiers'.[30] However exaggerated, this underlines an important fact: the *pronoia* was a new form of property rights, interposed between the state and the taxpayer. Its creation altered the legal status of the peasantry subject to it and threatened the rights of established landowners. This is apparent from the surviving details of one or two cases which came to the notice of the imperial administration.

Choniates's criticisms seem to have been solidly based, but they have the advantage of hindsight. His main concern was to trace the origins of the difficulties the Empire faced at the end of the century when he was chief minister. The weaknesses of Manuel's government were less apparent in his lifetime. Only occasionally did currents of criticism surface along lines similar to those indicated by Choniates. To counter them Manuel laid great stress from the middle of his reign on the rule of law. The main fruit of this preoccupation was the reorganization in 1166 of the law courts at Constantinople. The aim was to make them more efficient by cutting out delays. Presiding judges and their assessors were to sit three times a week. Assessors were not to be attached exclusively to any single court, but were to go to whichever needed their services. The same was to apply to barristers, who were in addition forbidden to indulge in lawyers' quibbles. The due process of law was speeded up. Oaths were to be administered within fifteen instead of thirty days. Petitions brought before the emperor were to be dealt with within eight days. A defendant who failed to appear within thirty days was deemed to be guilty.

There seems to be no reason to disbelieve the emperor's protestations that these measures were prompted by a regard for his judicial responsibilities before his subjects. But the wording of the prologue seems to suggest that the emperor was under some pressure to reform the organization of justice: 'Now seeing how many have been the victims of greed and injustice and have had to endure the loss of lands and dwellings and other things as well, but hammering on the gates of justice have wasted time and effort to no purpose. ...'[31] Manuel's judicial reforms coincided with a series of disturbing events: the final overthrow of Theodore Styppeiotes; the accusations of high treason against Alexius Axoukh; and the agitation led by Andronicus Comnenus against the oath to be taken to the Hungarian Prince Bela. Manuel Comnenus set out to crush all internal opposition, but he also needed to justify himself against criticism of his rule. His judicial reforms served as an earnest of his desire to restore moral direction to his government. He was fashioning a new image for himself, which corresponded to the more high-minded, not to say more autocratic, style of government of the last part of his reign. It had much in keeping with the rule of the emperors of the tenth century. He revived and even emended some of their legislation. Nicetas Choniates specifically affirms that he renewed Nicephorus Phokas's legislation designed to prevent property passing into the 'dead hand' of the monasteries. The text does not survive, but Choniates probably had in mind a measure of 1176 which deprived the monasteries of some of the legal protection their estates had previously enjoyed.

MANUEL COMNENUS AND THE CHURCH

This was in contrast to the generosity which Manuel had accorded to the church at the beginning of his reign. In 1144 he issued priests with a general exemption from the payment of extraordinary taxes to the state. In 1148 he confirmed the titles of property held by bishops, metropolitans, and the patriarch himself. Then in 1153 the patriarchal church of St Sophia received still more extensive privileges. Even its property where the title was defective received imperial confirmation. The emperor ordered a general survey of all the patriarchal estates to be carried out. Thereafter imperial agents were forbidden to set foot on those estates nor were they to raise any taxes from them. These measures were then extended in 1158 to the monasteries of the Constantinopolitan region. The net result was that the state lost much property and many rights to the church and monasteries. The emperor tried to limit the ill-effects of his generosity through a series of rescripts designed to protect the interests of soldiers, senators, and imperial agencies. These measures reflect the increasing competition there was towards the end of his reign for lands and revenues, but this was only a symptom of the strain that Manuel's policies were placing upon his Empire. But why should Manuel have been so foolishly generous towards the church in the early part of his reign? It was a case of necessity. There were many who felt that his elder brother Isaac should have succeeded to the throne. In such circumstances, Manuel needed the moral support of the patriarch and church and had to pay for it.

In one particular the new emperor was fortunate. The old patriarch died at the beginning of 1143 and Manuel returned to Constantinople to find the patriarchal throne vacant. After canvassing opinion among his own family, the senate, and the episcopal bench, his choice fell on Michael, the respected abbot of the monastery of Oxeia. He could be counted on to go through with the coronation. He was an unworldly man, who found the responsibilities of his office too burdensome. In March 1146 he abandoned the patriarchal throne and retired to the peace of the monastery of Oxeia. He had been faced with what was taken to be a recrudescence of the Bogomil heresy, but was, in fact, more complicated. The details of the case are unimportant; they concern two obscure Cappadocian bishops. Their fault seems to have been to introduce the mysticism then fashionable in certain monastic circles in Constantinople into the backwaters of the Byzantine world. This was the cause of consternation to the local church. Their condemnation was followed by that of one of their supporters in Constantinople, a monk called Niphon. He was to be kept in total seclusion in the monastery of the Peribleptos. It may be that he was from the first the intended victim, for he clearly had a considerable following in Constantinople. It included Cosmas Atticus, then a deacon of the patriarchal church. He was to succeed Michael of Oxeia on the patriarchal throne in April 1146. One of his first actions was to release Niphon. Underlying the charge of heresy that had been made against the monk were clearly political considerations.

The new patriarch was on intimate terms with the emperor's brother Isaac and, for that reason alone, one would have thought, suspect. We can only speculate as to why the Emperor Manuel should have been willing to allow his election to go ahead. Perhaps it is best seen as a gesture of reconciliation on the eve of the great expedition he was preparing against the Seljuqs. While the emperor was away, there was a whispering campaign against the patriarch. He was supposed to be plotting to put Isaac on the throne and his intimacy with Niphon was used to underline his unsound character. Manuel returned to find the church in an uproar. He intervened to settle the dispute, finally calling a council in the palace of the Blakhernai on 26 February 1147. Manuel interrogated the patriarch on his dealing with Niphon. The patriarch insisted in reply that the monk was not a heretic, but was orthodox. The opinion of the bishops who were present was that the patriarch was guilty of consorting with a man already condemned by a synod for his heretical teachings. He was therefore declared deposed. Cosmas refused to accept the validity of the assembly. He excommunicated those who took part in it and cursed the empress's womb – may she never bring forth a male child. It was not until the end of the year that the emperor was able to fill the patriarchal throne and even then his actions were the object of bitter criticism. The new patriarch was Nicholas Mouzalon. It was a strange choice. At the most conservative estimate he must have been well over seventy, having resigned the see of Cyprus some thirty-six years before. It is perhaps an indication of how difficult it was for the emperor to find anybody willing to become patriarch. It was a critical point in Manuel's reign, just as he was preparing to come to grips with the 'Sicilian Dragon'. He needed the moral support of the church and he was willing to buy it in the form of the novel he issued in February 1148 in favour of the church. This was made out in very general terms. Its workings were queried by the administrators of the church of St Sophia and in August 1153 in response he issued another novel, defining, protecting, and extending its rights. This was followed in March 1158 with very similar provisions for the monasteries of Constantinople and its environs.

To this point Manuel's dealings with the church were not very happy. He had had six patriarchs in fourteen years. One is known to have abdicated and at least two had been deposed. This is in contrast with later on in his reign, when from 1157 to 1178 there were only two patriarchs. He was then reasonably secure on his throne. His foreign policy too was often brilliantly successful. He no longer needed to buy the support of the church and he could adopt a more masterful approach to it. He also discovered a taste and a certain aptitude for theological controversy. He is even supposed to have given public lectures on theological topics. In good Comnenian fashion he used theological disputes to establish his credentials as a defender of orthodoxy and to confirm his mastery of the church.

The first serious theological dispute of his reign occurred in the mid-1150s. It revolved around the meaning of the words taken from the liturgy, 'Thou art He who offers and is offered and receives'. Did this mean that Christ's sacrifice was made to God the Father alone or to the Trinity as a whole? In that case was it possible for Christ to sacrifice Himself to Himself? There opened up a whole series of trinitarian and christological problems that the church hoped had been closed once and for all by the early general councils. There is the smack of logic-chopping about the whole affair. It did indeed begin as part of the rivalry between different groups among the deacons of St Sophia. In January 1156 the patriarch convoked a synod to consider the points at issue. It produced a compromise formula, which underlined that Christ's sacrifice was offered by the 'Word made flesh' to the Holy Trinity.

The emperor was not involved. He was away with his army in winter quarters at Pelagonia. In his absence the dispute continued. One of the deacons, Soterichos Panteugenos, patriarch-designate of Antioch, refused to accept the ruling of the synod on the matter. He composed a dialogue, supposedly in Platonic form, against it. He feared that it undermined the doctrine of the essential unity of Christ's being by presenting His sacrifice as made by His humanity to His divinity. He hoped to guard against this by presenting it as offered by God the Son to God the Father. He got himself into further difficulties by arguing that the sacrifice on the cross was not identical to that celebrated in the liturgy, thus denying the real presence in the Eucharist. A court theologian, Nicholas, bishop of Methone, was delegated to refute him. Soterichos protested his complete orthodoxy and demanded that his views should be properly examined. This time the emperor intervened. He called a council which met on 12 May 1157 under his presidency to consider the matter. He interrogated Soterichos himself. The patriarch-designate was condemned along lines already indicated by Nicholas of Methone. The bishop then composed a speech to celebrate the emperor's victory over heresy.

In his refutation of Soterichos, Nicholas of Methone hinted that his opponent had drawn some of his arguments from Plato. This is reminiscent of the charges made against John Italos and Eustratios of Nicaea. It is not at all clear that Soterichos owed very much to the Platonic tradition. It was merely a useful ploy on the part of the bishop, whose major work was the refutation of the Neoplatonic philosopher, Proclus. He claimed in his introduction to this work that he had undertaken it to protect those coming into contact with Proclus's ideas. He probably had in mind people, such as John Italos and Eustratios of Nicaea, but also the *Sebastokrator* Isaac Comnenus, who was an accomplished Platonist. The identity of this man remains in doubt. Professor Browning[32] has recently urged that he was not the brother of the Emperor Alexius I Comnenus, as has usually been supposed, but the uncle of Manuel I Comnenus, and the father of his most feared opponent, Andronicus Comnenus. The condemnation of Soterichos Panteugenos and his supporters was of immense value to Manuel Comnenus. It confirmed him as a defender of orthodoxy in the mould of his grandfather Alexius Comnenus. It may also have been used to place his opponents in a dubious light.

He thenceforth showed much greater confidence in dealing with ecclesiastical affairs. Whereas in the dispute involving Soterichos Panteugenos he only intervened towards the end, in a second theological controversy he was prominent from the start. It concerned the meaning of John 14, 28: 'for my Father is greater than I'. This dispute has already been touched upon, in so far as it reflects the influence of western currents of thought on Byzantine theology. A Byzantine diplomat, Demetrius of Lampe, who had travelled extensively in the West, criticized what he took to be the official Latin exegesis of these words. It amounted, in his opinion, to an admission that Christ was both inferior and equal to God the Father, which seemed nonsensical. He unfolded his ideas to the emperor, who was not impressed. There seemed rather to be a great deal of sense in the western formulation, for was not Christ inferior to the Father in His humanity, but equal in His divinity? The emperor found he had very little support for his views in the church. Even the patriarch dared not speak out openly on his behalf. Demetrius's views on the matter appeared to have won the day, perhaps just because of their anti-Latin character. The Byzantine sources conceal how heavily the emperor was relying on the advice of the Latin theologian, Hugh Eteriano. Rather than allow the dispute to drag on and thus emphasize his isolation, the emperor called a synod to be held in the Great Palace under his presidency. It duly met in March 1166. At the first meeting the emperor produced a tome backed up by a wealth of quotation from the fathers of the church to support his view that only in his 'created and concrete nature' was Christ inferior to God the Father. This produced a barrage of criticism from various bishops and members of the patriarchal administration. Another session was held four days later, packed with members of the imperial family and administration. There was again opposition, but a formula was agreed and signed just in time to be proclaimed on the Feast of Orthodoxy a week later. To still opposition Manuel Comnenus drew up an imperial edict or *ekthesis*, which imposed adherence to the ruling of the synod on pain of severe punishment: a bishop was threatened with dismissal from office, as was any official; the ordinary citizen with exile. To add force the edict was inscribed on stone and set up in the narthex of St Sophia. Amazingly the tablets survive to this day.

Manuel Comnenus's actions were high-handed in the extreme, but opposition was quelled. There was a brief flare-up on the death of the Patriarch Luke Chrysoberges in 1169, but it did not amount to very much. The emperor had mastered the church and could now afford to be less generous towards it. He put forward projects for a union of churches with the Latins and with the Armenians, in order to further the needs of his foreign policy. The response from the church was surprisingly mute. At the very end of his reign he bullied the patriarch into accepting a radical change in the formula of abjuration from Islam. Previously, a Muslim converting to christianity was called upon to renounce and anathematize the God of Mohammed. The emperor thought that this demand deterred potential converts to christianity. He therefore had a tome drawn up, removing this stipulation. He required the patriarch and bishops to append their signatures. They protested. So the emperor had a new and shorter version drawn up. He threatened that if they did not approve it, he would call a council of the church to consider the matter and the pope would be invited to give his opinion. The demand was too much for that great scholar, Eustathios, archbishop of Thessalonica. He declared, missing the point rather in his anger, that he would be unworthy of his cloth if he 'accepted as the true God that sodomite of a camel-driver'.[33] The emperor was furious, but once his temper had cooled he was induced by the patriarch to forgive the archbishop of Thessalonica. The patriarch and the bishops agreed to the removal of the offending anathema against the God of Mohammed, though they insisted that an anathema against Mohammed and his teachings should be included in its place. Once again, the emperor had been able to overawe the church, but he had not long to live. On his death-bed the patriarch extracted some small revenge by forcing the dying emperor to abjure his notorious interest in astrology.

Critics of Manuel may have complained that he went close to wrecking the harmony that was supposed ideally to exist between church and emperor in Byzantium, because of the way he meddled in matters of dogma. Yet the truth is that over the last part of his reign he was able to master any opposition to his interference with comparative ease. In other epochs of Byzantine history his conduct would have called forth bitter and sustained action from sections of the church, but this was noticeably absent. Why should this have been? Like his grandfather Alexius I Comnenus, Manuel was able to pose as the true defender of orthodoxy and like him used the Feast and *Synodikon* of Orthodoxy to calculated effect. He built on the suspicion there was of a speculative approach to theology. The methods he favoured were traditional to a degree with their concentration on citing authority. He was able to pit his court theologians against those deacons and professors of the church of St Sophia, who were the repositories of a more 'scientific theology'. There is an anecdote preserved by Nicetas Choniates, which catches the suspicion there was in court circles over the intellectual activities of the deacons of St Sophia. When the views of some of their number were condemned by the synod of January 1156, the emperor was absent with his army in winter quarters at Pelagonia. It was said that at the very moment of condemnation there was a crack of thunder overhead. One of the emperor's circle immediately went to consult a 'Thunderbook' to discover the meaning of the thunder. It told of 'the overthrow of the wise men'.[34] The events of 1156–57 went some way towards discrediting the intellectual pretensions of the deacons of St Sophia.

This allowed Manuel's allies and supporters within the church of St Sophia to assert themselves. Indicative of their victory is the work of the influential canon lawyer Theodore Balsamon, who held the position of *chartophylax* of St Sophia. He subscribed to a frankly caesaropapist view of imperial authority. The emperor was subject neither to the civil nor the canon law. He also held that the patriarch was in the last resort responsible for his actions to the emperor, whom he described as the 'disciplinarian of the church'.[35] He insisted that, if the patriarch was in the wrong, then he was subject to the judgement of the emperor. Such views come close to a betrayal of the traditions of orthodoxy with their insistence on the ultimate independence of the church. The defenders of orthodoxy against imperial encroachment had in the past been first and foremost theologians, men such as Maximus the Confessor, John of Damascus, Theodore of Stoudios, even perhaps Photius himself. Balsamon was no theologian, he was a canonist; and his perspective was different. He was less concerned with the dogma of the church, much more with its privileges, in particular with the privileges of his own office of *chartophylax*, to which he devoted a special treatise. The deeds of his office, so to speak, were provided by a novel of the Emperor Alexius

Comnenus, as were those of the other patriarchal offices. The emperor was seen as the guarantor of an administrative order. The patriarchal church had changed radically since the early eleventh century. It had become a complicated administrative organization almost on a par with that of the imperial government itself. But as a legal entity it needed the support and recognition of the emperor. From this point of view Manuel Comnenus was an excellent emperor. He protected and extended the legal rights and fiscal privileges of the church of St Sophia. In the end, this is what counted most.

BYZANTINE MONASTICISM UNDER MANUEL COMNENUS

These considerations help to explain why there was so little opposition to Manuel Comnenus from within the patriarchal administration, at least during the second half of his reign. They apply with almost equal force to Manuel's patriarchs. Professor Hussey has written that in the twelfth century 'the duties of the Patriarch were such that they demanded qualities of statesmanship and capacity for administration, rather than those gifts usually associated with the monastic vocation'.[36] In the past, it was usually the monks who had stood up to the emperor and had provided the patriarch of the day with the necessary backing to oppose the actions of an emperor. Under Manuel Comnenus Byzantine monasticism did not possess, nor was it able to discover, the moral force to oppose the emperor. A clue to why this should have been is provided by Theodore Balsamon.[37] He noted that in contrast to the West there was no 'common life' in Byzantine monasteries. They were, in the main, tiny communities, whose members lived and worshipped as individuals. Even allowing for a certain amount of exaggeration, Balsamon's observation brings out the fragmented character of Byzantine monasticism in this epoch.

Even more exaggerated was Eustathios of Thessalonica's account of the appalling state of the monasteries under his care. Their inmates were distinguished only by their ignorance and greed. He was disheartened by their wilful neglect of their studies. He tells of how he learnt of the existence of a volume of St Gregory of Nazianzus's works in a monastic library. He went and asked the abbot if he could consult it, only to be told that it had been sold. It was of no use to the monastery. He was dismayed to discover that monks were motivated by hatred of their bishop and by an 'unabashed search for ever more property'.[38]

His last stricture receives a surprising degree of support from perhaps the most successful Byzantine monastery of the twelfth century – the monastery of St John the Theologian on the island of Patmos. In contrast to the general run of Byzantine monasteries it was a large community. In 1157 there were no less than seventy-six monks, who witnessed the last testament of Abbot Theoktistos. Its contents are instructive. There is an almost complete absence of any spiritual advice to the brethren. Instead, the dying abbot concentrated on his administrative achievements: his voyages to Constantinople to visit the imperial court and the concessions and privileges that he was able to win for his monastery from a succession of Byzantine emperors. He was concerned to give an account of his stewardship. He claimed never to have wasted the monastery's wealth needlessly. Only in emergencies had he drawn on it. On one occasion he had bought off some Saracen pirates who were besieging the monastery. His main grief was not against the pirates, but against a vexatious imperial official who had entered the monastery and had confiscated 78 lb of gold, which had been deposited with the monks. The material interests of the monastery were the abbot's first concern.

Eustathios recommended the monasteries of Constantinople as a model of monastic order. And in a sense they were. There have survived from the twelfth century a surprisingly large number of *typika* or monastic rules for monasteries founded or refounded in the capital. They would seem to bear Eustathios out, with their detailed recipes for the efficient ordering of the monastic life and the smooth running of their estates and administration. What with the security provided for their estates by Manuel's chrysobull of 1158, it must have been a golden age of sorts for the monasteries of Constantinople. It was a time of consolidation; there was no longer the intense interest in monasticism and philanthropy that there had been at the court of Alexius I Comnenus. No monastic reformers were coming forward. The rules of the *typika* closely followed earlier rules, the *typikon* of the monastery of the Theotokos Evergetis of the mid-eleventh century being particularly favoured. The last major Comnenian foundation in Constantinople was the monastery of the Pantokrator, which the Emperor John Comnenus founded in 1136 in memory of his Empress Eirene. It enshrined the philanthropic ideals of his father. He had a teaching hospital attached to it. In good aristocratic fashion he also intended it as his burial-place and a family shrine.

In contrast, Manuel Comnenus showed little interest in the foundation of monasteries. He made no new foundations in Constantinople. He came to see monastic estates as an unnecessary burden upon his Empire. In his view, the wealth of the monasteries could only be justified if it was used to benefit society. 'Otherwise it would be better for the monks to die the most miserable death from famine than to possess disproportionate wealth.'[39] He preferred to work through the patriarchal church, very probably, as Paul Magdalino[40] judiciously notes, in order to emphasize his imperial status and to distance himself from the rest of the imperial clan. Its members continued to found monasteries. The emperor's uncle, the *Sebastokrator* Isaac, founded a monastery dedicated to the Kosmosoteira at Vera in Thrace. He meant it as a peace-offering to God in recognition of a stormy life, but it also provided an answer to a problem that must have exercised many aristocrats: what was to happen to his household and retinue after his death? The monastery would care for them and they would serve the monastery as they had previously their lord. In much the same way Manuel's cousin the *Protosebastos* John Comnenus was to turn his palace in Constantinople into a monastery. Such monasteries were a necessary extension of the aristocratic household. They served to commemorate the founder and his family and enshrined a sense of family.

Members of the aristocracy continued to act as patrons of holy men. Apart from any spiritual considerations this was one way of building up a popular following. The *protosebastos* was a patron of a monk who took up residence in the church of the Holy Apostles along with his drunken and dissolute following. As always, the streets of Constantinople were alive with holy men and Fools for Christ's sake garbed in the most bizarre manner. John Tzetzes complained about the way noblewomen and, sometimes even their husbands, had icons of these people set up in their private chapels. Worse, they collected, as relics of these holy men, the iron collars, and chains, and padlocks which served as instruments of their ecstatic bondage. Manuel Comnenus preferred to disassociate himself from such aristocratic enthusiasms.

THE PATRIARCHAL CHURCH

The ecclesiastical authorities regarded such activities with the deepest suspicion and with imperial support were able to clamp down on them. The condemnation of Constantine Chrysomallos in May 1140 was symptomatic. He seems to have been a genuine follower of the teaching of St Symeon the 'New Theologian', but he was condemned as a heretic who subscribed to Bogomil and Messalian doctrines. In the face of official disapproval the inspiration provided by St Symeon's writings petered out in the exhibitionism of the ascetic riff-raff of the capital. The mystical and ascetic tradition was not strong enough under Manuel Comnenus to provide the church with major figures while monastic life, at least in the capital, was geared to material well-being. There is more than a grain of truth in Theodore Prodromos's satire on monastic life in the capital. Monks and abbots showed too much concern for their stomachs: a charge that received ample confirmation from the abbot of Petra's ability to produce both red and black caviare at a moment's notice in the middle of the night and in Lent. Entry into some monasteries depended upon wealth and status. Theodore claimed to have been turned away from one because 'he was not the scion of a noble house, nor one of the "Great and the Good", nor was he able to endow the monastery with estates'.[41]

The men who dominated the Byzantine church were distinguished not so much for their spiritual qualities, more for their administrative and pastoral abilities. Michael Italikos is a good example. He was metropolitan of Philippopolis at the time of the second crusade. Thanks to his gifts of diplomacy the passage of the crusaders through the town went relatively smoothly. He conformed to a very typical pattern of appointment to the episcopal bench. He had worked in the patriarchal church and had been nominated to a series of official teaching posts before crowning his career with a bishopric. A great many, perhaps the majority, of the holders of the most important sees at this time started their careers in the patriarchal administration, often as deacons of St Sophia. Why they were willing to exchange the comforts and companionship of Constantinople for provincial rigours has to be explained. They almost invariably complain of life in the provinces and their letters are full of yearning for Constantinople and their friends. Their life was often dangerous. The metropolitan of Dristra, that important Byzantine base on the lower Danube, had been a deacon of St Sophia. He would be seized by some of the local people, tied up, and beaten. It was not the hope of material gain that spurred a patriarchal official to accept a bishopric. Few were rich; the cathedrals were often in need of repair. George Tornikes who was appointed metropolitan of Ephesus after a distinguished career in the patriarchal church says as much. He writes to a friend who held high office in the patriarchal administration. He beseeches him to stay in Constantinople, whatever inducements there might be to take up a post in the provinces, 'for there is nothing anywhere around here that is worthwhile either spiritually or materially'.[42] With such warnings ringing in their ears why did deacons of St Sophia continue to go out as bishops to the provinces? They went out of a sense of duty reinforced by a recognition of the mutual self-interest that united the patriarchal clergy. Since the reign of Alexius I Comnenus its members had come close to monopolizing power within the Byzantine church. This depended in the end upon their achieving an ascendancy over the patriarchal synod, whence the need for their most senior and respected members to take up the burdens of episcopal office. They understood, as well as their western counterparts, that the price of power was duty and they did not shirk their responsibilities.

There are similarities in the development during the twelfth century between the patriarchal church at Constantinople and the papacy at Rome. The accent in both was upon administration, reflected in the attention paid both at Constantinople and in Rome to canon law. The parallels cannot be pushed too far, if only because the relationship between the secular and spiritual arms was so different. A pope could hardly have tolerated the ascendancy that Manuel Comnenus sought to establish over the Byzantine church. At least, one Byzantine contemporary realized that papal precedents could be used to justify developments within the patriarchal church. He was the great canon lawyer Theodore Balsamon who held the office of *chartophylax* in the patriarchal administration. The *chartophylax* was the patriarch's deputy. He was 'the Patriarch's hand and mouth ... for which reason the keys of the kingdom of heaven are given to the *chartophylax*',[43] to quote the extravagant claims of Theodore Balsamon, as he set out the privileges of his office. He claimed among other things that its holder had the right to wear a golden tiara after the manner of a cardinal. His argument was that cardinals enjoyed this privilege as representatives of the pope. The *chartophylax* was the patriarch's representative – a 'patriarchal cardinal' to use Balsamon's words[44] – and should therefore enjoy the same privilege in this matter as a cardinal, given that in his opinion the patriarch of Constantinople enjoyed the same rights as the pope.

It may well be that Balsamon's views were a little eccentric, but they do catch the way that the chief officers of the patriarchal administration were coming to resemble the college of cardinals. They did not, of course, have the same rights in the election of the patriarch that the cardinals had in the election of the pope. In Byzantium the final decision rested with the emperor, but they were able to influence the names put forward to the emperor by the patriarchal synod. In contrast to the eleventh century and before, when the majority of patriarchs came from a monastic background, the reign of Manuel Comnenus saw at least three patriarchs chosen from members of the patriarchal administration. No patriarch was a prisoner of the patriarchal clergy, but Theodore Balsamon believed that the patriarch should leave details of administration and judicial business to his deputy, the *chartophylax*. Such things were, in his opinion, too mundane to merit the attention of a patriarch. He would clearly have liked to isolate the patriarch from the business of government.

Despite internal bickerings and personal rivalries the patriarchal church emerged under Manuel Comnenus with a sense of constituting an élite within the Byzantine church. Nothing contributed quite so effectively to this feeling of superiority as the intellectual ascendancy which it claimed. Whereas in the eleventh century the intellectual élite was to be found within the imperial administration, under Manuel Comnenus it was provided by the deacons of St Sophia and at their head the patriarchal professors or *didaskaloi*. There were three professorial chairs; in order of precedence – the Gospels, the Apostles, and the Psalter. There were also some supernumerary posts. These professorial posts first appear in Alexius I Comnenus's reign and seem to have been connected with his reform of the clergy in 1107. This envisaged that the first responsibility of the newly created order of *didaskaloi* was to preach the word of God to the people, but to be effective this demanded a higher standard of instruction in the scriptures. The *didaskalos* of the Psalter lectured on the Old Testament; the *didaskalos* of the Apostles lectured on the Acts of the Apostles and the Epistles of St Paul, while the *didaskalos* of the Gospels had overall responsibilities. Whether their activities were connected with a patriarchal academy is difficult to say. There is a description of the church of the Holy Apostles dating from the very end of the twelfth century, which suggests that there was an academy attached to this church at that time. It catered for primary and possibly secondary education. There is no evidence before this for a school attached to this church, so it may well be, as Professor Browning has argued,[45] that its creation was a relatively recent development, perhaps connected with the Emperor Alexius III Angelos (1195–1203) and his restoration of the church.

The strongest evidence for the existence of a patriarchal academy comes from the pen of a German bishop, Anselm of Havelberg. He knew Constantinople fairly well, visiting it on two occasions, the first time in 1136, when he disputed with Nicetas, metropolitan of Nicomedia. He described his opponent as 'chief among the twelve *didaskaloi*, who organize studies in both the liberal arts and the Holy Scriptures, as is the custom among the learned Greeks. They are superior to all in matters of doctrine and superintend the work of other learned men. To them are referred all difficult questions. Their solutions are thenceforward held as established doctrine and are enshrined in writing.'[46] Taken at face value, this certainly suggests that a college of *didaskaloi* were responsible for the organization of both secular and religious education. The information provided by Anselm of Havelberg cannot be dismissed out of hand. He may only have been a visitor to Constantinople, but he is known to have had informants who were well acquainted with its intellectual life. He is most likely guilty of confusing the *didaskaloi* with the sophists. This was an easy enough mistake to make, since 'sophist' was a general term applied to the highly educated and many of the sophists would have been *didaskaloi* and deacons of St Sophia. A college of twelve sophists did exist in the mid-twelfth century. Its main function was to adjudicate on matters of style, but other matters might be referred to it: for instance, a dispute over the application of the *schedographia* to the teaching of rhetoric. At best, the college of sophists would only have had semi-official status. It did not control the system of education.

Despite the creation of the patriarchal chairs the organization of education remained much as it had been in the late eleventh century. There was no academy, as such. Only a loosely connected collection of schools and schoolmasters. Many of the same churches had schools attached to them, the church of the Chalkoprateia, for instance. The orphanage of St Peter and St Paul continued to have its own school, as in the days of Alexius Comnenus. In this case, the emperor seems to have retained rights of appointment. At least, we find a future metropolitan of Trebizond appointed there by imperial decree to the position of assistant to his brother who held the professorial chair (*didaskalos thronos*). He would later be advanced to this position. To judge by other examples his official title would have been *maistor* of the rhetors or just possibly *maistor* of the philosophers. Virtually all those attested holding these positions would then go on to hold a position in the patriarchal church, normally including one of the patriarchal chairs. Teaching in the 'private schools' was now a prelude to a successful ecclesiastical career. It is this which constitutes the greatest change: the patriarchal church came to dominate the various 'private' institutions of education.

A man such as John Tzetzes did eke out a livelihood as a private tutor, but his complaints and his envy of those with established posts show that it was very much second best. He had to rely upon the uncertainties of aristocratic favour. The career of Nicephorus Basilakes provides another cautionary tale. He was a renowned teacher and advanced to one of the patriarchal chairs, but he was involved on the wrong side in the theological controversy about the meaning of the words, 'Thou art He who offers, and is offered, and receives'. He was dismissed from his post and sent briefly into exile. He ended his days in Constantinople, poor and embittered, never able to pick up the threads of his career.

Manuel Comnenus seems to have been happy to accept that education in Constantinople now came under the auspices of the patriarchal church. When he revived the post of consul of the philosophers in the 1160s, he chose a deacon of St Sophia, Michael Ankhialou, who would also receive the patriarchal office of *sakellarios*. In the eleventh and early twelfth century the post of consul of the philosophers was held by laymen. Its duties were not entirely honorific, but included both some teaching responsibilities and some general supervision of the 'schools' of Constantinople. Michael Ankhialou was ostensibly given the task of reviving the study of philosophy, or rather of asserting official control over its study. The appointment came in the wake of a series of heresy trials, which had revealed the dangers of speculative theology. Its practitioners were, like John Italos, misguided mythmakers who subscribed to 'Hellenic' beliefs. Philosophy was not to be reckoned for its own sake, but to be placed firmly at the service of theology. For this reason the new consul of the philosophers was to concentrate on the study of Aristotle. Not a word was said about the more dangerous Plato. It looks very much as though Manuel intended his revival of this office as a reproach to the patriarchal church. It had failed to control noxious teachings, but it was still preferable to work with it, rather than against it. The emperor had come to rely upon the expert knowledge of members of the patriarchal administration.

Alexius Aristenos is one example, if exceptional. He was a canon lawyer of renown. He combined a successful career in both the patriarchal and the imperial administrations, thanks to his legal skills.

Under John II Comnenus he was both a deacon of St Sophia and *nomophylax*, the emperor's legal adviser. He would then rise to the positions of *orphanotrophos* and *dikaiodotes*, which put him at the head of both the welfare organization and the legal service. At the same time, his career in the patriarchal administration culminated in its highest position, the office of Grand *Oikonomos*, who was responsible for the financial administration of the patriarchal church.

In the opposite direction, members of the imperial administration found sinecures for their relatives in the patriarchal church. There was a case that came before the patriarchal court in November 1145, which dealt with promotion within the *skevophylakion*, the sacristy of St Sophia. It ended with the establishment of a list of candidates for promotion. Six names are given. Three were sons of imperial officials and possibly a fourth; the other two were nephews of bishops. It could also work the other way around. Clergy were following secular callings. This was the cause of great disquiet to the Patriarch Luke Chrysoverges. One of his first acts on ascending the patriarchal throne in 1157 was to issue a decree forbidding such a practice. In part, he had people such as Alexius Aristenos in mind. Aristenos used all his legal skill to vindicate his occupation of posts in the imperial administration. To no avail: he was forced to resign them, after being summoned three times before the patriarchal synod to explain himself. The abuse also existed on a humbler level: members of the clergy acted as factors for aristocratic houses, engaged in tax collection, and even served as sea-captains. Such activities were specifically forbidden. Manuel Comnenus also legislated to prevent members of the clergy occupying changers' stalls and acting as bankers. Rascally monks, we know, went from door to door in Constantinople, flogging fruit and vegetables at exorbitant prices.

Before this the promiscuity of secular and clerical pursuits does not seem to have been the cause of much disquiet, but it was a problem that the Patriarch Luke Chrysoverges kept coming back to. Under his successor Michael Ankhialou it was even decided that the prohibition against clergy engaging in secular activities should apply to readers – the lowliest members of the clergy. It is possible that the general prosperity of Constantinople in the twelfth century opened up new opportunities for the clergy, but, at best, this would only have been a contributory factor. The real pressures came from within the church and from the emperor himself. Privilege and status went together. No patriarch would wish to endanger the privileges that were won from Manuel Comnenus by condoning such promiscuity. The emperor's interest was rather different. His ascendancy over his Empire depended in the end on his ability to maintain a balance between the orders into which the society of his capital divided – the court aristocracy, the bureaucracy, the patriarchal clergy, and the monks of Constantinople. To this end he sought to keep each distinct. The property and fiscal rights enjoyed by the patriarchal church and the monasteries of

Constantinople were carefully laid down. The emperor also insisted that imperial gifts of property made to members of the senate or the army were not to be alienated to others.

To hold the balance of society Manuel needed to stress the themes of imperial grandeur. He set himself above society. This was partly a matter of temperament but also in response to the political system he inherited from his father and his grandfather. They ruled in the end as the head of a family, which monopolized power. Manuel found it increasingly difficult to maintain this pattern. As his father's youngest son his right to ascend the throne was questioned by many and left him vulnerable. Throughout the early part of his reign he faced opposition from within the imperial family; most dangerously in the shape of his cousin Andronicus Comnenus. This impaired the cohesion of the imperial clan. In any case, unlike his father, grandfather, and great-grandfather before him, Manuel failed to sire a large family. This meant that the core of the imperial family was not being replaced. To that extent, it was a matter of biology. Many of his most trusted lieutenants came from outside the narrow confines of the Comnenian family. To them can be traced the fortunes of not a few of the aristocratic families who would dominate later Byzantine history. The court aristocracy was beginning to split up into a series of clans, producing new pressures. While Manuel lived they could be contained, but after his death ...

NOTES

1. William of Tyre (transl. by E A Babcock and A C Krey), II, p. 382
2. Nicetas Choniates (ed. by Van Dieten), p. 48
3. Odo of Deuil (ed. and transl. by V G Berry), p. 65
4. Eustathios, p. 230–1
5. Tzetzes, *Epistulae* (ed. by P A M Leone), p. 66
6. Georges et Dèmètrios Tornikès, *Lettres et Discours*, pp. 173–4
7. Nicetas Choniates (ed. by Van Dieten), p. 158
8. E Legrand, *Bibliothèque grecque vulgaire*, I (Paris, 1880), p. 2, ll. 45–6
9. Cinnamus (transl. by C M Brand), p. 206
10. Legrand, *op. cit.*, p. 2, l. 47
11. Georges et Dèmtrios Tornikès, *Lettres et Discours*, p. 301
12. A Maiuri, 'Una nuova poesia di Teodoro Prodromo in greco vulgare', *Byzantinische Zeitschrift*, 23 (1920), p. 399, ll. 15, 20–1
13. *Heliodori Aethiopica* (ed. A Colonna) (Rome, 1938), p. 367
14. E M Jeffreys, 'The Comnenian Background to the "Romans d'Antiquité"', *Byzantion*, 50 (1980), pp. 455–86
15. Maiuri, *art. cit.*, p. 399 , l.40
16. Nicetas Choniates (ed. by Van Dieten), p. 206
17. *Poèmes prodromiques en Grec Vulgaire*, (ed. by D C Hesseling and H Pernot) (Amsterdam, 1910), pp. 55, 67

18. Nicetas Choniates, (ed. by Van Dieten), p. 60
19. *Digenes Akrites* (ed. and transl. by J Mavrogordato) (Oxford, 1956), pp. 136–7
20. *Ibid.*, pp. 218–19
21. Cinnamus (transl. by C M Brand), p. 49
22. Nicetas Choniates (ed. by Van Dieten), p. 141
23. *Ibid.*, p. 104
24. Cinnamus (transl. by C M Brand), p. 141
25. Zepos, *Jus*, I, p. 386
26. Nicetas Choniates (ed. by Van Dieten), p. 204
27. *Ibid.*
28. *Ibid.*, p. 209
29. G Ostrogorskij, *Pour l'histoire de la féodalité byzantine* (Brussels, 1954)
30. Nicetas Choniates (ed. by Van Dieten), p. 208
31. Zepos, *Jus*, I, p. 390
32. R Browning, *Church, State, and Learning in Twelfth Century Byzantium* (London, 1981), p. 18
33. Nicetas Choniates (ed. by Van Dieten), pp. 216–17
34. *Ibid.*, p. 211
35. Migne, PG, 137, c. 1312
36. J M Hussey, *Church and Learning in the Byzantine Empire 867–1185* (Oxford, 1937). p. 133
37. Migne, PG, 138, c. 176
38. Eustathios, p. 22
39. *Ibid.*, p. 231
40. P Magdalino, 'The Byzantine Holy Man in the Twelfth Century', in S Hackel (ed.), *The Byzantine Saint* (London, 1981) pp. 51–66
41. *Poèmes prodromiques* (ed. by Hesseling and Pernot), p. 65
42. Georges et Dèmètrios Tornikès, *Lettres et Discours*, p. 170
43. G A Rhalles and M Potles, *Syntagma ton theion kai hieron kanonon*, IV (Athens, 1856), p. 534
44. *Ibid.*, I, p. 149
45. R Browning, *Studies on Byzantine History, Literature, and Education*, no. X, p. 177
46. Migne, PL, 188, c 1141

Chapter 13
CAPITAL AND PROVINCES

Foreign visitors to Constantinople in the reign of Manuel I Comnenus were impressed. The Spanish Jew Benjamin of Tudela considered that only Baghdad could compare with Constantinople in size and splendour. Equally impressionable was his contemporary, William of Tyre, who visited the city on a number of occasions on diplomatic business. He singled out the approach to the Great Palace from the sea: 'Marble steps descending to the water's edge, and statues of lions and columns, also of marble, adorning the place with royal splendour.'[1] He would have seen the city at its most stunning, for the Byzantines were adept at stagemanaging official visits. Odo of Deuil also experienced an official tour of the city. He duly registered the splendours of the Blakhernai Palace and the beauty of the churches, but he used his eyes. He saw beneath the glitter the squalor of a great city and the extremes of wealth and poverty. He noted how 'the wealthy overshadow the streets with buildings and leave these dirty, dark places to the poor and to travellers'.[2] These were the haunts of thieves and murderers.

Travelling the streets of Constantinople could be a hazardous business. The great avenue leading down to the Kharsianon Gate was cut by a mire, from which travellers could only rescue their animals with the help of ropes and tackle. In the winter there was a good chance that the beasts would die of cold before they could be got out. A petition was sent to the Emperor John II Comnenus asking him to repair the highway. It was the emperor's responsibility to maintain the chief thoroughfares of the city and public amenities in general. Eustathios of Thessalonica addressed a petition to Manuel Comnenus on behalf of the citizens of Constantinople about the city's water supply. He complained that there was now an inadequate supply of water even in the winter months. He connected this with the mounting incidence of disease. The trouble seems in part to have been that the system of reservoirs, conduits, and aqueducts inherited from the late Roman Empire was beginning to break down. Manuel responded by constructing a new

244

underground reservoir on the outskirts of Constantinople, whence water was piped into the old conduits.

Such information about the state of Constantinople in the twelfth century is amplified by the experiences of the littérateur John Tzetzes. He had to beg the loan of a mule from an influential friend because overnight rain had made the streets impassable on foot. He was unable to get in or out of his dwelling because monks from the nearby monastery of the Pantokrator were digging up the road. He stayed in a three-storied building, which was divided into flats. Above him lived a member of the minor clergy, who not only kept pigs, but also had numerous children. Tzetzes[3] wrote to his landlord anticipating instant disaster. Either he was going to be swamped from above by a flood of ordure or the long grass outside his flat was going to catch fire and he would be burnt alive. He therefore requested his landord to clear the grass and to repair his ceiling, which had been damaged by a leaking down-pipe.

What are we to make of these fragmentary impressions of Constantinopolitan life? That little had changed? There were difficulties over the water supply when Liutprand of Cremona visited Constantinople in the mid-tenth century and there were always troublesome neighbours in the flat above, for just as in Justinian's day the Constantinopolitan middle class of minor clergy, civil servants, literati, and teachers continued to live in flats, while the poor condition of the roads and of housing and what seems to have been a general squalor were an inseparable part of a thriving and populous metropolis. This was above all true of the area down towards the Golden Horn, where the Venetians, Genoese, and Pisans were granted their factories. The detailed descriptions of the area which have survived from the twelfth century plot the maze of alleys and courtyards. Workshops and dwellings cheek by jowl, lean-tos and stalls and outshuts. Housing was of an immense variety from apartment houses to hovels and basements, the exteriors decorated with wooden columns, balconies, solars, and terraces. Other parts of the city had a different character. While there is only a single great house described down by the quays along the Golden Horn, around the Blakhernai Palace they seem to predominate with their spacious gardens and walks. Around the church of the Holy Apostles, near the physical centre of the city, there were wide open spaces. There was an abundance of water, good agricultural land, fruit trees, gardens, 'and houses hidden in trees'. We are assured by a contemporary that for those that lived near the church of the Holy Apostles 'the wheat alone which grows in the land about their houses is sufficient for their nourishment'.[4] They had no need to fear pirates or rely upon shippers for their supplies. But, above all, Constantinople was a city of churches and monasteries, hidden behind high walls.

Provincials streamed into Constantinople to the disgust of John Tzetzes. He observed that 'those dwelling in imperial Constantinople are not of one language or one race, but use a mixture of strange tongues. There are Cretans and Turks, Alans, Rhodians, and Chiots, notorious thieves.'[5] Understandably, if inconsistently, Tzetzes also prided himself on his ability to operate in the half a dozen languages necessary to conduct business on the streets of Constantinople – Scythian, Persian, Latin, Alan, Arabic, Russian, and Hebrew. Constantinople under the Comneni was thoroughly cosmopolitan. The historian Nicetas Choniates was also struck by the polyglot character of Constantinople. He found in it an explanation for the unruliness and the fickleness of its inhabitants.

To some it seemed that the natural order of society was dissolving. Tradespeople no longer showed respect to their betters. One contemporary wished that he had never followed his father's advice and acquired a good education. He was now starving while tradesmen of all kinds were doing well for themselves. The envy is done for comic effect, but it does contain a grain of truth. Education was no longer a guarantee of a lucrative position in the imperial administration. The lot of the poor schoolmaster was not an enviable one. At one stage John Tzetzes was forced to sell off his books in order to eat.

It has to be said that it is easier to find poor schoolmasters than to document prosperous Byzantine merchants and businessmen in twelfth-century Constantinople. Yet a Byzantine poet of the time can employ the image of the 'big merchant wishing to make large profits, who disdains all terrors and defies the sea'.[6] He might almost be thinking of the money-changer Kalomodios, who made a fortune at this time, 'often setting forth on long and arduous journeys from his home [at Constantinople] for the sake of commerce'.[7] Another successful businessman was that Chrysiobasilius who in 1148 owned the quay of St Marcianus, with all its buildings and workshops. But these are exceptions. The normal run of tradespeople operated from rented workshops. The *emphyteusis* lease seems to have been very popular. This lease seems normally to have been employed in cases where the workshop had been built by the lessee. In return the rent was fixed at about half the normal rate. The attractions of such an arrangement are obvious, but it demanded favourable business conditions. The names of the lessors are not given. It is known that the church of St Sophia leased out a great deal of property in Constantinople.

Monasteries too were major owners of property. They tended to rent rather than to lease out, but they seem to have been more actively engaged in business than the church of St Sophia. As in the eleventh century, they owned many of the quays along the Golden Horn. They played an important role in supplying the city with foodstuffs. A peculiarity seems to have been that the bakeries were now attached to monasteries. Monks also went from door to door selling fruit and vegetables. There was no check on their activities by the prefect and his staff. In contrast, street traders suffered from their competition as a vignette of Constantinopolitan life preserved by John Tzetzes[8] reveals. A fishmonger or a greengrocer might buy mackerel or apples down at the quay for twelve to the obol and then sell them in the main street at ten to the obol. For their pains they were likely to be denounced to the prefect's office and beaten for contravening price control regulations. This seemed unfair to Tzetzes for, not only did these traders have to cart their wares up from the quay, but they were also forced to pay a cut to the prefect and his staff.

This all suggests that the prefect retained a large measure of control over areas of the economic life of the capital. He still possessed a formidable staff of inspectors and other agents. The Book of the Prefect, which regulated the guilds of Constantinople, also preserved its legal validity, being cited in an imperial ruling of 1148. Does this mean that the guild system continued to function? If it did, then it has left very few traces in the sources. There is a chance reference to the head of the goldsmiths from the turn of the twelfth century. It may be, as we shall see, that the chaotic conditions of those years allowed the guilds a greater prominence than they had enjoyed under Manuel Comnenus. Indicative of their weak position was Manuel's intervention to prevent members of the clergy occupying bankers' stalls. He did not insist that they be returned to members of the guild of bankers, only to 'trustworthy Byzantine persons'.[9] The man selected had to be presented to the prefect, who would enrol him as a banker. Not a word is said about any guild. This suggests that the powers of the prefect had increased at the expense of the guild organization. Guilds would have continued to exist, but as unofficial bodies. They would have lost their privileged position.

What were the economic implications of the eclipse of the guilds? It may well have stimulated individual enterprise, but, most of all, it favoured those who were able to escape from the control of the prefect's administration: the monks of Constantinople, for example. The real beneficiaries were the Italians. Their privileges exempted them from the supervision of the prefect. This, as we have seen, was the cause of considerable friction with the Byzantine authorities. Their presence in Constantinople may have produced some resentment, but it had its compensations. As an example of the benefits the natives of Constantinople derived from the Latin presence there were the large number of workshops described as *koparika* owned by Byzantines along the edge of the Genoese quarter. They turned out oars and other naval gear for Italian shipping. As shippers, sea-captains, and merchants, the Italians were a positive benefit to the Byzantine economy. They contributed to the continuing growth of the Empire's internal trade. With their seasonal fleets (*mudua*) the Venetians opened up regular trading links by sea between Constantinople and the Greek lands. They had an obvious interest in the region because it lay athwart the main routes from the Adriatic to Constantinople. It was also the most prosperous part of the Empire. The Venetians were attracted by the possibilities there were for the commercial exploitation of its agricultural potential.

THE GREEK LANDS IN THE TWELFTH CENTURY

In the Greek towns and ports the Venetians normally worked through local middlemen, but they might on occasion deal directly with the landowners, whose estates produced the crops they were interested in. In 1150 we find a Venetian buying up no less than 400 measures of olive oil from the *archontes* of Sparta for despatch to Constantinople. The *archontes* were the key figures in the provincial towns of the Byzantine Empire. They were local landowners with their property concentrated around the town where they had their residence. They played an active part in local administration. They, more than any other group, must have benefited from the presence of the Venetians in the towns of Greece.

By the twelfth century the town was well and truly established as the focus of the economy and society of the Greek lands. As we have already seen, this had its roots back in the tenth century. One of the attractions which Greece must have had for the Venetians was that the growth of towns was already beginning to stimulate agriculture. The Venetian interest in the region meant that its economic growth would continue, perhaps even accelerate. Archaeology suggests that at Athens and Corinth the rapid growth of the medieval town began in the middle of the eleventh century and continued with the occasional interruption, such as the Norman sack of the two towns in 1147, until the close of the twelfth century. As we know, it was in this period that the deserted *agorai* began to be built over. There was a maze of alleys, leading off into a series of courtyards surrounded by a complex of rooms. These served promiscuously as dwelling and workshop. New churches were built. Many survive in Athens. They seem to date in the main from the mid-eleventh to the late-twelfth century, reflecting the growth of the town. There were still some fields within the walls of Athens, but all around they were hemmed in with buildings and churches.

Archaeology suggests that the physical growth of Corinth and Athens over the twelfth century was not just a matter that can be explained by their role as markets for agricultural produce. They also functioned as centres of manufactures. Corinth produced textiles: cottons, linens, and silks. A glass workshop has been found in its *agora* and there were also potters working there. Athens concentrated on producing dyes and soap. One of its quarters was named Konkhyliariai after its fishers for purple, and a dyehouse with vats and basins has been discovered by archaeologists. We can just detect the beginnings of specialization, for the soap and dyes of Athens must have gone to supply the textile workshops of Corinth and, above all, the silk workshops of Thebes. By the middle of the twelfth century Thebes had almost certainly outstripped Constantinople as the main producer of silks within the Byzantine Empire. Theban silks were prized above all others for the quality of their workmanship. It was the women of Thebes who were renowned for 'the daintiness of their weaving'.[10] For this very reason they were driven off into exile by the Normans when they sacked the city in 1147. The descriptions of the booty they took away with them are ample testimony to the wealth of Thebes in the middle of the twelfth century.

The triangle formed by Thebes, Athens, and Corinth was almost certainly unique in the Byzantine Empire for its concentration on manufactures, which produced specialization and a division of labour. This worked its way down to quite a humble level. Athens, for instance, lacked smiths. Its archbishop would complain towards the end of the twelfth century: 'the bellows have failed us; there is no worker in iron among us, no worker in brass, no maker of knives'.[11] So he turned for help to the bishop of the small town of Gardiki, which was renowned for the manufacture of agricultural implements and carts. Why the theme of Hellas should have developed in this way is hard to say. It has something to do with the comparative security it enjoyed. The upheavals of the later eleventh century more or less passed it by. Unlike most other parts of the Empire it retained the administrative structure that had evolved in the early eleventh century, an indication of continuity. Jews were attracted to the region in considerable numbers. The Spanish Jew Benjamin of Tudela passed through in the middle years of the twelfth century. He noted a community of 300 Jews at Corinth and no less than 2,000 Jews at Thebes. This was the largest Jewish community in the Byzantine Empire, outside Constantinople, where 2,500 were settled. The Jews of Thebes dominated the production of silk there according to Benjamin of Tudela. He may well have been exaggerating. The best weaving was done by the women of Thebes, but the cleansing and dyeing of the raw silk, a dirty and unpleasant job, may well have been in the hands of the Jews. The presence of Jews and the commercial interest of the Venetians in the agricultural riches of the region combined with the talents of its inhabitants to promote it as a centre of manufactures. Sufficient local wealth was generated to foster the growth of industry.

Some impression of conditions in other parts of the Greek lands can be derived from the *Geography* of Edrisi, which was completed at the Sicilian court in 1154. His information for the European provinces of the Byzantine Empire seems to be up to date, but there are serious lacunae. He only mentions the town of Thebes in passing, but he has left a detailed description of the Peloponnese. It was a prosperous place, and he singles out Sparta, Arcadia, a port on the western coast, and Corinth, as towns of some size. There were plenty of market towns, which were centres for the surrounding villages and castles. Edrisi also notes that their inhabitants possessed their own boats. There can be little doubt that the agricultural potential of the Peloponnese was fully mobilized at this time.

Edrisi's way of describing the interior of Greece and the southern Balkans is by following the routes leading from Dyrrakhion or Avlona on the Adriatic to the ports of the Aegean. It is clear that most of the main towns along these routes were prospering in the mid-twelfth century. Ohrid is 'a city notable for the number of its public buildings and the importance of its trade'.[12] Skoplje is a large town, surrounded by vineyards and cultivated fields. Ioannina is a town, 'built on an eminence, well populated, and surrounded by water and orchards',[13] while Kastoria is a pleasant town, 'rich, well populated, surrounded by villages and hamlets. It is situated on a promontory bathed by the waters of a large lake, where plenty of fish is caught with the help of boats.'[14] Larissa, the chief town in Thessaly, is a large town, 'surrounded by fig-trees, vineyards, and arable land'.[15] These inland towns prospered as the centres of rich agricultural areas. Commerce and manufactures seem to have been of hardly any importance. This is in contrast to the ports along the Aegean coasts. Halmyros is described as an entrepôt, and Benjamin of Tudela correctly noted that it was frequented by Italian merchants. Chrysopolis was noted 'for the beauty of its markets and the importance of its trade'.[16] Philippi was built on an outcrop some 10 miles from the sea. 'There was plenty of industry and trade there, both in exports and imports.'[17]

Thessalonica remains an enigma. Edrisi limits himself to a brief note. It was 'a pleasant town, well-known and possessing a large population'.[18] This is hardly adequate for the second city of the Empire. It possessed a Jewish community some 500 strong according to Benjamin of Tudela, but they were badly treated by the local people. There was also the famed fair of St Demetrius. It was held every year in October and lasted for six days. It took place outside the city walls in the direction of the river Vardar. It was described in the early twelfth century by a contemporary as 'the greatest of the fairs held among the Macedonians. It was not just local people who came, but people from all corners of the world: Greeks, Bulgarians, Campanians, Italians, Georgians, Lusitanians, and Celts from beyond the Alps. Its fame resounded throughout Europe. There were lines of tents opening up into a big square, where merchants did business. It was possible to buy all kinds of cloths from Thebes and the Peloponnese and from Italy; indeed, from Egypt and Spain too. Merchants distributed them to Macedonia and Thessalonica. The Black Sea sent its own products via Constantinople.'[19] Thessalonica's geographical position made it a natural outlet for the products of the Balkans and a centre of distribution. No doubt, the people of Thessalonica benefited.

Otherwise, it is very difficult to gain much impression about the economy of Thessalonica in the twelfth century. The Jews recorded by Benjamin of Tudela worked in silk, but their position was fairly miserable. They were oppressed by the local people and seem to have been isolated in a suburb of the city. There was a guild of hatters, which suggests that there was at least the vestiges of a guild system.

Out of these bits and pieces of evidence it is scarcely possible to build up a coherent picture of society in Thessalonica in the twelfth century, but there are some useful pointers. Like other towns, Thessalonica had its archontic families, who, given Thessalonica's prestige, were probably rather grander than those of other provincial cities. The core of solid citizenry was formed by the *oikodespotai* or householders. They were men of substance. Their property was made up of land around Thessalonica and urban property, dwellings and workshops, which they leased out. They were *rentiers*. Eustathios, archbishop of Thessalonica, has left a nice sketch of how the city was run. He was delineating the local politicians. They took great care to ingratiate themselves with both the assembly and the people by pretending to be both concerned and honest. 'As a result all public business comes into their hands and not a little private.... Thousands frequent them on all kinds of matters: marriages, commerce, and exchange.'[20] The archbishop went on to complain that they then used this influence for their private advantage. His division of the city into the assembly and the people is very interesting. It seems to point to the beginnings of some communal organization. The city was divided into quarters which centred on parish churches and at the head of each was an official known as the *geitoniarches*. There was also some kind of market organization. The duke, the imperial governor, seemed a rather distant figure. On the Feast of St Demetrius on 26 October he would go in solemn procession on horseback surrounded by his gaily decked retinue to the church of St Demetrius to pay his respects to the patron saint of the city. It was the cult of St Demetrius which united the city. There was a confraternity of St Demetrius. Some of its members distinguished themselves in the defence of the city against the Normans in 1185.

An equally fragmented picture emerges from other provincial towns in Greece, but many of the same features can be paralleled. Athens was divided up into quarters, though they did not correspond with parishes as in Thessalonica, very probably because no parish organization ever existed in Athens. To judge by two mid-eleventh-century inscriptions local churches were in private hands at Athens. There is an echo of something similar in a division of property among the members of a substantial Thessalonican family. To the share of one of the brothers fell the church of St Stephen with all its fittings and plate. It was specified that the latter must remain in the church. It has recently been suggested[21] that the tiny churches erected outside the walls of Kastoria from the ninth to the twelfth century were family shrines. The church of St

Nicholas tou Kasnitze was put up around the middle of the twelfth century by Nicholas Kasnitzes. Like many of the provincial *archontes* of the time he had somehow acquired the right to a redundant court title, that of *magistros*.

The existence of private chapels and monasteries must not be allowed to obscure the importance of the cathedral clergy in the towns. Their position within the town depended on several considerations, not least that they provided the notariate. It has to be confessed that it is difficult to establish the kind of family from which they were drawn, simply for want of evidence. Slightly later evidence would suggest that they came from substantial local families, connected with the archontic ascendancy. It is clear that these families managed to keep ecclesiastical office in the family. Such a privileged position was on occasion backed up by chrysobull. This is known to have been the case both at Athens and at Mesembria, on the Black Sea coast. It could lead to scandal, with members of the clergy being succeeded by their children, even if they had not been ordained. They simply found themselves deputies to carry out their duties, while pocketing the perks and salary of office. When Michael Choniates became archbishop of Athens, he tried to limit the independence of his clergy. He had a heated exchange with the *sakellarios* of his church, who had been passed over for promotion to the office of *skevophylax* because of blindness. He protested that this went against all the traditions and procedures of the church of Athens. The archbishop in reply wanted to know who had appointed the *sakellarios* as *archon* and judge over him. It was his business as archbishop to decide such appointments. This is a clear example of a prelate attempting to assert his authority over his clergy. It fits with the greater authority that bishops were beginning to enjoy in the twelfth century. This is a development which finds echoes in the iconography of the period, as Father Christopher Walter has recently shown.[22]

The most tangible sign of this increasing prestige is to be seen in the chrysobulls which were issued in ever larger numbers to the bishoprics of the Empire. They were concerned first and foremost with the episcopal estates. In 1163 the property of the bishopric of Stagoi, the modern Kalambaka, was carefully delineated. It consisted of a notional 1,000 *modioi* of good land and there were 46 peasant families settled there. There was other property further afield and some mills on the river Salavria. Stagoi was almost as unimportant a bishopric as one could find in Thessaly. Yet it was clearly a substantial local landowner. Proof of its new-found wealth is the cathedral, which dates from the twelfth century. At the end of the eleventh century the church of Athens came close to losing control over all its estates and monasteries. By the end of the twelfth century it had considerable property and seems also to have brought back many of the monasteries and abbeys of Attica under its control. Episcopal power in the towns of Greece was based upon landed wealth.

THE LAND AND THE PEASANTRY

Land was very little use without the peasants to work it. The Comnenian emperors, from Alexius I Comnenus on, were extremely generous in their grant of peasants to the holders of great estates. These peasants were often described as free and unknown to the state. They were landless, uprooted peasants, who had suffered from the turmoils of the late eleventh century. Their settlement on great estates was part of the way Alexius I Comnenus was gradually able to bring some degree of stability to the countryside in the Empire's European provinces. One result was the completion of a process that went back to the tenth century: the free peasantry virtually disappeared. The peasants met in the sources are invariably described as *paroikoi* or dependent peasants. They owed their dues and services either to the state, in which case they were referred to as *demosiakoi*, or to the holder of some privileged estate. If there were free peasants, they had escaped the long arm of the Byzantine administration, or, as we shall see, they had special military duties.

It is not at all clear that there were in the twelfth century any real differences between state *paroikoi* and private *paroikoi*, beyond the fact that the former were subject to the state, and the latter to a landowner. Both were divided up into the same classes according to their substance. The *zeugaratoi* held plots of land known as *zeugaria*; this was roughly equivalent to the amount of land that could be cultivated with a pair of oxen, which, it was assumed, the *zeugaratoi* possessed. Next came the *boidatoi*, with a single ox and the land to go with it. Then the *aktemones* who are also sometimes called *kapnikarioi*. These might be divided into those that had some animals and those that did not. Bringing up the rear were the *aporoi*, those without means of support. For fiscal purposes one *zeugaratos* was the equivalent of either two *boidatoi* or four *aktemones*. In addition, to the tax owed originally to the state, the *paroikoi* were expected to pay a tithe to their landlord. They also owed corvées, which could be a cause of difficulties. The dispute between the Lavra monastery and Adrian, brother of the Emperor Alexius I Comnenus, was in part over the labour services of the monastery's *paroikoi*. The emperor ruled that, if the taxes of the *paroikoi* had to go to his brother, their labour was owed to the monastery alone. The exact amount is not given. Much later in the early fourteenth century the number of days that a *paroikos* was expected to work for his lord is specified. By western standards labour services were light – twelve days in the year being the customary norm, though this might rise in some cases to as many as fifty-two days in the year. In the twelfth century labour services were regulated by custom or private agreement; they may not even have been on a regular basis. Byzantine landowners did not possess large domains, so there was little demand for peasant services. It looks, in any case, as

253

though they preferred to cultivate their domains with the aid of labourers bound in their service. Landowners were interested in their peasantry mostly as a source of revenues.

The *paroikos* was not unconditionally dependent upon his lord. He could not be deprived of his holding and he could pass his land on, as he chose. His heir would naturally have to take on his obligations to his lord. The judicial status of the *paroikos* and his family was, like so much else, uncertain. It was not clear that the lord automatically had any rights over the children of his *paroikoi*. Manuel Comnenus had to rule that this was only the case while they remained part of their father's household. *Paroikoi* were not necessarily denied access to the public courts, but, in practice, most cases involving *paroikoi* would have come before the village courts. They were run by the elders of the village, as had always been the case. The lord seems only to have possessed supervisory powers and rights to the profits of justice.

The village community was beginning to regain its equilibrium after the dislocation caused in most parts of the Empire by the troubles of the late eleventh century. All the signs are that for most of the twelfth century the peasantry of Macedonia and the Greek lands, for which we have the best evidence, was reasonably prosperous. The evidence is anecdotal. It cannot be subjected to statistical analysis in the way that the Athonite estate surveys of the fourteenth century can be. We are dealing with 'hints followed by guesses'. One such hint concerns the peasants settled on the estates of the monastery of the Eleousa in the Strymon valley. The Emperor Alexius I Comnenus granted the founder the right to settle twelve landless peasants. By the middle of the century they or their descendants had become fully-fledged *zeugaratoi*. Surely a sign that the colonizing activities of the early twelfth century were bearing fruit. In the disparate lists of peasants that have survived from the twelfth century the proportion of *zeugaratoi* to other categories of peasants is surprisingly high, providing a rough-and-ready index of the general prosperity of the Byzantine peasantry.

The wealth of the Byzantine Empire in the twelfth century was founded on the prosperity of its countryside. It is no good looking to technological improvements in order to explain this. There were not any. The techniques needed had long ago been perfected. The scratch plough was more than adequate for Mediterranean soils. It was rather a question of the right balance being struck between population and land and between peasant, lord, and state. This was achieved during the Comnenian reconstruction of the countryside. Even the reduction of the vast majority of the peasantry to dependent status, which was part and parcel of this, worked in their favour, because it gave them greater security than they had previously enjoyed. Its disadvantages would become apparent later on. As we shall see, it was problematical how long this balance could be maintained. By the end of Manuel Comnenus's reign there are signs that it was beginning to be lost.

There was only one new factor in the equation: the growing demand from provincial towns. Nothing reflects this better than the large number of water-mills to be found in the vicinity of towns, great and small, in the Greek lands. They were one of the best investments, prized by bishop and *rentier* alike. Along with the growing demand of the towns went the increasing trade in agricultural products that we associate with the presence of Italian merchants in the towns of Greece. In the past, only levels of taxation stimulated the peasantry into putting more of their produce on to the market. It is highly unlikely that peasants would have responded to the commercial opportunities being opened up by the towns and the Italians, but landowners, both lay and monastic, certainly did. Both the Lavra and the monastery of St John the Theologian on the island of Patmos obtained exemptions from customs duties and harbour taxes. Lavra was granted this privilege for seven boats with a total capacity of 16,000 *modioi*; Patmos for a single ship of 500 *modioi*, to be raised in 1186 to three ships and 1,500 *modioi*. These privileges were ostensibly to help the monks provision their monasteries.

The aristocracy too was interested in the possibilities of trade. Manuel Comnenus's uncle Isaac Comnenus enjoyed exemptions for his twelve ships with a total capacity of 4,000 *modioi*. Among his properties was the port of Sagoudaous with its ships and *fondaco*. These were to pass after his death to his foundation, the monastery of the Kosmosoteira. It was sited at Vera, not far from Ainos on the Thracian coast. The place was uninhabited. The prince tells us that 'the place where this holy monastery has been founded was completely devoid of men and dwellings, a haunt of snakes and scorpions, just rough ground, overgrown with spreading trees'.[23] Near the monastery a new settlement was established. In this case the foundation of a monastery was in some sense a colonizing venture. It was part of the way that deliberately or not monasteries were instruments of the agrarian reconstruction that occurred in the European provinces under the Comnenian emperors. It has left its own memorial in the impressive scattering of twelfth-century churches from the Greek lands to Macedonia. Occasionally we know who founded them. Sometimes it was the local bishop, as in the case of the nunnery of Hagia outside Nauplion in the Argolid, but there is one famous example of a church founded by a member of the court aristocracy. This was the church of St Panteleimon at Nerezi, near Skoplje in the Vardar valley. Its frescos are among the greatest achievements of Byzantine art in the twelfth century. They were executed in 1164 on the orders and at the expense of Alexius Comnenus, the son of Constantine Angelos and Theodora Comnena, the daughter of Alexius I Comnenus. He gives himself no official title in the inscription which records his largesse. This can be taken to mean that he did not hold the position of governor of the region. The presumption is that, like Isaac Comnenus around Ainos in Thrace, he possessed estates in the district and patronized a local church. The presence of a member of the court aristocracy in the upper reaches of the Vardar valley marks the probable northern limits of aristocratic interest. Other evidence suggests that their estates were to be found much further south in Thessaly, southern Epiros, and the Peloponnese, but it was in the reign of Manuel Comnenus that they established themselves in force in the European provinces of the Empire.

THE ANATOLIAN PROVINCES

Agrarian reconstruction in the Anatolian provinces of the Empire had a different rhythm and, in some respects, a different character. Whereas recovery in the European provinces began fairly quickly after the restoration of political control, in Anatolia it was delayed because of the need to create a new frontier with the Turks who had occupied central Anatolia. This was not completed until the reign of Manuel Comnenus and involved a complete overhaul of the provincial administration. The Turkish occupation at the end of the eleventh century obliterated the old administrative divisions. The reconquest was largely a matter of occupying key points, which became the centre of local administration. In 1133 a start was made towards installing a regular provincial administration in western Asia Minor, when the theme of Thrakesion was restored. Those parts south of the river Maiander were united with remnants of the theme of Kibyrraiotai to form the new theme of Mylasa and Melanoudion. Manuel Comnenus completed this reorganization with the creation of the theme of Neokastra, which was centred on the fortresses of Khliara, Pergamon, and Atramyttion. These he strengthened and he established garrisons in the surrounding countryside to provide protection against marauding bands of Turks. Neokastra consisted of the Kaikos (Bakir) valley and the coastlands opposite the island of Mitylene. It was one of the most exposed sections of the frontier. According to the historian Nicetas Choniates, who is full of praise for the emperor's measure, the region was soon flourishing. The countryside which had been almost deserted began to teem with life. Manuel Comnenus was completing the work of his father John Comnenus, who fortified the key points to the north at Lopadion (Ulubad) and at Akhyraous (Balikesir). In addition to major works of this kind a large number of smaller fortresses were founded in the frontier districts from the region of Mount Olympus (Ulu Dag) southwards. They were built high up commanding the passages through the mountainous rim of the Anatolian plateau to the coastal plains. The garrisons were recruited from landless peasants and they were given plots of land in the neighbourhood of the fortress in full possession.

What little we know of the army of the theme of Neokastra suggests that it was recruited from these free peasants. After 1204 the emperors of Nicaea inherited this system of border defence. Thanks to it the Nicaeans gained the upper hand in the broad band of no man's land that formed the real frontier between them and the Turks. Protected in this way the coastal plains and river valleys flourished. The great prosperity of western Asia Minor under the Laskarids of Nicaea can be traced back to the work of the Comnenian emperors. The essentials were all present from the middle of the twelfth century. Recovery was only momentarily slowed down by a renewal of Turkish raids in the aftermath of the defeat at Myriokephalon in 1176.

In comparison with the European provinces of the Empire there survives relatively little building from the twelfth century. Churches are much more likely to be of the thirteenth century than of the twelfth. A great church, such as that of St John the Theologian at Ephesus, was allowed to fall into disrepair. Its upkeep was to be a responsibility of George Tornikes who was metropolitan of Ephesus in 1155–56. He was far from complimentary about his new home. His first impression was that he had been sent to a benighted land, where the inhabitants were 'more savage than leopards and wilier than foxes'.[24] He found the church organization in danger of collapse. He was slowly learning how tough life was for a bishop, far from the comforts of Constantinople and the support of friends. However reluctantly, he carried out the duties of his office, undertaking exhausting journeys to protect the interests of his church, and reprimanding local governors for interfering in ecclesiastical affairs. The effort, though, seems to have killed him, for he disappears abruptly from the scene in 1156, only a year after becoming bishop.

A bishop accustomed to life in Constantinople may well have found conditions in one of the major centres of Anatolia harsh, nor would Ephesus have compared very well with the Thebes that George Tornikes had known in his youth. This does not mean that there were no signs of improvement. There were the beginnings of a phase of new construction around the church of St John the Theologian. Recent excavations at Pergamon have pinpointed the middle of the twelfth century as the time when the medieval town began to expand. When Odo of Deuil passed down the western coast of Anatolia in the autumn of 1147, he 'found many cities in ruins and others which the Greeks had built up from the ancient level above the sea, fortifying them with walls and towers'.[25] He also noted the presence of ships in their harbours. The ports of western Asia Minor attracted the interest of Venetian sea captains. There were expeditions to Atramyttion and to Smyrna. There may even have been, at least temporarily, a Venetian factory at Smyrna. The division of property made there between Romano Mairano and his brother Samuel was witnessed by Giovanni da Plebe, priest and notary. The list of goods that the brothers had in their possession at Smyrna is instructive. It consisted of gold, silver, copper, iron, lead, tin, gold *hyperpyra*, slaves, male and female, and pearls. The problem is to know how many of these items were acquired locally. Iron was mined in the Smyrna region. Slaves are most likely to have come from the Turkish-held interior. There is therefore a chance that Smyrna was already an outlet for the products of central Anatolia. In the thirteenth century the prosperity of the Nicaean Empire owed something to its trade with the Seljuqs, who paid in gold for the corn produced in the coastal plains of western Asia Minor. This interdependence of coast and plateau already existed in the twelfth century. The fair of St Michael the Archangel at Chonai, in the upper reaches of the Maiander valley, played much the same role for the exchange of goods between coast and interior as the fair of St Demetrius at Thessalonica for the southern Balkans. Just as the Venetians seem to have found it hard in the twelfth century to break into the trade of Thessalonica, so they had little permanent impact on the trade of western Asia Minor. It may be that in both cases the main orientation of trade from the coast to the interior did not suit them, while the central role of autumn fairs did not favour seafarers.

For what sea-borne trade there may have been the Venetians almost certainly had as rivals the Jews established in considerable numbers along the Anatolian coast and on the offshore islands. Benjamin of Tudela noted that there were 400 Jewish families at Chios, 300 on the island of Samos, and about 400 at Rhodes. There were smaller communities scattered along the Anatolian coasts – at Strobilos for instance. It was the centre of a community of Jews scattered through the Empire. They were subject to the church of St Sophia and would seem to have operated the ships belonging to the patriarchal church. This is reminiscent of the Jews of Chios in the mid-eleventh century who were subject to the monastery of Nea Moni on the island. Attaleia on the south coast of Asia Minor also had a Jewish community. Although apparently well positioned for trade, the importance of this town seems to have been mostly strategic. John II Comnenus used it as a base from which to mount his Cilician campaigns. As the crusader historian William of Tyre noted, it was very much an outpost of the Empire, hard pressed by the Turks: 'It possesses very rich fields, which are, nevertheless of no benefit to the townspeople, for they are surrounded on all sides by enemies who hinder their cultivation.'[26] The grain supply had to be brought in by sea. The overland route from the upper Maiander was hard to keep open.

The situation of Attaleia underlines the insecurity of the whole of the south-western corner of Asia Minor. The famous monastery of St Paul on Mount Latros was more or less destroyed by a Turkish raid of the early 1140s and was temporarily abandoned by its monks. The countryside suffered too. One of the estates of St Paul's was described as 'formerly heavily populated and well-stocked, ideally suited to producing herds of cattle and other sorts of revenue, but these estates and the rest of the monastery's property have suffered under the barbarian knife, and have become as nothing'.[27] With imperial support the monastery was able to recover much of its property. Peasants were attracted on to its estates. It acquired some abandoned holdings. It obtained an olive plantation paying the relatively high tax of 36 *hyperpyra* per annum. The Emperor Manuel Comnenus exempted it from payment. They then leased out the olive plantation to a local *archon* for an annual rent of 24 measures of oil. As we shall see, this deal was to bring the monks nothing but trouble. There were to be difficult times ahead after the death of Manuel Comnenus, but the impression is that during his reign one of the more exposed parts of his Anatolian provinces prospered.

Only a little supplementary evidence can be gleaned from the documents of the monastery of St John the Theologian on the island of Patmos. The Emperor Alexius I Comnenus granted the monastery twelve landless peasants for its estates on the small island of Leipso. By the beginning of Manuel Comnenus's reign these peasants or their descendants had become *zeugaratoi*. The monastery begged to be allowed to settle more landless peasants and the emperor was willing to grant it another six. It is quite clear that the monastery was not able to support itself from its exiguous estates. It received grants of corn from Alexius I Comnenus and his son John, which were to be supplied by the governor of Crete. Under Manuel Comnenus the monks were able to obtain in lieu of this a grant of 144 *hyperpyra* from the revenues of Crete, with which to buy up corn on their own account. What this tells us is that the monks considered it more profitable to work through the market rather than through the state machinery. It is just a sidelight on the way in which the trade in agricultural products increased over the twelfth century.

CONCLUSION

Conclusions can only be tentative, given the lack of evidence that is amenable to statistical analysis. It is only possible to deal in impressions, but there remains the strongest impression that the Byzantine Empire enjoyed a period of great prosperity in the twelfth century. This seems to hold good for all parts of the Empire from the capital to frontier regions. There is some variation. The Greek lands saw a more sustained growth than other areas and this led to a greater development of towns, trade, and manufactures. The full potential of regions, such as western Asia Minor, was not realized until after 1204 under the Laskarids of Nicaea, while Thessalonica and Macedonia had to wait until the middle of the thirteenth century. The foundation of the Byzantine economy remained its agriculture, but it was now more open to a market economy and more likely to be stimulated by the demands of the growing towns than had been the case in the past. The *archontes* who dominated the provincial towns saw the advantages of selling the produce of their estates. This generated larger supplies of money locally, which helped to foster local manufactures. Urban development was most noticeable in the Greek lands, where the Venetians were especially active.

If the underlying situation was, on this reading, so favourable, what went so wrong that less than a quarter of a century after the death of the Emperor Manuel Comnenus (1180) the Byzantine Empire was overturned? There is, of course, no necessary correlation between economic and political success. Sometimes the reverse, for economic growth will produce strains that weaken political structures. Well before the end of Manuel Comnenus's reign signs of strain were becoming apparent. After his initial generosity to the church and monasteries at the beginning of his reign he found it necessary to prevent monasteries acquiring more property. He had also to insist that those who had received grants of landed property from the emperor should alienate them only to members of the senate and the army. The stock of land the emperor had at his disposal was clearly diminishing. If he was to reward his soldiers and the aristocracy, he had to restrict the amount of land passing into the dead hand of the church.

Land was no good without peasants to work it. There seems to have been just as much competition for peasants as there was for land. Not for nothing were *pronoiai* described as grants of *paroikoi*. By the end of his reign the administration had to check the number of *paroikoi* settled on monastic estates. In 1175 an official sent to survey the estates of the monastery of St Paul of Latros discovered that the monastery had settled far more *paroikoi* on its estates than its entitlement allowed. He immediately transferred the *paroikoi* illegally held by the monastery to the public registers.

Two different things are involved. In the first place, the state was struggling to maintain its rights over the available manpower. In the second, there was perhaps not sufficient manpower in any case. This does not necessarily mean that the population of the Byzantine Empire was falling. It was more that there was a greater demand for manpower. The state competed with landowners for the services of the peasantry, as more land was brought into production. In a free society this would have been to the advantage of the peasantry, but their dependent status told against them. To meet the demands made upon them by the state and their lords they were forced to bear an increasingly heavy burden of taxes and rents. The army, trade, and manufactures, all competed for skilled labour. It was not possible to satisfy this demand for skills from among the native population, whence the prominence of the Jews; whence, more to the point, the way westerners were sucked into the Byzantine Empire as soldiers and merchants. By the end of Manuel

Comnenus's reign there were signs that the Byzantine Empire was reaching an impasse. The prosperity of its trade depended upon the skills of westerners, which was the cause of increasing resentment in some circles. The prosperity of its agriculture rested on the backs of the peasants, but it was being undermined by the demands being placed on them by the state and by landowners. It might have been possible to restore the necessary balance by cutting down on government expenditure and state grants of lands and peasants, but this was an operation that almost inevitably produced the bitterest political rivalries. This was the lesson of the mid-eleventh century and it would be reiterated in the closing years of the twelfth.

NOTES

1. William of Tyre (transl. by E A Babcock and A C Krey), II, p. 379
2. Odo of Deuil (ed. and transl. by V G Berry), p. 64
3. Tzetzes, *Epistulae* (ed. by P A M Leone), no.18, pp. 31-4
4. G Downey, 'Nikolaos Mesarites: Description of the Church of the Holy Apostles at Constantinople', *Transactions of the American Philosophical Society*, N.S.47 (1957), p. 863
5. John Tzetzes, *Chiliades* (ed. by T Kiessling) (Leipzig, 1826), XIII, vv.360-8
6. E Legrand, *Bibliothèque grecque vulgaire* (Paris, 1880), I, p. 18, ll. 8-9
7. Nicetas Choniates (ed. by Van Dieten), p. 523
8. Tzetzes, *Epistulae* (ed. by P A M Leone), no.57, pp. 79-84
9. Zepos, *Jus*, I, p. 416
10. Nicetas Choniates (ed. by Van Dieten), p. 74
11. Michael Choniates (ed. by Sp Lambros), II, p. 12, ll. 2-22
12. *Géographie d'Idrisi* (transl. by P Jaubert) (Paris, 1836), II, p. 288
13. *Ibid.*, p. 291
14. *Ibid.*
15. *Ibid.*, p. 292
16. *Ibid.*, p. 297
17. *Ibid.*
18. *Ibid.*, p. 296
19. Pseudo-Luciano *Timarion* (ed. by R Romano) (Naples, 1974), pp. 54-5
20. Eustathios, p. 92
21. A Epstein, 'Middle Byzantine Churches of Kastoria: Dates and Implications', *Art Bulletin*, 62 (1980), pp. 190-207
22. C Walter, *Art and Ritual of the Byzantine Church* (London, 1982), pp. 237-49
23. L Petit, 'Typikon du monastère de la Kosmosotira près d'Aenos (1152)', *Izvestija russkogo arkheologitcheskogo Instituta v Konstantinopole*, 13 (1908), p. 19
24. Georges et Dèmètrios Tornikès, *Lettres et Discours*, p. 153

25.   Odo of Deuil (ed. and transl. by V G Berry), p. 107
26.   William of Tyre, (transl. by E A Babcock and A C Krey), II, p. 178
27.   Miklosich and Müller, *Acta et Diplomata*, IV, p. 324

Chapter 14

BYZANTIUM 1180–1203: THE FAILURE OF THE COMNENIAN SYSTEM

Manuel Comnenus died in 1180 'on a melancholy September day'. He had been well aware of the dangers that lay in wait for his young son and heir Alexius. As his health failed, so he did all he could to safeguard the boy's succession. He had married him to a French princess, as prestigious a match as he could find. At the same time he arranged for his daughter, the Porphyrogenite Maria, to marry Renier of Montferrat, who came from the greatest house of northern Italy. In this way he hoped to preserve Byzantine influence in the West. Nearer home he sought to safeguard the frontiers of his Empire by getting his allies, such as Bela of Hungary, Kilidj Arslan, the Seljuq sultan, and various crusader princes to guarantee the succession of his young son. There remained his cousin Andronicus Comnenus, a mortal enemy of his family. He was lurking in exile beyond the north-eastern frontiers of the Empire. Manuel induced him to come to Constantinople, where in an emotional scene the old enemies were reconciled. Andronicus took an oath to protect the young emperor and received most of Paphlagonia as an apanage.

These were sensible measures, but they were based on the fatal assumption that the emperor's prestige would ensure that they were respected after his death. Such a hope was undermined by his choice of his wife Maria as guardian of their young son Alexius. She was a crusader princess. She was, in Eustathios of Thessalonica's words, 'ripe for love',[1] however hard she may have tried to conceal it. Eustathios, the foremost Homeric scholar of his age, was appropriately casting her in the role of a new Helen. As he put it, 'Burning love, almost consciously, loosed evil upon the world.'[2] Is such an explanation just fanciful? Not perhaps entirely. Byzantine political life depended upon a delicate balance of interests, which Manuel Comnenus had managed to preserve. Now that he was gone, political rivalries were likely to flare up at the slightest pretext. Far from being able to control them, the empress herself became a political prize. She was to fall, ensnared by love, to the *Protosebastos* Alexius Comnenus, one of her late husband's nephews.

He became her lover and effective ruler of the Empire. His promotion split the house of Comnenus into warring factions. The empress's chief rival was her stepdaughter, the Porphyrogenite Maria, who for so long had been the heiress to the Byzantine throne. She was the natural focus of opposition to the new regime and therefore immediately suspect. Learning that her supporters had been seized she fled with her husband to seek sanctuary in the church of St Sophia. She was warmly welcomed by the Patriarch Theodosius Boradeiotes, who resented the way he had been ignored by the empress, even though he was nominally head of the regency council.

The Porphyrogenite Maria enrolled under her banner Italians and Georgians and attracted much popular support. She turned the precinct of St Sophia into an armed camp. Troops loyal to the empress launched an assault on it which was only partially successful. Finally, in May 1181 the patriarch was able to negotiate a truce between the Porphyrogenite and the empress's party. The Porphyrogenite and her husband were allowed to go free, but their supporters were left in prison.

During this 'Holy War', as Eustathios called it, the opponents of the empress's regime increasingly looked towards Andronicus Comnenus, who remained in his Paphlagonian lair. His sons Manuel and John were supporters of the Porphyrogenite and were now in prison. Their sister escaped from the capital to her father's court and persuaded him that Constantinople would welcome him as a deliverer from the tyranny of the present regime. Andronicus had little difficulty in convincing himself that it was his duty to go to Constantinople to protect the interests of the young emperor. He was clearly in danger from his mother and her lover, the *protosebastos*. Andronicus met very little resistance as he advanced upon Constantinople in the early spring of 1182. Once he arrived opposite the capital, all he could do was wait, since the crossing to Constantinople was barred by the navy. The decisive event was the desertion of the commander of the fleet to Andronicus. The empress and her lover were abandoned by their supporters and then seized by their Frankish bodyguard who handed them over to Andronicus. The city was Andronicus's for the asking, but before he formally entered, he sent in his Paphlagonians, whom even the Byzantines regarded as barbarians. They at once set about massacring the Latins settled there. They were assisted by the Constantinopolitan populace, who envied the Latins their wealth and resented their mounting influence in the capital. The initiative for the massacre came from Andronicus. He regarded the Latins, who had supported the empress's regime, as potential opponents. Their removal was a necessary step on the way to power. In the past Andronicus had been a leader of anti-western opinion at the court of Manuel Comnenus. He must have hoped to gain the support of those most bitterly opposed to the Latins. These included men of influence, bureaucrats and churchmen. Andronicus capitalized on rumours that were floating about that the empress had been bidding for the support of the Latins, 'promising that she would hand over the city to them and would place the Byzantines under their authority'.[3] Andronicus's motives were political, but he unleashed Byzantine resentment against the Latins. A religious element soon entered into the massacre. Latin priests and monks were singled out by the mob. A cardinal who happened to be in Constantinople was murdered. The hospital of the knights of St John was sacked. The Byzantine clergy were prominent in directing attacks on the Latins.

Though Eustathios might claim to be horrified by the massacre of Latins, it was very much to Andronicus's short-term political advantage. It cowed potential opposition and won him the support not only of the people, but also of an influential section of the bureaucracy. For a time he could do more or less as he pleased. The Porphyrogenite and her husband were treated as a potential threat. They were confined in the imperial palace, where they died mysteriously, perhaps poisoned by one of Andronicus's eunuchs. The empress was accused of plotting with enemies of the state. She was found guilty. She was first consigned to a nunnery and then secretly drowned. The Patriarch Theodosius did not possess the stomach to face Andronicus and preferred to go into retirement. He knew that he would be called upon to sanction Andronicus's elevation to the imperial office. This duly occurred in September 1183 and the young emperor was strangled at the first convenient opportunity. The ageing Andronicus completed his triumph by marrying the eleven-year-old Agnes of France, the young emperor's consort. It was a bloody path to the throne, but not quite unparalleled in the annals of Byzantium. In the past, such blood-letting ushered in a period of political stability, but not on this occasion. Within two years Andronicus would be overthrown by those forces which had raised him up and he would be put to death in ways more revolting than even he had devised for his opponents.

Andronicus came to power with the support of both the court aristocracy and the populace of Constantinople. The former soon learnt that their trust had been misplaced. The alienation of the populace took longer, for Andronicus cultivated their support. He used the Constantinopolitan mob as a political weapon. He manipulated it through demagogues, whom 'he encouraged to consult with him. They were a wretched class of persons, brawlers and agitators, kings in their own company.'[4] He boasted to his sons that in this way he had been able to rid himself of the 'Giants' and they would be able to rule over Pygmies. It was a bitter jest, which he had cause to regret, but one that revealed an anti-aristocratic programme.

His intentions were apparent in the fresco he had put up of himself in the church of the Forty Martyrs, which he restored as his family shrine. It portrayed him dressed in the smock and long white boots of a Byzantine peasant, holding a sickle (*drepanon*) in his hand. Because the sickle allegedly curved round the bust of a handsome man, the composition was interpreted at the time as betraying Andronicus's intention to murder the young emperor, Alexius II Comnenus. This is hardly likely to have been the meaning that Andronicus intended. The fresco was designed for public consumption, since it was painted on the gate of the church looking towards the great avenue of Constantinople, the Mese. It is much more likely that Andronicus wished to present himself as the good husbandman with the interests of the peasantry at heart. He went out of his way to publicize the punishment he meted out to one of his trusted agents, who had stopped with his retinue in a peasant household and had not only failed to pay for his board and lodging, but had also taken all the peasant's carts.

Andronicus's plans for reforms were directed towards the provincial administration and the well-being of the peasantry. He was meeting the mounting criticism there had been at the end of Manuel Comnenus's reign about the condition of the peasantry, who were suffering at the hands of oppressive squads of tax-collectors. Andronicus tried to ensure that the provincials only paid their regular taxation and were protected from the surcharges which were imposed by unscrupulous tax-collectors. He made sure that these fiscal posts went to honest men and were not simply sold to the highest bidder, as had been the case previously. He appointed good men to provincial governorships and paid them decent salaries in the hope that they would not oppress the cities.

Only for Attica do we possess material which enables us to test how genuine or how effective these reforms were. Michael Choniates, the archbishop of Athens, has left the distinct impression that a real effort was made in Attica to improve the standard of the administration. The provincial governors who had been drawn almost without fail from the great court families now came from more modest administrative backgrounds. If there was a genuine desire for reform, practical considerations ruled out any real alleviation of the lot of the peasantry. A new tax register was drawn up for Athens, which took into account tax exemptions granted by the imperial government, but an official at Constantinople refused to enrol the new register. It was clear that the financial needs of government precluded real concessions.

Andronicus's reforms might well have foundered on this financial impasse, even if his energies were not increasingly taken up with the need to crush aristocratic opposition. The usual assumption is that Andronicus was intent upon eradicating the aristocracy or, at least, aristocratic privilege from the outset. At least one of the measures he is known to have taken as regent for the young emperor can be construed as an indirect attack upon the aristocracy's landed property. In December 1182 he repealed a law of Manuel Comnenus, by which imperial grants of landed property could only be alienated to members of the senate and army. The aristocracy built up its estates very largely through imperial grants of property. Manuel's legislation was designed to protect aristocratic estates. It would be easy to interpret Andronicus's measure as a first step towards dismantling the system of aristocratic privilege which was at the heart of the Comnenian system of government.

Aristocratic opposition to Andronicus was apparent several months before he had recourse to this measure. A conspiracy was hatched in August or September by Andronicus Angelos and Andronicus Kontostephanos. They had been Andronicus's two main backers among the aristocracy. They had engineered his seizure of power to rid themselves of the empress's regime. They found that they were still excluded from power. Worse, it was becoming clear that Andronicus was using demagogues and the mob to make himself independent of his aristocratic supporters. Andronicus learnt of the plot and pounced. The Angeloi managed to escape his clutches and got away to Syria, but Andronicus Kontostephanos and many of the other conspirators were taken and blinded.

Outside the capital several of the towns of Asia Minor had been opposed to Andronicus from the start. When he was marching on Constantinople in the spring of 1182 the city of Nicaea refused to open its gates to him and soon afterwards the Grand Domestic John Batatzes came out in open revolt, making Philadelphia his base. His rebellion divided the Anatolian cities into pro- and anti-Andronican factions. Even though the rebellion was put down with relative ease, there was an undertow of discontent in the Anatolian cities, which opponents of Andronicus might be able to exploit.

In September 1183 Isaac Angelos and Theodore Cantacuzenus seized Nicaea, while Isaac's brother Theodore established himself in neighbouring Prusa. The fortress-town of Lopadion soon went over to the rebels. It remains a mystery why these Bithynian towns should so willingly have lent their support to the rebel cause. There is nothing to suggest that the Angelos or Cantacuzenus families had estates in the region. They might nevertheless have been able to count on some local support, because their allies, the Kontostephanos family, possessed the Bithynian monastery of Elegmoi, and this must have been a centre of local influence.

Andronicus took his time. He had to rally support. In retrospect, his benevolence seemed so extraordinary that this period of his rule was referred to as the 'Halcyon Days'. He also had to stress his right to rule, now that he had ridded himself of the young emperor. He went on a pilgrimage to the monastery of the Kosmosoteira at Vera in Thrace. This was founded by his father, the *Sebastokrator* Isaac Comnenus, and there he had been buried. Andronicus was underlining that he had a legitimate claim to the throne, inherited from his father. Andronicus's circumspection worked. The western armies and their commander, Alexius Branas, remained loyal. With their support the rebellion was easily crushed. Andronicus would seem to have eradicated all internal opposition. Members of the aristocracy were sullenly loyal, under lock and key, or had fled the country. Yet scarcely a year later he was to be overthrown.

Two sets of circumstances conspired to bring this about. Andronicus allowed himself to become increasingly isolated. He relied upon an inner circle of advisers and agents. They were not drawn from the great families, whether of the court or of the bureaucracy. Some of them may have come from the fringes of the court, but the majority were of obscure origins: they were loyal and prompt to obey Andronicus's often harsh orders. They were only too quick to mutilate and impale those that Andronicus felt to be a threat. In his isolation he became increasingly suspicious and reacted to his suspicions with needless cruelty. At the same time, he became more openly contemptuous of the people. For their part the people of Constantinople were beginning to be sickened by Andronicus's cruelty.

Andronicus's hold on power depended upon a reign of terror. It left him isolated from all but his trusted servants, but apparently in command. The weakness of his position was immediately revealed by the first major foreign challenge that he faced. It came from the Normans of Sicily. The Sicilian court sheltered many Byzantine aristocrats, who sought Norman backing to overthrow Andronicus. The Normans were happy to have an excuse to invade the Byzantine Empire. A pretender claiming to be the murdered Alexius II was duly produced to give greater respectability to the undertaking. In June 1185 the Norman expedition arrived before the city of Dyrrakhion. It fell with scarcely a blow. The disaffection of the Byzantine aristocracy was evident. The commander of the garrison, John Branas, preferred to be led away to comfortable captivity in Sicily, rather than to return to face Andronicus's wrath. The Norman army advanced on Thessalonica, which they reached in August and where they linked up with the Norman fleet. The people of Thessalonica heartened by their Archbishop Eustathios's decision to stay with them offered spirited resistance, but the imperial governor, David Comnenus, conducted a defence of the city that was negligent to the point of treachery. Andronicus sent an army to the relief of the city, but its commanders, largely drawn from the great aristocratic houses, proved half-hearted either deliberately or out of loss of morale.

The fall of Thessalonica sealed Andronicus's fate. He pretended to be unmoved by the Norman invasion, but one action showed how it had affected his confidence. A well-connected reader of St Sophia unwisely criticized Andronicus for his cruelty and he was led off for execution, but Andronicus then relented, when news came that the Normans had taken Dyrrakhion and were now advancing unopposed on Thessalonica. In the face of failure he withdrew more and more into the pleasures of his suburban palaces. This was to be his undoing. The details of Andronicus's overthrow are sickening, but the outline is simple enough. He sent one of his agents to arrest Isaac Angelos who was confined to his mansion and was suspected, probably rightly, of being the centre of any remaining aristocratic opposition to Andronicus's regime. Isaac killed the emperor's agent and fled for sanctuary to St Sophia, where other members of his family joined him. They appealed to the people of Constantinople, who rose up on their behalf and proclaimed Isaac emperor. Andronicus was slow to react, because he was away from Constantinople, staying in one of his palaces. He hurried back to the Great Palace, but the situation was quite out of control and he decided to flee to Russia. He was taken near the mouth of the Bosporus, brought back to Constantinople, and delivered up to the malevolence of the mob. He was subjected to the most appalling indignities and died horribly in the Hippodrome.

There is no evidence that Isaac Angelos came to power through some carefully laid coup. It seems to have been a spontaneous reaction on the part of the people of Constantinople. For the historian Nicetas Choniates it was further proof of their notorious fickleness. Pure emotion had a part to play. They were alarmed by Andronicus's failure to deal with the Norman invasion. They had begun to disapprove of his cruelty. The mob could also be manipulated, as Andronicus had shown. He had played upon their self-regard and had given them a glimpse of their power. To withdraw his favour was to play a dangerous game; to show his outright contempt was foolish. It is often urged that much more important than any such explanations for the mob's changing mood was Andronicus's willingness to countenance the return of Latins to Constantinople. This is to assume that the main motivating force behind the activities of the Constantinopolitan crowd was blind hatred of the Latins. There is no denying that it was a factor, but only one among many. In 1185 there is no sign that anti-Latin feeling had any part to play. This is in contrast to what happened two years later, when there was an attack upon the Latin quarters of Constantinople. That whole episode is very instructive for the motivation of the Byzantine mob. Isaac Angelos put down a dangerous revolt thanks to the support of a western prince, Conrad of Montferrat, and a scratch body of Latin knights and mercenaries. To celebrate their victory the Latins began to plunder Constantinople and invited the proletariat of the city to join in, which they did with a will. There was a reaction on the part of the craftsmen of the city. They suffered from the mob going on the rampage and they could not stand the way the Latins boasted of their victory over a Byzantine general, rebel that he might have been. They accordingly organized an attack upon the Latin quarters, it has to be said, with scant success. The lesson both of this incident and of the massacre of 1182 is that the people may have resented the presence of the Latins in Constantinople, but they only turned on them on those occasions when they had been drawn into Byzantine politics. They were suspect, less because they were foreigners and catholics, more because they had become a political force. In 1185 this did not apply. The people turned on Andronicus because he had failed, because he had isolated himself, and because he had offended them.

Andronicus exercised a fascination for contemporaries. The story of his downfall was soon circulating in semi-legendary form in the West. Byzantines tried to explain him, but his Protean character seemed to defy explanation. They were amazed by his apparent inconsistency, but this was as much a reflection of the price paid for consistent opposition to his cousin Manuel Comnenus. He was forced out of Byzantium and was blown along by chance. His opposition to Manuel Comnenus may have sprung from an envy rooted in the accident of birth, but he became identified with currents of criticism, opposed to the system of government presided over by Manuel Comnenus. These are reflected in the history of Nicetas Choniates. They amounted to a demand for less Latin influence, for a fairer system of taxation, and more equitable provincial government. It was a call for a return to the ideal of the Macedonian emperors and it was most likely to have appealed to the bureaucracy.

One of the most persuasive interpretations of Andronicus's reign has been put forward by Professor A P Kazhdan.[5] He sees Andronicus as trying to re-establish a bureaucratic regime in key with the ideals of the Macedonian emperors. To do this he had to sweep aside the privileged position of the aristocracy. Kazhdan views the emergence of a hereditary aristocracy under the Comneni as part of the 'natural' development of the Byzantine Empire. Andronicus's reactionary policies were therefore, in his view, bound to fail. The exhaustive *enquête* that Kazhdan carried out on the Byzantine aristocracy shows that Andronicus's reign was something of a watershed. It was then that the grip of the Comneni on the highest positions of state began to relax and new names appear. Eunuchs, so redolent of Byzantine government under the Macedonian emperors, reappear in the higher reaches of government.

This analysis has to be taken further if the real importance of Andronicus's reign is to become apparent. The first point to be made is that in political terms bureaucrats are not very powerful under Andronicus, certainly not as powerful as they were to become under the emperors of the house of Angelos. Bureaucrats had become accustomed to being servants of the state. They welcomed the reforms introduced by Andronicus, while regent for the young emperor. But disillusion soon set in. Nicetas Choniates, who approved of the reforms in principle, preferred to retire from the administration rather than to continue to serve Andronicus. His disapproval was directed against the style of Andronicus's government and the role accorded to his agents. It was also a recognition that the reforms could not work. They were being used in the end as publicity material to justify a cruel regime.

A positive desire for reform changed into the revenge of an outsider on the society which had rejected him. The careful balance of privilege, order, and obligation, which had characterized Comnenian government, was undermined. Hopes of reform in the common interest had proved to be empty. It would be left to Isaac Angelos to try, in vain, to restore the balance that had existed under Manuel Comnenus and to give to the government of the Byzantine Empire a new purpose and sense of direction.

ISAAC II ANGELOS (1185–1195)

It would have needed a ruler of the highest abilities to surmount the difficulties that faced the Byzantine Empire in 1185. Isaac was still comparatively young when he was thrust so unexpectedly into supreme office. His main asset seems to have been his amiability, which rescued political life from the brutality which had characterized it under Andronicus. It favoured his guiding aim which was a return to the compromises that had underpinned Manuel Comnenus's rule. The difficulty was that he had at the same time to establish a new dynasty in power. The Angeloi were only one of a series of competing families which had emerged out of the fragmentation of the Comneni family. They were usually closely connected with the imperial dynasty; their fortunes depending on a marriage to a Comnenian princess. The rise of the Angeloi began with the marriage of the obscure Constantine Angelos to the youngest daughter of Alexius I Comnenus. Their stock had risen markedly because of the way they had led the opposition to Andronicus Comnenus. They clearly had a following in both the capital and the provinces. Having secured the throne Isaac would face the jealousy of other aristocratic families. This would in the end prove his undoing, for they objected to the way he concentrated power in the hands of a small clique. They were able to overthrow him and to replace him with his worthless elder brother Alexius.

The most pressing problems that Isaac faced on coming to power were ironically in the realm of foreign policy. Andronicus's usurpation had provided a pretext for those that had guaranteed the young Emperor Alexius II's succession to invade the Byzantine Empire. The Hungarian King Bela invaded the Balkans and had penetrated as far as the key fortress-town of Sofia, thus beginning the destabilization of the Balkan provinces. And, of course, there were the Normans, who were advancing pell-mell on Constantinople. Isaac put Alexius Branas, the most respected of the Byzantine generals, in sole command of the Byzantine forces. On 7 November 1185 he suddenly attacked the Normans and won a complete victory. The Normans evacuated Thessalonica in panic and fell back on Dyrrakhion. The next spring Isaac took charge of the siege of Dyrrakhion, which soon fell. The Normans suffered enormous losses, both in killed and captured.

Alexius Branas emerged from this victory with the greatest credit. He was remembered as 'small in stature, but colossal in the depth and the deviousness of his understanding and by far the best general of his time'.[6] The Branas family had been prominent since the middle of the eleventh century, but they had largely steered clear of the Comnenian court, preferring to dominate their native city of Adrianople. Alexius Branas reckoned that he now had the power and the prestige to make a bid for the throne. His first attempt was a fiasco. He sought sanctuary in St Sophia, hoping that his exploits in battle would win him the support of the people of Constantinople. None was forthcoming and he had ignominiously to throw himself on the emperor's mercy. His military talents were too valuable and he was soon restored to command of the western armies. In 1187 he raised the standard of revolt once again, but this time he made Adrianople his base. He advanced on Constantinople meeting no opposition. Isaac was saved by his brother-in-law Conrad of Montferrat, who had recently married his sister Theodora. His energy and dash proved too much for the tactical skill for which Branas was renowned. Branas was left dead on the field of battle.

THE FOUNDATION OF THE SECOND BULGARIAN EMPIRE

Just at the moment when Isaac seemed at last thoroughly in command of his Empire, the situation in the Balkans began to deteriorate alarmingly. He had managed to dispose of the threat from Bela of Hungary very neatly. He negotiated a marriage with Bela's daughter Margaret and received back as her dowry the Balkan provinces that the Hungarians had occupied. A special tax was then levied on these provinces to pay for the wedding festivities. The Vlachs of the Balkan mountains (Stara Planina) refused to pay. At much the same time, two chieftains Peter and Asan came to Isaac who was encamped on the plains of Kypsella and requested the grant of a village somewhere in the Balkans. Their demand was turned down. One of the emperor's uncles hit Asan across the face for his insolence. The brothers returned home, determined on revenge. They found the Vlachs of the Balkans reluctant to join in any revolt, even though the demand for a special tax had left them disaffected. To win them over the brothers took a most remarkable step. They annexed the cult of St Demetrius to their cause. 'In order to overcome the reluctance of their fellow countrymen the brothers erected a chapel dedicated to the good martyr Demetrius. There they brought together many ... from both races.... They stoked up their enthusiasm by assuring them that the God of the Bulgarian and Vlach nation had vouchsafed them their freedom and assented to the shaking off of their age-old yoke, for the Christ-martyr Demetrius had abandoned the city of Thessalonica along with his church there and his residence among the Byzantines, in order to dwell among them and to act as a guide and a collaborator in their undertaking.'⁷

An appeal couched in these terms rings true. The loss of Thessalonica to the Normans must have made a great impression throughout the Balkans. The cult of St Demetrius was by no means limited to the citizens of Thessalonica but spread throughout the Balkans. Serbs were numbered among the confraternity of St Demetrius, who resisted the Norman assault upon the city. The cult of St Demetrius had the added advantage of uniting the Vlachs and the Bulgarians, the two peoples who took part in the uprising. They shared a common pastoral life among the mountains of the Balkans, but they were separated by language and traditions. The Bulgarians could look back to the glories of the Bulgarian Empire. The Byzantine occupation did not put an end to the use of Old Church Slavonic as a liturgical language and the Gospels in Old Church Slavonic continued to be copied. The Vlachs had their own traditions of an origin among the Roman colonists of Dacia.

The testimony of Nicetas Choniates suggests that Peter and Asan were Vlachs rather than Bulgarians. In the opening stages of the rebellion the Vlachs played a more prominent part than the Bulgarians, simply because it was centred on the hilly interior of the Balkans, where the Vlachs were dominant. As the rebels established themselves, so the Bulgarian element came to the fore and the Bulgarian traditions of empire asserted themselves. In its origins the rebellion owed much to the traditional suspicion and dislike of the pastoralist for established order. This can only have intensified as the Byzantine administration tightened its grip on the interior of the Balkans. At the same time, aristocratic and monastic estates were spreading inland into the pastures of the Balkans. The Vlachs had to pay various dues, the most important of which was a tithe on their beasts and flocks. This went either to the state or to a landowner. Byzantine control over the pastoralists of the Balkans was threatened by a new element in the population – the Cumans. The main bulk of these Turkish tribesmen were encamped beyond the Danube in southern Russia, but large numbers were recruited into the Byzantine armies and some were given *pronoiai* in the Balkans. They were a disturbing influence, contesting or usurping the rights of neighbouring landowners. In the theme of Moglena, to the north-west of Thessalonica, they seized the planina or pastures of Pouzouchia and subjected the Vlachs and Bulgarians settled there to their authority. They built a sheep-fold and refused to pay the tithe on flocks. In 1184 the imperial government had to issue an order restoring control of the region to the rightful owner, the Athonite monastery of the Lavra. It is not likely to have had much effect.

The Cumans would prove a decisive factor in the opening stages of the rebellion. Without their support it would probably have been crushed. In 1187, fresh from his triumph over Alexius Branas, Isaac Angelos set out to deal with the rebels once and for all. He managed to get his army into the hilly centre of the Balkans and to defeat Peter and Asan, who fled to the Cumans beyond the Danube. Isaac returned to Constantinople, convinced that the country had been pacified. He did not even see the need to leave any garrisons behind to hold the country down. Peter and Asan returned with Cuman support and soon re-established themselves. This time Isaac failed to get to grips with the enemy and was lucky to extricate his army from the interior of the Balkans. The chance to nip the rebellion in the bud had gone. Negotiations with Peter and Asan came to nothing and the rebellion spread, as other Vlach chieftains asserted their independence. The initiative had passed into the hands of the rebels and it was all that the Byzantines could do to protect the regions of Adrianople and Philippopolis in the Maritsa valley. The passage of Frederick Barbarossa's crusade across the Balkans in the summer of 1189 confirmed this state of affairs. It also encouraged Stefan Nemanja, the Serbian ruler, who had been content to sit on the sidelines, to repudiate his alliance with Byzantium and to attack Byzantine territory. He sacked the key point of Skoplje.

The whole of the Balkans was slipping out of the Byzantine grasp. In 1190 Isaac made a desperate attempt to recover the initiative against the rebels. Once again he led an army into the interior of the Balkans. The Vlachs obstinately refused to fight, but they caught the Byzantine army as it was retreating southwards through the passes of the Balkan mountains and inflicted a heavy defeat. Isaac could not wipe his hands of the Balkans. He had devoted too much of his energy to suppressing the rebellion; he had invested too much of his prestige in the effort to subdue the Balkans. As a last desperate throw he organized a joint operation with his father-in-law, the Hungarian King Bela. It came to nothing because Isaac was dethroned before he took the field. His failure against the rebels was a contributory factor in his overthrow. He lost the support of the army, which was unwilling to endure the discomforts of another unsuccessful campaign.

Isaac was supplanted by his elder brother Alexius, who in all things took the line of least possible resistance. He called off the campaign against the Vlachs and Bulgarians and used the war chest to buy himself support. He was content to contain the rebels. There was sense behind his minimalist approach. The Vlach chieftains had begun to quarrel among themselves and Alexius exploited their squabbles. He was also fortunate that the Cumans were defeated in 1201 by the Russians of Galicia and this deprived the rebels of the Cuman aid on which they relied. The original leaders of the rebellion, Peter and Asan, split with one another in 1193. Asan was murdered by one of his boyars in 1196 and the next year Peter was assassinated. Leadership now passed to their youngest brother Joannitsa. He had been a hostage at the Byzantine court. His energies were to be directed towards laying the foundations of the second Bulgarian Empire. In 1202 Alexius came to an agreement with Joannitsa. The Byzantines were left in control of Thrace, the Rhodope mountains, and Macedonia, but in return they recognized Bulgarian independence. Alexius was a realist and it was all that he could reasonably hope to salvage.

In its beginnings the rebellion of Peter and Asan was not all that different from other rebellions that occurred at this time in other parts of the Empire. It was an assertion of local interests at a time when central authority seemed to be in eclipse. Whereas the other rebellions usually collapsed in the face of determined efforts on the part of the central government to restore their authority, the Bulgarian rebellion led to the creation of a new state. The rebels were favoured by a number of factors. They could look for help across the Danube to the Cumans; they were building on the resentments of the pastoralists of the Balkans at their treatment by the Byzantine authorities, and, however obscurely, there was still a clear recollection of Tsar Symeon and the first Bulgarian Empire to which they could appeal.

LOCAL SEPARATISM UNDER THE ANGELOI

Conditions in Asia Minor were not so very different from those existing in the Balkans. Beyond the frontiers were Turcoman nomads who were only too happy to have an excuse to raid the Byzantine provinces in search of plunder and winter pastures for their flocks. The Byzantine frontiers in western Anatolia were subjected to increasing pressure. The understanding which had existed for much of Manuel Comnenus's reign with the Seljuq Sultan Kilidj Arslan was breaking down. Andronicus's usurpation provided a pretext for Turkish aggression. A series of pretenders, claiming to be the murdered Emperor Alexius II, appeared along the frontiers. They were given unofficial Turkish backing and found some local Byzantine support. The cities of Asia Minor had been a scene of unrest since the reign of Andronicus. The new wave of Turkish raids meant that the border towns had more than ever to fend for themselves. A place like Philadelphia looked for its defence to its own inhabitants, who were famed for their skill at archery. Rather than rely on the doubtful support of Constantinople the people of Philadelphia preferred to raise up their own ruler. His name was Theodore Mangaphas, a local man. He was proclaimed emperor and even minted his own coins. He soon brought under his control the inland areas of the theme of Thrakesion. Isaac Angelos could not let this challenge to his authority go unchecked and he led a punitive expedition against Philadelphia. News of the approach of Frederick Barbarossa's crusade forced him to withdraw. He recognized Mangaphas as *de facto* ruler of Philadelphia on condition that he gave up his imperial claims and sent his sons as hostages to Constantinople. When Frederick Barbarossa's crusade passed by in the spring of 1190, Philadelphia acted as though it was an independent state. It was only some three years later that Mangaphas was driven out and Philadelphia was brought back under the nominal control of the imperial government. Mangaphas fled to the Seljuqs of Konya and with their backing did much damage along the frontiers. He was able to re-establish himself as ruler of Philadelphia in the chaos that accompanied the arrival of the fourth crusade and the overthrow of Alexius III Angelos in 1203.

It was at exactly this juncture that Theodore Laskaris, a son-in-law of Alexius Angelos, escaped from Constantinople to Asia Minor. He began to lay the foundations of what was to become the Nicaean Empire, the most successful of the Byzantine successor states after 1204. He was able to come to terms with local rulers, such as Theodore Mangaphas at Philadelphia, and in this way harnessed the separatist tendencies of the Anatolian cities. In much the same way, the grandsons of the Emperor Andronicus Comnenus were able to get away to the Pontus region, where they built on the traditions of local independence associated with the Gabras family to create the Empire of Trebizond. The political fragmentation of the Byzantine Empire after 1204 was anticipated by such traditions.

The emperors of the house of Comnenus were normally able to check local independence, but there were some provinces that were always likely to flare up in rebellion; the island of Cyprus, for example. In May 1123 the imperial governor was murdered in an uprising and a Byzantine emissary to the court of Antioch only just escaped with his life. The Cypriots were regarded as a separate people by the Byzantines. Their church of St Barnabas was autocephalous. The island was on the very fringes of the Byzantine Empire and its interests seemed to lie with the crusader states and Cilician Armenia rather than Constantinople. It was treated very much as a colonial territory. Its bishops and governors were sent out from Constantinople and were not chosen locally. The Byzantine government was mainly concerned to get as much as it could out of the island by way of taxation and, in order to do so, treated the peasantry abominably. The contempt of the Constantinopolitan for the Cypriot is evident in Constantine Manasses's account[8] of his stay on the island. At church he found himself next to a local man, who smelt so strongly of dung and garlic that he had to order him to move away. Since this had no effect, he hit him, with the desired result. There would seem to be all the ingredients of a rebellion, but, when it came, it surprisingly had no local support. In 1184 the island was seized by Isaac Comnenus, a nephew of the Emperor Manuel Comnenus. He forged letters purporting to show that the Emperor Andronicus had appointed him governor of Cyprus. Once in power, he assumed the imperial title. A Cypriot monk remembered his rule thus: 'He not only completely ruined the land and plundered the property of the rich, but even harassed and oppressed the *archontes* themselves.'⁹ Many of the archontic families fled abroad. When Richard Cœur de Lion stopped at Cyprus in 1191 he was welcomed by the local people as a deliverer.

Isaac Comnenus's tyranny sets in relief some of the more positive features of the Byzantine administration of Cyprus during the twelfth century. It respected the rights of the people who counted, the local *archontes*. In addition, its governors and bishops proved to be generous patrons of the church in Cyprus. To judge by material remains the twelfth century was a golden age of Cypriot monasticism. Artists of considerable talent were brought in from Constantinople to decorate the monasteries of Koutsovendi, Asinou, Lagoudera, and the hermitage of St Neophytos outside Paphos. Where evidence has survived, the patrons of this work were the Byzantine bishops and governors. Such benefactions mollified local opinion. Much less is known about Crete, but the pattern seems to have been much the same. The governors and their staff were sent out from Constantinople, but society was dominated by a series of archontic families. Isaac Angelos found it prudent to confirm them in their estates and privileges.

Under the Angeloi the imperial government found it more and more difficult to control local power, whence the increasing lawlessness in many provinces. In the south-eastern corner of Asia Minor an *archon* of the town of Mylasa simply appropriated an olive plantation, which he leased from the monastery of St Paul on Mount Latros. After his death his heirs proved no more amenable to the demands of the monastery for the return of their property. The monastery had the support of the imperial administration, but this seems to have had no effect. The local *archontes* did much as they pleased. In Epirus a local magnate backed by an armed retinue carried off a rich widow and forced her to marry him. He obtained a statement from his fellow *archontes* of the town of Koloneia to the effect that no force had been used to acquire his wife. The upshot was a vendetta between the magnate and his bride's family. Her brother came and seized him. He then married his sister off to somebody of his own choice. The Angeloi were learning to condone the excesses of local power rather than risk open rebellion. How else were they to ensure the continuing collection of taxes, which was the primary function of the imperial administration!

The fatal weakness of provincial administration under the Angeloi was a willingness to connive at local power combined with oppressive and erratic taxation. Judith Herrin¹⁰ has shown what sorry consequences this combination had for the Greek lands. The *praitor* of the theme of Hellas descended upon Athens, demanding to be put up with all his train. Tax commissioners wanted payment for the privilege of assessing the taxpayer for taxation. Demands were made for additional taxes. Worst was perhaps ship-money. This was raised by three different agencies – the *praitor's* staff, the Grand Duke's agents, and by Leo Sgouras, who was in control of the town of Nauplion. Athens was apparently more vulnerable than its neighbours, Thebes and Eurippos, which were able to fend off the demands for taxation. In the end, the people who paid were the peasantry, and Michael Choniates, the archbishop of Athens, ended a petition that he addressed to Alexius III Angelos in 1198 with a plea that the *archontes* of Athens should be prevented from acquiring more peasant land. The peasants were in danger of being 'blown hither and thither like leaves before the wind'.[11] Michael Choniates bewails the failing prosperity of Attica. The main cause was the oppressive fiscal administration. Worse still, for all their demands the imperial government failed to protect the region from the depredations of the pirates who now swarmed through the Aegean. The failure of the imperial government was reflected in the way local men established themselves as independent rulers in the Peloponnese. Such a man was Leo Sgouras. He inherited control over the town of Nauplion in the Argolid from his father and he took advantage of the chaos existing at the end of the century to extend his authority to Argos and Corinth. He almost certainly had local backing. His opponents were bishops, such as Michael Choniates, who kept alive traditions of loyalty to the imperial government at Constantinople. The truth was that by 1203 the imperial government had lost effective control over most of the provinces of the Empire. It was just one sign of the way the Empire was collapsing from within.

COURT, CAPITAL, AND POLITICS – DEMORALIZATION AT THE CENTRE

The woefully poor standard of provincial administration under the Angeloi can only be understood in the light of the politics of the court and capital. Isaac Angelos tried to hold the balance between different factions, interests, and families in Constantinople after the manner of Manuel Comnenus, but unlike Manuel he had no obvious foundation for his authority. He did not trust his brothers and other relatives and his children were still too young to be useful to him. His solution was to seek the support of the bureaucracy. He put his maternal uncle Theodore Kastamonites in charge of the administration with the title of Grand Logothete. He was then succeeded by Constantine Mesopotamites, who was still a young man, and his ascendancy over the emperor was the cause of some resentment. He was singled out for particular criticism by the 'holy man', Basilakios, who seems to have been a spokesman for those opposed to Isaac. His criticisms were very soon followed by the coup that brought Alexius Angelos to the throne. It was engineered by a powerful faction among the court aristocracy. Its leaders were Theodore Branas, George Palaiologos, John Petraliphas, Constantine Raoul, and Manuel Cantacuzenus. It was the first time that a group of aristocratic families had openly got together at Byzantium to decide upon the succession. They agreed that Isaac had failed both the Empire and themselves. They expected Alexius Angelos to rule in their interests.

Alexius Angelos was only too well aware of the interlocking factions that existed at court and threatened the throne. His strategy for survival was, we know, to take the line of least resistance, to be as generous and malleable as he could. He made grants of landed property and state revenues to those that asked. He almost never refused a request. Whether he was in a position to carry out his promises was another matter. Almost as a matter of course, his immediate family were among the beneficiaries of his bounty; his wife, in particular, upon whom he relied very heavily. She came from the great bureaucratic family of Kamateros. Thanks to her he left the bureaucracy very much to its own devices. There were some able men in charge of affairs in his reign. They included among others the historian Nicetas Choniates, who became chief minister. The task that he set his civil service was wellnigh impossible, because of the ludicrously generous way in which he granted away the tax revenues of the state. They were reduced to slapping surcharges on to the basic land tax to raise more revenue or exploiting special taxes, such as ship-money. Alexius's slack administration was paid for in fiscal abuse, with terrible consequences for the provinces. Alexius also expected the administration to make up its lost revenues by checking all manner of possible infringement of privileges that had been issued. The monastery of the Lavra on Mount Athos was involved in a tedious lawsuit with the maritime bureau over the question of whether it paid customs duties on wine transported in its ships. Before the case was finally settled in the monastery's favour there were no less than four sessions, each involving a minimum of five assessors and seven judges. The administration was getting choked with time-consuming detail.

The failure of Andronicus Comnenus's reforms was bad for civil service morale. Any claim to be working for the common good disappeared. Civil servants seemed now to be motivated by a desire to show off their technical expertise and to line their pockets. This state of affairs was aggravated by the freedom of action that the bureaucracy enjoyed under the Angeloi emperors. Increasing paper-work demanded an increase in staff. The lists of officials in different departments leave the distinct impression that at the end of the twelfth century the civil service was expanding and abuses that had perhaps been kept in check were now rampant. Isaac Angelos was accused of 'putting up offices for sale, like a street trader with a barrow load of fruit'.[12] Nepotism was rife; Constantine Mesopotamites used his influence to find various members of his family jobs in the administration. The most flagrant example comes from the maritime bureau, where a John Mesopotamites is found acting on behalf of his brother Michael. It was a common practice at this time for a civil servant to get a relative to carry out his duties in a particular office. The civil service was a battleground for competing cliques. The Mesopotamites would be ousted by Nicetas Choniates's clique. This included his brother-in-law John Belissariotes, who held the position of Grand Logariast, in other words the head of the financial administration. His brother Michael Belissariotes held the office of prefect of the city. Civil service families began to monopolize different offices. When Demetrius Tornikes, the logothete of the drome, died in 1201, he was succeeded in his office by his son Constantine. Not surprisingly the Tornikes had a strong sense of family. One of them was urged to imitate his father and his grandfather 'so that those who had not seen them with their own eyes could be sure that their noble blood flowed in his veins'.[13] They preferred to stress their personal achievements rather than their descent from an ancient family. This stress on ability gave these civil service dynasties a sense of moral superiority, which marked them out as an élite, but set them apart from the court aristocracy.

For all that, they were preoccupied with their own struggles and interests in Constantinople. Their members had very little time to spare for the problems of the provinces. It was even difficult to get them to leave the comforts of the capital and take up posts which they had been given in the provinces. Michael Choniates put it very well: 'The luxury-loving citizens of Constantinople have no desire to peep out from behind the safety of their gates and walls and take regard for neighbouring cities, so that they can benefit from their good fortune. All they do is to send out tax-collectors ... wave upon wave of them to strip the cities of their remaining wealth.'[14] Constantinopolitan indifference was cause for bitterness.

At one point it seemed as though Alexius and his government might be brought to heel. At Christmas 1196 Alexius was confronted by a demand from the German Emperor Henry VI that unless a sum of 5,000 lb of gold was paid immediately he would invade the Empire. Alexius temporized and was able to get the sum reduced to 1,600 lb of gold, still a hefty sum. In order to raise it, he proposed to impose a special levy to be known as the German tax. He sought to gain popular assent to this measure by calling a 'parliament'. It consisted of members of the senate, but reinforced by representatives of the clergy and guilds of Constantinople. He presented his plans for the apportioning of the new tax. His proposal was greeted with uproar. He was accused of squandering public funds and of appointing his relatives to provincial governorships, 'all of them useless creatures',[15] blind in some cases. He hurriedly dismissed the assembly and looked for other means of raising the money. He at last hit on the idea of plundering the imperial tombs in the mausolea on either side of the church of the Holy Apostles. They were broken open and their treasures disgorged. The emperor's agents were just beginning to prise open the tomb of Constantine the Great, when word came that enough treasure had been collected. It amounted to over 7,000 lb of silver. It turned out to be something of a windfall, because Henry VI died in September 1197 and the money was never despatched. It gave Alexius a breathing space. He had cash in hand and could afford to ignore his critics from the safe distance of the Blakhernai Palace. He became increasingly isolated from his capital.

This is apparent in the festivities he arranged to celebrate the double wedding of his two daughters in the spring of 1199. It was at carnival time, when races were traditionally held in the Hippodrome, but Alexius refused to allow these to go ahead. Instead, he put on a travesty of the games in a special theatre that he had constructed at the Blakhernai Palace. The prefect of the city who was a eunuch disported himself on a gaily caparisoned cock-horse, as the master of ceremonies. There were foot-races, from which the ordinary citizens were excluded. These were contested by the golden youth of the court. The spectacle was reserved for the emperor, the empress, and their courtiers. It was this kind of tomfoolery which so alienated people from the imperial office. When after 1204 men came to consider the causes of the fall of the Byzantine Empire they singled out the luxury and vice of the imperial court.

'What was it', asked a scholar at the Nicaean court, 'that gave our great city as a prey to the Latins and filled the world with all manner of misfortunes? It was nothing but the culpable conduct of those who were then on the throne and the slackness and cowardice which it bred.'[16]

The failings of the Byzantines, their factiousness and their love of luxury, seemed to contemporaries, such as Nicetas Choniates, to compare unfavourably with the sterner virtues of the Latins. If Nicetas Choniates recorded the growing gulf between the Byzantines and the Latins – 'we do not have a thought in common'[17] – he also used the example of westerners as implicit criticism of Byzantine society. He has preserved an exchange between the ambassadors of Henry VI and Alexius Angelos, when they came to demand the payment of tribute. To impress, Alexius had dressed in his full regalia; he was dripping with jewels. The Germans looked at him and dismissed his finery as high fashion fit only for women. They challenged the emperor with these words, 'Now the time has come to put away these effeminate gowns and array yourself in iron, not gold.'[18] The charge of effeminacy was one of the stock slurs against the Byzantines, but one which had some force, when Byzantine luxury was compared with western dynamism. Western society seemed more effectively organized. This seems to be the lesson that Nicetas Choniates drew from an incident involving Frederick Barbarossa and a Byzantine embassy. The German emperor made the emissaries all sit down with their servants and grooms, in order to stress that at Byzantium there was no distinction of rank; that under the emperor all were equal, 'like pigs in a sty'.[19] Like it or not the feudal ordering of society seemed to the historian Nicetas Choniates capable of producing a more effective, a less factious society. The Latins seemed to be able to organize themselves so much better than the Byzantines. This was a point taken up in a different context by Nicetas Choniates's brother, Michael, the archbishop of Athens. He was commenting on a riot in the town of Eurippos. He contrasted this lack of order with the self-discipline that Latins were able to show: 'Now order has been overturned. One sees Celts, Germans, and Italians assembling in an orderly fashion and debating with a sense of decorum, but, as for the Byzantines, they get infuriated at the slightest pretext and reduce any meeting called for the common good to a shambles.'[20]

The Byzantine Empire was disintegrating, not for the first time. Renewal and decay were the rhythm of Byzantine political history, but the Empire had never been quite so vulnerable. This was not only because of disillusion with the imperial institution. Never had the rhetoric of imperial ideology been made to work so hard as under the Angeloi and never had it appeared so hollow. It was also because of the penetration of Byzantine society at so many different levels by westerners: they were needed for their military and commercial skills. *Faute de mieux*, it was natural to turn to them for help in the internal affairs of the Empire. The upshot was that a crusade would be sucked into the decaying Byzantine Empire with disastrous consequences. The instrument was to be Alexius's nephew, also called Alexius. He had been kept in confinement with his father, the ex-emperor Isaac, who still nourished hopes of regaining the throne. Early in the autumn of 1201 the young Alexius was able to evade his guards and was spirited away on a Pisan ship. It has all the marks of a well-organized escape. He made his way to Sicily and then to the court of his brother-in-law Philip of Swabia. There at Christmas 1201 he would meet Boniface of Montferrat, the newly elected leader of the fourth crusade. It was a fateful encounter.

NOTES

1. Eustazio di Tessalonica, *La espugnazione di Tessalonica* (ed. by St Kyriakidis), p. 18
2. *Ibid.*
3. *Ibid.*, p. 34
4. *Ibid.*, p. 42
5. A P Kazhdan, *Sotsialjnyj sostav gospodstvujushchego klassa Vizantii XI–XII vv.* (Moscow, 1974), pp. 263–5

6. Nicetas Choniates (ed. by Van Dieten), p. 376
7. *Ibid.*, p. 371
8. K Horna, 'Das *Hodoiporikon* des Konstantin Manasses', *Byzantinische Zeitschrift*, 13 (1904), p. 344
9. *Excerpta Cypria* (transl. by C D Cobham) (Cambridge, 1908), p. 12
10. J Herrin, 'Realities of Byzantine provincial government: Hellas and the Peloponnesos, 1180–1205', *Dumbarton Oaks Papers*, 29 (1975), pp. 253-84
11. Michael Choniates (ed. by Sp. Lampros), II, p. 99
12. Nicetas Choniates (ed. by Van Dieten), p. 444
13. Michael Choniates (ed. by Sp. Lampros), II, p. 357
14. *Ibid.*, p. 83
15. Nicetas Choniates (ed. by Van Dieten), p. 478
16. Quoted in E Barker, *Social and Political Thought in Byzantium from Justinian to the Last Palaeologus* (Oxford, 1957), p. 156
17. Nicetas Choniates (ed. by Van Dieten), p. 301
18. *Ibid.*, p. 477
19. *Ibid.*, p. 410
20. Michael Choniates (ed. by Sp. Lampros), I, p. 183

Chapter 15

THE FALL OF CONSTANTINOPLE AND THE FOURTH CRUSADE

By the turn of the twelfth century Byzantium had become the 'Sick Man of Europe'. It had ceased to be useful to western christendom. In the days of the Emperor Manuel, to which westerners looked back with increasing nostalgia, the Byzantine Empire provided effective support to the crusader states and western knights were welcome at the Byzantine court. Italian merchants grew rich in the comparative security provided by the Byzantine administration and fleet. Innocent III recalled with affection Manuel's devotion to Rome. None of this held good now that the throne of Constantinople had passed to the Angeloi. Rather than support the crusade they preferred an alliance with Saladin. They constantly prevaricated on the question of the union of churches. The Italian maritime republics could no longer trust the Byzantines to observe solemn and binding treaties. Instead, the Byzantine emperors deliberately played off one republic against another. To make matters worse, they no longer possessed a fleet capable of patrolling Byzantine waters. As a result, piracy was rife and commerce uncertain. Looked at in this way, the destruction of the Byzantine Empire was the logical outcome of the needs of the West. Only a Latin Empire established at Constantinople could safeguard western interests in a part of the world, which over the twelfth century had become vital to the West. This is rather too neat an explanation of the fall of the Byzantine Empire in 1204 to be entirely convincing. This is only how it appears in retrospect, rather in the way that Innocent III hailed the news of the conquest of Constantinople as a miraculous vindication of the papal claims to supremacy over the Byzantine church.

The pursuit of western interests provides only part of the logic behind the events. The outcome depended even more on the resolution of opposing currents of attraction and repulsion created by the crusade. Byzantine and Latin eyed one another suspiciously, but with respect. The Byzantines admired the prowess of the western knight. The Latins respected Byzantine wealth and subtlety. The Emperor Manuel Comnenus was a figure they whole-heartedly admired. During his reign

Latins came to play an important part in the affairs of state. This was the cause of resentment in some circles. Byzantine hatred of the Latins deepened after Manuel's death, when they were seen to be the main prop of the Empress Maria's regime. Few Byzantines were willing to tolerate the exercise of political power by the Latins within the Empire. These political resentments were soon strengthened by religious prejudices against the Latins, which had always existed, but only burst forth in the massacres of 1182.

The crusade gave, in Byzantine eyes, a much clearer sense of identity to the westerners. They were united under the papacy in a common enterprise, which experience suggested might turn into a threat to Byzantium itself. The natural reaction was to stress the differences separating the Byzantine and the Latin, but these were not incorporated into official ideology until the end of the twelfth century. Manuel Comnenus, in contrast, preferred to stress the Roman or, more correctly, Justinianic elements in Byzantine ideology. Quite different are the 'Hellenic' ideas that are beginning to creep in to the official phraseology under the Angeloi. In 1199 the podestà and consuls of Genoa were informed by the Byzantine emperor that 'the apophthegms and maxims of Hellenic philosophers are not just accurate; they are penetratingly true. Their wise poet Hesiod declared that the whole city suffers on account of a single wicked man.'[1] To invoke Hesiod in a diplomatic exchange seems bizarre, but it was clearly done because it was expected to impress. It underlined that the Byzantines were the heirs of 'Hellenic Wisdom'. It was something that set them above the Latins. Such ideas would have a future after 1204. They may have been confined to a small circle of intellectuals and bureaucrats at the centre of government. They nevertheless reflect how under the Angeloi an effort was being made to create an identity for the Byzantines that set a gulf between them and the Latins. The possibility of compromise that existed under the Comneni became more remote.

Suspicion of Byzantium grew in the West. There had always been a current of opinion that condemned the Byzantines as schismatics and considered that Constantinople was a legitimate target of the crusade, but this was balanced by the conviction that the crusade was a cooperative venture between western and eastern christendom. It was on this notion that Manuel Comnenus had based much of his diplomacy. It remained part of the verbiage of diplomacy, but the crusade itself was changing in a way that made such cooperation more or less impossible. Objectives, other than the security of eastern christendom and the rescue of the Holy Places, began to be considered. At the Third Lateran Council of 1179 it was agreed that the fight against heresy deserved the same spiritual rewards as participation in a crusade. This was but a short step from the idea that the crusade might be employed for any undertaking that was morally justified, that restored right order to Christian society. The schism that existed between Rome and Constantinople was to western eyes a breach of that right order upheld and safeguarded by the successor of St Peter.

But for the fact that Frederick Barbarossa was a Staufer the experience of his crusade would have provided incontrovertible proof that the Byzantines were enemies of christendom. For the Byzantines the passage of his crusading armies showed once again that the crusade was hostile to Byzantium. Frederick was an old enemy, the more dangerous for the understanding that he had built up with the Seljuqs of Rum. To counter this it was a natural move to ally with Saladin, who was not on the best of terms with the Seljuqs of Rum. The Byzantine Emperor Isaac Angelos agreed to oppose Frederick Barbarossa's passage through the territories of his Empire. Byzantine opposition was brushed aside by the Germans in the summer of 1189. Barbarossa made Adrianople, the capital of Thrace, his base. One party at court was convinced that he intended an assault upon Constantinople, but another which finally prevailed suggested that he merely wished an unimpeded passage through the Empire. In November 1189 a treaty was concluded, guaranteeing his safe passage across the Dardanelles and on through the Anatolian provinces.

Frederick Barbarossa insisted that the treaty should be signed by the Patriarch Dositheos. He was the leader of opposition to the passage of the crusade. He was supposed by the Germans to have preached against them, calling them dogs and assuring convicted murderers that they could wipe away their guilt by killing crusaders. The patriarch came from a Venetian family, but he became a monk in the monastery of Stoudios, where his holiness attracted the attention of the future Emperor Isaac Angelos. He predicted his elevation to the imperial throne. As a reward Isaac made him titular patriarch of Jerusalem, soon after he became emperor in 1185. Isaac then tried to foist him on the church of Constantinople, when the patriarchal throne fell vacant at the beginning of 1189. This caused a furore because it was hardly canonical and he was forced to resign. The new patriarch proved incompetent and by June Dositheos was back on the patriarchal throne. Though he had only been titular patriarch of Jerusalem, Dositheos must have been aware of the situation of the Orthodox church in the crusader states. It had more to gain from Saladin than from the Franks. In 1187 it was the orthodox of Jerusalem who had opened the gates of the city to Saladin. There were plans afoot in Constantinople to persuade Saladin to restore the church of the Holy Sepulchre and the other churches of Jerusalem to the orthodox patriarch. In the end Saladin turned this request down, but when in 1192 a party of crusaders visited the church of the Holy Sepulchre, they found to their dismay that it was in the possession of orthodox clergy. The experience of the third crusade suggested that the Byzantines were enemies of the crusade. They opposed its passage in the interests of Saladin and hoped to exploit the loss of Jerusalem to the Muslims to the advantage of their church.

Add to this the massacre of Latins in 1182, which made a great impression in the West, and there seemed little chance of any reconciliation between Byzantium and the West. A new set of circumstances would conspire, however, to throw Byzantium and the papacy together once more. In November 1189 William II of Sicily died, leaving Frederick Barbarossa's son and heir, Henry VI, with a very good claim to the crown of Sicily. The papacy had no desire to see Sicily united with the German Empire; the Byzantines hardly less so. Feelers were put out on both sides. Isaac resorted to the diplomatic rhetoric of Manuel Comnenus's time. He claimed that 'what touched him most deeply and grieved him continually'[2] was the fate of the Holy Places, now occupied by the infidel. Such sentiments were not expected to be taken seriously; they were the small change of diplomatic exchange. The Byzantines had reckoned without Innocent III who ascended the throne of St Peter in January 1198. The Byzantine emperor, now Alexius Angelos, sent him a polite letter of congratulation. He got in return a fierce reply. The Greeks had betrayed the Holy Sepulchre and took delight in the schism which separated their two churches. To prove their good faith they should use their wealth and position to give protection to the crusader states. The launching of a crusade was one of Innocent's guiding aims and Byzantium was included in his plans from the very beginning. For the Byzantines the prospect of another crusade was alarming. Alexius Angelos's reply was a study in prevarication. He was, in principle, all in favour of the liberation of the Holy Sepulchre, but it was very much in God's hands. The pope must remember how much damage Frederick Barbarossa's crusade had inflicted upon the Byzantine Empire. Then there was the question of the union of the churches. This did not seem a difficult matter, because in his opinion the essential union had been preserved in the person of Christ. There were petty differences, but these could be resolved at a general council of the church.

Innocent III cut through to the essentials. Alexius was rebuked for not wishing to further the cause of the Holy Sepulchre: 'His negligence would incur divine displeasure.'[3] His desire to end the schism was welcome, but he was advised that the apostolic see was the 'divine head and mother of all Churches'.[4] It was not subject to the authority of a general council, but was empowered to convene it. The Byzantines would have to come to a general council fully accepting papal supremacy. Alexius found himself entangled in plans that were not of his own choosing and in ideas that he could not countenance. His attempt to back out earned him the contempt of the pope. Innocent's crusading plans were from the outset muddled up in his mind with what seemed to him to be Byzantine intransigence and bad faith.

Innocent's call for a new crusade only found enthusiastic response among the barons and princes of northern France. Their leaders turned to Venice for the transports which would take them to the East. The necessary agreements were concluded in April 1201 with Enrico Dandolo, the doge of Venice. The destination was fixed in a secret treaty as Egypt. The participation of Venice in the fourth crusade has usually been regarded as the key to the diversion of the crusade against Constantinople. The Byzantine historian Nicetas Choniates was in no doubt about this. He presents the Doge Enrico Dandolo as the guiding figure in the enterprise.

'Not the least threat was the then doge of the Venetians, Enrico Dandolo. His eyesight was impaired and he was bowed with age, but he was full of envy against the Byzantines and desired revenge. He had a sharp eye for a shady deal, claiming that he was the shrewdest of the shrewd. It was his boast that failure to revenge himself on the Byzantines for their senseless treatment of his people was tantamount to a sentence of death. He kept going over in his mind, time and time again, all that the Venetians had suffered at the hands of the Angeloi brothers, when they were ruling, and before them at the hands of Andronicus, and even when Manuel reigned over the Byzantines. Being well aware in his own mind what would happen if he undertook some treacherous enterprise against the Byzantines with only the help of his fellow-countrymen, he sought to bring in others as collaborators and communicated with them secretly. These were men, whom he knew to nourish an implacable hatred towards the Byzantines and to gaze covetously on their wealth. It so happened that chance brought certain noble princes, who were setting out for Palestine. He induced them to conspire with him in a common venture against the Byzantines. They were Boniface, marquis of Montferrat, Baldwin, count of Flanders, Henry, count of St Pol, Louis, count of Blois, and many other daring warriors, who seemed to be as tall as their lances were long.'[5]

There we have set out the official Byzantine interpretation of the diversion of the crusade against Constantinople. It should not be dismissed out of hand, for Nicetas Choniates was chief minister for much of the time and was as well informed on events as any Byzantine. If it is difficult to find hard evidence for the conspiracy sketched by Nicetas Choniates, there is little doubt that the commercial interests that Venice had in the Byzantine Empire were another factor tilting the crusade towards Byzantium. Their aim was to recover the position within the Byzantine Empire that they had enjoyed before their expulsion by Manuel Comnenus in 1171. Serious negotiations began again under Andronicus Comnenus. It was agreed that reparation for the losses suffered by the Venetians in 1171 should be fixed at 1,500 lb of gold. This concession was hastened by the Norman invasion of 1185. It underlined the importance to Byzantium of the Venetian alliance. When a treaty was formally concluded under Isaac Angelos in 1185, the details of the naval assistance to be provided by the Venetians were to the fore. They were to come to the aid of the Empire with a fleet of from 40 to 100 ships. The emperor promised to respect the privileges previously enjoyed by the Venetians and to set up a commission to ensure the return of the property that had been confiscated from the Venetians. The last provision turned out to be unsatisfactory. After a lapse of sixteen years, it was very difficult to find the property in question. Instead, Isaac agreed in 1189 to concede to the Venetians the neighbouring quarters occupied by the Germans and the Franks. These had an annual income of 50 lb of gold. Isaac also agreed to honour the sum of the damages agreed with Andronicus. He paid 100 lb of gold immediately. The remainder was to be paid off in instalments.

Isaac next set about regularizing relations with the Pisans and the Genoese, which had been disturbed by the massacres of 1182. His foreign minister, the logothete of the drome, Demetrius Tornikes, masterminded two parallel sets of negotiations, which culminated in the spring of 1192 in the issue of chrysobulls to the Pisans and the Genoese. Their old privileges were confirmed; they received additions to their quarters in Constantinople; customs duties remained at the old rate of 4 per cent. Isaac had cause to congratulate himself on the way that he had restored the situation existing under Manuel Comnenus, all purchased at a very moderate cost. It soon became evident that an efficient display of diplomatic skills was not sufficient to wipe away the legacy of the breach that had occurred. The Latins took to piracy to revenge themselves on the Byzantines after the massacres of 1182. The Norman invasion of 1185 unleased a swarm of privateers who preyed upon the Aegean coasts. They made their base along the south-western shores of Asia Minor. Their depredations were evident when the fleets carrying the contingents of Philip Augustus and Richard Cœur de Lion to the Holy Land in 1191 passed that way. In November 1192 Isaac Angelos protested to Genoa about the activities of a Genoese pirate called William Grasso. Along with a Pisan ship he entered the harbour at Rhodes. They were to all appearances merchants going about their business. Once ashore they attacked and plundered the harbour quarter. They then waylaid a convoy of Venetian ships bringing an embassy from Saladin. They murdered the crews and the Greek and Syrian merchants that they found on board. They also set upon a Sicilian ship that was carrying Byzantine envoys from Cyprus. The Genoese were not willing to accept responsibility for Grasso's actions, because he had been exiled from Genoa several years before. The people of Constantinople were infuriated at the fate of the Byzantine merchants and the loss of their goods. It represented a major commercial undertaking for the Byzantines. They threatened to attack the Genoese quarter. Isaac was able to calm them down by exacting pledges from the Genoese of Constantinople to the tune of 20,000 *hyperpyra*, which was reckoned to cover the value of the goods that had been lost. In the end, Isaac allowed himself to be convinced by the Genoese authorities that they had no way of controlling Grasso's activities and he did not realize the pledges.

Isaac dealt equally leniently with the Pisans, who on the pretext of war with Venice had attacked Byzantine shipping in the sea of Marmora and had raided the coasts and islands. Isaac demanded reparations from the commune of Pisa, which countered with exactly the same argument as that used by the Genoese. They could not be held responsible for the misdemeanours of individual citizens, acting on their own account. The lesson was that Genoa and Pisa were not able to control the activities of their citizens. The suspicion was that they may not have been interested in doing so, because of their struggle for commercial mastery with the Venetians. The naval weakness of Byzantium meant that Italians were waging a covert war for control of Byzantine waters.

Isaac was only too glad to accept the services of a Calabrian pirate called John Steiriones, 'the worst pirate of them all'.[6] He nearly met his match in Gafforio, who had commanded a Genoese flotilla during the third crusade and had then turned to piracy. He was powerful enough to sack the Anatolian port of Atramyttion. Steiriones was sent against him by Alexius Angelos, but was defeated. Alexius tried to buy Gafforio off with the offer of 600 lb of gold and revenues from the coastal provinces to support his crews which numbered some 600 sailors. This offer lulled him into a false sense of security and Steiriones fell on him and killed him. Alexius had decided that the only way to beat the pirates was quite literally to join them. He fitted out a privateer which preyed on shipping in the Black Sea. When in 1201 he heard of the approach of a pirate fleet bound for Byzantine waters from Sicily he hired a Genoese corsair to hunt them out.

The Byzantines suffered from the activities of the pirates, though many, taking a leaf out of their emperor's book, were able to profit by them. It was the Venetians who stood to lose most, because they still had the largest commercial stake in the Byzantine Empire. Their ancient privileges seemed to give them little protection against Byzantine officials, still less against Pisan and Genoese pirates. In order to check the depredations of the Pisans a Venetian naval expedition was despatched in 1196 to Abydos at the entrance to the Dardanelles. It must also have been intended to overawe the Byzantine government in an effort to obtain more favourable treatment, as well as payment of the reparations which were now well in arrears. Another form of pressure that the Venetians could bring to bear on Alexius was the threat that they would support his nephew, the young Alexius, against him. According to Venetian tradition it was this which finally persuaded Alexius to ratify Venetian privileges in a chrysobull issued in November 1198. This was a far more detailed document than any of the previous chrysobulls issued to the Venetians. It was intended to block any loopholes that the Byzantine administration might seek to exploit. Instead of a rather restricted list of ports where the Venetians' right to free trade was specified, a comprehensive and up-to-date gazetteer of the provinces of the Empire was included in the new chrysobull, as was a current list of the dues from which the Venetians were exempted. The legal rights enjoyed by the Venetians were equally carefully defined. The Venetians ran the risk of being cited before a Byzantine court in their suits with Byzantines and, if the case went against them, landing up in a Byzantine gaol. It was now agreed that in cases involving money the hearing should be in the defendants' court. This gave the Venetians the protection they wanted. The Byzantine courts were to keep jurisdiction in cases involving murder and public order generally.

In theory, the Venetians now had more or less all that they could possibly want. In practice, their position had changed very little. Alexius still vacillated on the question of the payment of the reparations. His agents continued to harass Venetian merchants, while the emperor clearly favoured the Pisans and Genoese at the expense of the Venetians.

The approach made by the leaders of the fourth crusade to Venice in the spring of 1201 must have seemed to offer a way out of the difficulties in which the Venetians found themselves. This does not mean that they automatically thought of turning the crusade against Constantinople. More attractive was the possibility of stealing a march on their rivals by securing the ports of the Nile delta, where an increasingly large share of Venice's overseas trade was now concentrated. The crusaders envisaged some massive undertaking, for they demanded transport for 4,500 knights and horses, 9,000 squires, and 20,000 sergeants. This is to be compared with the 650 knights and horses and 1,300 squires of Philip Augustus's crusade to the Holy Land. It has been estimated that the core of St Louis's first crusade of 1249–50 only comprised 2,500 knights; and this by all accounts was the largest and best organized crusade ever to go by sea. There was therefore a certain lack of realism about the figures put forward by the leaders of the crusade, but it is not likely that at the time anybody appreciated this, not even the Venetians. They agreed a price only slightly above the going rate for the transport of knights and horses overseas and they offered to supply fifty ships at their own expense. In return, any conquests made were to be shared equally between the Venetians and the crusaders.

All the resources and energies of Venice were directed towards building and equipping this armada. Venetians were forbidden to trade overseas while preparations were going ahead. There can be little doubt that a substantial portion of the wealth of Venice was invested in the fleet for the fourth crusade. Embarrassingly, the knights and troops did not turn up in the numbers anticipated. Many preferred to make their own way to the Holy Land. Only a third of the force reckoned on had arrived at Venice by the late summer of 1202. They managed to find 41,000 out of the 85,000 marks they had contracted to pay. Even so, the Venetians were faced with financial disaster and the Doge Enrico Dandolo with ruin. Why so comparatively few crusaders made their way to Venice remains a matter of speculation. Secrecy over the destination was one possible cause. Another was the death in May 1201 of the original leader of the crusade, Thibaut, count of Champagne. He was eventually replaced in September by Boniface of Montferrat. He came from a northern Italian family with impeccable crusading credentials, but not from the nobility of northern France, which provided the bulk of the crusaders.

The Venetians were in an impossible position. They could not back out of the enterprise because they had invested so much in its preparation. With the reduced numbers available they could hardly think of mounting an assault upon Egypt, but they had to keep the crusade together if they were to recoup their losses. At the end of August, when it seemed that the crusade might break up, Enrico Dandolo took the cross and was joined by a crowd of enthusiastic Venetians. In return, Dandolo was able to get the leaders of the crusade to agree to an attack upon the Dalmatian city of Zara, once a Venetian dependency, but now in the hands of the king of Hungary. The doge would have been aware of the presence in Italy of the young Alexius, who was trying to get the support of the crusaders and was willing to promise almost anything. He had the good offices of Boniface of Montferrat, who had his own interests in the Byzantine Empire.

The Byzantine government was reasonably well informed about events in western Europe and was justifiably alarmed by news that the young Alexius was in touch with the leaders of the crusade. The Emperor Alexius III turned to Pope Innocent III in the hope of preventing the crusade being turned against Byzantium. Innocent III replied to the emperor's representations in a letter sent on 16 November 1202. One can assume that the imperial embassy must have left Constantinople about a month previously and was despatched in response to information originating in the West a month or so before that. On this reckoning the piece of news that was likely to have caused alarm at Byzantium was the doge's taking of the cross at the end of August. The worry produced at the Byzantine court is perhaps reflected in the decision to go straight ahead with the handing over of a large extension to the Genoese quarter.

In his reply to the Byzantine emperor Innocent III admitted that the young Alexius had appealed to him for his support, but he had sent him away to his brother-in-law, Philip of Swabia. Philip had in his turn put the young prince in touch with the leaders of the crusade. They refused to do anything on his behalf unless they had the approval of the pope. Innocent III assured the Emperor Alexius that he had withheld his approval, 'though there were several who urged that we ought to look favourably upon such a proposal seeing that the Greek Church is less than obedient and devoted to the Apostolic See'.[7] It was a transparent threat. Unless the Emperor Alexius was able to accept papal terms for the reunification of the churches, it might not be possible to restrain the crusade from attacking the Byzantine Empire. Innocent III did not wish the diversion of the crusade to Constantinople and certainly played no active part in its diversion. His sin, if sin it was, was one of omission. He said one thing, but seemed to intend another. If he sternly forbade any attack upon the Byzantine Empire, he foresaw that 'some just or necessary cause might perhaps arise'[8] that made this unavoidable. The crusaders understood by this that the pope wished to bring the Byzantine church back into the Roman obedience.

Innocent's ambivalent attitude towards Byzantium gave the leaders of the crusade the latitude to impose upon the crusading army acceptance of the proposals made formally by Boniface of Montferrat on behalf of the young Alexius. Only twelve men from the whole army came forward in support but they happened to be the leaders of the crusade. Their insistence that they would be shamed if they did not accept the proposals hints at some informal understanding reached earlier. The whole debate had to be reopened when the crusaders reached Corfu in April 1203 and were joined by the young Alexius. Rumours were flying around the camp that Boniface of Montferrat desired to go to Constantinople only 'to avenge himself for an injury that the Emperor of Constantinople who was then holding the Empire had done to him'.[9] He certainly possessed certain claims upon the Byzantine Empire, inherited from his father. The leadership prevailed once again and on 23 June 1203 the crusading fleet hove to in sight of Constantinople.

The diversion of the crusade to Constantinople can hardly be labelled a conspiracy. If there was a conspiracy, it was probably hatched in Constantinople. It seems unlikely that Alexius's escape at a time when it must have been known in Constantinople that over the next year a new crusade would be assembling can have been a complete coincidence, but there was no certainty that Alexius would be able to win the support of the crusade. That he did can only be ascribed to chance. His offer to pay the crusaders 200,000 marks seemed a godsend at a time of financial embarrassment and his willingness to assent to the union of churches and to provide military assistance to the Holy Land provided some moral justification for accepting his proposals. The Venetians who had the biggest stake in the crusade saw an opportunity of recouping their position at Constantinople at the expense of their rivals, the Pisans and the Genoese. They were well informed about conditions at Constantinople and would have reckoned on considerable opposition to the regime of Alexius Angelos.

Their gamble worked, for at the first demonstration of concerted force Alexius Angelos's nerve broke and he abandoned Constantinople, eventually finding refuge at Adrianople. Isaac Angelos was brought out of confinement and restored to the imperial throne. Then on 1 August 1203 the young Alexius was crowned emperor. He did his best to meet his obligations to the crusaders. The Venetians got the 34,000 marks that were still due to them from the crusaders and he paid other sums, amounting to a grand total of 100,000 marks. This was enough to convince the crusaders of the genuineness of his intentions and they agreed to take service with him for a full year until Michaelmas 1204. Only the support of the crusaders gave any hope that Alexius and his father would be able to master the situation. The Empire was falling to pieces, with Alexius III Angelos established in Thrace and the provinces falling into the hands of different 'dynasts'. While Isaac and his supporters held Constantinople, the young Alexius went with the bulk of the crusading army on a sweep through Thrace, in order to establish the authority of the new regime in the provinces.

Relations between the crusaders and the Byzantines had changed dramatically by the time the crusading army returned in November. Soon after it had departed in August, a group of Latins descended on Constantinople and attacked the mosque there. It was a symbol of the double-dealing of the Byzantines. The local people came to the rescue of the Muslims. The riot that ensued soon got out of hand. Vast stretches of the harbour area of the capital were burnt down. Virtually all the Latins were driven out of Constantinople and had to find refuge across the Golden Horn in the crusader camp. Given the history of relations between the people of Constantinople and the Latins over the past twenty years, such a clash was more or less inevitable.

It left the young Alexius in an almost impossible position. He was caught between the need to placate public opinion in Constantinople, which was bitterly hostile to the crusaders, and reliance upon the support of the crusaders, who were not likely to let him forget who it was that set him up in power. The young Alexius tried to distance himself from the crusaders, visiting their camp and joining in their carousing less frequently, because of the way it had offended Byzantine opinion. He was encouraged by a court orator to break with the Latins: 'Let them not grow wanton, but because they, restoring the lord emperor, have fulfilled servants' roles, let them be bent to servile laws.'[10] The crusaders were alarmed by their lord Alexius's growing coolness and, to bring him to heel, issued him, in good feudal fashion, with a formal *diffidatio*. The result was predictable. Without the support of the crusaders Alexius was soon overthrown and murdered. The new emperor was another Alexius – Alexius V Mourtzouphlos. He came to power to destroy the crusaders, who were now in a desperate plight. They were isolated in their camp outside Constantinople and in the middle of winter supplies were running low. They did not quit because they were convinced of the rightness of their cause. The murder of the young Alexius by Alexius Mourtzouphlos horrified them. In western eyes the murder of one's lord was the most heinous of crimes. Their preachers assured them of this and taught them that it was part of their crusading duty to attack the Byzantines, because they were schismatics, who had deliberately separated themselves from Rome. The crusading leaders proceeded to draw up a partition treaty. Then on Friday 9 April 1204 they launched their first assault, which was a failure. The next on 12 April gained some towers along the sea walls and a narrow space within. It was a tenuous foothold. Byzantine morale failed once again in the face of the crusaders. Mourtzouphlos was quite unable to rally any support to continue the fight the next day and fled the city. A half-hearted attempt to find a new emperor came to nothing. The crusaders found that the city was theirs. It had fallen almost by default.

The city was put to the sack. Terrible things happened. The accumulated treasure of nearly 1,000 years was seized and dispersed. Among the Byzantines there was complete disorientation. It was a 'cosmic cataclysm'.[11] There was almost no sympathy for the Constantinopolitan élite which had ruled the Empire increasingly badly. When a column of aristocratic refugees headed by the patriarch and his clergy wound out of Constantinople making for Selymbria, the reaction of the Thracian peasants was eloquent testimony to the state of Byzantium: 'The peasants and common riff-raff jeered at those of us from Byzantium and were thick-headed enough to call our miserable poverty and nakedness equality, learning nothing from the suffering of their neighbours. Many were only too happy to accept this outrage, saying, "Blessed be the Lord that we have grown rich", and buying up for next to nothing the property that their fellow-countrymen were forced to offer for sale, for they had not yet had much to do with the beef-eating Latins and they did not know that they served a wine as pure and unmixed as unadulterated bile, nor that they would treat the Byzantines with utter contempt.'[12]

With these bitter words Nicetas Choniates closes his account of the fall of Constantinople to the Latins. His history was completed in exile after 1204. In it he tried to make sense of the Empire's fall from grace. It is a triumph from both an artistic and a historical point of view. He is the true successor of Michael Psellos in his psychological penetration and surpasses him in the vividness of his descriptions and the pungency of his comments. His explanations for the downfall of the Byzantine Empire are eminently sound. He traces the weaknesses in the fabric of government back to the exigencies of Manuel Comnenus's foreign policy. He indicates the factiousness of the upper reaches of Byzantine society and the fickleness of the lower classes. He underlines how the Byzantines succeeded in alienating the West by their bad faith. But much more valuable is the way he presents through his own experience the Byzantine predicament. He hated the Latins with their short hair and shaven cheeks and their swaggering presumption. Yet he admired their dynamism and ability. He approved of the reforms of Andronicus Comnenus, but looked to the court aristocracy as the natural leaders of society. These contradictions were built in to the political system created by the emperors of the house of Comnenus. While the Comneni retained their cohesion, it produced an effective system of government, but it was always curiously fragile. Its disintegration in the closing years of the twelfth century was predictable, part of the curious political cycle at Byzantium of decay and renewal.

NOTES

1. Miklosich and Müller, *Acta et Diplomata*, III, p. 46
2. Georges et Dèmètrios Tornikès, *Lettres et Discours*, p. 341
3. Tafel and Thomas, *Urkunden*, I, p. 243
4. *Ibid.*, p. 245
5. Nicetas Choniates (ed. by Van Dieten), pp. 538–9
6. *Ibid.*, p. 482
7. Tafel and Thomas, *Urkunden*, I, p. 406
8. *Ibid.*, p. 417
9. Robert of Clari (transl. by E H McNeal), p. 59
10. C M Brand, 'A Byzantine Plan for the Fourth Crusade', *Speculum*, 43 (1968), p. 467
11. J Darrouzès, 'Les discours d'Euthyme Tornikès (1200–1205)', *Revue des Etudes Byzantines*, 26 (1968), pp. 82–3
12. Nicetas Choniates (ed. by Van Dieten), pp. 593–4

REFERENCES

Texts cited in an abbreviated form in the chapter notes:

The Alexiad of Anna Comnena (transl. E R A Sewter). Penguin Classics 1969.

Eustathii opuscula (ed. T L F Tafel). Frankfurt 1832.

Georges & Dèmètrios Tornikès, *Lettres et Discours* (ed. J Darrouzès). Paris 1970.

Ioannes Tzetzes, *Epistulae* (ed. P A M Leone). Leipzig 1972.

John Kinnamos (Cinnamus), *Deeds of John and Manuel Comnenus* (transl. C M Brand). New York 1976.

Kekavmenos, *Strategikon: Cecaumeni Strategicon et incerti Scriptoris De Officiis regiis Libellus* (ed. B Wassiliewsky & V Jernstedt). St Petersburg 1896; *Sovety i rasskazy Kekavmena* (ed. G G Litavrin). Moscow 1972.

Michaêl Akominatou tou Chôniatou ta sôzomena (ed. Sp P Lampros). Athens 1879–80, 2 vols.

Michael Psellos, *Chronographia;* Michael Psellus, *Fourteen Byzantine Rulers* (transl. E R A Sewter). Penguin Classics 1966.

Michaelis Pselli scripta minora (ed. E Kurtz & F Drexl). Milan 1936–41, 2 vols.

J P Migne, *Patrologia Graeca*. Paris 1857–66.

J P Migne, *Patrologia Latina*. Paris 1844–80.

F Miklosich & J Müller, *Acta et diplomata graeca medii aevi sacra et profana*. Vienna 1860–90, 6 vols.

Nicetae Choniatae Historia (ed. I A Van Dieten). Berlin/New York 1975.

Odo of Deuil, *De profectione Ludovici VII in Orientem* (ed. and transl. V G Berry). New York 1948.

Otto of Freising, *The Deeds of Frederick Barbarossa* (transl. C C Mierow). New York 1953.

Robert de Clari, *The Conquest of Constantinople* (transl. E H McNeal). New York 1936.

K N Sathas, *Masaiônikê Bibliothêkê (Bibliotheca graeca medii aevi)*. Venice/Paris 1872–94, 7 vols.

G L F Tafel & G M Thomas, *Urkunden zur älteren Handels- und Staatsgeschichte der Republik Venedig*. Vienna 1856–57, 3 vols.

William of Tyre, *A History of Deeds Done Beyond the Sea* (transl. E A Babcock & A C Krey). New York 1943, 2 vols.

J & P Zepos, *Jus graecoromanum*. Athens 1931, 8 vols.

BIBLIOGRAPHY

1. WORKS OF GENERAL INTEREST

H Ahrweiler, *Byzance et la mer.* Paris 1966.

H Ahrweiler, *L'idéologie politique de l'Empire byzantin.* Paris 1975.

H G Beck, *Kirche und theologische Literatur im byzantinischen Reich.* Munich 1959. [Excellent bibliography.]

R Browning, *The Byzantine Empire.* London 1980.

Cambridge Medieval History, IV, parts 1–2 (ed. J M Hussey). Cambridge 1966–67. [Good bibliographies.]

F Chalandon, *Les Comnènes. Etudes sur l'Empire byzantin aux XIe et XIIe siècles, I: Essai sur le règne d'Alexis 1er Comnène (1081–1118); II: Jean II Comnène (1118–1143) et Manuel I Comnène (1143–1180).* Paris 1900–12, 3 vols.

Ch Diehl, *Byzantine Portraits* (transl. H Bell). New York 1927.

H W Haussig, *A History of Byzantine Civilization.* London 1971.

H Hunger, *Die hochsprachliche profane Literatur der Byzantiner.* Munich 1978, 2 vols. [Exhaustive bibliography.]

A P Kazhdan, *Vizantijskaja Kul'tura (X–XII vv.)* Moscow 1968.

A P Kazhdan, *Sotsialjnyj sostav gospodstvujushchego klassa Vizantii (XI–XII vv).* Moscow 1974.

A Kazhdan & G Constable, *People and Power in Byzantium.* Washington, D.C. 1982.

P Lemerle, *Cinq Etudes sur le XIe siècle byzantin.* Paris 1977.

C Mango, *Byzantium. The Empire of New Rome.* London 1980.

C Neumann, *Die Weltstellung des byzantinischen Reiches vor den Kreuzzügen.* Berlin 1894.

D Obolensky, *The Byzantine Commonwealth.* London 1971. [Useful bibliography.]

G Ostrogorsky, *History of the Byzantine State.* Oxford 1968. [Helpful bibliography.]

S Runciman, *A History of the Crusades.* Cambridge 1951–54, 3 vols.

S Runciman, *The Eastern Schism.* Oxford 1955.

S Runciman, *The Byzantine Theocracy.* Cambridge 1977.

K M Setton (General Editor), *A History of the Crusades,* I–II. Philadelphia 1955–62.

A A Vasiliev, *History of the Byzantine Empire*. Madison 1952. [Interesting bibliogaphy of older literature.]

2. BYZANTINE FOREIGN RELATIONS IN THE ELEVENTH CENTURY

THE RUSSIANS

D Obolensky, 'Byzantium, Kiev and Moscow. A study in ecclesiastical relations', *Dumbarton Oaks Papers,* 11 (1957), pp. 21–78. [Reprinted in D Obolensky, *Byzantium and the Slavs.* London 1971, no. VI.]
A Poppe, 'La dernière expedition russe contre Constantinople', *Byzantinoslavica,* 32 (1971), pp. 1–29, 233–68.
A Poppe, 'The political background to the baptism of the Rus', *Dumbarton Oaks Papers,* 30 (1976), pp. 197–244. [Reprinted in A. Poppe, *The Rise of Christian Russia.* London 1982, no. II.]
A Poppe, 'The building of the church of St Sophia in Kiev', *Journal of Medieval History,* 7 (1981), pp. 15–66. [Reprinted in A Poppe, *The Rise of Christian Russia,* no. IV.
J Shepard, 'Why did the Russians attack Byzantium in 1043?', *Byzantinisch-neugriechischen Jahrbücher,* 22 (1979), pp. 147–212.

THE PETCHENEKS

P Diaconu, *Les Pétchenèques au Bas-Danube.* Bucarest 1970.

THE SELJUQS

C Cahen, *Pre-Ottoman Turkey.* London 1968. [Good bibliography.]
C Cahen, *Turcobyzantina et Oriens Christianus.* London 1974.

MANTZIKERT AND THE LOSS OF BYZANTINE ANATOLIA

W C Brice, 'The Turkish colonisation of Anatolia' *Bulletin of John Ryland's Library,* 38 (1955) pp. 18–44.
J C Cheynet, 'Mantzikert. Une désastre militaire?', *Byzantion,* 50 (1980), pp. 410–38.
G Dagron, 'Minorités ethniques et religieuses dans l'Orient byzantin à la fin du Xe et au XIe siècle: l'immigration syrienne', *Travaux et Mémoires,* 6 (1976), pp. 177–216.
G Dedeyan, 'L'immigration arménienne en Cappadoce au XIe siècle', *Byzantion,* 45 (1975), pp. 41–117.
A Friendly, *The Dreadful Day. The Battle of Mantzikert, 1071.* London 1981.

Sp Vryonis, Jr, *The Decline of Medieval Hellenism in Asia Minor and the Process of Islamization from the Eleventh through the Fifteenth Century.* Berkeley/Los Angeles/London 1971.

SOUTHERN ITALY AND THE WEST

H Bibicou, 'Une page d'histoire diplomatique de Byzance au XIe siècle: Michel VII Doukas, Robert Guiscard et la pension des dignitaires', *Byzantion,* 29/30 (1959/60), pp. 43–75.

H Bloch, 'Monte Cassino, Byzantium and the West in the earlier Middle Ages', *Dumbarton Oaks Papers,* 3 (1946), pp. 165–224.

A Guillou, 'Production and profits in the Byzantine province of Italy (10th–11th Centuries): an expanding society', *Dumbarton Oaks Papers,* 28 (1974), pp. 89–109. [Reprinted in A. Guillou, *Culture et Société en Italie byzantine (VIe–XIe siècles).* London 1978), no. XII.]

B Leib, *Rome, Kiev et Byzance à la fin du XIe siècle.* Paris 1924.

R Mayne, 'East and West in 1054', *Cambridge Historical Journal,* 11 (1953–55), pp. 133–48.

D M Nicol, 'Byzantium and the Papacy in the eleventh century', *Journal* of Ecclesiastical History, 13 (1962), pp. 1–20. [Reprinted in D M Nicol, *Byzantium: its Ecclesiastical History and Relations with the Western World.* London 1972, no. II.

M H Smith III, *And Taking Bread… Cerularius and the Azyme Controversy.* Paris 1978.

3. THE INTERNAL HISTORY OF THE BYZANTINE EMPIRE IN THE ELEVENTH CENTURY

POLITICAL AND ADMINISTRATIVE HISTORY

J B Bury, 'Roman emperors from Basil II to Isaac Komnênos', *English Historical Review,* 4 (1889), pp. 41–64, 251–85. [Reprinted in *Selected Essays of J B Bury* (ed. H Temperley). Cambridge 1930, pp. 126–214.]

P Charanis, 'The Byzantine Empire in the eleventh century', in K M Setton & M W Baldwin (eds), *A History of the Crusades,* I. Philadelphia 1955, pp. 177–219. [Reprinted in P Charanis, *Social, Economic and Political Life in the Byzantine Empire.* London 1973, no. XVI.]

J M Hussey, 'The Byzantine Empire in the eleventh century: some different interpretations', *Transactions of the Royal Historical Society.* 4th series, 32 (1950), pp. 71–85.

J M Hussey, 'The later Macedonians, the Comneni and the Angeli 1025–1204', in *Cambridge Medieval History,* IV, part 1. Cambridge 1966, pp. 193–249.

R J H Jenkins, *The Byzantine Empire on the Eve of the Crusades.* London 1953.

R J H Jenkins, 'A cross of the Patriarch Michael Cerularius', *Dumbarton Oaks Papers,* 21 (1967), pp. 233–49.

P Lemerle, '"Roga" et rente d'état aux Xe–XIe siècles', *Revue des Etudes Byzantines,* 25 (1967), pp. 71–100. [Reprinted in P Lemerle, *Le Monde de Byzance.* London 1978, no. XVI.]

N Oikonomidès, 'Le serment de l'impératrice Eudocie (1067). Un épisode de l'histoire dynastique de Byzance', *Revue des Etudes Byzantines,* 21 (1963), pp. 101–28. [Reprinted in N. Oikonomidès, *Documents et études sur les institutions de Byzance (VIIe–XVe siècles)* London 1976, no. III.]

N Oikonomidès, 'L'évolution de l'organisation administrative de l'Empire byzantin au XIe siècle (1025–1118)', *Travaux et Mémoires,* 6 (1976), pp. 125–52.

D I Polemis, *The Doukai.* London 1968.

Sp Vryonis, Jr, 'Byzantine Δημοκρατία and the guilds in the eleventh century', *Dumbarton Oaks Papers,* 17 (1963), pp. 287–314. [Reprinted in Sp Vryonis, Jr, *Byzantium: its Internal History and Relations with the Muslim World.* London 1971, no. III.]

G Weiss, *Oströmische Beamte im Spiegel der Schriften des Michael Psellos.* Munich 1973.

ECONOMIC AND SOCIAL HISTORY

H Ahrweiler, 'Recherches sur la société byzantine au XIe siècle: nouvelles hiérarchies et nouvelles solidarités', *Travaux et Mémoires,* 7 (1976), pp. 99–124.

G I Bratianu, 'Une expérience d'économie dirigée. Le monopole du blé à Byzance au XIe siècle', *Byzantion,* 9 (1934), pp. 643–62.

P Grierson, 'The debasement of the Bezant in the eleventh century', *Byzantinische Zeitschrift,* 47 (1954), pp. 379–94.

C Morrisson, 'La dévaluation de la monnaie byzantine au XIe siècle: essai d'interprétation', *Travaux et Mémoires,* 6 (1976), pp. 3–30.

N Svoronos, 'Société et organisation intérieure dans l'Empire byzantin au XIe siècle', in *Thirteenth International Congress of Byzantine Studies.* Oxford 1966: Main Papers XII. [Reprinted in N Svoronos, *Etudes sur l'organisation intérieure, la société et l'économie de l'Empire byzantin.* London 1973, no. IX.]

N Svoronos, 'Remarques sur les structures économiques de l'Empire byzantin au XIe siècle', *Travaux et Mémoires,* 6 (1976), pp. 49–67.

Sp Vryonis, Jr, 'Byzantium: the social basis of decline in the eleventh century', *Greek, Roman and Byzantine Studies,* 2 (1959), pp. 159–75. [Reprinted in Sp Vryonis, Jr, *Byzantium: its Internal History and Relations with the Muslim World,* no. II.]

LAW, EDUCATION, AND INTELLECTUAL LIFE

R Browning, 'Byzantine scholarship', *Past and Present,* 28 (July 1964), pp. 3–22. [Reprinted in R Browning, *Studies on Byzantine History, Literature and Education.* London 1977, no. XIII.]

W Conus-Wolska, 'Les écoles de Psellos et de Xiphilin sous Constantin IX Monomaque', *Travaux et Mémoires,* 6 (1976), pp. 223–43.

W Conus-Wolska, 'L'école de droit et l'enseignement du droit au XIe siècle. Xiphilin et Psellos', *Travaux et Mémoires*, 7 (1979), pp. 1–107.

J Gouillard, 'La religion des philosophes', *Travaux et Mémoires*, 6 (1976), pp. 305–24. [Reprinted in J Gouillard, *La vie religieuse à Byzance*. London 1981, no. III.]

J M Hussey, *Church and Learning in the Byzantine Empire 867–1185*. London 1937.

J M Hussey, *Ascetics and Humanists in Eleventh-century Byzantium*. London 1960.

C Niarchos, 'The philosophical background of the eleventh-century revival of learning in Byzantium', in *Byzantium and the Classical Tradition* (ed. M Mullett and R Scott). Birmingham 1981, pp. 127–35.

D Simon, *Rechtsfindung am byzantinischen Reichsgericht*. Frankfurt 1973.

MICHAEL PSELLOS

J Grosdidier de Matons, 'Psellos et le monde de l'irrationel', *Travaux et Mémoires,* 6 (1976), pp. 325–49.

J M Hussey, 'Michael Psellus, the Byzantine historian' *Speculum*, 10 (1935), pp. 81–90.

Ja N Ljubarskij, *Mihail Psell*. Moscow 1978.

F Tinnefeld, '"Freundschaft" in den Briefen des Michael Psellos. Theorie und Wirklichkeit', *Jahrbuch österreichischen Byzantinistik*, 22 (1973), pp. 151–68.

ST SYMEON THE NEW THEOLOGIAN

I Hausherr & G Horn, *Un grand mystique byzantin. Vie de Syméon le Nouveau Théologien (949–1022) par Nicetas Stéthatos*. Rome 1928.

K. Holl, *Enthusiasmus und Bussgewalt beim griechischen Mönchtum*. Leipzig 1898.

A P Kazhdan 'Predvaritel'nye zametchanija o mirovozzrenii vizantijskogo mistika X–XI vv. Simeona', *Byzantinoslavica*, 28 (1967), pp. 1–38.

KEKAVMENOS

P Lemerle, *Prolégomènes à une édition critique et commentée des 'Conseils et Récits' de Kekauménos*. Brussels 1960.

4. BYZANTINE FOREIGN RELATIONS UNDER THE COMNENI

BYZANTIUM AND THE CRUSADES

P. Charanis, 'Byzantium, the West and the origin of the First Crusade', *Byzantion*, 19 (1949), pp. 17–36. [Reprinted in P Charanis, *Social, Economic and Political Life in the Byzantine Empire*, no. XIV.]

F-L Ganshof, 'Robert le Frison et Alexis Comnène', *Byzantion*, 31 (1961), pp. 57–74.

F-L Ganshof, 'Recherche sur le lien juridique qui unissait les chefs de la 1ère croisade à l'empereur byzantin', in *Mélanges P-E Martin*. Geneva 1961, pp. 49–63.

J M Hussey, 'Byzantium and the Crusades, 1081–1204', in K M Setton, *A History of the Crusades*, II. Philadelphia 1962, pp. 123–51.

E Joranson, 'The problem of the spurious letter of Emperor Alexius to the Count of Flanders', *American Historical Review*, 55 (1949–50), pp. 811–32.

P Lemerle, 'Byzance et la croisade', in *Relazioni del X Congresso Internazionale di Scienze Storiche*, III. Florence 1955, pp. 595–620. [Reprinted in P Lemerle, *Le Monde de Byzance*, no. XIV.]

R J Lilie, *Byzanz und die Kreuzfahrerstaaten*. Munich 1981. [Comprehensive bibliography.]

M de Waha, 'La lettre d'Alexis 1er Comnène à Robert 1er le Frison. Une revision', *Byzantion*, 47 (1977), pp. 113–25.

J G Rowe, 'Paschal II, Bohemund of Antioch and the Byzantine Empire', *Bulletin of John Ryland's Library*, 49 (1966–67), pp. 165–202.

BYZANTIUM AND THE WEST

M V Anastos, 'Some aspects of Byzantine influence on Latin thought', in *Twelfth-century Europe and the Foundations of Modern Society*. Wisconsin 1961, pp. 131–87. [Reprinted in M V Anastos, *Studies in Byzantine Intellectual History*. London 1979, no. XIII.]

A Bryer, 'The first encounter with the West–A.D. 1050–1204', in P. Whitting, *Byzantium. An Introduction*. Oxford 1971, pp. 83–110.

A Bryer, 'Cultural relations between East and West in the twelfth century', in D. Baker (ed.), *Relations between East and West in the Middle Ages*. Edinburgh 1973, pp. 77–94.

P Classen, 'Das Konzil von Konstantinopel 1166 und die Lateiner', *Byzantinische Zeitschrift*, 48 (1955), pp 339–68.

P Classen, 'Die Komnenen und die Kaiserkron des Westens', *Journal of Medieval History*, 3 (1977), pp. 207–24.

A Dondaine, 'Hugues Ethérien et Léon Toscan', *Archives d'histoire doctrinale et littéraire du moyen âge*, 19 (1952), pp. 67–134.

A. Dondaine, 'Hugues Ethérien et le concile de Constantinople de 1166', *Historisches Jahrbuch*, 77 (1958), pp. 473–83.

J. Ferluga, 'La ligesse dans l'Empire byzantin', *Zbornik Radova Vizantoloshkog Instituta*, 7 (1961), pp. 97–123.

C H Haskins, *Studies in the History of Mediaeval Science*. Cambridge, Mass. 1924.

P. Lamma, *Comneni e Staufer* (Rome, 1955–57), 2 vols.

Marquis de la Force, 'Les conseillers latins du Basileus Alexis Comnène', *Byzantion*, 11 (1936), pp. 153–65.

W Ohnsorge, *Das Zweikaiserproblem im früheren Mittelalter*. Hildesheim 1947.

W. Ohnsorge, *Abendland und Byzanz*. Darmstadt 1958.

J. Parker, 'The attempted Byzantine alliance with the Sicilian Norman Kingdom, 1166–1167', *Papers of the British School at Rome*, 24 (1956), pp. 86–93.

A A Vasiliev, 'Manuel Comnenus and Henry Plantagenet', *Byzantinische Zeitschrift*, 29 (129–30), pp. 233–44.

BYZANTIUM AND THE PAPACY

P J Alexander, 'The Donation of Constantine at Byzantium and its earliest use against the Western Empire', *Zbornik Radova Vizantoloshkog Instituta*, 8, i (1963), pp. 11–26, [Reprinted in P J Alexander, *Religious and Political History and Thought in the Byzantine Empire*. London 1978, no. IV.]

J Darrouzès, 'Les documents byzantins du XIIe siècle sur la primauté romaine', *Revue des Etudes Byzantines*, 23 (1965), pp. 42–88. [Reprinted in J Darrouzès, *Littérature et histoire des textes byzantins*. London 1972, no. X.]

W Holtzmann, 'Die Unionsverhandlungen zwischen Alexios I. und Papst Urban II.', *Byzantinische Zeitschrift*, 28 (1928), pp. 38–67.

D M Nicol, 'The papal scandal', *Studies in Church History*, 13 (1976), pp. 141–68.

BYZANTIUM AND HUNGARY

R Browning, 'A new source on Byzantine–Hungarian relations in the twelfth century', *Balkan Studies*, 2 (1961), pp. 173–214. [Reprinted in R Browning, *Studies on Byzantine History, Literature and Education*, no. IV.]

G Moravcsik, 'Hungary and Byzantium in the Middle Ages', in the *Cambridge Medieval History*, IV, part 1. Cambridge 1966, pp. 567–92.

G Moravcsik, *Studia Byzantina*. Amsterdam 1967.

G Moravcsik, *Byzantium and the Magyars*. Amsterdam 1970.

A B Urbansky, *Byzantium and the Danube Frontier*. New York 1968.

THE VENETIANS

S Borsari, 'Il commercio veneziano nell'Impero bizantino nel XII secolo', *Rivista Storica Italiana*, 76 (1964), pp. 982–1011.

S Borsari, 'Per la storia del commercio veneziano col mondo bizantino nel XII secolo', *Rivista Storica Italiana*, 88 (1976), pp 104–26.

H Brown, 'The Venetians and the Venetian Quarter in Constantinople to the close of the twelfth century', *Journal of Hellenic Studies*, 40 (1920), pp. 68–88.

R Cessi, 'Venice to the eve of the Fourth Crusade', in the *Cambridge Medieval History*, IV, part 1. Cambridge 1966, pp. 251–74.

E Frances, 'Alexis Comnène et les privilèges octroyés à Venise', *Byzantinoslavica*, 29 (1968), pp. 17–23.

P Lamma, 'Venezia nel giudizio delle fonti bizantine dal X al XII secolo', *Rivista Storica Italiana*, 74 (1962), pp. 457–79.

M E Martin, 'The chrysobull of Alexius I Comnenus to the Venetians and the early Venetian Quarter in Constantinople', *Byzantinoslavica*, 39 (1978), pp. 19–23.

A Pertusi, 'Venezia e Bisanzio: 1000–1204', *Dumbarton Oaks Papers*, 33 (1979), pp. 1–22.

F Thiriet, *La Romanie vénitienne au moyen âge*. Paris 1959.

O. Tüma, 'The dating of Alexius's chrysobull to the Venetians: 1082, 1084, or 1092?', *Byzantinoslavica*, 42 (1981), pp. 171–85.

5. THE INTERNAL HISTORY OF THE BYZANTINE EMPIRE UNDER THE COMNENI

HERESY

R Browning, 'Enlightenment and repression in Byzantium in the eleventh and twelfth centuries', *Past and Present*, 69 (Nov. 1975), pp. 3–23. [Reprinted in R Browning, *Studies on Byzantine History, Literature and Education*, no. XV.]

L Clucas, *The Trial of John Italos and the Crisis of Intellectual Values in the Eleventh Century*. Munich 1981.

N G Garsoian 'Byzantine heresy. A reinterpretation', *Dumbarton Oaks Papers*, 25 (1971), pp. 85–113.

N G Garsoian, 'L'abjuration du moine Nil de Calabre', *Byzantinoslavica*, 35 (1974), pp. 12–27.

J Gouillard, 'L'hérésie dans l'Empire byzantin des origines au XIIe siècle', *Travaux et Mémoires*, 1 (1965), pp. 299–324. [Reprinted in J Gouillard, *La vie religieuse à Byzance*. London. 1981, no. I.]

J Gouillard, 'Le synodicon de l'Orthodoxie', *Travaux et Mémoires*, 2 (1966), pp. 1–316.

J Gouillard, 'Constantin Chrysomallos sous le masque de Syméon le Nouveau Théologien', *Travaux et Mémoires*, 5 (1973), pp. 313–27. [Reprinted in J Gouillard, *La vie religieuse à Byzance*, no. XI.]

J Gouillard, 'Quatres procès de mystiques à Byzance (vers 960–1143). Inspiration et autorité', *Revue des Etudes Byzantines*, 36 (1978), pp. 5–81.

M Loos, *Dualist Heresy in the Middle Ages*. Prague 1974.

D Obolensky, *The Bogomils*. Cambridge 1948.

S Runciman, *The Medieval Manichee*. Cambridge 1947.

THE CHURCH

P Charanis, 'Monastic properties and the state in the Byzantine Empire', *Dumbarton Oaks Papers*, 4 (1948), pp. 53–118. [Reprinted in P Charanis, *Social, Economic and Political Life in the Byzantine Empire*, no. I.]

P Lemerle, 'Un aspect du role des monastères à Byzance: les monastères donnés à des laics, les charisticiaires', *Comptes rendus de l'Academie des Inscriptions et Belles-Lettres*, 1967, pp. 9–28. [Reprinted in P Lemerle, *Le Monde de Byzance*. London 1978, no. XV.]

P Magdalino 'The Byzantine holy man in the twelfth century', in *The Byzantine Saint* (ed. S Hackel). London 1981, pp. 51–66.

N Svoronos, 'Les privilèges de l'église à l'époque des Comnènes: un rescrit inédit de Manuel 1er Comnène, *Travaux et Mémoires*, 1 (1965), pp. 325–91. [Reprinted in N Svoronos, *Etudes sur l'organisation intérieure, la société et l'economie de l'Empire byzantin*, no. VII.]

V Tiftixoglu, 'Gruppenbildungen innerhalb des Konstantinopolitanischen Klerus während der Komnenenzeit', *Byzantinische Zeitschrift*, 62 (1969), pp. 25–72.

C Walter, *Art and Ritual of the Byzantine Church*. London 1982.

SCHOLARSHIP, EDUCATION, AND LAW

A Angelos, 'Nicholas of Methone: the life and works of a twelfth-century bishop', in *Byzantium and the Classical Tradition* (ed. M Mullett & R Scott) Birmingham 1981, pp. 143–48.

M Angold, 'The date of the *Synopsis Minor* of the Basilics', *Byzantine and Modern Greek Studies*, 4 (1978), pp. 1–7.

R Browning, 'The Patriarchal School at Constantinople in the twelfth century', *Byzantion*, 32 (1962), pp. 167–202; 33 (1963), pp. 11–40. [Reprinted in R Browning, *Studies on Byzantine History, Literature and Education*, no. X.]

R Browning, 'An unpublished funeral oration on Anna Comnena', *Proceedings of the Cambridge Philosophical Society*, New Series, 8 (1962), pp. 1–12. [Reprinted in R Browning, *Studies on Byzantine History, Literature and Education*, no. VII.]

R Browning, *Church, State and Learning in Twelfth-century Byzantium*. London 1981.

G Buckler, *Anna Comnena*. Oxford 1929.

R Macrides, 'Four novels of Manuel I Komnenos', *Fontes minores*, 6 (1983).

G Podalsky, 'Nikolaos von Methone und die Proklosrenaissance in Byzanz 11/12. Jahrhundert', *Orientalia Christiana Periodica*, 42 (1976), pp. 509–23.

COMNENIAN COURT AND PALACES

Ch Diehl, *La société byzantine à l'époque des Comnènes*. Paris 1929.

P Magdalino, 'Manuel Komnenos and the Great Palace', *Byzantine and Modern Greek Studies*, 4 (1978), pp. 101–14.

P Magdalino & R Nelson, 'The Emperor in the Byzantine art of the twelfth century', *Byzantinische Forschungen*, 8 (1982), pp. 123–83.
S Runciman, 'Blachernae Palace and its decoration', in *Studies in Memory of David Talbot Rice* (ed. G. Robertson & G. Henderson). Edinburgh 1975, pp. 277–83.

THE LITERATURE OF THE COMNENIAN COURT

M Alexiou, 'A critical reappraisal of Eustathios Makrembolites' *Hysmine and Hysminas', Byzantine and Modern Greek Studies*, 3 (1977), pp. 23–43.
H G Beck, *Geschichte der byzantinischen Volksliteratur.* Munich 1971. [Excellent bibliographical guide.]
H G Beck, 'Der Leserkreis der byzantinischen "Volksliteratur" im licht der handschriftlichen Überlieferung', in *Byzantine Books and Bookmen.* Washington, D.C. 1975, pp. 47–67.
C Cupane, 'Un caso di giudizio di Dio nel Romanzo di Teodoro Prodromo (I 372–404)', *Rivista di studi bizantini e neoellenichi*, 10/11 (1973/74), pp. 147–68.
H Hunger, *Antiker und byzantinischer Roman.* Heidelberg 1980.
E M Jeffreys, 'The Comnenian background to the *Romans d'Antiquite', Byzantion*, 50 (1980), pp. 455–86. [Reprinted in E & M Jeffreys, *Popular Literature in Late Byzantium.* London 1983, no. X.]
N Oikonomides, 'L' "épopée de Digénis" et la frontière orientale de Byzance aux Xe et XIe siècles', *Travaux et Mémoires*, 7 (1979), pp. 375–97.
S B Poljakova, *Iz istorii vizantijskogo romana.* Moscow 1979.

ECONOMY AND RURAL SOCIETY

M F Hendy, 'Byzantium, 1081–1204: an economic reappraisal', *Transactions of the Royal Historical Society*, Fifth Series, 20 (1970), pp. 31–52.
M F Hendy, *Coinage and Money in the Byzantine Empire 1081–1261.* Washington, D.C. 1969.
C Morrisson, 'La logarikè: reforme monétaire et reforme fiscale sous Alexis 1er Comnène', *Travaux et Mémoires*, 7 (1979), pp. 419–64.
G. Ostrogorsky, *Quelques problèmes d'histoire de la paysannerie byzantine.* Brussels 1956.
G Ostrogorsky, 'La commune rurale byzantine: loi agraire–traité fiscal-cadastre de Thèbes', *Byzantion*, 32 (1962), pp. 139–66. [Reprinted in G Ostrogorsky, *Zur byzantinischen Geschichte.* Darmstadt 1973, pp. 44–71.]

PRONOIAI AND OTHER GRANTS

A Hohlweg, 'Zur Frage der Pronoia in Byzanz', *Byzantinische Zeitschrift*, 60 (1967), pp. 288–308.

P Lemerle, 'Recherches sur le régime agraire à Byzance: la terre militaire à l'époque des Comnènes', *Cahiers de Civilisation Médiévale*, 2 (1959), pp. 265–81.

N Oikonomides, 'The Donation of Castles in the last quarter of the eleventh century (Dölger, *Regesten*, No. 1012)', in *Polychronion: Festschrift Franz Dölger zum 75. Geburtstag.* Heidelberg 1966, pp. 413–17. [Reprinted in N Oikonomidès, *Documents et études sur les institutions de Byzance (VIIIe–XVe siècles),* no. XIV.]

G Ostrogorsky, *Pour l'histoire de la féodalité byzantine.* Brussels 1954.

G Ostrogorsky, 'Pour l'histoire de l'immunité à Byzance', *Byzantion*, 28 (1958), pp. 165–254.

G Ostrogorsky, 'Die Pronoia unter den Komnenen', *Zbornik Radova Vizantoloshkog Instituta*, 12 (1970), pp. 41–54.

6. THE BYZANTINE PROVINCES

THE GREEK LANDS

A Bon, *Le Péloponnèse byzantin jusqu'en 1204.* Paris 1951.

R Davidson, 'A medieval glassfactory at Corinth', *American Journal of Archaeology*, 44 (1940), pp. 297–324.

A W Epstein, 'Middle Byzantine churches of Kastoria: dates and implications', *Art Bulletin*, 62 (1980), pp. 190–207.

M A Frantz, *The Middle Ages in the Athenian Agora.* Princeton, 1961.

J Nesbitt & J Wiitta, 'A confraternity of the Comnenian era', *Byzantinische Zeitschrift*, 68 (1975), pp. 360–84.

R L Scranton, *Medieval Architecture in the Central Area of Corinth (Corinth,* XVI). Princeton 1957.

K M Setton, *Athens in the Middle Ages.* London 1975.

THE BALKANS

J V A Fine, Jr, *The Early Medieval Balkans.* Ann Arbor, 1983.

J Ferluga, *Byzantium on the Balkans.* Amsterdam 1976.

D A Xanalatos, *Beiträge zur Wirtschafts- und Sozialgeschichte Makedoniens im Mittelalter.* Munich 1937.

ANATOLIA

H Ahrweiler, 'L'histoire et la géographie de la région de Smyrne entre les deux occupations turques (1081–1317)', *Travaux et Mémoires*, 1 (1965), pp. 1–204. [Reprinted in H Ahrweiler, *Byzance: les pays et les territoires.* London 1976, no. IV.]

H Ahrweiler, 'Choma-Aggelokastron', *Revue des Etudes Byzantines*, 24 (1966), pp. 278–83. [Reprinted in H Ahrweiler, *Etudes sur les structures administratives et sociales de Byzance.* London, 1971, no. X.]

A Bryer, 'A Byzantine family: the Gabrades, *c.* 979–*c.* 1653', *University of Birmingham Historical Journal*, 12 (1970), pp. 164–87. [Reprinted in A A M Bryer, *The Empire of Trabizond and Pontos.* London 1980, no. IIIa.]

C Foss, *Byzantine and Turkish Sardis.* Cambridge, Mass. 1976.

C Foss, *Ephesus after Antiquity.* Cambridge 1979.

H Glykatzi, 'Les forteresses construites en Asie Mineure face à l'invasion seldjoucide', *Akten des XI. Internationalen Byzantinisten-Kongresses.* Munich 1958, pp. 182–9. [Reprinted in H Ahrweiler, *Etudes sur les structures administratives et sociales de Byzance,* no. XVII.]

CYPRUS AND THE AEGEAN

H Ahrweiler, 'L'administration militaire de la Crète byzantine', *Byzantion*, 31 (1961), pp. 217–28. [Reprinted in H Ahrweiler, *Etudes sur les structures administratives et sociales de Byzance,* no. XI.]

C Mango & E J W Hawkins, 'The Hermitage of St Neophytos and its wall paintings', *Dumbarton Oaks Papers*, 20 (1966), pp. 122–9.

C Mango, 'Chypre carrefour du monde byzantin', in *XVe Congres International d'Etudes byzantines.* Athens 1976, V, 5.

7. THE COLLAPSE OF THE BYZANTINE EMPIRE 1180–1204

C M Brand, 'The Byzantines and Saladin, 1185–1192: opponents of the Third Crusade', *Speculum*, 37 (1962), pp. 167–81.

C M Brand, *Byzantium confronts the West 1180–1204.* Cambridge, Mass. 1968. [Excellent bibliography.]

C M Brand, 'A Byzantine plan for the Fourth Crusade', *Speculum*, 43 (1968), pp. 462–75.

J Folda, 'The Fourth Crusade, 1201–1203. Some reconsiderations', *Byzantinoslavica,* 26 (1965), pp. 277–90.

A Frolow, *Recherches sur la déviation de la IVe croisade vers Constantinople.* Paris 1955.

J Godfrey, *1204. The Unholy Crusade.* Oxford 1980.

J Herrin, 'The collapse of the Byzantine Empire in the twelfth century: a study of medieval economy', *University of Birmingham Historical Journal*, 12 (1970), pp. 188–203.

J Herrin, 'Realities of Byzantine provincial government: Hellas and the Peloponnesos, 1180–1205', *Dumbarton Oaks Papers,* 29 (1975), pp. 253–84.

O Jurewicz, *Andronikos I. Komnenos.* Amsterdam 1970.

The Byzantine Empire

P Lemerle, 'Notes sur l'administration byzantine à la veille de la IVe croisade d'après deux documents inédits des archives de Lavra', *Revue des Etudes Byzantines*, 19 (1961), pp. 258–72. [Reprinted in P Lemerle, *Le Monde de Byzance*, no. XXIV.]

D E Queller, *The Fourth Crusade. The Conquest of Constantinople, 1201–1204*. Leicester 1978. [Good, up-to-date bibliography.]

R L Wolff, 'The "Second Bulgarian Empire". Its origin and history to 1204', *Speculum*, 24 (1949), pp. 167–206. [Reprinted in R L Wolff, *Studies in the Latin Empire of Constantinople*. London 1976, no. III.]

MAPS

MAP 1. The Byzantine Empire *c.* 1025

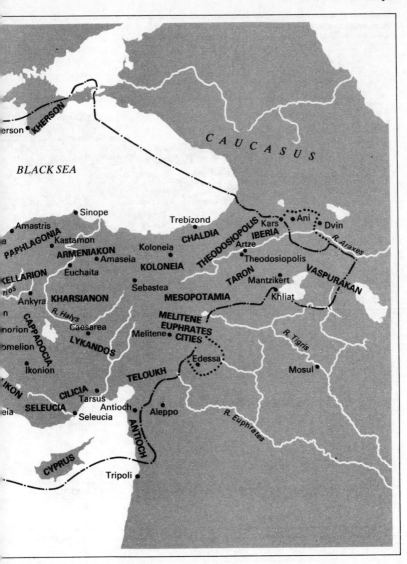

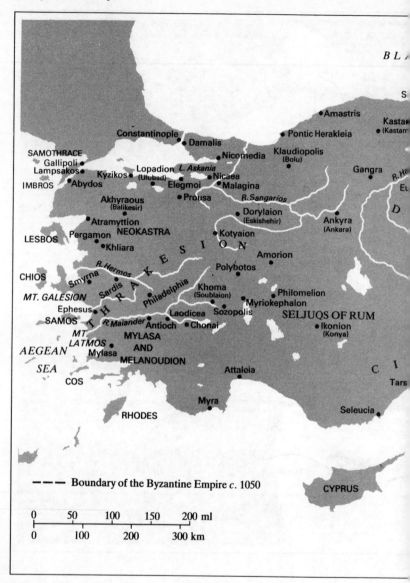

MAP 2. Byzantine Asia Minor in the eleventh and twelfth centuries

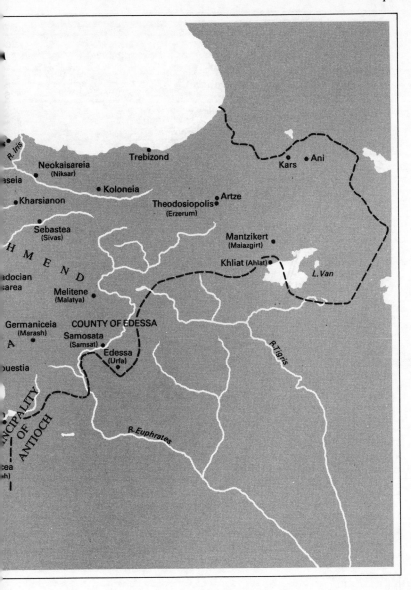

R.Iris

Neokaisareia
(Niksar)

Trebizond

Kars   ● Ani

...aseia

● Kharsianon

● Koloneia

Theodosiopolis ● Artze
(Erzerum)

Mantzikert
(Maiazgirt)

Sebastea
(Sivas)

Khliat (Ahlat)

L. Van

H M E N D

...adocian
...sarea

● Melitene
(Malatya)

Germaniceia
(Marash)

COUNTY OF EDESSA

Samosata
(Samsat)

A

● Edessa
(Urfa)

R.Tigris

...uestia

...NCIPALITY
OF
ANTIOCH

R. Euphrates

...cea
...sh)

The Byzantine Empire

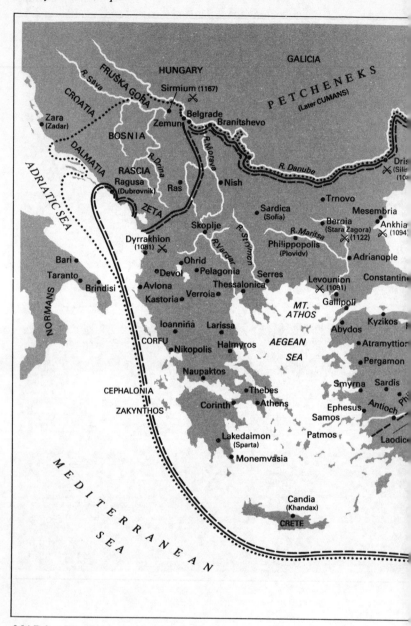

MAP 3.   The Empire under the Comneni

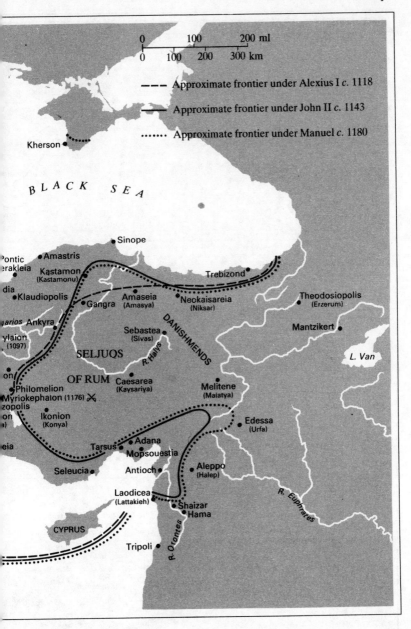

0 100 200 ml
0 100 200 300 km

– – – Approximate frontier under Alexius I *c.* 1118

——— Approximate frontier under John II *c.* 1143

· · · · · · Approximate frontier under Manuel *c.* 1180

Kherson

BLACK   SEA

Sinope

Pontic
erakleia

Amastris

Kastamon
(Kastamonu)

Trebizond

dia

Klaudiopolis

Gangra

Amaseia
(Amasya)

Neokaisareia
(Niksar)

Theodosiopolis
(Erzerum)

arios

Ankyra

Sebastea
(Sivas)

R. Halys

DANISHMENDS

Mantzikert

ylaion
(1097)

SELJUQS

L. Van

on

Philomelion

OF RUM

Caesarea
(Kaysariya)

Melitene
(Malatya)

Myriokephalon (1176) ✗

zopolis

Ikonion
(Konya)

Edessa
(Urfa)

on
a)

eia

Tarsus

Adana

Mopsouestia

Aleppo
(Halep)

Seleucia

Antioch

Laodicea
(Lattakieh)

Shaizar
Hama

R. Euphrates

CYPRUS

Tripoli

R. Orontes

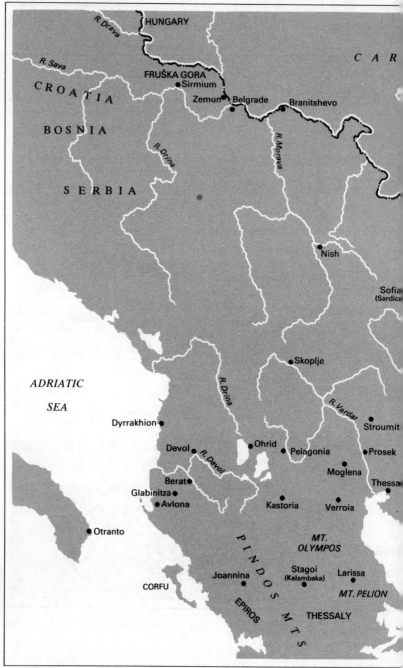

MAP 4. The Balkans in the twelfth century

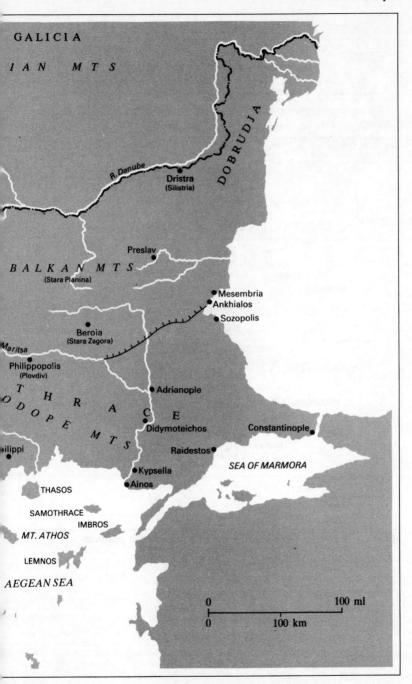

GALICIA

I A N   M T S

R. Danube

Dristra
(Silistria)

DOBRUDJA

Preslav

B A L K A N   M T S
(Stara Planina)

Mesembria
Ankhialos
Sozopolis

Beroia
(Stara Zagora)

Maritsa

Philippopolis
(Plovdiv)

T H R A C E

O D O P E   M T S

Adrianople

Didymoteichos

Constantinople

ilippi

Raidestos

SEA OF MARMORA

Kypsella
Ainos

THASOS

SAMOTHRACE

IMBROS

MT. ATHOS

LEMNOS

AEGEAN SEA

0   100 ml
0   100 km

The Byzantine Empire

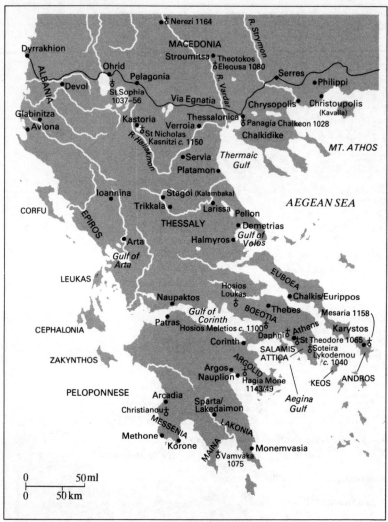

MAP 5. Byzantine Greece in the eleventh and twelfth centuries

INDEX

331

The Byzantine Empire